SURPRISING
NEWS

SURPRISING
NEWS

HOW THE MEDIA AFFECT—AND DO NOT AFFECT—POLITICS

Kenneth Newton

LYNNE
RIENNER
PUBLISHERS

BOULDER
LONDON

To Clare,
who made this book
and many other things possible

Published in the United States of America in 2019 by
Lynne Rienner Publishers, Inc.
1800 30th Street, Boulder, Colorado 80301
www.rienner.com

and in the United Kingdom by
Lynne Rienner Publishers, Inc.
Gray's Inn House, 127 Clerkenwell Road, London EC1 5DB

Library of Congress Cataloging-in-Publication Data
Names: Newton, Kenneth, 1940– author.
Title: Surprising news : how the media affect—and do not affect—politics /
    Kenneth Newton.
Description: Boulder, Colorado : Lynne Rienner Publishers, Inc., [2019] |
    Includes bibliographical references and index.
Identifiers: LCCN 2018053714 | ISBN 9781626377660 (hardcover : alk. paper) |
    ISBN 9781626377707 (pbk. : alk. paper)
Subjects: LCSH: Mass media—Political aspects. | Press and politics. |
    Public opinion—Political aspects.
Classification: LCC P95.8 .N49 2019 | DDC 070.4/4932—dc23 LC record
    available at https://lccn.loc.gov/2018053714

British Cataloguing in Publication Data
A Cataloguing in Publication record for this book
is available from the British Library.

Printed and bound in the United States of America

The paper used in this publication meets the requirements
of the American National Standard for Permanence of
Paper for Printed Library Materials Z39.48-1992.

5 4 3 2 1

Contents

Tables and Figures

Tables

Figures

Preface

This book is not a standard academic research monograph that presents the results of a tightly defined study dealing with a specific aspect of how the media might affect a particular element of political life. Such a piecemeal approach has not resolved a controversy that has bedeviled political science for more than sixty years. Instead, this book surveys the large and diverse range of in-depth, case-study research on the topic as a whole. This research has accumulated in varied academic disciplines over a long period of time, most of it in the past couple decades. Comparing and contrasting studies that have used different methods in different countries makes it possible to draw out general conclusions about what sorts of media have what sorts of effects on what sorts of people. Thus, my work leans heavily on the research of others who have published work on the topic in detailed case studies, drawing together the myriad threads of a controversial topic that has puzzled and perplexed two or three generations of political scientists.

To be certain I have not misrepresented their work, draft chapters were sent to other authors for their comments and corrections. I am grateful to the following for taking the time and trouble to read these drafts, confirm my accounts of their research and results, and often to make useful comments and point me in the direction of publications I had missed: Kees Aarts, Malcolm Brynin, Nick Cauldry, Russ Dalton, Paul Dekker, Richard Gunter, Jon Krosnick, Staffan Kumlin, Jeff Mondak, Helmut Norpoth, Pippa Norris, Rudiger Schmitt-Beck, and Holli Semetko. Lance Bennett, Ivor Crewe, Robert Entman, Marc Hooghe, Ellen Mickiewicz, Jacob Neiheisel, Samuel Popkin, Markus Prior, and Ranjit Sondhi were particularly generous with their time and deserve special thanks. I was also lucky enough to have the helpful and thoughtful comments of three anonymous readers, whose reports resulted in important changes.

Some of these kind souls disagree with several points of my argument (perhaps most or all of them), but I cannot blame them for any of the errors, oversights, and failures of the book. These, unfortunately, are mine alone. It would be nice to follow the crowd and blame the media for all my faults and failings, but that is not possible either given the main thrust of my argument.

Most of all I would like to thank Caroline Wintersgill for being such a good and helpful publication adviser, John Smith for being such a true and trusty friend, and Clare Dekker, for whom the book's dedication is a poor reward for all the time, support, and patience she has given me in the long, sometimes painful and exhausting, business of writing and rewriting. Like the swan sailing effortlessly upstream, an awful lot of hard work is done out of sight.

—*Ken Newton*
Wivenhoe

1

Surprising News

Few would argue with the claim that free news media should be a vital part of democracy, but many believe they undermine it instead. Some newspapers proudly proclaim their decisive influence over election results and their ability to make or break even powerful politicians. Research finds evidence of the agenda-setting power of the media and of the videomalaise, distrust, alienation, and political apathy they induce. Some eminent academics go so far as to state that the media use their monopoly of news and information to control what the population thinks and does. Politicians evidently believe them or, at least, are unwilling to risk ignoring them, so they spend huge amounts of time, energy, and money trying to control the news and keep media owners and editors on their side. There is widespread concern about the declining quantity and quality of news available in the mainstream media and how their influence has been supplanted by the divisive and corrosive effects of partisan television, biased journalism, fake news, foreign interference, and the hate-laden prejudices of a multitude of websites.

The importance of the media for democracy continues to produce a huge volume of comment on the subject. Opinions are often expressed with conviction, and yet (or perhaps because?) it is actually exceedingly difficult to pin down media power with any certainty. If the commercial media must produce what consumers are able and willing to buy, and if consumers are free to self-select what they want and are able and willing to pay for, then which is the chicken and which the egg?

Consequently, social science is divided. Some assert the power of the press, sometimes without evidence; some produce facts and figures that suggest strong, even massive, media effects; some find little more than modest consequences for public opinion and behavior; and some discover positive, others negative, media effects on democratic politics and government.

1

The result has been a hotly debated and unresolved issue ever since modern research took off some eight decades ago.

The difficulty of arriving at definitive and acceptable conclusions based on hard evidence has produced two divergent responses. One is to make plausible but speculative generalizations, though this has resulted in an assortment of contradictory claims that seem reasonable but are difficult to prove, or are sometimes disproved by subsequent developments. The other response, resulting from the pressures of modern academic life, is to engage in ever more specialized research on one particular set of circumstances in one country at one time, which is then summarized neatly in eight thousand words for publication in a journal. This sort of research, though it may be a valuable addition to knowledge, usually relates to a limited and specific time, place, and set of circumstances, so its relevance to higher level generalization about media effects in other times, places, and circumstances are obscure or unknown.

This volume takes a different approach. It is a slow book that marshals a great deal of empirical evidence drawn from a large and diverse range of studies, placing them in a broader picture and drawing out their common features and conclusions. As it turns out, diverse studies in different subfields reach some strikingly similar conclusions. In addition, trying to sketch out the bigger picture, the book ventures into fields of research directly relevant to media effects that are sometimes neglected by specialists in the field. This strategy reveals important gaps in media effects research and highlights the work that starts filling them in. Most important, perhaps, it sheds the harsh light of fact-based social science research on the influence of different kinds of media with different kinds of messages on different types of people in different sorts of circumstances. The results turn out to have a lot in common with the standard model of the behavioral sciences established by social psychology, political science, and sociology over two or three generations of research. The standard model is built upon a very large body of work that establishes such things as class, education, religion, income, occupation, age, and sex as the most important causal variables in most explanations of mass attitudes and behavior. In political science, the list also includes partisanship, party identification, and political interest. This book shows that the standard model, rather than the media, is generally the most powerful when it comes to explaining political attitudes and behavior.

In Chapter 2, the book lays down its foundations with a review of a large body of experimental psychology research on how and why individuals can preserve their beliefs, sometimes in the face of all evidence, logic, and argument to the contrary. The second part of the chapter shows that millions of people do the same in the real world outside the laboratories, whatever the media say. Disbelieving what the mainstream media tell us and believing things that find little or no support in the mainstream media are common behaviors in modern society, although so also is accepting, absorbing, and acting upon media messages. This suggests that media effects are the product of interactions between audiences and media messages, and any attempt to understand these effects must take account of the relationship between media producers and consumers.

Chapter 3 considers political partisanship and party identification—that is, strong attachments to political ideas, values, and organizations. Experiments show that people are likely to engage in belief preservation where partisan opinions are concerned, and the same seems to be true of partisans in the outside world. Pre-existing political beliefs and values exercise a strong influence on what news individuals get and how they react to it, accepting it, rejecting it, or ignoring it according to their prior political attachments and attitudes.

Most people do not have strong partisan or political party attachments. Chapter 4 broadens the scope of the inquiry to examine how non-partisanship and non-party political beliefs and values can influence the ways the majority of individuals receive and process news reports and draw conclusions from them.

Building on evidence about personal values and beliefs, Chapter 5 examines the largely neglected role of everyday knowledge and experience as sources of political information and opinion that can reinforce or over-ride the messages of the news media. It is widely assumed that citizens depend heavily on the news media for political information and opinion, but it seems that this is not always the case.

Chapter 6 continues with this line of inquiry by examining how one aspect of everyday life—political talk with friends, family, neighbors, and colleagues—can also be a source of political information and opinion that moderates the impact of the news media. Political talk can guide individuals to accept, ignore, or reject media messages.

Since trust is so important for the credibility of a news source, Chapter 7 discusses how it can limit or enhance media influence and how it interacts with individual characteristics to moderate media effects.

Chapter 8 explores the ways the media—especially the entertainment media—might influence political life indirectly with subtle messages that come in under the radar of conscious awareness. It covers an array of possible effects and compares those of newspapers and television, and news and entertainment television.

The first eight chapters deal mainly with the micro, demand side of the equation—the individual characteristics of media audiences—but there is also the macro, supply side of news media systems. Supply and demand are often analyzed separately, although understanding media effects requires examining the interaction between them. Besides, the contours of the producer side have changed radically in recent decades, giving the media a new shape, possibly new powers. Therefore, Chapters 9 to 11 analyze three important aspects of the news media supply side and their consequences for political attitudes and behaviors.

Chapter 9 compares commercial and public service broadcasting, showing that they have different effects on political knowledge, trust, participation, and democratic support. Chapter 10 turns to the classic theory of news media pluralism as a cornerstone of modern democracy—one that requires news to be produced by a variety of sources, reflecting a diversity of political opinions. A pluralist news media maximizes the power of citizens to make up their own minds and minimizes the power of the press over public opinion. The chapter discusses how a new information-rich digital era has outflanked the growing concentration of ownership and control of the old media and the importance of internal pluralism within a single news organization. In brief, Chapter 9 estimates the extent to which the contemporary news media systems of Britain and the United States are pluralist in terms of their organization and news content.

A vital but largely unexplored aspect of both media pluralism and media effects concerns the news-gathering habits of citizens and the political diversity of their news diets. The importance of news diets has been raised by claims that the new media have a divisive, polarizing effect because they make it possible for individuals to self-select news sources that reflect their own opinions back to them. Chapter 11 presents evidence about the extent to which citizens use different news sources and whether they are trapped in echo chambers of their own making.

The first chapters of the book give insufficient attention to what are often called the "new media," so Chapters 10 and 11 expand on this topic, explaining why the term *new media* is misleading and confusing. Avoiding the plausible speculation of many digital utopians and dystopians as much as possible, they explore what little we know about the political content and effects of digital news, social websites, cable news, and fake news.

Chapter 12 draws together the threads of previous chapters, summarizing the main findings of the book in brief and general terms.

The postscript argues that media power is not just of academic interest, but a practical issue that lies at the heart of democracy, involving how political leaders behave. Democratic government and politics could be greatly improved if politicians and the public better understood the real nature of media influence and power.

Each chapter reviews a set of empirical studies that deal with a subset of media effects research. The studies are chosen for their high quality and because they reveal a key aspect of the subject. The research strategy for exploring media effects is to take the best cases, not necessarily the most recent ones simply because they are contemporary. To take just two examples: The Clinton-Lewinsky scandal resulted in what has been described as a "feeding frenzy of attack journalism." Although the case is now twenty years old, it provides us with one of the clearest test cases in modern history of the news media's ability to undermine, even destroy, elected leaders. As such, it has been subjected to close scrutiny by dozens of social scientists, with surprising results.

The second example comes from the other side of the Atlantic. The role of the tabloid paper, *The Sun*, in the British election of 1997 was highly controversial. *The Sun* was Britain's biggest-selling paper, it was highly partisan, and, unusually for national dailies in the United Kingdom, it switched its party support for the 1997 election. If newspapers influence the voting patterns of their readers, this should show up with unusual clarity in a larger-than-average increase in Labour voting among *Sun* readers. Because Labour won an unprecedented landslide, and because it is widely believed that newspapers have a lot of influence over their readers' voting choices, it is entirely plausible to speculate, as *The Sun* did, that "It was *The Sun* wot won it." Because it is a key test case for gauging media influence, the 1997 election also attracted a great deal of careful research in the United Kingdom, also with surprising results.

The chapters that follow dwell on these and other significant case studies of media power that tell us a lot about the subject. Some of the case studies are old, some new, but in all cases the argument of the main research piece is augmented with evidence drawn from other sources, often more recent publications and especially up-to-date websites and survey evidence where it exists. One purpose of case studies is to lay down markers that can be checked against subsequent studies and new developments, so these chapters deal with, among other things, newspaper endorsements of Donald Trump, fake news, the content of the most popular news websites, the political effects of partisan cable news channels, and the politics of social media sites.

The research strategy of this book, therefore, involves comparing and contrasting a large number of studies of media effects on political attitudes and behavior in order to compare and contrast the conclusions they reach. The book does not merely triangulate in order to reach reliable conclusions, but it polyangulates, using many different studies written by sociologists, political scientists, psychologists, and economists who employ a variety of methods to investigate many possible media effects on politics. American and British research is used in the main, but single-country research on Russia, the Netherlands, Canada, France, Italy, Spain, Germany, and Belgium is included, as are comparative studies of European Union member states.

The book covers the work of more than 50 main authors in some detail and reinforces them with shorter accounts of other work and many references to related work. The methods used in these studies include laboratory experiments, participant observation, questionnaire surveys, focus groups, single-country and comparative studies, and cross-sectional, time-series, and multilevel analysis.

The research strategy requires a comparison of different kinds of media—broadsheet and tabloid newspapers, print and TV news, commercial and public broadcasting, and news and entertainment content. It also requires a careful distinction between the means of delivering news (old media and new media) and their content, as well as examination of how the demand and supply sides of the media equation interact to produce media effects.

Because media effects may vary from one political matter to another, the case studies cover an assortment of issues, including the Korean and Vietnam Wars, the Clinton-Lewinsky scandal, priming and agenda setting, how Russians use their TV news, judgments about the national economy, election campaigns and voting patterns, televised incivility, political knowledge, social and political trust, the mean world effect, democratic attitudes, political activity, political polarization, political cynicism, and alienation.

In short, this book is a meta-analysis and synthesis that marshals a large and diverse body of evidence and argument about the power and influence of the media on mass political attitudes and behavior. The results are often counterintuitive and contrary to received wisdom. In a word, they are surprising.

2

Belief Preservation

We see the world not as it is but as we are.

—Attributed to Leo Rosten

An impressive weight of experimental psychological research demonstrates that individuals are able to ignore, suppress, misinterpret, forget, misremember, misunderstand, avoid, or deny information and opinion that does not accord with their own view of the world. The basic idea is not at all new. In *The New Organon* published in 1620, Sir Francis Bacon wrote, "The human understanding when it has once adopted an opinion (either as being the received opinion or as being agreeable to itself) draws all things else to support and agree with it." This is confirmed by the accumulated evidence of six decades of experimental research since the 1950s, showing how people are equipped with an elaborate and subtle array of psychological mechanisms that can protect them from information and opinions that conflict with their own values and beliefs. As a result, those who have formed an opinion or made a decision are often unwilling or unable to change it.

Research of this kind has powerful implications for the ability of the media to shape or create public opinion and behavior. Therefore, the first part of this chapter briefly reviews the psychological mechanisms of belief preservation, also known as cognitive bias, heuristics, and motivated reasoning. The next section takes a closer look at research on the psychology of belief preservation and what can occur when attempts are made to correct misinformation.

The third section moves out of the psychology laboratories and into the real world to consider how some individuals stick doggedly to beliefs and forms of behavior that are inconsistent with all evidence and rational argument. Although "true believers" form small minorities on any given

7

subject—flat-earthers and alien abductees, for example—they are collectively a large minority. The fourth part of the chapter provides evidence of less extreme forms of such beliefs and behavior that are common in modern society. Some involve rejecting almost everything found in the mainstream media on a given subject, and some involve resolute faith in ideas that find little or no support there. In some cases, millions of individuals do this, even to the point of considerable expense and self-harm.

The fifth section makes the point that many popular beliefs are variations on themes that predate—sometimes by centuries—the modern era of communications, so the media cannot be held responsible for originating them, though they may help sustain these beliefs and spread them. Neither can genes, evolution, advertising, or the pursuit of fun and curiosity explain more than a small percentage of such beliefs, thus leaving room for media effects.

The chapter ends with the crucially important observation that although some people are able to close their ears and eyes to the political information they receive from the mainstream media, others accept it and may change their minds. Different people respond in different ways to the same media message, and the same person can respond in different ways to the same message from different sources.

Cognitive Bias and Heuristics

Reason is and ought only to be the slave of the passions and can never pretend to any other office than to serve and obey them.
                                    —*David Hume,* Treatise on Human Nature

One account of cognitive bias lists over 50 types that contribute to a "lack of active open-mindedness [when we] ignore possibilities, evidence, and goals that we ought to consider, and we make inferences in ways that protect our favored ideas."[1] Fortunately, six decades of research on the subject are documented by Fine in her marvelous book *A Mind of Its Own: How Your Brain Distorts and Deceives,* where she writes, "The brain biases, evades, twists, discounts, misinterprets, even makes up evidence—all so that we can retain that self-satisfying sense of being in the right."[2] Or as the neuroscientist Burnett puts it, "The brain has a strong egocentric bias: it makes it and us look good at every opportunity."[3]

Daniel Kahneman, a coinventor of the term cognitive bias, distinguishes between two basic types of thinking.[4] Type 1 is fast, intuitive, emotional, subconscious, automatic, and instinctive. Type 2 thinking is slower, more deliberative, logical, calculating, and conscious. It is also more demanding of effort and concentration and less frequently used. Type 1 thinking is typically used in the ordinary course of events, especially when complex issues are involved, little time is available for thought, and there is either a lack or an excess of information. Type 1 thinking cannot be switched off. It works fast by simplifying, makes the WYSIAYG (what you see is *all* you get) assumption, and is good at jumping to conclusions, correct or otherwise. It is built out of a wide array of biases that cut corners at high speed and without much thought. According to Kahneman, most of our daily decisions and judgments are produced by type 1 thinking. He does not mention the news, but it is likely that we respond to that in the same way.

Kahneman applies his observations about type 1 thinking to laypeople, experts, highly trained professionals, and seasoned specialists. So does Tetlock in his book *Expert Political Judgment.* He classifies experts as foxes at one end of a continuum and hedgehogs at the other. Foxes know many things; hedgehogs know one big thing. Hedgehogs are the grand theorists who believe that their approach explains a great many events; they tend to be intellectually aggressive and confident. Foxes are skeptical about grand theories; they pick and choose from different theories, are cautious in their judgments, and modify their ideas according to experience.

Hedgehogs have their value, but they are less likely to admit to being wrong and rarely change their theory, rationalizing their failures with a "formidable combination of defences" that enable them to stick to their original theory.[5] They are similar to ordinary people in their ability to preserve their view of the world even in the face of incontrovertible evidence to the contrary. As Mlodinow observes, "We all create our own view of the world and then employ it to filter and process our perceptions. . . . And we often make errors."[6] Moreover, we tend to think that we know more than we actually do, and those who know the least are prone to be more certain of their own judgment. Americans with only the vaguest idea of where the Ukraine is geographically were the most likely to support the idea of US military intervention in response to problems between it and Russia.[7] For the same sort of reason, political extremists often suffer from the illusion that they understand political problems.[8]

Observing that "anyone who has made a decision is usually extremely reluctant to change it, even in the face of overwhelming evidence that it is wrong," Sutherland lists a handful of mental mechanisms that explain why opinions are resistant to change.[9] First, there is selective perception, which enables individuals to avoid inconvenient evidence. Second, evidence may be rejected as unbelievable. Third, individuals may twist evidence to fit their own views. Fourth, they may selectively remember those things that confirm their opinion. Fifth, people are adept at inventing explanations for events.[10] He adds a sixth, more general reason, which is the self-serving or confirmation bias that may be the root cause of other forms of cognitive bias.[11] Ariely comes to the same conclusion when he says, "We persist in deceiving ourselves in part to maintain a positive self-image."[12] The self-serving bias has another little twist. People are more critical of other people's arguments than their own. They are not necessarily overcritical, but they are better able and much more likely to spot failings in the arguments of others.[13] As Mercier and Sperber put it, "Human reason is both biased and lazy."[14]

According to Westen, the self-serving bias has a neurological and chemical basis.[15] In his brain-scanning research, he presented committed Republicans and Democrats with information that was in head-on conflict with their own beliefs and traced the neural activity in the brain that it caused. Threatening information activated neural paths that produce stress, so participants' brains quickly searched by means of faulty reasoning for ways of reducing the stress. This turned off stress-producing brain cells and turned on brain circuits involved in positive emotions. Westen concludes that, "When partisans face threatening information, not only are they likely to 'reason' to emotionally biased conclusions, but we can trace their neural footprints as they do it."[16] Conversely, encountering beliefs that are consistent with our own induces a shot of dopamine-induced pleasure in the brain so that we feel good about ourselves even if we are wrong.[17]

Self-serving bias can produce amusing outcomes. When asked to compare themselves with others, many say that they are better drivers, more popular than their friends, have healthier lifestyles, are endowed with better memories, and have superior problemsolving and leadership skills.[18] Two-thirds of the faculty of the University of Nebraska placed themselves in the top 25 percent of teachers in their university, and more than three-quarters of MBA students at Stanford claimed to be above the median in academic performance.[19] Virtually all Germans believe they are very good or quite good drivers.[20] Many believe that others are foolish enough to believe what they read in the papers, though they themselves are too well-informed and clever to fall into this stupid trap.[21] Most Americans believe that they are good at spotting fake news, although some evidence shows otherwise.[22] Correspondingly, the Dunning-Kruger effect occurs when those who are unable to do a mental task well overrate their performance; they are ignorant of their own ignorance and not intelligent enough to rate their own intelligence.[23] The final irony of the self-serving bias is that most people believe they are less susceptible to the self-serving bias than others. Even when they are aware that the bias is a general tendency, they deceive themselves into thinking they are objective and others are not.[24]

An early experiment showed fans of opposing teams a film of an American football game in which each side committed a lot of fouls. Each set of fans thought the other team had committed more fouls. The authors concluded that "there is no such 'thing' as a 'game' existing 'out there' in its own right which people merely 'observe.' . . . For the 'thing' simply is *not* the same for different people whether the 'thing' is a football game, a presidential candidate, Communism, or spinach."[25] The tribal loyalties of the fans led them to see what they wanted to see. Similarly, Rahn's experimental work shows how partisanship and party labels often trump hard information, allowing individuals to avoid the stress of confronting inconvenient political facts.[26]

It is to be expected that football fans are biased in their judgments about the game, but neutral photographs and pictures are no less subject to interpretation. A picture may be worth a thousand words, but people typically use a different thousand words to describe it. "If you ask a number of observers to look at a photograph," writes the pioneer of this research, "the variability of their reports will be amazingly high."[27] It is often said that photographs don't lie (though, actually, they can be manipulated), but people can see different things in them, focus on different parts, ignore others, and assign different meanings to the same photo. As Edelman puts it, "The audiences for news are ultimate interpreters, paying attention to some stories, ignoring most, and fitting news accounts into a story plot that reflects their respective values."[28] Seeing may be believing, but people see different things to believe in.[29]

Once an idea or a "fact" has taken root, it can be hard to change or correct, partly because of the confirmation and disconfirmation biases.[30] According to Fine, "Evidence that fits with our beliefs is quickly waved through the mental border control. Counter-evidence, on the other hand, must submit to close interrogation and even then will probably not be allowed in."[31] This helps to explain why those who initially supported the invasion of Iraq—because they believed it had weapons of mass destruction—were more likely to believe that such weapons had been found, despite repeated news stories to the contrary.[32]

Memory often plays tricks.[33] According to Mlodinow, we give "unwarranted importance to memories that are the most vivid and hence most available for retrieval—our memory makes it easy to remember the events that are unusual and striking not the many events that are normal and dull."[34] The self-serving bias works because, as Trivers observes, "There are also many processes of memory that can be biased to produce welcome results. Memories are continually distorting in self-serving ways."[35] A recent study argues that several forms of cognitive bias cause distortions in storing and retrieving memories.[36] This, in turn, has a bearing on theories of agenda setting, priming, and framing, which argue that how people respond to the news is strongly influenced by what is most easily and readily accessible from their memories. But what if memories about news stories are faulty and distort, forget, or invent what was actually reported? In such cases, it may be the manipulation of memories in individual minds that primes, frames, and sets the agenda, not the original news stories. Chapter 7 returns to the subject of priming, framing, and agenda setting.

The Persistence of Beliefs

"I have always abided by my first opinion," answered Pangloss, "for, after all, I am a philosopher, and it would not become me to retract my sentiments; especially as Leibnitz could not be in the wrong."
                                                            —*Voltaire,* Candide

A classic study of cognitive bias selected capital punishment as the controversial topic of study because it elicits strong and widely discussed opinions.[37] Forty-eight students, half with pro–capital punishment and half with anti–capital punishment views, were presented with three rounds of information. First, they were shown a brief statement about the results of an invented study of the deterrent effects of the death penalty. Next, they were presented with a more detailed account of the study, its methods, and some prominent criticism of the study in an invented literature plus a rebuttal of those criticisms. In the third round, the whole process was repeated, this time with a different piece of fictitious research reporting results that were the reverse of the first. Each round was followed by questions probing attitudes and attitude change about capital punishment.

Both the pro– and the anti–capital punishment groups were biased in favor of studies that confirmed their initial attitudes, each group interpreting the same information to support their opposing views. They said that the evidence they disagreed with was unreliable or invalid, but accepted the evidence they agreed with at face value. Moreover, attitudes toward the death penalty were more polarized at the end of the research than at the start. The authors conclude, "In everyday life, as well as in the course of scientific controversies the mere availability of contradictory evidence rarely seems sufficient to cause us to abandon our prior beliefs or theories."[38]

In another classic study, counterinformation was found to immunize people against subsequent doses of the same sort of information.[39] In later research, experimental subjects were provided with a small and weak refutation of their beliefs, which made it possible for them to resist stronger refutations afterward.[40] Immunity theory has been tested on a variety of political issues and in various election campaigns, and it works well, allowing people to hold on to their opinions and dismiss opposing information, especially if they are aware counterattacks may be possible in the future—a normal occurrence in political controversies.[41]

Other experimental studies shed light on the persistence of political misperceptions and how attempts to correct them can backfire.[42] Individuals with opinions about weapons of mass destruction in Iraq, stem cell research, and tax cuts were presented with mock news articles containing false and misleading information about these issues. The effectiveness of attempts to correct this misinformation varied according to participants' original beliefs. The most committed were the most resistant to correction, and in several cases, correcting false information not only failed to change minds but had a "backfire" or "boomerang" effect of strengthening mistaken beliefs. So, trying to correct mistakes can have the opposite effect of reinforcing them. Whereas positive reinforcement—when opinions are strengthened by information that supports them—is well recognized in the political science literature, the reverse effect of negative reinforcement strengthening mistaken beliefs has gone largely unnoticed. It turns out to be quite a common phenomenon and important for an understanding of media effects, and we return to it in Chapter 3.

It does not follow that all attempts to correct misinformation fail, but once again, it seems that this depends on the source of the correction insofar as individuals are more likely to accept the word of people with whom they have personal connections than that of strangers.[43] The validity of the message is judged by who is delivering it.

Munro's study of the rejection of science takes belief persistence a step further.[44] After sorting a hundred students into two groups according to their views about homosexuality, he gave them fake research evidence that either confirmed or contradicted their opinions about the association between homosexuality and mental illness. Those who associated homosexuality with mental illness were not only more likely to reject the evidence of no association but were also more likely to reject the relevance of scientific investigation to this and other empirical questions. In this way, they were able to hold strong and erroneous opinions about a wide variety of subjects by denying the relevance and reliability of science itself—a stance that is not uncommon in modern society. Believers in extrasensory perception (ESP) can maintain their faith by claiming that the particular ESP phenomenon under investigation disappears when placed under the scientific microscope.[45] Similarly, practitioners of homeopathy claim their treatments cannot be tested using normal methods of medical science.[46] When some people are confronted with simple logical errors in their beliefs, they can escape their dilemma by denying the validity of the logic and the validity of the science.[47]

Some argue that belief confirmation can result from the solitary activity of thinking about an issue. It is not necessarily limited to occasions when we read newspapers, watch the news, or discuss matters with others but also occurs when we engage in the satisfying job of knocking down the straw men we create in our own minds.[48]

Some personal beliefs are like cherished possessions, not to be given up without a mental struggle.[49] The more cherished the possession and the more central it is to a person's core personality, the harder it is to give it up.[50] Conversely, neutrals and partisans whose beliefs are weaker are likely to be more open-minded.[51] This raises an important point: experimental research carefully selects participants who hold strong beliefs in order to study how people preserve their beliefs. But not many people hold strong beliefs on all topics. How do these ambivalent partisans or neutrals react to information that attempts to correct misperceptions and erroneous ideas? One set of experimental studies shows how.

Belief Preservation, Attractive Faces, and Moral Issues

Early research demonstrates that once formed, impressions can be resistant to new information, even when strongly held and partisan opinions are not involved.[52] More recently, 120 people were shown a pair of photos of female faces and asked to pick the one they found more attractive.[53] They were then shown the photos again and asked to explain why they preferred the faces they picked. But in some cases, unknown to participants, a "magic card trick" was used to switch the cards, so that they were now asked to explain why they preferred a face they had not picked. Most participants failed to notice the switch and nevertheless proceeded to explain in detail why a face they had not chosen was more attractive than the one they in reality had chosen. When the photo switch was revealed, some people refused to believe it and insisted their behavior was consistent and reasonable.

Subsequent research demonstrates the same mental agility operates on a variety of matters, including opinions about abstract paintings, the taste of jam, and the smell of tea. It is not difficult to imagine why people want to protect pet theories and strong beliefs about religion and politics, but the fact that they do the same with trivial matters suggests that self-delusion and the need to be right can triumph over undeniable evidence and logic, all because of "the vain brain that excuses your faults and failures, or simply rewrites them out of history."[54]

In one experiment, participants were asked to agree or disagree with a set of controversial political statements (for example, the appropriateness of government surveillance of citizens to combat crime and terrorism).[55] Then, by means of a trick, they were invited to defend exactly the opposite opinion. A small minority detected the trick, but some endorsed and explained the view opposite the one they had just expressed and offered firm and coherent arguments that contradicted what they had said before.

The evidence about belief preservation in the face of truth is overwhelming, but nevertheless has its limitations and shortcomings. First, psychology labs create a simplified world in which a few variables are systematically manipulated, while others are held constant. That is the strength and the weakness of experimentation; the real world is a more complex place where all other things are rarely constant or equal. Consequently, we cannot automatically extrapolate from experiments to the real world. Second, it is clear that people do not always or inevitably use these mental mechanisms to protect their opinions. On the contrary, experimental and other research finds that some people do change their opinions in response to evidence and argument.[56] Therefore, the next section explores cognitive bias and belief preservation in the world outside experimental laboratories, starting with some extreme and clear-cut cases of "true believers"—those who hold to certain ideas and theories, even if these are inconsistent or in head-on conflict with practically everything known about the issues.

True Believers

A fanatic is one who won't change his mind and won't change the subject.
                                        —Attributed to Winston Churchill

When Prophecy Fails tells how Marian Keech (pseudonym) received messages in the form of automatic writing from advanced aliens on the planet Clarion, telling her how the world would be destroyed by a great flood before dawn on December 21, 1954.[57] The messages said that Mrs. Keech and the Seekers, her small group of followers, would be saved at midnight just before the cataclysm by a stranger, who would carry them off to safety on Clarion in a flying saucer. The Seekers prepared for their departure from Earth, some by giving up jobs, college enrollment, spouses, and money, and waited as midnight approached for the stranger to whisk them away.

When the stranger had not arrived by five past midnight, the group sat in stunned silence, and Mrs. Keech began to cry. But shortly before dawn she received another automatic message telling her that the little group sitting all night long had shown so much faith and spread so much light that the world would be saved from destruction for the time being. The group reorganized itself around this revelation. Two members left, but the others were convinced that their example had saved the world. To eliminate the cognitive dissonance caused by the failure of the prophecy, they set out to convince the rest of the world of their belief. Festinger concludes that when faced with undeniable refutation of a deep conviction, an individual will frequently emerge, not only unshaken, but even more convinced of the truth of his beliefs than ever before. Indeed, he may even show a new fervor about convincing and converting other people to his view.[58]

Mrs. Keech and her Seekers are an extreme case, but not an exceptional one. Many others in the Western world are convinced of ideas that are contrary to all known evidence as reported by most information sources, including the mainstream media. Examples pack the pages of the following books:

• *Counter-Knowledge: How We Surrendered to Conspiracy Theories, Quack Medicine, Bogus Science and Fake History*[59]

- *Paranormal America: Ghost Encounters, UFO Sightings, Bigfoot Hunts, and Other Curiosities in Religion and Culture*[60]
- *Invented Knowledge: False History, Fake Science and Pseudo Religions*[61]
- *Egyptomania: A History of Fascination, Obsession and Fantasy*[62]
- *The March of Unreason: Science, Democracy, and the New Fundamentalism*[63]
- *Follies of the Wise: Dissenting Essays*[64]
- *Flat Earth: The History of an Infamous Idea*[65]
- *Voodoo Science*[66]
- *Superstition: Belief in the Age of Science*[67]
- *Voodoo Histories: The Role of the Conspiracy Theory in Shaping Modern History*[68]
- *How Mumbo-Jumbo Conquered the World: A Short History of Modern Delusions*[69]
- *Snake Oil Science: The Truth About Complementary and Alternative Medicine*[70]
- *Conspiracy Theories: Secrecy and Power in American Culture*[71]
- *Why People Believe Weird Things: Pseudoscience, Superstition, and Other Confusions of Our Time*[72]
- *Flim-Flam! Psychics, ESP, Unicorns, and Other Delusions*[73]
- *Trick or Treatment: The Undeniable Facts About Alternative Medicine*[74]
- *Killing Us Softly: The Sense and Nonsense of Alternative Medicine*[75]
- *Abducted: How People Come to Believe They Were Kidnapped by Aliens*[76]
- *When Prophecy Never Fails: Myth and Reality in a Flying-Saucer Group*[77]

These volumes discuss Holocaust deniers; UFO believers; fake nutrition; biblical prophecies; 9/11 conspiracy theories; astrology; witchcraft; Satanism; Martian civilizations; airstrips in the Andes; pseudohistory; fake archaeology; fantastical astronomy; lost tribes; ESP; a flat earth; a hollow earth; the Ark of the Covenant; the healing power of crystals; myths about AIDS; Merovingian kings descended from Mary Magdalene; the Holy Grail; lay lines; perpetual motion; the law of attraction (the universe adjusts itself around your thoughts); cult leaders; the QLink pendant that protects us from radiation; chemical analysis of the hair; homeopathy; and how space travelers built the Egyptian pyramids, the Easter Island statues, Stonehenge, and the Andean temples of Tiahuanaco. Thompson refers to these as counterknowledge, and the economist John Quiggin refers to them as zombie ideas.[78]

This is only a small part of the true believer phenomenon. Some claim to have been abducted by space aliens; others are convinced that the world will be destroyed by a wrathful God on a date calculated from biblical text, Aztec ruins, the pyramids, or Nostradamus. There are those who believe in near-death or prebirth experiences, miracle diets, orthomolecular medicine, applied kinesiology, and the therapeutic touch of healing hands. According to some, we should all eat more bilberries or follow the rainbow diet or realign our biorhythms on the astral plane. The Unarius Academy of Science teaches evolutionary physics and the fourth-dimensional level of understanding. Quack medicine is a huge industry with a large and steady demand for expensive snake oils and books on alternative medicine. These are firmly held beliefs for which the mainstream media offer little, if any, support and little, if any, coverage of any kind.

Conspiracy theories form a large and popular subset of true beliefs. Some assert that the Kennedys murdered Marilyn Monroe, the CIA murdered the Kennedys, and the British government and/or Royal Family murdered Princess Diana. One theory states that President Franklin Roosevelt was responsible for the attack on Pearl Harbor, another that the Apollo moon landing was faked in a Hollywood film studio, and another that Communists/Muslims/Jews have penetrated every level of American government. For some, *The Protocols of the Elders of Zion* reveals a Jewish plot to take over the world, but others know that the world is actually run by the secret society of the Illuminati. According to some, miniature cameras are hidden in TV sets to spy on us, but others fear the mind-controlling rays and subliminal messages that TV sets emit. Some are convinced that the Holocaust never happened; others, that the Bermuda Triangle exists. According to one theory, President Bill Clinton had at least 50 of his political opponents murdered.[79] The belief that 9/11 was planned and carried out by people inside government is not uncommon, and a video series about it (*Loose Change*) is said to have sold more than a million copies and to have been watched by 10 million people on the web.[80] Also, the secret truth about how to cast out demons is expounded for all to discover on a website.[81]

Some of these strange beliefs have been taken seriously by the US government and military and funded by them. In *Voodoo Science,* the Nobel Prize winner Robert Park reports that the US military has sponsored research on perpetual motion.[82] *The Men Who Stare at Goats* tells how the First Earth Battalion of the US Army was set up in defiance of all known laws of physics to research walking through walls, becoming invisible, and killing goats by staring at them.[83]

True believers can always find support for their ideas in highly specialized sources that cater to small minorities, but very few of the ideas listed in the previous paragraphs are seriously advocated or even mentioned in the mainstream media. How is it, as Schudson asks, "that half of the American people believe in devils when there is not a trace of the devil to be found in the relentlessly secular mainstream media?"[84] People in their millions are capable of believing things that do not appear in the mainstream media.

Mass Attitudes and Behavior

Mundus vult decipi, ergo decipiatur.
(The world wants to be deceived; let it be deceived.)
    —*Attributed to various people including, incorrectly, Petronius*

Numerous popular sayings tip us off to the possibility that blindness to evidence, argument, and influence is all around us in daily life. People say, "There is no sense in trying to reason with him," or there is "no talking to her," or "it's like talking to the deaf," or "it's all water off a duck's back," and "it's like talking to a brick wall." The same thought is expressed as "you will never make him see sense," or "you might as well talk to yourself," and "you might as well save your breath" because "there's none so blind as will not see." It is well known that love is blind, that you can lead a horse to water, but you can't make it drink. We commonly say a person is in denial, stubborn as a mule, pig headed, suffers from tunnel vision, has a one-track mind, is thick-headed and that it doesn't matter what you say, that person always has to be right, will always have the last word, and is so certain. Of course, it is possible that the people saying these things are projecting their own faults onto others, but this simply confirms that mulishness might be a common feature of normal life, which includes political life; perhaps it is a special feature of political life.[85]

In *States of Denial: Knowing About Atrocities and Suffering,* Stanley Cohen documents examples of how people can ignore or suppress information they do not want to know:

> One common thread runs through the many different stories of denial: people, organizations, governments or whole societies are presented with information that is too disturbing, threatening or anomalous to be fully absorbed or openly acknowledged. The information is therefore somehow repressed, disavowed, pushed aside or reinterpreted. Or else the information "registers" well enough, but its implications—cognitive, emotional or moral—are evaded, neutralized or rationalized away.[86]

There are many other examples of such mass denial. In the United States, about 40 to 45 percent of the adult population (90 to 100 million individuals) believes that God created the world about 10,000 years ago. In Britain, the same belief is held by only 9 percent of the adult population, amounting to about 4.5 million people, and in Canada the figure is 15 percent, or about 5 million adults.[87] Across 33 European countries, one in five of the population or approximately 150 million individuals do not accept the theory of evolution.[88]

A Harris poll (December 16, 2013) shows that 84 percent of those polled believed in miracles, two-thirds believed in the devil and hell, and half in ghosts.[89] Surveys in the United States find that three out of four people profess at least one paranormal belief from a list of ten, including ESP (41 percent), haunted houses and ghosts or spirits (37 percent and 32 percent, respectively), and telepathy (31 percent). Between a fifth and a quarter believe in clairvoyance, astrology, witches, and communication with the dead. More than a fifth (22 percent) believe in 5 of the list of 10, and more than half (57 percent) believe in at least 2 of them.[90] These numbers remain constant over time. New York City is replete with mentalists, astrologists, palm readers, clairvoyants, forecasters, star gazers, mind readers, hand readers, celestial travelers, clairaudients, diviners of individual essence, and technical astrologers who specialize in the spiritual life of people and animals. Demand for their skills allows them to charge $100 to $250 an hour.[91]

Polls conducted in the United Kingdom report that 16 percent of people believe in witches and wizards, 42 percent believe in ghosts, 24 percent believe that Princess Diana's death was the result of conspiracy, and 30 percent believe that evidence of UFO landings on Earth is being hidden from the public.[92] A Gallup study shows that 45 percent of people in Western Europe believe in telepathy, 34 percent had experienced telepathy, 21 percent had experienced clairvoyance, and 25 percent claimed to have had contact with the dead.[93] ESP, psychokinesis, psychic detectives, levitation, psychic surgery, UFOs, and dowsing can be added to the list of not uncommon beliefs. A CNN/Time poll reports that 80 percent of Americans believe that their government is hiding its knowledge of extraterrestrial life-forms. One Roper poll found that at least 1 in 50 Americans claims to have been abducted by aliens, and a quarter in a Gallup poll survey believed that space aliens have visited Earth.[94]

Other mass beliefs and behaviors defy almost everything to be found in the mainstream media. For years, the media have broadcast warnings about the danger of skin cancer caused by sunbathing, but millions of people continue to lie on beaches in the midday sun. Few in the Western world can possibly have missed the steady drumbeat of the media telling us not to overeat, not to smoke, not to abuse alcohol, to get enough exercise, and to eat a healthy diet. Yet the number of unhealthy and obese couch potatoes grows daily, heavy drinking is a problem, and tens of millions of people persist with their aversion to exercise. It is estimated that more than a quarter of British and more than a third of American adults are obese, and numbers are rising.[95] In the United Kingdom, 20 percent of adults smoke an average of 12 cigarettes a day.[96] In the United States, 15 percent of adults smoke, and 16 million have a smoking-related disease, which accounts for an estimated 480,000 deaths annually.[97]

Government announcements on TV and thousands of notices on the roads warn drivers not to follow the vehicle in front too closely: "Keep your distance." But on any journey in my car, I generally find at least one person driving dangerously close to my rear bumper. These drivers must have missed the great mass of messages about dangerous driving either because they are blind and deaf or illiterate (which would normally exclude them from getting a driver's license in the first place) or because they are impervious to the endlessly repeated warnings in the mass media about the dangers of tailgating. Drinking and driving is the same story. According to official statistics, roughly 11 percent (28.7 million) of the American population *owned up* to driving at least once in the previous year while over the legal limit. One person is killed every 45 minutes and 1 person injured about every 2 minutes in car accidents involving drink.[98] Few can have missed media reports about the dangers and penalties of using handheld phones while driving, but one survey reports that some 70 percent of Americans did this in 2015.[99]

Less harmful but no less surprising, men continue to buy hair-restoring potions that are known to have no effect at all, and women spend even more on useless beauty products. In 2012 in the United Kingdom, the facial skin care market was estimated at £1 billion thanks partly to a growth in spending on expensive antiaging and antiwrinkle products, most of which are known to have little or no physical effect.[100] As Helen Mirren, the face of L'Oreal, is reputed to have said, "Using moisturiser probably does f**k all."

There are many such political examples, as well. According to a Scripps Howard poll in 2006, most young Americans and 36 percent of adults suspect that it is "very likely" or "likely" that federal officials either assisted in the 9/11 attacks on the World Trade Center and the Pentagon or took no action to stop them because they wanted the United States to go to war in the Middle East.[101] In 2015, 43 percent of American Republicans and 29 percent of all Americans believed Obama was a Muslim, and 20 percent of all adults believed he was not American by birth.[102] A month after Baghdad was captured in April 2003, a third of Americans believed that weapons of mass destruction had been found in the country, and about a fifth believed that they had been used in the war.[103] These figures declined, but months later, a fifth still believed it was true. Almost half (48 percent) believed that Iraq had supported Al Qaeda.[104] The United States has its birthers, 9/11 conspiracy theorists, believers in Palin's death panels, and those who are convinced of the Clintons' involvement in a pedophile ring.

Surveys in Britain show that 56 percent of British Muslims thought that Arabs were innocent of any connection with 9/11, but a quarter believed that the British government was involved with the London terrorist bombings of July 7, 2005, and only 29 percent thought the Holocaust happened "as history teaches it."[105]

The fact is that most of us seem to be all but bulletproof against at least one, if not more, of the messages repeated over and over again by the mass media and other sources of information. This applies to political life as much as or perhaps more than other areas of human activity. Achen and Bartels find that "Even on purely factual questions with right answers, citizens are sometimes willing to believe the opposite if it makes them feel better about their partisanship and vote choices."[106] Nor is belief preservation limited to those with less education and lower intelligence. It also includes highly intelligent, well-educated, carefully trained, and well-paid experts and the full array of professionals, high-ranking military leaders, judges, shrewd political advisers, top businesspeople, and learned scholars.[107] The list, dear reader, includes you and me. And, it should be stressed, not all our belief preservation abilities are exercised in aid of outlandish and preposterous ideas. The chapters that follow provide many examples of where sections of the general public have rejected or ignored the messages of the mainstream media for perfectly understandable, sane, and sensible reasons, even if we don't personally agree. Belief preservation is a value-neutral mental tool. The point made here is that its use is widespread throughout the population.

The Hostile Media Effect

Political scientists have written extensively about one of the mental mechanisms used by some people to reject news stories that do not match their beliefs—the hostile media effect. This refers to the tendency of some people with strong ideological positions to regard media reports as negative about their own view and favorable to opposing views. The effect has been observed so often that it is judged to be a reliable finding.[108]

It is usually strongest among those with deep-rooted beliefs, less so among those with weaker beliefs and those who face new issues.[109] Partisans are likely to recognize when a report is biased in their own favor, but they may still claim that it favors the other side more than it should.[110]

One much-quoted study presented pro-Palestinian and pro-Israeli students at Stanford University with the same video report of a massacre of Palestinian refugees in Lebanon.[111] Both sides believed the report was biased, and whereas some students thought the content was loaded against their view, others thought the content was fair but claimed it still did not acknowledge the superiority of their own position. Both sides believed that a neutral observer would see the report as more critical of one or the other side's view. Similarly, a study of the 1992 US presidential election found that Republicans were more likely to believe that their newspaper favored Bill Clinton, while Democrats thought it favored George H. W. Bush.[112] Content analysis of the papers found little evidence of such bias.

The hostile media effect is commonly used selectively. Liberals and socialists do not complain that other liberals or socialists have been brainwashed by the liberal or socialist press. As far as they are concerned, only right-wingers and those with the wrong views are subjects of media bias. Right-wingers do not complain that those who share their views have been hoodwinked into thinking this way by the right wing or conservative press.

Only liberals and left-wingers fall into this error. Each claims that media effects explain the wrong and misinformed views of others, but not their own opinions. Committed partisans often make use of this argument selectively as a quick and easy way of discrediting opposing opinions and preserving their own beliefs, especially if they are in a minority. Ironically, complaining that others behave like sheep in mindlessly believing what the media tell them is itself behaving in a sheep-like manner by repeating the dogma that others believe everything they read in the papers.

In recent years the effects of biased cable news channels have become a concern. Research finds that those who believe the mainstream news is biased against their own views turn to these channels to find news that is more congenial. They also say that these programs are more interesting and more informative. More recently still, the issue of fake news and tweets about "dishonest journalists" have become major news items. This is an extreme version of the hostile media effect in which people believe that the mainstream media are not merely biased against them but also use false news (lies) as a propaganda weapon. We return to the hostile media effect and fake news in later chapters of this book. Meanwhile, the hostile media effect is another way in which individuals can reject news reports that do not fit their own view of the political world. As Gunther and Schmitt observe, the hostile media effect also underlines the importance of audience reactions to the media messages they receive and challenges what they call "the simplistic view of powerful and homogenizing effects of mass media."[113]

Belief Preservation and the Media

Some people want to be fooled all of the time.
All people want to be fooled some of the time.
But not all people want to be fooled all of the time.
                    —Attributed to Dr. Otto I. Q. Besser-Wisser

A lot of the evidence produced so far in this chapter relies on the answers that respondents give in opinion polls, but can we always be sure that people really believe what they say? Even if we can, can we assume that they act on what they claim to believe?

Do People Always Believe What They Say?
Some may not be entirely serious when they claim exotic beliefs and experiences that are given no credibility in the mainstream media. In the 2001 UK census, 390,127 people registered themselves as Jedi knights in order to make it an official religion in the country, but in all likelihood no more than 7 believed they actually were Jedi knights. Sometimes respondents say the

first thing that comes to mind to get rid of the pollsters—doorstep opinion. Some may have amused themselves by visiting a palm reader or playing with an Ouija board at a drunken party. There is also a difference between passing fads and fancies and long-lasting convictions. The mass media may influence short-lived crazes, of the hula hoop and Pokémon Go variety, although many other factors in the funnel of causality have to be taken into account.[114]

These examples suggest caution when perusing survey numbers for flat-earthers, UFO spotters, and Jedi knights. Nevertheless, curiosity, fun, and fleeting fashion do not explain the huge amounts of money, time, energy, danger, or self-harm involved with smoking, alcohol abuse, drugs, obesity, excessive sunbathing, lack of exercise, dangerous driving, and the costs of ineffective beauty products, miracle medicines, and diets.

Besides, beliefs range on a continuum from deep-seated convictions to superficial beliefs of convenience. Some who claimed that Obama was not an American by birth used it as a cover for gut feelings of a different, less acceptable kind.[115] Some may have used "death panels" to justify their opposition to Medicare legislation in the United States to bolster or hide their rejection of "creeping socialism and communism." The palpably false promise of £350 million a week for the National Health Service (NHS) after Brexit was, for some, a convenient smokescreen for views about immigration or to rationalize protest voting. Beliefs of convenience can be dropped and forgotten with ease, leaving beliefs of conviction untouched. Some partisans construct beliefs of convenience out of fake news, and some politicians and journalists construct fake news knowing it will be used this way and is unlikely to come back to haunt them. None of this suggests that no one is convinced by fake news, only that some may use it for temporary convenience. The influence of the news may vary according to how hard or soft opinion is.

Denying and Ignoring

There may also be a gap between what people know and believe and what they do. The majority of smokers can scarcely be unaware of the proven link between smoking and ill health, which has been a constant topic of media reports since the 1960s, yet they choose to ignore the warnings and continue to self-harm. In this respect, they are different from the creationists, who are also aware of the scientific view about evolution but reject it. It seems that some preserve their beliefs by denying the evidence; others accept the evidence but ignore it. Most flat-earthers, creationists, and believers in the occult and paranormal are deniers, while many smokers, drinkers, and drug addicts are ignorers.

Denying and ignoring were features of political life in Britain and the United States in 2016–2017. When Donald Trump Jr. stated that he had a meeting with Russians, who had promised information harmful to Hillary Clinton, only 45 percent of Trump supporters believed he had this meeting, while 55 percent denied it or were not sure. These figures reveal a "don't know, don't care" reaction.[116] Often denial is supported by conspiracy theory, whereas ignoring can be achieved by treating the news as a trivial matter of no concern. Once again, this is not to overlook the fact that a third group of Trump voters support him because they believe in what he claims to stand for. They have made their choice and they stick with it despite all the news in the mainstream media. At the time of this writing, about 34 percent of adult Americans, some 70 million people, approve of Trump's presidential performance. Party identification explains much of this. In July 2017, more than 80 percent of Republicans approved of his performance and about the same percentage of Democrats disapproved.[117]

The same ability to deny or ignore was demonstrated in the 2016 European Union (EU) referendum campaign in Britain. It was not difficult to avoid the truth behind many of the false claims and figures of the campaign, but many voters chose either to believe the untruths or to ignore them. The leave campaign's key promise that £350 million a week would be available for the NHS was untrue and widely reported to be so, but the facts counted for little. When the promise was dropped a day after the referendum result was announced, few of those who voted "leave" seemed to notice or care.

In both the United States and United Kingdom, the willingness of some electors to accept or ignore political lies, fake news, and impossible election promises raises concerns that some voters will believe six impossible things before breakfast and the hard facts, logic, and honest reporting in the media, or elsewhere, are powerless to do anything about it.

Counter-Knowledge and Mass Behavior in Ancient and Premodern Times

There are more reasons to doubt the power of the media to shape mass opinion and behavior on some matters. Many (probably most) of the beliefs detailed in this chapter—including faith in love and beauty potions, beliefs in the supernatural, witchcraft, Satanism, Armageddon, fake archaeology, the Second Coming, astrology, ESP, spiritualism, superstitions, and ghosts— are updated versions of beliefs commonly held long before media of any kind were invented. Most undesirable attributes of the general population— racism, sexism, greed, violence, prejudice, bigotry—said to be propagated by the yellow press, hate radio, and the worst websites, predate the Gutenberg Bible by centuries. Insatiable demands for tobacco, potatoes, and sugar raced across whole continents soon after Columbus returned from North America and all without the help of TV commercials and modern marketing techniques.[118] Cohn's study of social movements in the late middle ages in Europe shows how there were frequent outbreaks of millenarial beliefs and behavior, including manias like Saint Vitus's dance (Sydenham's chorea), mass fantasies, peasant revolts, collective violence, visions, and hysteria, some of them involving tens of thousands of people and all without the advantage of going viral on the web. Mass-market consumerism developed in the Netherlands in the seventeenth century—without the assistance of *Mad Men* and multimillion-dollar advertising campaigns.[119] The enduring myth of Atlantis goes back at least to Plato and lives on still in different forms because of some people's deep-seated need for the "assurance that somewhere, sometime, there can exist a land of peace and plenty, of beauty and justice, where we, poor creatures that we are, could be happy. In this sense Atlantis . . . will always be with us."[120]

The historian Robert Darnton tells us that the marvels of modern communication often blind us to the fact that information can travel far and fast by word of mouth, even in semiliterate societies.[121] Just as the poet Phillip Larkin said, that "sexual intercourse began in nineteen sixty-three," so there is a tendency amid all the excitement about the digital revolution to forget that communication of all kinds, including the verbal sort, has a long history and that some quite important things have happened in the world without the help of TV and the Internet. Although fake news and alternative facts became front-page topics in 2016, there is nothing new about them. Ramses the Great used them to persuade people that he had a stunning victory in the Battle of Kadesh. The beginnings of Christianity caused all sorts of rumors, fake news, and misinformation to spread in ancient Rome.[122] Mark Antony and Octavian employed fake news and misinformation in their struggles for power.[123] Shakespeare's historical plays about Britain are grounded in Holinshed's Tudor propaganda. Since the earliest times, anti-Semitism has often been accompanied by lies and bogus information. The popular English language press has been printing fake news and made-up stories for more than a century. Fake news has been widely and quickly spread by word of mouth and without the help of Facebook, Twitter, viral videos, the yellow press, hate radio, spin doctors, and cable TV. These media may help fuel and spread it, but they are not the motive force behind fake news or the public appetite for it.

Why Some, Not Others?

The fact that some people preserve their beliefs and habits in certain circumstances doesn't mean that everyone does, even if a lot of people do it some of the time and some do it a lot of the time. Faced with evidence and argument, some change their minds. Many have responded to health warnings by giving up smoking, by eating and drinking more healthily, by getting more exercise, and by avoiding sunburn. Doesn't this testify to media power, at least in some cases?

Let us assume, for the moment, that the media have influenced large minorities to drop their smoking habits but have encouraged others to keep it. This used to be possible when the media spoke with forked tongue about health risks while carrying lots of glossy advertising for cigarettes. The fact that cigarette advertising has been supplanted by health warnings has not deterred a stubborn 18.8 percent of the population who continue to smoke in the United Kingdom.[124] This raises the question of why some accept the antismoking message and others reject or ignore it. Similarly, why do some change their eating and drinking patterns and their exercise regime, while others do not?

Genes and evolution are possible explanations.[125] Perhaps we are hardwired by evolution to like salty, fatty, and sweet foods, which made it possible to survive as hunters and gatherers, but if so, how do some overrule their genetic imperative? Besides, genes, mental hard-wiring, and evolution cannot explain why some believe that weapons of mass destruction were discovered in Iraq after the invasion of 2003, that federal officials were complicit in 9/11, or that Obama is a Muslim. Nor do genes and evolution explain the ability of large numbers to accept or discount the lies and fake news of the 2016 presidential election and the EU referendum in the United Kingdom, or that two-thirds of Americans claim to believe in the devil, while 4 out of 10 Americans doubt or reject evolution. In this respect, genes, advertising, and evolution cannot be the whole story and may not be even part of it. In the absence of plausible genetic and evolutionary explanations, we are left with the question of what part the media play, if any, in shaping mass attitudes and behavior.

Conclusions

Individuals can preserve their beliefs even if these beliefs fly in the face of all available evidence. They can reject simple logic, hard facts, and compelling argument; avoid, forget, or misinterpret information they do not like; and even invent evidence (alternative facts) that confirms their misinformed beliefs. As a result, they override the information and opinion routinely found in the mass media to protect their values and beliefs and to continue behaving as they always have. At the same time, millions in Britain and the United States hold steadfastly to ideas that are not advocated or are rarely even mentioned by the mainstream media. Small minorities—such as flat-earthers, alien abductees, and outlandish conspiracy theorists—are true believers in ideas that defy logic and evidence. Large majorities are creationists, abusers of their own health, and believers in the paranormal and supernatural.

All this points to the fact that people can believe strongly in ideas that do not appear in the media. Can we claim, then, that the media can create or strongly influence beliefs about what does appear in the media? This point is deliberately posed as a question, given that many of the mass attitudes and behaviors commonly ascribed to media influence—racism, nationalism, sexism, militarism, religious intolerance, conspiracy theories, consumerism, overeating, a taste for sugar and salt, belief in the occult and supernatural, willingness to buy love potions and magic medicines, and not least the fake news that has flowered in the last few years—have a history that predates the media and modern advertising by centuries. Those who believe that the media are responsible for such attitudes might reflect on the fact that they were common long before even the first printed bible.

Observations about belief preservation are based on the mountain of evidence produced by a great many experimental psychologists over the past 60 years or so. Although it cannot be assumed that what occurs in the psychology laboratories necessarily occurs in the outside world, it is clear that belief preservation in the face of opposing mainstream media messages is a common feature of everyday life. In some experiments, researchers provide subjects with fake news—made-up news supported by invented evidence—and find that some individuals swallow it whole because it is consistent with what they already believe, while others reject it because it is not consistent with their beliefs. When those who reject it are presented with correct evidence or irrefutable logic, they often are able to preserve their original beliefs by rejecting the real evidence as fake, mistaken, or irrelevant. In some cases, they strengthen their views and come out of the experiment even more convinced than when they went in.

This raises doubts about the idea that the mass media are a powerful force able to create or influence public opinion and behavior. It suggests that people pick and choose what they want to believe in the news on the matters that are close and important to them. If we were to add up all the true believers of the flat-earth kind, they would probably amount to a large minority of the population. If we then add the creationists, believers in the occult, users of quack medicine and fad diets, those who drink too much, who smoke, who do not exercise, who do take drugs, who eat unhealthily, and those who drink before driving or use handheld devices and tailgate while driving, the result is a clear majority of the adult population. Since 40 percent of Americans are creationists, some 75 percent harbor one or more kinds of paranormal belief, and 80 percent claim that the US government is hiding its knowledge of extraterrestrial life-forms, it is also clear that some individuals embrace more than one of these beliefs. And this is only a small portion of the total universe of counter-knowledge beliefs.

It is important to stress that individuals do not protect their beliefs all the time and that they have beliefs about many issues they don't want to protect. Most people have no strong beliefs about a wide array of issues, and many are probably prepared to be flexible about some beliefs they do hold. Some change their minds about strongly held beliefs, but it can be difficult to distinguish between those who stick and those who change at any given point in time because of sleeper effects that cause some to revert slowly to their previous beliefs and cause others to change slowly to a different belief. It sometimes takes a long time for information to be absorbed and acted upon. Beliefs also vary in strength. Convictions are firmly rooted and difficult to change, whereas beliefs of convenience are superficial rationalizations, useful smokescreens that can be dropped without a thought when they are no longer convenient. Convictions are integral to an individual's core personality and include expressions of tribal loyalty to a religion, party, class, ethnic group, or place.[126] These are likely to be fairly resistant to media influence compared with beliefs of convenience.

It is easy to exaggerate the power of the media, as the media often do.[127] But it is also easy to exaggerate the power of public resilience in the face of media influence. Many deny or ignore news reports, but equally many accept them and change their beliefs as a result. The past two decades have seen many examples of opinion change, including global warming, sexual relations, same-sex marriage, feminism, abortion, healthy lifestyles, corruption and public accountability, and political distrust. And, of course, there is a variable element of vote churning in most elections. Whether the media alone are responsible for these opinion changes is a different matter, taken up in later chapters; the point here is that citizens display plentiful evidence of their ability to accept, reject, or ignore media messages. This leaves us with unresolved questions about how powerful the news media are and what their political effects are likely to be.

Three preliminary points emerge from the evidence. First, news media effects can vary in kind and strength. They may be strong, weak, or neutral. They may reinforce existing beliefs either positively or negatively. They may be enduring or short-lived. They may have an impact on attitudes or behavior, or both, or neither. They may have no effects whatsoever on some mass beliefs—perhaps because they have little or nothing to say about them.

Second, news media effects are highly dependent on the attitudes, values, and opinions of individual consumers, which also vary in kind and strength. Partisans, especially those of the true believer kind, are less susceptible to news media influence that conflicts with their opinions. The news media are likely to have less influence on beliefs of conviction than beliefs of convenience. Similarly, they may have less influence on beliefs that are already formed than on those that are not yet settled. Some people may be predisposed to strong or dogmatic opinion; some seem to be more open-minded in general. Knowledge and education seem to be important here: those who are less well informed about politics often claim to be well informed, even as they are more likely to be misinformed.[128] Nevertheless, there is also evidence that people who are better and more accurately informed are capable of seeking out information that is consistent with their own ideas and are more creative in inventing reasons to justify their beliefs.[129] Highly intelligent individuals among them might be called clever fools.

Third, different people can react in different ways to the same message from the same medium, and the same person can react in different ways to the same message from different media. Therefore, in trying to understand media effects, it is essential to consider both the source and content of the message as well as the characteristics of the individuals receiving it. It is neither the media alone nor their audiences alone that explain media effects, but the interaction between them. If the media are the supply side and audiences are the demand side, then media effects can only be understood as the interplay between the two sides. Any attempt to explain media effects that focuses on one or the other is open to suspicion.

The chapters that follow attempt to unravel the complexity of these interactions in order to establish the nature and strength of media effects on mass political attitudes and why these vary according to circumstances. The results are sometimes surprising, unanticipated, and inconsistent with conventional wisdom.

Notes

1. Baron 2007: xiii, 56.
2. Fine 2006: 104.
3. Burnett 2017: 260.
4. Kahneman 2011.
5. Tetlock 2005: 187.
6. Mlodinow 2009: ix.
7. Gorman and Gorman 2017.
8. Fernbach et al. 2013.
9. Sutherland 2009: 95–110.
10. Some are also good at inventing facts to fit the theory. As Jastrow (1935: 132) writes, "Create a belief in the theory and the facts will create themselves."
11. See also Shepperd, Malone, and Sweeny 2008.
12. Ariely 2012: 158.
13. Trouche et al. 2016.
14. Mercier and Sperber 2017: 9.
15. Westen 2008.
16. Westen 2008: xiii.
17. Gorman and Gorman 2017.
18. Fine 2006: 6.
19. Cross 1977; Zuckerman and Jost 2001.
20. "German Driving Laws—Fines for Speeding, Drunk Driving, Parking Violation Etc.," https://www.bussgeldkatalog.org/german-driving-laws/.
21. I am an intelligent, well-informed realist. You are sometimes quite sensible but misinformed. They are gullible fools. On this third-person effect, see Davison 1983.
22. http://www.journalism.org/2016/12/15/many-americans-believe-fake-news-is-sowing -confusion/. This evidence is open to doubt because it presents people with fake and real news stories and asks them whether they believe the fake ones. In real life, however, most people come across fake news in conjunction with mainstream media discussion about its reliability, so giving the audience a chance to judge it.
23. Kruger and Dunning 1999; Dunning 2011.
24. Cohen 2001; Hansen et al. 2014.
25. Hastorf and Cantril 1954: 132–133. Italics in the original.
26. Rahn 1993.

27. Leibowitz 1965: 37.
28. Edelman 1988: 95.
29. Philo 2014.
30. Edwards and Smith 1996.
31. Fine 2006: 106.
32. Lewandowsky et al. 2005.
33. Ecker et al. 2011.
34. Mlodinow 2009: 28–29.
35. Trivers 2011: 143.
36. Hilbert 2012.
37. Lord, Ross, and Lepper 1979.
38. Lord, Ross, and Lepper 1979: 2107–2109.
39. Lumsdaine and Janis 1953.
40. Papageorgis and McGuire 1961; McGuire and Papageorgis 1961.
41. Compton and Ivanov 2012; Ivanov et al. 2012; Compton, Jackson, and Dimmock 2016.
42. Nyhan and Reifler 2012. See also Thorson 2015; Borah 2014.
43. Margolin, Hannak, and Weber 2018.
44. Munro 2010.
45. Randi 1982.
46. Goldacre 2007.
47. Edwards and Smith 1996; Nichols 2017.
48. Kuhn and Lao 1996; Redlawsk 2002; Goodin 2000.
49. Abelson 1986.
50. Nyhan and Reifler 2012.
51. Lavine, Johnston, and Steenbergen 2012.
52. Ross, Lepper, and Hubbard 1975. See also Anderson, Lepper, and Ross 1980.
53. The original work by Johansson, Hall, Sikström, and Olsson (2005) has been replicated and developed with the same results by Johansson, Hall, Tärning, Sikström, and Chater (2014).
54. Fine 2006: 4.
55. Hall, Johansson, and Strandberg 2012.
56. Kuklinski et al. 2000; Gilens 2001; Howell and West 2009; Ditto and Lopez 1992.
57. Festinger, Riecken, Schachter 1956: 3.
58. Festinger, Riecken, Schachter 1956: 3.
59. Thompson 2008.
60. Bader, Mencken, and Baker 2017.
61. Fritze 2009.
62. Fritze 2016.
63. Taverne 2005.
64. Crews 2006.
65. Garwood 2008.
66. Park 2002.
67. Park 2008.
68. Aaronovitch 2010.
69. Wheen 2005.
70. Bausell 2009.
71. Fenster 1999.
72. Shermer 2002.
73. Randi 1982.
74. Singh and Ernst 2008.
75. Offit 2013.
76. Clancy 2005.
77. Tumminia 2005.

78. Thompson 2008; Quiggin 2012. The demand for books on voodoo medicine, miracle diets, fake history, and pseudoscience is huge.

79. A. Tsoulis-Reay, "Bill Clinton Killed 50 People," *New York,* November 17, 2013, http://nymag.com/news/features/conspiracy-theories/clinton-body-count/.

80. https://www.vanityfair.com/news/2006/08/loosechange200608. See also J. Kaminski, "9/11 Was a Hoax: The American Government Killed Its Own People," *Serendipity* (blog), http://www.serendipity.li/wot/911_a_hoax.htm; and BBC News, "Why the 9/11 Conspiracy Theories Have Changed," *BBC News Magazine*, August 29, 2011, http://www.bbc.co.uk/news/magazine-14572054.

81. G. Morris, "Satan and Evil Spirits: *You* Can Beat Them," http://www.net-burst.net/demons/cast_out.htm.

82. Park 2002.

83. Ronson 2009. It does not follow that the US military believed in such things, only that it thought the chance worth taking, given that it cost a negligible amount of its multibillion-dollar budget.

84. Lodge and Taber 2013.

85. S. Blancke, H. H. Hjermitslev, J. Braeckman, P. C. Kjærgaard, "Creationism in Europe: Facts, Gaps and Prospects," https://biblio.ugent.be/publication/3239297/file/6790625; S. Blancke and P. C. Kjærgaard, "Creationism Invades Europe," *Scientific American,* October 1, 2016, https://www.scientificamerican.com/article/euro-creationism/.

86. Cohen 2001: 1.

87. Gallup Poll, November 19, 2004; F. Newport, "In U.S., 42% Believe Creationist View of Human Origins," Gallup, June 2, 2014, https://news.gallup.com/poll/170822/believe-creationist-view-human-origins.aspx.aspx; A. Hall, "Results of Major New Survey on Evolution" (press release), Science & Religion, September 5, 2017, https://sciencereligionspectrum.org/in-the-news/press-release-results-of-major-new-survey-on-evolution/#more-1366.

88. "Americans' Belief in God, Miracles and Heaven Declines," Harris Poll, December 16, 2013, https://theharrispoll.com/new-york-n-y-december-16-2013-a-new-harris-poll-finds-that-while-a-strong-majority-74-of-u-s-adults-do-believe-in-god-this-belief-is-in-decline-when-compared-to-previous-years-as-just-over/.

89. D. W. Moore, "Three in Four Americans Believe in Paranormal," Gallup, June 16, 2005, http://www.gallup.com/poll/16915/three-four-americans-believe-paranormal.aspx; Live Science Staff, "Americans' Beliefs in Paranormal Phenomena (Infographic)," LiveScience, October 28, 2011, https://www.livescience.com/16748-americans-beliefs-paranormal-infographic.html.

90. "Mystical City," *New York,* http://nymag.com/nymetro/news/culture/features/n_8624/.

91. https://www.ipsos.com/ipsos-mori/en-uk/survey-beliefs; http://news.bbc.co.uk/1/hi/programmes/conspiracy_files/6217136.stm.

92. M. Potscka, "Human Values Study: Incidence of Telepathy," http://homepage.univie.ac.at/martin.potschka/EVSSG.pdf.

93. Dean 1998: 3; Kim et al. 2015.

94. https://digital.nhs.uk/data-and-information/publications/statistical/statistics-on-obesity-physical-activity-and-diet/statistics-on-obesity-physical-activity-and-diet-england-2012; https://www.cdc.gov/obesity/data/.

95. https://digital.nhs.uk/data-and-information/publications/statistical/statistics-on-smoking/statistics-on-smoking-england.

96. https://www.cdc.gov/tobacco/data_statistics/fact_sheets/adult_data/cig_smoking/index.htm.

97. US Department of Health and Human Services 2014; National Highway Traffic Safety Administration, "Drunk Driving," https://www.nhtsa.gov/risky-driving/drunk-driving.

98. L. Chang, "70 Percent of Drivers Use Their Smartphones While on the Road," *Digital Trends*, May 19, 2015, https://www.digitaltrends.com/mobile/70-percent-of-us-use-our-phones-while-driving/.

99. "UK Beauty Industry Worth Over £15bn," Cosmetics Business, February 29, 2012, http://www.cosmeticsbusiness.com/news/article_page/UK_beauty_industry_worth _over_15bn/76258.

100. T. Hargrove, "Third of Americans Suspect 9-11 Government Conspiracy," Scripps Howard News Service, August 1, 2006, http://aldeilis.net/english/wp-content /uploads/sites/3/2014/02/nj012.pdf.

101. P. Schroeder, "Poll: 43 Percent of Republicans Believe Obama Is a Muslim," The Hill, September 13, 2015, http://thehill.com/blogs/blog-briefing-room/news/253515-poll -43-percent-of-republicans-believe-obama-is-a-muslim.

102. S. Kull, *Misperceptions, the Media, and the Iraq War,* Program on International Policy Attitudes and Knowledge Networks, October 2, 2003, https://web.archive.org/web /20060210232719/www.pipa.org/OnlineReports/Iraq/IraqMedia_Oct03/IraqMedia_Oct03 _rpt.pdf.

103. See Brendan Nyhan, "New Surveys Show the Persistence of Misperceptions," *Huffington Post*, December 6, 2017, https://www.huffingtonpost.com/brendan-nyhan/new -surveys-show-the-pers_b_1718794.html?guccounter=1.

104. Thompson 2008: 26.

105. Achen and Bartels 2016.

106. Tetlock 2005; Crews 2006; Sutherland 2009; Westen 2008.

107. Gunther and Schmitt 2004: 55–70; Vallone, Ross, and Lepper 1985; Perloff 1989; Gunther et al. 2001; Giner-Sorolla and Chaiken 1994; Christen, Kannaovakun, and Gunther 2002; Coe et al. 2008; Gunther, Miller, and Liebhart 2009; Arpan and Raney 2003.

108. Nyhan and Reifler 2012; Schmitt, Gunther, and Liebhart 2004.

109. Gunther and Chia 2001; Gunther et al. 2001; Coe et al. 2008; Gunther, Miller, and Liebhart 2009.

110. Vallone, Ross, and Lepper 1985.

111. Dalton, Beck, and Huckfeldt 1998: 120.

112. Coe et al. 2008.

113. Gunther and Schmitt 2004: 56.

114. Smelser 1965.

115. J. Sanchez, "Symbolic Belief," Julian Sanchez, August 3, 2009, http://www .juliansanchez.com/2009/08/03/symbolic-belief/.

116. "Health Care a Mine Field for Republicans; Many Trump Voters in Denial on Russia," Public Policy Polling, July 18, 2017, http://www.publicpolicypolling.com/pdf /2017/PPP_Release_National_71817.pdf.

117. Packer and Wohl 2017.

118. Mann 2011.

119. Schama 1988: 2.

120. De Camp 2012: 277.

121. Darnton 2000.

122. Wilken 2003.

123. Kaminska 2017.

124. M. Wilkerson, "More Young Women Smoking Cigarettes in the UK, as More Young Men Quit," The Fix, February 23, 2016, https://www.thefix.com/more-young-women -smoking-cigarettes-uk-more-young-men-quit.

125. Trivers (2011) argues that self-deception is an evolutionary advantage.

126. Kahan 2017; Achen and Bartels 2016.

127. See, for example, Cathcart 2017.

128. Nyhan 2010.

129. Taber and Lodge 2006; Nyhan and Reifler 2012: 8.

3

Partisans and
Party Identifiers

In short, citizens are often partisan *in their political information processing, motivated more by their desire to maintain prior beliefs and feelings
than by their desire to make accurate or otherwise optimal decisions.*
—*M. Lodge and C. S. Taber,* The Rationalizing Voter[1]

If the conclusions emerging from the experiments on cognitive bias and
belief preservation apply in the political world outside the psychology laboratories, it is likely that those with strong political beliefs will be likely to
avoid, reject, ignore, or misinterpret the news they do not agree with. And,
indeed, in the real world, this sort of behavior is commonplace. As Achen
and Bartels put it,

> We find that partisan loyalties strongly colour citizens' views about candi-
> dates, issues, and even "objective" facts. . . . Insofar as they [partisans] do
> consider new issues or circumstances, they often do so not in order to chal-
> lenge and revise their fundamental commitments, but in order to bolster those
> commitments by constructing preferences or beliefs consistent with them.[2]

This chapter explores how partisanship moderates the impact of the news
media on public opinion.

A *partisan,* as the term is used here, is someone with strong beliefs
about a matter. In politics, party identification is the most widespread
form of partisanship and one that has a pervasive influence on how individuals react to the news. According to Bartels, "Partisanship is . . . a pervasive dynamic force shaping political perceptions of, and reactions to,
the political world."[3]

The chapter presents five main bodies of research about how partisans
and party identifiers react to the news. In the first, John Zaller shows how

33

hawks and doves in the United States reacted in different ways to news about the Vietnam War between 1964 and 1970.[4] This is a revealing and important study because many senior military officers, politicians, and writers claimed that press reports lost America that war by turning public opinion against it. If this is the case, then the media are indeed a powerful force in politics. The second and third sections of the chapter examine the ways in which partisanship and party identification moderate the influence of the British media—especially national newspapers—on voting behavior in the general elections of 1992, 1997, 2001, and 2005. It is often claimed that British newspapers are particularly influential in shaping political opinion and behavior, so if the press does have a strong impact on voting, we are more likely to see it in the United Kingdom than in other Western countries.

The fourth section of the chapter returns to the 1997 election in the United Kingdom because it is thought to present a crucial test case of newspaper influence given that *The Sun,* the best-selling paper in the country, switched its party allegiance. If newspapers can influence the voting patterns of their readers, this should show up clearly in *The Sun*'s about-face. The fifth section looks briefly at the role and influence of newspaper endorsements in the 2016 US presidential election, and a final section considers the way in which political awareness and identity are associated with the use of the new electronic forms of communication. It is brief because the subject is considered at greater length in Chapter 11.

Hawks, Doves, and Vietnam War News

The Vietnam War is an important test case of media influence. Many claimed that the United States lost the war because the media turned the public against the conflict, which, in turn, suggests that the media are no longer the fourth estate but have usurped the power of the state and have the ability to control a key issue of public policy. However, John Zaller has meticulously researched the links between how the American media reported the Vietnam War and the changing attitudes of the American public toward the war.[5] He shows that coverage of the war gradually increased between 1964 and 1970 in *Time, Newsweek, Life,* and the *New York Times.* Whereas in 1964 scarcely any antiwar reports appeared in the press, by 1966 the balance had shifted to antiwar coverage both in the press and on TV, and by 1970 the proportion of negative stories about the war had increased nine times in the *New York Times.*

In 1964, politically aware people were more likely to support the war. This was true of both hawks and doves, although support was substantially stronger among the hawks. As the antiwar news accumulated after 1966, however, highly aware doves began to change their opinions, and by 1970 their support was at its lowest level and less than a third of that of the most aware hawks.[6] After a while the attitudes of the less-aware doves, who paid less attention to the news, also switched, so by 1970 their support was also comparatively low. No surprises here. Doves were predisposed to accept antiwar news messages and duly did so.

It is the behavior of the hawks that is most interesting, especially that of the most aware among them. In 1964, almost all hawks supported the war, and as antiwar news grew in volume, the strength of their support scarcely wavered. By 1970, support among hawks was barely lower than its 1964 level.

Three preliminary points can be made about Zaller's study. First, hawkishness and dovishness were values that predated heavy press coverage and the increase in antiwar messages. In any case, low-aware citizens were not paying much, if any, attention to the war news at that time, so they were not much if at all affected by it. Second, whereas experiments on belief persistence are able to control both the content of communications and the people receiving it—they know who is reading what—Zaller's study was unable to do this. His study includes no information about what kinds of news and from which sources was absorbed by hawks and doves. He shows a correspondence between antiwar feelings of a population sample and antiwar news in the media, but correlations between trends over time are circumstantial evidence, no more. Third, his results are consistent with the experimental research showing that some individuals—the hawks, in this case—are capable of rejecting opinion they do not agree with.

In his 1996 publication, "The Myth of Massive Media Impact Revived: New Support for a Discredited Idea," Zaller argues for "a complete break with the old 'minimal effects'" tradition. He goes on to say,

> At least in the domain of political communication, the true magnitude of the persuasive effect of mass communications is closer to "massive" than to "small to negligible" and . . . the frequency of such effects is "often." Exactly as common intuition would suggest, mass communication is a powerful instrument for shaping the attitudes of the citizens who are exposed to it, and it exercises this power on an essentially continuous basis.

It is worth looking more closely at this statement. The correspondence between the increase in antiwar messages and the rise of antiwar opinion among the doves suggests, if anything, a reinforcement effect of the media, although there is no direct evidence of this in the study. Yet reinforcement is not usually described as a massive effect because it does not take a massive effort to swim with the tide. Reinforcement is part of the minimal effects tradition that Zaller seeks to break with.

The aware hawks, in contrast, did fight the increasingly frequent antiwar messages of the press, and Zaller offers this explanation for the durability of their hawkish attitudes: they were a reflection of the fact that antiwar messages were, owing to the ideological coloration of war critics both on the street and in the US Congress, unambiguously tagged as liberal, which led highly aware conservatives to reject them. . . . Such doggedness in the face of extremely frustrating real-world outcomes is explained by the fact that the highly aware conservatives received a consistent set of pro-war messages and cues from people they respected.[7]

According to experimental research, this sort of behavior is evidence of the capacity of individuals to protect their beliefs, even in the face of real-world outcomes, but Zaller sees this "as evidence of massive media effects." Is this correct?

At a minimum, that hawks and doves reacted in opposite ways to war news suggests an interaction between individual predispositions and political communications. It was not the media alone but the way that hawks and doves either accepted or rejected antiwar media messages that caused their attitudes to diverge. At most, because hawks and doves drew opposite conclusions from the news it suggests that media effects in this case were highly dependent on how different audiences treated the media messages. The way the hawks behaved is another example of the hostile media effect that underlines the weakness of the press for some people, not its power.

Another aspect of partisanship—party identification—came into play in 1968 when Lyndon Johnson was replaced as president by Richard Nixon, making it more comfortable for Democratic doves and liberals to switch to opposing a war that was then being waged by a Republican president. Combining the partisan effect (doves vs. hawks) with the political party effect (Republicans vs. Democrats) and the political awareness effect explains both the levels of support and changes in the levels of support for the war. Media effects—and certainly media effects alone—do not. In fact, this combination of factors suggests that media effects were less important than the predispositions of doves and Democrats, hawks and Republicans.

But then, a completely different explanation for the spread of the antiwar movement in the United States is also possible. The "real-world" events in Vietnam and the rising number of US military casualties suggested to some that the United States was not winning the war and might never win it, or that the cost of winning was too high. Perhaps it was simply the hard facts of real-world outcomes that weighed most heavily on American doves—facts that were denied, ignored, or deemed less important by hawks. This is not to deny that the way the war was reported, how it was framed, and how this primed news audience reactions was important, but it is odd to ascribe the shift in public opinion to a massive media effect when a more important cause might easily have been the impact of death, destruction, and the horror of war, not to mention the ethical problems and costs it entailed for the American public. This cannot be the whole story because it does not explain the difference between aware hawks and doves, but it might well be a more important part of the story than media effects.

Can we weigh the effects of real-world events against the way the media report them? This turns out to be a difficult, perhaps impossible, question to answer, and we return to it in Chapter 5, which explores how the real world and daily life experiences shape the ways citizens treat the news and media agendas. There is also more to be said about the Vietnam War and how it throws light on media influence, and this is also discussed in Chapter 5. Meanwhile, this chapter continues with an examination of the impact of British newspapers on the voting behavior of their readers.

British Newspapers and Party Voting

The British case is a clear-cut one for exploring newspaper effects on the politics of readers. In the United Kingdom, the newspaper market is highly centralized, and two out of three people read a national daily or Sunday paper regularly (three or more days a week). In addition, most national papers in Britain are party political by Western standards, pinning their political sympathies firmly to their mastheads and endorsing a party on election day. If newspapers swing votes, then the British national press surely does.

This, however, magnifies the cause-and-effect problem that bedevils so much research on media influence: readers are free to self-select the papers they read, and political partisans are likely to select a paper that supports the party aligned with their views. At the same time, newspapers are bound by the golden chains of the market to give their readers what they want and are willing to pay for. As there is a close correspondence between the supply and demand for partisan papers, how can we tell which is cause and which is effect?

There is a way around this chicken-and-egg problem, because the fit between the politics of newspapers and their readers is not always tight. Some people do not select their paper for its politics, and newspapers do not always please the political preferences of some of their readers. The result is that large minorities of readers do not share the party-political sympathies of the paper they read.[8] The size of the minority varies among papers and over time. Table 3.1 shows that almost half of the readers of Conservative-supporting newspapers in 1992, and almost two-thirds in 1997, did not have a Conservative ID. Conversely, 40 percent of Labour paper readers in 1992 did not have a Labour ID, and neither did 28 percent in 1997. In 1997, 29 percent of Conservative *Daily Mail* readers intended to vote Labour, with 22 percent doing the same in 2001, and another 14 percent intending to vote Liberal Democrat.[9] *The Sun,* however, had a consistent 30 percent, 29 percent, and 33 percent of Conservative voters in the

Table 3.1 UK Newspaper Readership and Party Identification, 1992 and 1997

Party Identification	Conservative Papers (%)		Labour Papers (%)		Other Papers (%)		No Paper (%)	
	1992	1997	1992	1997	1992	1997	1992	1997
Conservative	53	35	13	6	34	22	33	19
Labour	18	33	60	72	34	43	29	38
Other	13	14	13	9	18	18	19	18
None	16	18	14	13	14	17	19	25
(*n*)	(2,994)	(2,995)	(1,502)	(1,117)	(1,649)	(1,068)	(2,526)	(3,383)

Sources: University of Essex, Institute for Social and Economic Research 2018.

Notes: "Other" voters are those who vote other than Conservative or Labour. All column percentages sum to 100. Party identification was determined a year before the general election: in 1991 for the 1992 election and in 1996 for the 1997 election. Similarly, the newspaper read was established a year before the election. Conservative papers were *Daily Telegraph, Times, Daily Express*, and *Daily Mail*. Labour papers were *The Guardian, Daily Mirror, Morning Star. The Sun* was Conservative in 1992 and Labour in 1997. "Other" papers were *The Independent, Financial Times*, and *Today* (1992 only).

general elections of 1997, 2001, and 2005, respectively, when it strongly recommended its readers to vote Labour.[10]

The correspondence between reader and newspaper politics is far from perfect for different reasons. Some do not know the allegiance of their paper, and some identify it incorrectly.[11] Others may know but don't care, because they choose their paper for other reasons—its sports pages, its price, out of habit, because family members read it, or because its politics do not matter. Choosing a newspaper is rather like choosing a favorite pub to drink in. Pubs sell beer, and many people in Britain are particular about the beer they drink, but it doesn't follow that everyone picks their pub for its beer. Some go to meet friends, some choose a place for its music, pub quizzes, or darts team. Some like a beer garden by a river, some like a noisy pub, others prefer a peaceful one. Some value a large parking lot or the most local pub. And some pick a pub because it sells good beer.

Because politics are not greatly important to many people, it is not surprising that some do not choose their paper for its politics. Political scientists probably do, but they should not assume that others do the same. Politics are one of the least appealing subjects covered by the media.[12] In addition, voting intentions can change in and between election campaigns, but there is little evidence that people change their paper accordingly.[13] If people stick to the same paper, yet change their voting intention, and if newspapers have changed their politics while some of their readers have not, what does this tell us about newspaper effects on voting?

It is difficult to know what conclusions to draw about media influence from this evidence. The presence of large minorities of people who do not share their paper's politics may be taken as evidence of a weak or minimal effect of newspapers on voting. But it also undermines the self-selection argument that people pick their newspaper for its politics and it, therefore, also undermines the argument that papers are inevitably restricted to the minimal role of preaching to the converted. However, the large minority provides a way of prizing open the problem of cause and effect. When people choose a paper that is not of the same politics as their own, the problem of self-selection does not apply and the paper may cross-pressure the politics of these readers. When they pick a paper with the same politics as their own, their politics will be reinforced rather than cross-pressured. We can, therefore, estimate the newspaper effect on voting by comparing the behavior of reinforced people, where the party ID of the newspaper and the reader coincide, with cross-pressured readers, where the party leanings of reader and newspaper are opposed.

Cross-pressure theory predicts that Conservative voting among Conservatives reading a Conservative paper should be higher than among Conservatives reading a Labour paper. Similarly, those with Labour sympathies reading a Labour paper should vote Labour in greater numbers than those with Labour sympathies reading a Conservative paper. Better still, we can estimate the newspaper effect more accurately by comparing the voting behavior of the reinforced and cross-pressured voters with a control group of party sympathizers who do not read a paper regularly or who read a party-neutral paper. It is difficult to draw any conclusions from media impact studies that lack a control group of people who are not exposed to the media. The introduction of a control group into the research design can change the results completely.[14] In the British Household Panel Studies of 1991–1992 and 1996–1997, 35 percent of respondents did not read a newspaper regularly (fewer than three times a week). This group is more weakly constrained by the politics of the paper they read. The predicted voting pattern of reinforced, cross-pressured, and weakly constrained voting is shown in Figure 3.1.

There is another way of tackling the cause-and-effect problem. British newspapers rarely change their party support, but *The Sun* did in 1997, when it came out strongly for Labour. It was also the largest-selling paper in the country, with a daily circulation of almost four million. If newspapers influence the voting behavior of their readers, this would be revealed in the way that *Sun* readers voted in 1997. Did *Sun* readers switch to Labour, voting in larger numbers than those reading equivalent Conservative papers?

A study of newspaper reading and voting patterns in the 1992 and 1997 general elections in the United Kingdom examines the hypotheses laid out in Figure 3.1 about cross-pressured, reinforced, and weakly conditioned

Figure 3.1 Hypothesized Levels of Party Voting Among Reinforced, Cross-Pressured, and Weakly Constrained Groups

	Conservative Paper	Labour Paper	Other Paper	No Paper
	1	2	3	4
Conservative ID and Attitudes	**Reinforcement** Highest Conservative vote	**Cross-pressured** Lowest Conservative vote	**Cross-pressured** Conservative vote similar to cross-pressured readers of a Labour paper	**Weakly constrained** Medium Conservative vote
	5	6	7	8
Labour ID and Attitudes	**Cross-pressured** Lowest Labour vote	**Reinforcement** Highest Labour vote	**Cross-pressured** Labour vote lower than reinforced readers' and similar to that of cross-pressured readers of a Conservative paper	**Weakly constrained** Medium Labour vote

newspaper readers, and readers of *The Sun* using data collected by the British Household Panel Study (BHPS), an annual survey of 5,500 households and 10,300 individuals.[15] The BHPS has two major merits: it identifies large numbers of readers of different newspapers and compares them with nonreaders; and it uses a panel survey, which interviews the same people every year, ensuring that hypothesized causes precede hypothesized effects.

The study measures partisanship by seven questions, one on party identification and six on attitudes toward left-right issues: the distribution of wealth, equality before the law, private enterprise, public services, the government's responsibility for full employment, and the need for strong trade unions. Answers are recorded for each participant in the year before an election. Similarly, newspaper readership patterns are also recorded a year before an election, both to establish cause-and-effect ordering and because reading a partisan paper for a week or two before an election is unlikely to have much impact. Reading the same partisan newspaper regularly over a period of time is what matters. Newspaper partisanship is often measured according to how the paper recommends its readers to vote on election day, but in the BHPS, newspapers are classified in a more reliable way—according to their long-term party support and their position on a variety of party-related political issues.

To isolate the newspaper effect, it is necessary to control for a wide variety of other variables associated with both voting behavior and newspaper reading. In this study, the control variables were party identification, attitudes toward the most salient political issues of the election, education, class, gender, age, political interest, and trade union membership. The study was unable to control for strength of party identification and attitude on issues, which is a weakness.

The results of statistical analysis show that the national press did influence voting patterns in the 1992 and 1997 elections, even after controlling for a list of six socioeconomic variables, party identification, and the six attitudes on important left-right political issues. Reinforced voters, who share the party preference of the paper they read, were more likely to vote for that preferred party than those who were cross-pressured by their paper. This was true of both Conservative and Labour voters who were reinforced. Moreover, as hypothesized, the voting patterns by party of the unconstrained voters, that is, those who did not read a specific paper, differed from those of the reinforced and cross-pressured voters. They generally cast their vote according to their own party identification, although they were less likely to do this than the reinforced voters and more likely to do it than the cross-pressured. Of the eight hypotheses in Figure 3.1, seven were confirmed by statistical analysis.[16]

Although the results for the impact of newspaper reading are statistically significant, they are usually substantively small, meaning that they are not to be ignored but neither can they be treated as major influences on voting. In most cases, the impact of newspaper reading is much less powerful than that of party identification and left-right attitudes, and sometimes less powerful than age, class, and education. Party identification and left-right political opinions are far stronger influences on voting behavior than newspapers.

The size of the newspaper effect seems to depend on the nature of the election. The 1992 election was a close-fought one, with the main parties getting much the same share of the opinion polls during most of the campaign. Many voters had trouble making up their minds, and the Conservatives drew ahead only in the last few days. Compared with this, the 1997 election was a foregone conclusion, with Labour maintaining its clear lead in the polls from the disastrous Black Wednesday, September 16, 1992, when the United Kingdom withdrew from the European Monetary Union, right up to election day on May 1, 1997. Voters knew their own minds, made their voting decision soon after the 1992 election, stuck to it, and had no need to take their cue from a paper. Newspaper impact on voting was small in both elections, but it was marginally larger when the parties were close in the polls and more voters were undecided.

Discussion of media influence in the United Kingdom often turns on claims about the impact of *The Sun,* which in 1992 backed the eventual winner, John Major, though not firmly until the final week of the campaign. This was thought by many to be decisive in the Conservative swing in the last few days of the campaign, leading to the paper's famous headline the day after the election: "It's *The Sun* wot won it." It is also notable that *The Sun* supported the Conservatives in 1992 when they won, but switched in 1997 when Labour won with a landslide victory. Because it is rare for a newspaper to switch sides, *The Sun* offers a good test case of newspaper effects on voting.

The research results are clear on this. First, *The Sun*'s effects on voting were smaller, not larger, than that of other papers, because when it is taken out of the regressions for 1992 and 1997, the newspaper effect is marginally larger, not smaller. An absence of *Sun* effects on voting is found in another study of the 1997 election, which observes, "The *Sun*'s conversion [to the Labour cause] did not bring the Labour Party new recruits. Equally Labour's new voters did not prove particularly keen to switch to *The Sun*."[17]

Perhaps this is no great surprise. After all, the political content of *The Sun* is relatively slim, highly partisan, and often outrageous and satirical.[18] This combination means that *Sun* readers often regard it as an amusing diversion—a bit of fun not to be taken seriously. According to a poll in January 2008, less than a third of *Sun* readers trusted the paper, the lowest trust rating of eight national dailies.[19] It may have undermined its political influence in the relentless pursuit of sales; its flippant, satirical style; and by attracting readers with a low level of political interest and trust (see also Chapter 7). Although it might be thought that *Sun* readers, being comparatively low on political awareness and information, are precisely the kinds of people who might be most influenced by their paper, it turns out that the paper does not have this kind of success.

The changing party allegiance of *The Sun* from Conservative to Labour in 1997 may also underline the power of market forces. The paper knew that many of its readers were going to vote Labour in 1997 and that it was in its economic interests to follow them. Meanwhile, *The Times,* also owned by Murdoch's NewsCorp, did not swing behind Labour, but then its readers were mainly Conservative faithfuls. *The Sun* reverted to supporting the Conservatives in 2009 when they had a large lead in the polls, but nevertheless the Party's lead declined substantially over the next six months. The paper's return to the Conservative fold was no surprise and neither was its support for two opposing parties in 2015, one in England and one in Scotland, ensuring it was on the side of most of its readers in each country.[20] The end result is, as Peter Kellner puts it, "Although *The Sun* newspaper is a great weather vane, it doesn't decide the direction of the wind."[21] This was well recognized by Lundberg in 1926 when he wrote, drawing on his own survey research, "A modern commercial newspaper has little direct influence in the opinions of its readers on public questions. It probably seeks to discover and reflect that opinion rather than make it."[22]

Murdoch's media in the United States are also of two minds about Donald Trump. Initially, both Fox News and the *Wall Street Journal* supported him, but then the *Journal* began to change its mind and started to converge with opinions of its readers once more. As one journalist pointed out, Murdoch "likes to support the party most likely to win *and* the one most likely to further his commercial interests."[23] Commercial interests also dictated Murdoch's Fox News coverage of the US presidential election of 2012, when, to the anger of Republican campaign managers, the channel persistently gave air time to the right-wing policies and unelectable candidates favored by its aging, white audience, but not the rest of the electorate.[24] When trying to understand the politics of Murdoch's media, it is best to follow the money and check the bottom line.

Another UK paper also demonstrates the power of market forces over newspaper content. Richard Desmond bought the *Daily Express* when its circulation was in steep decline and made it profitable again with a simple formula. He states that his policy is "to reinforce his ageing readers' opinions, and give them occasional hope of increased mobility and pain relief, with frequent front-page splashes that promise cures for arthritis." His motto is "Affirmation rather than information."[25] Affirmation comes cheap.

Voters and Newspapers in the 1983, 1992, 1997, 2001, and 2005 Elections

The conclusion that British newspapers have little or no impact on the voting behavior of their readers is repeated in six other election studies, though contested by a seventh. The first study comments, in passing, that it finds no evidence that the strident right-wing views of *The Sun* in the 1983 election influenced its readers.[26] The second focuses in greater depth on media effects in the 1992 election, with a panel study that matches voting intentions against newspaper reading over the course of the campaign. It finds that "Neither the *Sun* nor any other of the pro-Conservative tabloid newspapers were responsible for John Major's unexpected victory in 1992. There is no evidence in our panel that there was any relationship between vote switching during the election campaign and the partisanship of a voter's newspaper."[27] In common with most election studies around the world, with experimental studies summarized in Chapter 1, and with the attitudes of American hawks and doves about the Vietnam War, the study authors conclude, "many electors still appear to view newspaper reports (and watch television news) through a partisan filter that enables them to ignore uncongenial messages."[28]

The third study takes advantage of the fact that *The Sun* switched its support to Labour in 1997, and being a panel study it was able to track vote switching and newspaper reading to estimate the effect of *The Sun* coming out to shine on the Labour Party. As the author writes, "If newspapers can influence votes, then the one occasion on which we should be able to see their influence is when a paper changes sides."[29] But, again, the study found that "the pattern of vote switching during the campaign amongst readers of *The Sun* or any ex-Tory newspaper proved to be much like that of those who did not read a newspaper at all."[30] The presence of the control group of non–newspaper readers was vital as a foundation for reliable conclusions.

The fourth study concentrates on campaign communications in the 1997 election.[31] It found that 61 percent of the electorate remained faithful in 1997 to the party they voted for in 1992, and 39 percent switched their vote. But there is little evidence that shifts in electoral opinion had much to do with the media or that *The Sun*'s switch to Labour had much to do with vote churning. First, the mass media's agenda and that of the electorate diverged widely, and the public followed its own agenda, ignoring that of the media. Second, there is no evidence of a connection between variations in the tone of television coverage of the campaign and fluctuations in party preferences. Third, although more than a third of voters changed their paper between 1992 and 1997, the evidence suggests that they did so according to their long-held political affinities, not according to short-term shifts in their voting attitudes. Fourth, there is sparse evidence for the idea that newspapers influenced votes in the 1992–1995 period or during the 1997 campaign. And fifth, there is no significant or consistent evidence that *The Sun*'s switching to Labour converted its readers to the new cause. The study concludes, "Newspapers have but a limited influence on the voting behaviour of their readers" and "the *short term* impact of the news media, for good or ill, has been greatly exaggerated."[32]

The fifth study revisits the impact of *The Sun*'s change in political allegiance and plots the development of party support in the polls against the way 19 daily and Sunday national papers reported the campaign in the year before polling day.[33] It observes, as do others, that Labour lost a few percentage points of popularity during the period when some papers were changing to support it. In this time, its high point of popular approval fell from 57 percent in mid-1996 to 43 percent on polling day, while the Conservative Party stayed on or around 30 percent during this period, in spite of the fact that it lost a few of its usual press allies. It is normal for the gap between the two main parties to narrow in the months before the election, and so it did in 1996–1997, but this trend was the opposite of what would be expected if papers were able to recruit voters to their cause. In line with the other research, the study concludes that, "Panel data collected regularly since 1992 suggest that partisan newspapers have only a marginal influence on the voting preferences of individual readers and that they have little or no influence on overall outcomes."[34]

The sixth study examines the statistical links between three types of political communication and three kinds of political attitudes during the official British general election campaign of 2005.[35] It shows that where different channels of communication had any effects on opinions at all, these were scattered, varied, and substantively small, without any overall coherent pattern.

A report of the Electoral Commission makes a further point about media coverage of the 2005 election.[36] TV news was used by 89 percent of the population as their main source of political information, another 50 percent used radio, and 43 percent used national papers.[37] Whatever political messages people received from the papers must be set against what they got from TV and radio, which—with their different and largely nonpartisan content—may well reduce whatever influence the press has. Also, it should not be assumed that these three forms of political communication are the only, or even the main influence on what individuals know and think about politics, as we will see in Chapters 5 and 6.

Exploiting a Rare Communication Shift

The conclusion of the seventh election study, by Ladd and Lenz, contrasts strongly with the previous six. It is perhaps the most sophisticated and statistically complex piece of research of its kind on newspapers and voting and was published in a highly rated professional journal that subjects submissions to intense scrutiny by fierce critics.[38] This study takes advantage of the rare case of three British newspapers, *The Sun, Daily Star,* and *Financial Times,* switching party allegiance from Conservative to Labour in the 1997 general election. It controls for a large number of variables, employs a series of data going back to 1992, tests for placebo effects, and considers the possibility that these newspapers followed rather than led their readers' voting preferences. The persuasive effects of newspaper endorsement influencing readers to switch voting allegiance in 1997 ranged between 10 percent and 25 percent of readers, providing strong support for Zaller's suggestion of massive media effects. Although the conclusions of this study are out of line by a wide margin with the conclusions of almost all other research on the 1997 election, the sheer size of *The Sun*'s alleged effect makes it worthwhile to revisit the election.

First, the party endorsement of some papers is not always clear-cut. Some broadsheets try to keep fact and opinion separate, which can make it difficult to see which side of the fence they sit on. Their editorial and opinion pieces can also be mixed, strongly or weakly partisan, sometimes critical of and qualified in their party support. Some tabloids are better described as "papers" than "newspapers" because their political content is normally sparse throughout the year, even if they endorse during the official campaign period. Sometimes a paper's recommendation is not for one party, but for tactical voting, support of anti-EU candidates, a left-center alliance of Labour and Liberal Democrats, or just voting in general. Consequently, studies do not always agree on how to classify the national papers. All agree that the *Mail, Telegraph,* and *Express* were Conservative in 1992 and 1997, that the *Mirror* was for Labour in both elections, and that *The Sun* switched from Conservative to Labour. The allegiance or lack of it and how it changed, if at all, of the *Financial Times, The Independent, Independent on Sunday, The Guardian,* and the *Daily Star* in 1997 is open to debate, and consequently their endorsements have been classified in different ways, sometimes differently from how Ladd and Lenz classified them, which has consequences for the conclusions drawn.[39]

Second, large minorities of some newspaper readers are unable to identify correctly the political allegiance of the paper they read.[40] This may be the result of ignorance or the difficulties, just discussed, of knowing just where a paper stands. Prior to the 1997 election, 8 percent of *Sun* readers thought it supported the Conservatives, 6 percent thought it opposed Labour, and between a quarter and a third thought it supported no party or didn't know which party it did support. Overall, some 40 percent did not identify *The Sun* as a Labour paper.[41] If it is assumed that it is necessary to know which party a paper favors in order for readers to follow its voting cue, *The Sun,* along with some others, is likely to have had no influence over a large minority of its readers.

Third, to show a newspaper effect on party voting, it is necessary to compare the voting patterns of those people who read papers who clearly remained faithful to the Conservatives with those who clearly remained faithful to Labour and with those who clearly switched party allegiance. These three should also be compared with those people who did not read any paper in order to rule out the possibility of a common third factor affecting the voting behavior of readers and nonreaders.[42] For good measure, it is necessary to track voting intentions against newspaper endorsements and party support over a long time, because voting intentions may emerge well in advance of election years and the campaign period. The year 1997 is a case in which the public mood swung to Labour soon after the 1992 election and long before some papers switched their party support.

The figures in Tables 3.2 and 3.3 are Ipsos MORI polling data showing how the voting intentions of national newspaper readers and nonreaders changed in 1997 compared with 1992. The clear-cut cases of consistently Conservative, consistently Labour, and the switch by *The Sun* are picked out, but the more ambiguous cases are grouped together in an "other" category because of disagreement about how to classify them. To avoid category errors of any sort creeping in, however, the papers are listed individually to show, one by one, how the newspaper readers voted and how these voting patterns compare with those of nonreaders.

The numbers show that it does not matter how papers are grouped because readers of all papers and nonreaders behaved in pretty much the same way. Irrespective of the newspaper read and whether a paper was read

Table 3.2 Swing in Voting Intentions Between Labour and Conservative Parties, 1992–1997, by National Daily Papers

		Swing to Conservative (%)	Swing to Labour (%)
Consistently	*Daily Mail*	−16	15
Conservative papers	*Telegraph*	−15	9
	Express	−19	14
	Average	−16.7	12.7
Consistently Labour papers	*Mirror*	−6	9
Papers that switched from Conservative to Labour	*Sun*	−15	16
Others	*Times*	−22	13
	Financial Times	−17	12
	Independent	−9	10
	Guardian	−7	12
	Star	−15	13
	Record	−2	2
No paper		−12	9
All papers		−13.8	11
Total electorate		−12	9

Source: "How Britain Voted in 1997," Ipsos MORI, May 30, 1997, https://www.ipsos-mori.com/researchpublications/researcharchive/2149/How-Britain-Voted-in-1997.aspx?view=wide.

Table 3.3 Swing in Voting Intentions Between Labour and Conservative Parties, 1992–1997, by National Sunday Papers

		Swing to Conservative (%)	Swing to Labour (%)
Consistently	*Sunday Times*	−14	12
Conservative papers	*Sunday Telegraph*	−15	8
	Sunday Express	−13	12
	Mail on Sunday	−11	9
	Average	−13.3	10.3
Consistently Labour papers	*Observer*	−8	13
	Sunday Mirror	−5	8
	People	−9	11
	Average	−7.3	10.7
Papers that switched from Conservative to Labour	*News of the World*	−12	14
Others	*Independent on Sunday*	−11	9
	Sunday Mail	−4	4
	Sunday Post	−9	6
No Sunday paper		−11.0	10.0
All Sunday papers		−10.9	10.7
Total electorate		−12.0	9.0

Source: "How Britain Voted in 1997," Ipsos MORI, May 30, 1997, https://www.ipsos-mori.com/researchpublications/researcharchive/2149/How-Britain-Voted-in-1997.aspx?view=wide.

at all, there was a uniform swing against the Conservatives and a slightly smaller uniform swing to Labour. Newspaper endorsement and support made no difference to voting patterns, which were the same across all papers. The swing against the Conservatives was slightly smaller than the swing to Labour because many voters who voted Conservative in 1992 chose not to vote in 1997 rather than support Labour. To confirm this, the Ipsos MORI numbers (not presented here for reasons of space) also show that not only did all newspaper readers and nonreaders swing to Labour and against the Conservatives to a similar extent but also all demographic groups in the electorate did the same whether they are grouped by gender, age, class, region, phone ownership, work status, housing tenure, or trade union membership.

There was a little variation in the size of the swings, but they were still almost always within 5 percent of each other for each set of newspaper readers and nonreaders. Even these small differences do not support the claim that continued Labour endorsement or a switch to Labour produced a larger Labour swing. On the contrary. Among the daily papers, the average swing against the Conservatives of all three faithful Tory papers was larger than Labour's *Mirror* and *Sun*. The *Sun*'s swing to Labour was the largest among all dailies but only a percentage point higher than the *Mail*'s and two points above the *Express,* both consistently Conservative. The *Mirror*'s swing to Labour was the same as *The Telegraph*'s (also consistently Conservative). A larger percentage of *Express* readers than *Times* readers swung to Labour, and yet the *Express* stayed Conservative and the *Times* did not.

Among the Sunday papers, the readers of the four Conservative faithfuls registered a larger swing against the Conservatives than those who did not read either a daily or a Sunday paper. The *Sunday Mirror,* a Labour faithful, had one of the smallest swings against the Conservatives and a smaller-than-average swing to Labour, smaller than nonreaders and the same as for the electorate as a whole. The staunchly Tory *Sunday Telegraph* had a larger swing against the party than any other Sunday paper, and its swing to Labour was identical to that of Labour's *Sunday Mirror*. It is true that these variations are often within measurement error, but that underlines the point that swings in voting intentions were not associated with any pattern of political support and endorsements by the daily and Sunday newspapers.

Why do consistently Conservative papers show a bigger swing against the Conservatives and to Labour compared with the consistently Labour papers and those papers that switched to Labour? The obvious answer is the ceiling effect imposed by the party identification of most readers of any given paper. For example, the *Times, Telegraph,* and *Financial Times* have a very high percentage of Conservative readers compared with the *Mirror, Guardian,* and *Sun.* Seven out of 10 *Telegraph* readers voted Conservative, and 11 percent voted Labour in 1992, compared with the *Mirror,* which was 64 percent Labour and 20 percent Conservative. Consequently, the true-blue papers had a larger percentage of possible defectors from the Conservative Party when the national mood turned against it. Left and liberal papers (*Independent, Guardian, Mirror*) show a smaller swing to Labour because they had a larger proportion of core Labour readers to start with and, therefore, a smaller pool of readers who could switch their vote to Labour. However, not voting Conservative is one thing; taking the next step of voting Labour is quite another. Hence, slightly larger numbers of *Times, Telegraph,* and *Financial Times* readers swung against the Conservatives compared with the *Mirror* and *Sun,* but not all of them voted Labour.[43]

In sum, these figures provide no support for even a small newspaper effect on voting in the 1997 election. They do not even support the idea that partisan papers reinforce the voting intentions of their readers, because the consistently Conservative papers registered a larger swing against the Conservatives and to Labour than the national average. It might be argued that the defection rate would have been even larger but for a reinforcement effect, but this would invoke all the problems of counterfactual and somewhat complicated and implausible arguments to explain why defection rates from the Conservatives were high among readers of Conservative papers.

If newspapers had little effect on voting in 1997, what did? President Bill Clinton might be right if he said, "It's the economy, stupid." The election involved unusual circumstances that explain both voter behavior and newspaper endorsements. It starts with our old tried and tested friend, economic voting, which argues that the state of national and household economies—economic prosperity or decline—are a prime determinant of whether voters reward or punish government in elections, perhaps *the* prime determinant. The Conservative Party, being the party most closely attached to business interests, is often regarded as the most competent at handling the economy and delivering prosperity, but this belief took a battering on Black Wednesday, November 16, 1992. On that day the newly elected Conservative government was forced by market pressures to withdraw the pound sterling from the European Exchange Rate Mechanism (ERM). This was a major blow to the national economy and to the Conservative Party, which overnight lost its prized reputation for economic competence.[44] It didn't regain its status in the next five years.[45] Satisfaction with the Conservative government began to slide, falling from a high of 45–46 percent in May 1992 to a low of less than 30 percent in the last quarter of that year and staying below that level for most of the next four years. In that period, Labour maintained a clear and unbroken lead in the polls, a highly unusual occurrence.[46] The result was, as a long time, close observer of elections commented, that "this was never going to be the kind of election which the role of the press could sway."[47]

The Conservative government compounded its long-term unpopularity with scandals, deep internal division, and a reputation for indecision and ineffectiveness. At the same time, Labour moved to the center ground and Tony Blair enjoyed an unprecedented period of popular approval as leader of the opposition.[48] In the polling history of the United Kingdom, no other opposition party or leader has retained such a big lead for so long. As early as 1992, large numbers in the electorate formed a voting intention that mostly stuck for the next four years. Their decision was made long before many papers announced their endorsements.

The Conservatives then dug themselves a deeper hole with an uncharacteristically inept election campaign in 1997, while Labour conducted an uncharacteristically effective and slick one, dominated by the charismatic Blair. The result of political developments starting in 1992 and polished off in the 1997 campaign was a defection of some 4.5 million voters from the Conservatives and a landslide Labour victory.

As argued, the political line of Murdoch's media often follows the bottom line of their own economic interests. The polls conducted for Murdoch's papers, among others, showed a clear majority of *Sun* readers intending to vote Labour. Murdoch did not want to alienate them and did want the paper to be on the winning side. The same polls showed that Conservative support among *Times* and *Financial Times* readers declined somewhat as the election approached, although it never fell below a substantial majority. In the event, both equivocated and fudged their party allegiance, especially the *Financial Times,* which came under sharp criticism when it recommended voting Labour in a previous election.

Ironically, the 1997 election is a particularly poor one for uncovering media effects on voting because the political and economic circumstances that caused voters to switch also caused normally Conservative papers to desert the party or qualify their support for it. A detailed study of the election concludes that "Labour did not win because the *Sun* backed it; rather, the *Sun* backed Labour because Labour was going to win."[49] The outcome of the 1997 election was the product of a national mood that took root as early as 1992 and spread throughout the electorate irrespective of whether they read a paper or not, and which paper they read. The 1992 election is a better test of newspaper effects, but even then, these effects are small to negligible and *The Sun*'s are no stronger than any other national daily.

Ironically, too, the 1997 British election shows how difficult it is to pin down causes and effects and that this requires close attention to a mix of circumstances: how papers are classified according to the subtleties of their partisanship; how important are the political and economic circumstances of the election; how early voting intentions can be formed well in advance of newspaper endorsements; how important it is to compare readers and nonreaders explicitly to rule out the possibility that they may both behave in the same way; how to compare readers of newspapers with different partisan bias; and how to recognize that a significant proportion of readers do not know or misunderstand the partisan leaning of the paper they read—which is not difficult when papers are not always aligned on certain issues with the favored party, or when they practice balanced, impartial reporting.

Newspaper Effects in American Elections

Are things any different in the United States? During the 2016 presidential campaign, a total of 653 daily and weekly newspapers and magazines reported the news. Of these, 76.6 percent endorsed Hillary Clinton, 12.6 percent endorsed no candidate, 3 percent supported Trump, and 4.9 percent recommended not voting for Trump. The rest were divided in their support of Gary Johnson, Evan McMullin, split endorsement, and "not Clinton." Of the 100 newspapers with the largest paid circulations, Clinton had the support of all traditionally Democratic papers, plus 17 traditionally Republican ones, and some that had never endorsed before, making a total of 57 periodicals with a circulation of some 13.1 million copies. Among the top 100, the two papers that endorsed Trump had a circulation of 36,000.[50]

Despite this imbalance, Trump had an overwhelming proportion of media coverage, according to the *Washington Post,* although most of this coverage was of a neutral, nonpartisan nature.[51] It might be argued that all publicity is good publicity and that Trump's victory was built on the media's fascination with him, but this would need to explain Clinton managing to win 2.9 million more votes than Trump. Besides, the two main topics of Clinton's publicity spikes were ill health and official inquiries into her email use, and it is generally argued that this publicity did her nothing but harm.

The American evidence for newspaper endorsements in the 2016 election is no more than circumstantial, but it is consistent with a systematic study of newspaper effects on voting using a data set on newspaper turnover (entries and exits to the market) between 1869 and 2004.[52] This finds no evidence of a significant newspaper impact on party voting in the United States—not even a moderate one—and concludes that the persuasive impact of partisan newspapers is limited. Newspaper endorsement of political candidates seems to have little impact on the outcome of elections in much the same way that celebrity endorsements seem to have little effect.[53]

Partisanship and the New and Digital Media

Research on the digital media is hampered by rapid technological change and a vast and fragmented array of sources of political news and opinion, about which little is known. A conspicuous exception is Fox News, which has attracted a lot of research. However, partisanship and party identification seem to play as large a role for audiences of the new media as the old, notably for some partisan cable news channels. In the United States, those people who are consistently conservative in values and attitudes are likely to choose Fox News as their main source of news.[54] Asked if they have heard of 36 different sources of news—ranging from Fox News, CBS, and the *New York Times* to *BuzzFeed*, Al Jazeera, and the Drudge Report—the consistent conservatives know of fewer than those of liberal and moderate individuals, and their level of trust in them is lower, Fox News being the only trusted source for 72 percent of them. The six main sources trusted by consistent liberals are overwhelmingly distrusted by the consistent conservatives, some of whom get their news mainly, but not exclusively, from one source.

Social media show similar patterns of use among partisans and party supporters.[55] Facebook is most heavily used for political news, and liberals are more likely to use it and to get political news from it than are conservatives. However, some conservatives pay attention to its political content, and almost half of them say that the messages they get from it are consistent with their views compared with a third of liberals.

Belief confirmation seems to be as common among those who use websites as those who access the old media. A study that examined self-selected exposure of 227 subjects to web material in the weeks leading up to the 2012 US presidential election found this result.[56] Users were strongly biased toward selecting web material that confirmed their beliefs about health, minimum wage, gun control, and abortion. Opposing views were not wholly avoided, but participants in the study spent almost two-thirds of their time on messages that were consistent with their own attitudes. Confirmation bias was stronger in individuals with strong beliefs than in persons with weak ones, but Democrats and Republicans displayed the same propensity for selection bias.

These rather cursory remarks about the digital media are intended only to make the point that they are subject to the same sorts of partisan and party identification considerations as the old media. At any rate, little is new about them in this respect. But, of course, there is much more to the digital media than this, so the topic is taken up again in Chapters 10 and 11.

Conclusions

The case studies in this chapter show that large sections of the public in Britain and the United States are able to reject or ignore the political messages they receive from the news media. Newspapers and TV can—and often do—have little effect on political attitudes and voting choices, whether these concern the Vietnam War, British or American elections, and whether or not a newspaper or TV channel takes a political stand or endorses a political candidate. The partisanship, sales, and national organization of the British daily press make them a key test case of newspaper effects on voting behavior, but repeated in-depth studies have failed to confirm such an effect, even for *The Sun* in 1997—perhaps especially for *The Sun* in 1997.

Different groups in the population accept or reject media messages for their own reasons. In the United States, the increasing volume of anti–Vietnam War messages in the mainstream media in the 1960s was absorbed by the doves because they were predisposed to antiwar sentiments. But the hawks rejected these messages and, in Zaller's words, doggedly rejected news about extremely frustrating real-world events to preserve their hawkish politics. They demonstrated what experimental psychologists call the "boomerang" or "backfire" effect in which evidence against a belief is used to strengthen that belief. Negative reinforcement of this kind is not much discussed in the political science literature on media effects, which concentrates on positive reinforcement. The fact that the same message from the same source can have both effects turns attention from content of the media to the different ways people can perceive and process content according to their own beliefs. If people react in different ways to the same message, it is not the content so much as how it is received that counts. Trying to gauge the likely impact of a media message by considering only its content—judging a book by its cover—is a serious mistake, although concern about media effects is often based on this error.

The role of partisanship and party identification comes as no surprise to many political scientists, especially the large numbers who deal generally with elections, voting, parties, presidential approval, political participation, and public opinion and behavior. They often have little need to include media variables in their work because other factors do a better job of explaining these political attitudes and behaviors. For example, *Democracy for Realists* develops a well-documented theory of the part that partisanship and tribal party loyalties play in modern democracies, with only a few fleeting references to the media.[57] Similarly, a recent Pew Research Center report states, "Partisan divides dwarf demographic differences on key political values," with the implication that the media do not enter into consideration.[58]

When it comes to positive reinforcement, the numbers in Tables 3.2 and 3.3 provide no support for the idea that Conservative papers acted to reinforce the Conservative vote. On the contrary, readers of Conservative papers were *more likely* to swing to Labour and against the Conservative Party in 1997 than either readers of Labour papers or those who did not read any paper. This is likely to be because of the ceiling effect whereby the Conservative papers had a larger pool of readers available to swing against the Conservatives and toward Labour. The faithful Labour papers had far fewer Conservative readers who could desert their party.

Yet, we must not assume the media are always and everywhere without influence over mass attitudes and behavior any more than it is reasonable to assume the opposite. The evidence shows that the media are sometimes without much influence over political matters and that this is more likely to be the case when media messages face partisan beliefs and party identification in their audiences. The stronger the beliefs and party identification, the weaker the media's influence over them may be. Conversely, the weaker the beliefs and partisanship, the better the chances of media effects.

Partisan forces were muted in the special circumstances of the 1997 British election, when most voters had made up their minds well in advance of the poll, sometimes years in advance. In this election, even the minimal effects of positive reinforcement are not evident. In both elections the newspaper effect was small to insignificant.

One reason for weak media effects is the pressure commercial papers are under to follow the preferences of their consumers. This seems to be true of the Murdoch papers, *The Sun* and *The Times* in Britain, the different editions of his papers in England and Wales, and his Fox News channel in the United States. It is also a characteristic of the *Daily Express,* according to its owner. Sometimes these commercial pressures encourage nonpartisanship and political neutrality in the commercial media; sometimes they encourage partisan bias. This is discussed later in this book, especially Chapter 10.

All of this underscores the leaky, hit-or-miss nature of media effects: people who were the most politically aware picked up anti–Vietnam War news in the US media earlier than people who were the least aware, and hawks and doves reacted in opposite ways to this news; some in the United Kingdom do not read a daily newspaper and are not directly influenced by a paper; the national press played no more than a small part, if any, in voting decisions in the 1997 election; newspaper endorsements may have carried slightly more weight in the 1992 election, which presented voters with a more difficult decision; the media may have less influence over opinions about major events such as wars and elections, where opinions are formed and fixed, than over newer or less important matters, where public opinion is more fluid; individuals who are well informed and who hold strong opinions typically pay more attention to the news media but are better at protecting and rationalizing their beliefs, hence they are more impervious to opinions that differ from their own. These are only some of the causes of media leakiness, and they are picked up again in chapters that follow.

Meanwhile, it must be said that this chapter is based on only a small number of studies (plus supporting evidence from other sources), albeit important ones. Although research results are suggestive, they are not sufficient to draw firm conclusions, but they are consistent with the claim that the mass media can and do have mixed effects, both strong and weak, positive and negative, largely recognized and unrecognized, commonly understood and counterintuitive. The next chapter looks more closely at the way in which news media effects are shaped by individual values, attitudes, and opinions other than partisanship and party identification.

Notes

1. Lodge and Taber 2013.
2. Achen and Bartels 2016: 269, 294.
3. Bartels 2002. See also Levendusky 2017.
4. Zaller 1992, 1996.
5. Zaller 1992: 185–215; Zaller 1996: 17–78.
6. Zaller 1992: 202.
7. Zaller 1996: 57.
8. Heath, Jowell, and Curtice 1994: 44, 46; Curtice 1999: 10.
9. Hundal 2010.
10. S. Hundal, "What Happens to Politics After the Sun Dies?," *New Statesman America,* June 3, 2010, http://www.newstatesman.com/blogs/the-staggers/2010/06/sun-media-labour-politics.
11. Kellner and Worcester 1982: 61; Curtice 1998; Lord Ashcroft, "Which Party Does *The Sun* Support? Do *Sun* Readers Know?," Lord Ashcroft Polls, July 5, 2012, http://lordashcroftpolls.com/2012/07/which-party-does-the-sun-support-do-sun-readers-know/.
12. Seymour-Ure 2002: 119.
13. Curtice 1998: 12–14.
14. See the Haller and Norpoth (1997) research discussed in Chapter 5.
15. Newton and Brynin 2001. This study covers only the electorate 18 years and older.
16. The exception being Conservative readers of Labour papers in 1997, who had a higher level of Conservative voting than Conservatives reading Conservative papers. However, the Conservative/Labour paper cell contains only 0.07 percent (56 people) of the total sample, and the result may be unreliable.
17. Norris et al. 1999: 166–169.
18. Street 2001: 43, 61.
19. "BBC Survey on Trust," BBC, January 3–6, 2008, https://www.ipsos.com/sites/default/files/migrations/en-uk/files/Assets/Docs/Archive/Polls/bbc.pdf.
20. Greenslade 2009; "Election 2015: The Sun and the Scottish Sun Endorse Rival Parties," BBC News, April 30, 2015, http://www.bbc.co.uk/news/election-2015-scotland-32523804.
21. Quoted in "Sun's Circulation Down 35% from mid-1990s Peak," Left Foot Forward, September 30, 2009, https://leftfootforward.org/2009/09/suns-circulation-down-35-from-mid-1990s-peak/.
22. Lundberg 1926: 712.
23. J. Martinson, "As the Papers Loudly Declare Party Allegiances, It Won't Just Be One That Wins It," *The Guardian* (Manchester), May 1, 2015, https://www.theguardian.com/media/2015/may/01/election-newspapers-endorsements-sun-murdoch-conservatives-labour.
24. Coll 2014.
25. Jack 2015.
26. Heath, Jowell, and Curtice 1985: 149.
27. Curtice and Semetko 1994: 55.
28. Curtice and Semetko 1994: 56.
29. Curtice 1999: 4.
30. Curtice 1999: 17.
31. Norris et al. 1999.
32. Norris et al. 1999: 168.

33. Curtice 1997. See also Bartle, Crewe, and Gosschalk 1998: xix.

34. Curtice 1997: 9.

35. Norris 2006.

36. Electoral Commission 2005.

37. Electoral Commission 2005.

38. Ladd and Lenz 2009.

39. D. Boothroyd, "Newspaper Endorsements 1964–97," Politics Resources, October 22, 2012, http://www.politicsresources.net/area/uk/e97/pastpaps.htm; "Newspaper Support in UK General Elections," *Datablog* (blog), *The Guardian* (Manchester), https://www.theguardian.com/news/datablog/2010/may/04/general-election-newspaper-support; Seymour-Ure 1997.

40. Kellner and Worcester 1982: 61; Curtice 1998; Newton and Brynin 2001: 269.

41. "The Campaign and the Media, 1997," Ipsos MORI, May 29, 1997, https://www.ipsos-mori.com/researchpublications/researcharchive/2793/The-Campaign-and-the-Media-1997.aspx?view=wide.

42. See also Chapter 5 on the sometimes neglected importance of control groups in media research and how they can alter or reverse the conclusions drawn.

43. The size of the pool of possible defectors and vote switchers depends also on strength of party identification, but the poll reports no information about that.

44. Sanders et al. 2001.

45. Hilton 1998: 48.

46. "Polls 1992–1997," UK Polling Report, http://ukpollingreport.co.uk/historical-polls/voting-intention-1992-1997; "Political Monitor Archive," Ipsos MORI, January 18, 2017, https://www.ipsos-mori.com/researchpublications/researcharchive/103/Voting-Intention-in-Great-Britain-1976present.aspx. See also Perkins 1998: 225.

47. McKie 1998: 129.

48. "Political Monitor Archive," Ipsos MORI, January 18, 2017, https://www.ipsos-mori.com/researchpublications/researcharchive/poll.aspx?oItemId=2438&view=wide#1992.

49. Bartle, Crewe, and Gosschalk 1998: xix.

50. "2016 General Election Editorial Endorsements by Major Newspapers," American Presidency Project, http://www.presidency.ucsb.edu./data/2016_newspaper_endorsements.php.

51. J. Sides, "Is the Media Biased Toward Clinton or Trump? Here Is Some Actual Hard Data," *Monkey Cage* (blog), *Washington Post,* September 20, 2016, https://www.washingtonpost.com/news/monkey-cage/wp/2016/09/20/is-the-media-biased-toward-clinton-or-trump-heres-some-actual-hard-data/?utm_term=.df0c026cf14f.

52. Gentzkow, Shapiro, and Sinkinson 2011a.

53. Wood and Herbst 2007.

54. A. Mitchell, J. Gottfried, J. Kiley, and K. E. Matsa, "Section 1: Media Sources: Distinct Favorites Emerge on the Left and Right," Pew Research Center, October 21, 2014, http://www.journalism.org/2014/10/21/section-1-media-sources-distinct-favorites-emerge-on-the-left-and-right/.

55. A. Mitchell, J. Gottfried, J. Kiley, and K. E. Matsa, "Section 2: Social Media, Political News and Ideology," Pew Research Center, October 21, 2014, http://www.journalism.org/2014/10/21/section-2-social-media-political-news-and-ideology/.

56. Knobloch-Westerwick, Johnson, and Westerwick 2015.

57. Achen and Bartels 2016.

58. A. Geiger, "17 Striking Findings from 2017," Pew Research Center, December 26, 2017, http://www.pewresearch.org/fact-tank/2017/12/26/17-striking-findings-from-2017/.

4

When the Public
Is Not Buying

Media frenzies over personal shortcomings are not the driving force of American politics. Stories of personal scandal can sell newspapers and provide opposition politicians with ammunition for rhetorical attack, but they do not in the end seem to make much difference for public opinion or national politics.

—J. Zaller, "Monica Lewinsky and the
Mainsprings of American Politics"[1]

Because large numbers of the population do not have strong opinions about many matters, this chapter turns to the way in which audience characteristics other than partisanship and party identification can affect how people react to news items. Are people less likely to display belief preservation shown by the true believers, hawks, doves, and party identifiers of the previous chapter and, therefore, more susceptible to media influences?[2]

To answer this question, the chapter starts with reactions of the US public to press coverage of the scandal between President Bill Clinton and White House intern Monica Lewinsky. This case is now 20 years old but a prime example of a "feeding frenzy of attack journalism" that is thought to be capable of destroying the careers of even the most powerful politicians. The American media covered every twist and turn of events in detail for a 12-month period, making the drama a clear test of their power over the hearts and minds of the American people. However, Clinton survived the year with his popularity intact, something that puzzled political scientists who assumed this would not be possible. As a result, many of them examined the evidence carefully to explain the surprising outcome.

The chapter moves on to evidence on the ability of the press to influence the public's issue agenda during election campaigns. Even during hard-fought national elections, political agendas are probably not high voter priorities, and it would not be surprising if voters adopted media agendas to save themselves time and trouble. But what if reporters and politicians dwell on matters that do not resonate with the interests of voters? Do voters still follow the media agenda or do they ignore it and stick to what they think is more important? The second part of the chapter investigates how much influence the media have over the public's election agendas.

The last part of the chapter moves on to examine briefly the effectiveness of party election campaigns as widely reported in the British media. Political parties put an ever-increasing amount of time, effort, skill, and money into their election campaigns, and they rely heavily on the media to broadcast their messages. Many newspapers and television channels have their own political interests and promote their own preferred parties and candidates throughout the year—not just during election campaigns. How effective are these campaigns? Although political leaders increasingly bypass the media and communicate directly with voters via text messages, videos, emails, and social websites, the majority of voters still use the mainstream media as a main port of call for election information.

Before presenting evidence about what the media have done, however, the reader is invited to conduct some mental experiments about what the mass media cannot do and what happens to them if they try to do it.

The Limits of Media Acceptability

Could a media campaign persuade the public to support the idea of closing all public libraries, outlawing tobacco and alcohol, or introducing a window tax or salt tax or a poll tax, for that matter? Imagine how Western populations would react to media demands for reducing the minimum age for marriage, buying alcohol, smoking, and driving to 14 or 15 years, or else raising it to 25 or 30 years. How would the public respond to arguments for reducing the school leaving age to 14 or 15 and allowing people to go into full-time employment at that age? Would most of the public vote for slashing the nation's defense budget or banning all parking on public roads, making cremation compulsory, abolishing civil weddings, or state enforcement of vegetarianism if their newspaper or favorite TV channel advocated these positions?

These are a few extreme examples of the unthinkable, but there are cases of newspapers being punished for advocating less. In 1956, the UK daily paper the *Manchester Guardian* (now *The Guardian*) and its Sunday partner, *The Observer,* opposed the Suez invasion, which put its sales at risk, provoked denunciation and accusations of treason in Parliament, and caused a damaging advertising boycott of *The Observer*. Fifty years later, the editor of *The Guardian* asked, "Is it great editorship or reckless indulgence to hazard the viability if not the very life of your newspaper?"[3]

The front page of *The Sun* on April 19, 1989, ran a story about the behavior of Liverpool football fans in the Hillsborough disaster, with accounts of gruesome and inhuman acts that turned out to be fabrications.[4] A full-page apology was printed in 2004 and another in 2011, but a boycott of the paper in Liverpool was still operating in 2012.[5] In the same year as the Hillsborough disaster, some British papers initially joined a government campaign to promote the poll tax, a policy that provoked such widespread civil disturbance that the papers quickly fell into line with public opinion.

On April 28, 2005, the *Financial Times* endorsed Labour in the general election that year, provoking a sharp reaction from some readers and threats to cut subscriptions. On September 16, 2016, the *New York Times* reported that several normally Republican papers that were critical of Donald Trump came under attack from readers and started losing sales. The *Arizona Republic,* never once favoring a Democratic presidential candidate since its foundation in 1890, received subscription cancelations every 10 minutes, angry calls from outraged subscribers, and a death threat.[6]

Niche market media can pursue unpopular policies because they have self-selecting minority audiences that seek them out, but the risks for the mainstream media of bucking public opinion can be serious. As Schudson puts it, "Certainly the press more often follows than leads; it reinforces rather than challenges conventional wisdom."[7] Journalist Alexander Cockburn states it more bluntly: "The first law of journalism: To confirm existing prejudice, rather than contradict it."[8] In an era of declining newspaper sales, challenging conventional wisdom, even if it is palpably false, can be risky.

Of course, mental experiments are just that—hypothetical abstractions. The rest of the chapter sticks to real-life cases of real-life events that demonstrate real-life limits.

The Lessons of the Clinton-Lewinsky Affair

It has often been suggested that feeding frenzies of attack journalism have the power to cut short the public careers of politicians, even those in high office.[9] There are few better tests of this claim than the Clinton-Lewinsky scandal that led to a sustained, year-long media campaign against the president from January 1998, when the news broke, to February 1999, when the situation was brought to a conclusion by a Senate hearing. Every new episode of the scandal—and there were many—got blanket coverage in the American news media and, according to Miller, "For the most part, the public perceived the media, especially television, as promoting the removal of the president."[10] Many political scientists believed that no one, not even the most powerful man in the Western world, could withstand such an onslaught and assumed that it would do Clinton harm, if not destroy his career.

Clinton's popularity as president fell immediately after the scandal broke but bounced back a few days later, to reach 67 percent in late January 1998. His ratings for that year and beyond hovered around 60 percent, the highest of his term in office. An approval rating of 63 percent when he left the White House was the highest of any post-war president at the end of his second term.[11] In addition, only a few months after the Clinton-Lewinsky scandal hit the headlines, Clinton and the Democrats confounded normal midterm election expectations by gaining seats.

That Clinton was at the center of the biggest political scandal since Watergate, yet survived with his presidential popularity enhanced, puzzled media experts. Delli Carpini and Williams note that the failure of public opinion to respond to the media messages and instead to increase their support for the president was the opposite of what media specialists predicted.[12] So many political scientists set to work to solve the mystery of how Clinton completed a second term with his presidential reputation in good standing. They collected mountains of public opinion evidence, making the Clinton-Lewinsky affair one of the best researched issues in recent US political history. With few exceptions, most of that research arrived at the same conclusion: the news media are not as powerful in shaping mass attitudes and opinions as many journalists, politicians, and social scientists believed.[13]

After what has been said about belief preservation in previous chapters, it might be expected that Clinton loyalists would have preserved their faith by denying the facts of the case. Republicans might have been more likely to accept the facts and use the evidence to condemn the president. That did not happen. A Pew survey in August 1998 reported that 70 percent of the country believed that Bill Clinton had sexual relations with Monica Lewinsky, and 66 percent believed that he had lied about it. Almost half (48 percent) believed that he was involved in trying to get Lewinsky to lie. Most thought this was immoral behavior, and more than half (56 percent) said Clinton had set a poor moral example.[14] The same percentage said Clinton did not share their values or show good judgment, and 62 percent did not believe he was honest and trustworthy.[15] In other words, most Americans, including a large proportion of Democrats, were not in denial. On the contrary, they accepted the evidence as the media reported it, became more certain of Clinton's guilt, but turned more against impeachment.[16] This reaction to news of the scandal is not an example of how individuals can deny overwhelming evidence and argument to sustain their opinions. In this case, the public had other reasons for rejecting the media messages.

For a start, they had a low opinion of the press. Three out of four believed there was too much coverage of the controversy and that the press put a priority on being first to report rather than getting the facts right. A third of the population believed that the news media enjoyed Clinton's difficulties.[17] Pew Research Center evidence shows that public evaluation of the press had plummeted in the previous 15 years, with increased numbers saying it was immoral, unprofessional, and disrespectful.[18] Two-thirds believed the press displayed a disregard for the people in the news and tried to cover up its mistakes. Seven out of 10 believed the media propagated scandals, more than half (56 percent) thought it was biased, and 4 out of 10 thought it too critical of the United States. These views were common to a cross section of the public. The Pew report concludes, "It is no surprise that a solid majority of Americans give the media poor grades for their coverage of the investigation and impeachment trial of President Clinton." Other polls report similar figures for distrust and disapproval of the press.[19]

In spite of the blanket coverage, not many Americans followed the scandal closely.[20] Interest declined after an initial period, and only 20 to 30 percent followed the situation "very closely" over the next year.[21] Even 73 percent of Midwest Republicans complained about too much coverage of the story.[22] Whereas Nixon supporters developed a convenient lack of interest in Watergate,[23] most Americans, including Republicans, became bored by the Clinton-Lewinsky affair, and by August 1998 only 22 percent believed it to be of great importance to the country.

Nevertheless, the news media persisted in reporting the scandal at length, claiming this was what the public wanted.[24] Indeed, despite plentiful evidence to the contrary, one journalist displayed a capacity for belief preservation by complaining that the polls were wrong and underestimated real opposition to Clinton.[25] Reporters are professional news junkies who sometimes persist with stories that they, not their audience, find fascinating.

Many Americans supported Bill Clinton as a president but disapproved of Bill Clinton the man.[26] At the beginning of the scandal, in January 1998, 56 percent of the public said that Clinton did not share their values and did not show good judgment, but approximately the same percentage (55 percent) said that Clinton's personal life did not matter to them so long as he did a good job of running the country.[27] A large majority (70 percent) said he "was tough enough" for the job, 68 percent stated that he "could get things done," 59 percent believed that he "cared about people," and 53 percent thought he "could bring about change."[28]

The public's distinction between Clinton the man and Clinton the president hardened over time. Just after the release of the Starr Report, 73 percent rated Clinton poorly in ethical and moral terms, but 66 percent approved of his performance as president.[29] In August 1998, two-thirds said that his affair with Lewinsky had nothing to do with his job as president.[30] In September 1998, the *Washington Post* reported that barely more than one in five Americans thought Clinton was honest and trustworthy, but nearly three in five thought he understood their problems.[31]

The public also divided to some extent along party political lines. Republicans were less inclined to support Clinton than Democrats and Independents, but many of them were against impeachment. Between a third and a half were unwilling to see him impeached either for lying about the affair or for encouraging Lewinsky to lie. Irrespective of their party identification, Americans were generally more supportive than critical of Clinton.[32] Public opinion was shaped to some extent by party identification, but not mainly by it.

All these factors—trust in the media, growing boredom with the issue, the distinction between the man and the president, partisanship—played a part, but behind them was another basic and powerful reason. Zaller argues that the bedrock values of American citizens mainly account for Clinton's continuing popularity in the face of media attack.[33] The mainsprings of American politics are, he writes, peace, prosperity, and moderation.[34] Clinton was judged not by his personal conduct but by the fact that the economy at the time was the strongest it had been for 25 years, the federal budget was close to being balanced for the first time in 20 years, crime was falling for the first time in living memory, the country was at peace, and Clinton held to the center ground on issues such as welfare reform, the North American Free Trade Agreement (NAFTA), and a balanced budget. These factors, not a media feeding frenzy of attack journalism, account for America's approval of Clinton as a president.

Newman reaches the same conclusion when he writes about "the impotence of the mass media.[35] He notes that most experts assumed Clinton's approval ratings as president would collapse when the scandal broke. He also observes that past research—and there is an awful lot of it—finds that peace, prosperity, and probity (PPP) are what drives presidential approval ratings. He tests the PPP model against what might be called the attack journalism model and finds that the PPP model explains Clinton's ratings, and does so with surprising statistical ease. He concludes, "Political realities, actual outcomes in the real world, continue to drive presidential approval." Just as "actual outcomes in the real world" can explain why American opinion turned against the Vietnam War, so also it explains why opinion did not turn against Clinton as president. Evidence about the real world as a driver of public opinion is discussed again in the next chapter.

Having mostly decided that Clinton's behavior was a private and personal issue, not a public, presidential one, the public made a judgment about the man's personal shortcomings. It involved sexual behavior that most Americans encounter in films, novels, newspapers, and history books, and probably in their first- and secondhand experience as well. Most have attitudes and beliefs about such matters and do not need a newspaper journalist or TV reporter to tell them what to think about it.

We see the same sort of reaction to the personal and the political in recent reactions to President Trump. In a *Politico* interview, a leading figure in a conservative evangelical action group says that he would excuse Trump's personal reputation as long as he continued to represent the Right's policies on abortion, "religious freedom," Christian values, and liberal activism.[36] Policy, not personality, counts; the public is capable of making up its own mind, whatever the tenor of the mainstream media. A good deal has been written about the agenda-setting powers of the media, but the Clinton-Lewinsky affair is a conspicuous example of the failure of the US media in this respect. The next section demonstrates this point in a different context.

Agenda Setting in British Elections of 1987, 1997, 2001, 2005, and 2015

When research testing for direct media effects on public opinion produced mixed results, attention turned to the indirect effects of agenda setting, priming, and framing, which then became one of the most widely discussed examples of media effects. Summarizing 45 years of research, McCombs, the doyen of the theory, likens the media to teachers who repeat their lessons over and over again so that when "citizen students" are asked for their views on the most important issues facing their nation, their responses typically reflect the lessons they have learned from the media in the recent past.[37] The result is that "the news media set the public agenda."[38]

Setting aside how this statement is framed in terms of adults as "citizen students," not all political scientists accept McCombs's conclusion. In their review of 19 studies of political agenda setting at different levels of the political system, Walgrave and Van Aelst find that some studies show only a modest media impact, or none at all.[39] They conclude that agenda setting is contingent on a number of considerations, including the characteristics of individuals.[40] This is consistent with the conclusions of the two previous chapters, which note that what people learn and remember from the news may have more to do with their propensities for belief preservation than with what was actually presented in the media. Agenda-setting theory assumes that individuals accurately store and recall what they read or are told, but ample evidence shows that what people learn from the media depends on how they interpret it and whether they remember it accurately. Memory is capricious. Perhaps this is why there is little evidence of media agenda setting in a series of British elections, as we will now see.

Miller's panel study of the British general election of 1987 concentrates on the agenda-setting role of television, the most common source of news in the country. Television coverage focused heavily on defense, terrorism, and crime, though few voters gave these issues much priority.[41] Around two-thirds of the TV-viewing public in the study stuck to the view that unemployment was extremely important to their voting decision and should be widely discussed, but it got little coverage on television. After unemployment, voters prioritized health, education, and social services, with three out of four saying these were extremely important factors in determining their vote. However, television devoted 13 percent or less of election news time to these issues.[42]

Miller concludes that television had little influence on the public agenda. The public agenda did not follow changes in TV news focus, and although viewers were aware that the media had switched to stronger coverage of defense in the third week of the campaign, they had little interest in the issue. The result was that "Overall, therefore, the agenda set by television was miles away from the agenda of issues that the electorate rated important and wanted discussed."[43]

In their study of the British general election campaign of 1997, Norris and her colleagues conducted a content analysis of more than 6,000 articles in the national press during the six-week campaign. In the first three weeks, the papers gave most election space to corruption and social and economic policies.[44] Halfway through the campaign, Conservative Party splits on Britain and the European Union rose far above all other issues and stayed at the top of the press agenda until election day.[45] For 10 to 14 days, the front pages of the usually loyal Conservative press (*Daily Mail, Star, Express, Sun, Telegraph,* and *Times*) were dominated by Tory division on Europe and the spinoff controversies it generated.

As a result, 17 percent of newspaper space devoted to political issues during the campaign was about foreign policy, nearly all about the European Union, and almost a fifth of the column inches about the Conservative Party focused on the party split on Europe. Corruption slipped down the agenda as the campaign progressed to become a minor issue in the last week. Social and economic issues, at the top of the agenda in the first three weeks, also fell well below the European controversy.

The public did not follow the media agenda. It gave priority to health and education and emphasized these more strongly as election day approached. Economic issues of employment, taxation, and the macroeconomy followed, but far below health and education. Less than 3 percent of the sample mentioned the European Union in the first three weeks, and the EU issue rose to barely more than 3 percent of mentions in the last three weeks. Corruption, easily at the very top of the media agenda in the first two weeks, was never important for more than 1 percent of the electorate. A Mori poll concludes that many of the issues the media dwelled on at length were of no particular interest to voters. Indeed, the general public's focus on health and education did not waver over the whole campaign period.

A study of agenda setting in the 2001 election in the United Kingdom examines the relationships between what the public thought, what six national daily newspapers were publishing, and what the three main parties printed as press releases.[46] It finds that all three were relatively independent of each other. The press had little impact on the political priorities of the public, and party press releases had little general effect on the press agenda, with only two minor exceptions. The study concludes that the press had little impact on the public's political priorities, in the short term at least. But then, agenda-setting theory is based on what the public can remember about the news from the recent past.[47]

Norris also researched agenda setting for the 2005 election.[48] Since different forms of communication can have different effects on attitudes and behavior, the study pushes the research a step further by investigating the relationship between the media and party agendas, on the one hand, and the public's attitude toward political issues, campaign activity, and voting, on the other. This study finds, once again, that the public pursued an agenda that generally failed to converge with those of the media and parties. There was some correlation between what the press and the parties were putting out and public opinion and behavior, but even when statistically significant, the associations were generally weak, patchy, and of modest impact. The study concludes, "Contrary to the media agenda-setting hypothesis, the results indicate that none of the uses of campaign communications generated a significantly greater propensity for the public to alter their issue agenda."[49]

Using a large body of data collected at the start of the election year of 2015, a study of media and public agendas finds that the media agenda changed very little during the course of the campaign. The press and the two main parties focused mainly on the economy, and few stories emerged to disrupt this concern. Despite this, the public maintained its constant interest in health and immigration. The study concludes that there were clear discrepancies between what the public thought important and the issues the media focused on. Public opinion did not appear to converge with the media agenda as the campaign progressed.[50]

These examples of the Clinton-Lewinsky scandal and the British media in election campaigns demonstrate that the public can follow its own political concerns independently of mainstream media agendas. What sometimes fascinates political journalists and drives their professional lives within the Washington Beltway and the Westminster "Village" can fail to register with those whose main concern is making it through the routines and problems of ordinary life. The result is that the press ends up preaching to the uninterested.[51] Consistent with this idea is the finding that the agendas of (new) web-based social media and (old) legacy media—that is, printed newspapers, TV, and radio—are to a large extent separate and independent, with social media focusing more on personal issues of birth control, abortion, same-sex marriage, drugs, and guns.[52]

You Are What You Read?

Mori Social Research conducted another study of the agenda-setting role of British newspapers.[53] The study hypothesizes that if people with the same political, social, and economic characteristics choose to read different papers and have different political agendas, then the influence of the newspaper they read may explain their different agendas. The study identified the top five issues in British politics in 2004 as being security, the National Health Service (NHS), race and immigration, education, and crime/law and order. It then compared how individuals vary in the importance they attach to these issues according to their social, economic, and political characteristics and the newspaper they read. If the choice of newspaper is associated with the importance attached to an issue—even though other individual characteristics are the same—then it might be concluded that newspapers make a difference to the political agendas of their readers, that newspapers have the power to influence or set agendas of readers.

The results are summarized in Table 4.1. This table picks out the characteristics (social, economic, political, and newspaper read) that are most

Table 4.1 Variables Significantly Associated with the Political Agendas of National Newspaper Readers, 2004

Security	NHS	Race/Immigration	Education	Crime/Law and Order
Vote Labour	Vote Lib-Dem	Read *Mail*	Social class AB	Black
Vote Lib-Dem	Vote Labour	Read *Express*	Read *Guardian*	Vote Con
Read *Guardian*	Work part-time	Read *Sun*	One or more children in household	Read *Mail*
Age 16–24 years	Owner occupier	Owner occupier	Social class C1	Age 65+
Satisfied with Lib-Dem leader	Vote Con	Vote Con	Vote Lib-Dem	
Vote other	Satisfied with Lib-Dem leader	Work full-time		
Work part-time				

Source: Duffy and Rowden 2005.

Notes: Owner occupiers refers to those who own their accommodation rather than rent it. Social class AB is higher and C1 is lower. "Black" refers to ethnicity.

closely associated with the importance individuals attach to the five policy issues. So, for example, the security issue in the first column shows that those who vote Labour are most likely to attach high importance to the security issue. So also, but to a lesser extent, do Liberal Democrat voters, and finally (more weakly still) readers of *The Guardian*. The 16- to 24-year-olds and those satisfied with the Liberal Democrat leader are also likely to attach importance to security as an issue, but the association is the weakest in the security column list. No other social, political, or economic characteristic counts in this respect, including reading a national newspaper.

A simple count of the number of times that a given characteristic appears in the table shows that political variables appear nine times across all five issues. Various social characteristics appear nine times across all five issues, and newspaper reading appears six times across four issues. This suggests that newspapers might have some influence over the political agendas of their readers. This is what the authors of the research conclude, although they are careful to point out that their study cannot establish any causal relationship between agendas and newspaper reading.

Even so, there are difficulties with their conclusion. The newspaper effect is largely confined to race and immigration, and then only to the *Mail, Express,* and *Sun* readers. Moreover, as the study notes, all the variables combined explain very little of the difference between agendas, which means that other things, unknown and not taken into account, are far more important for an understanding of political agendas. Consequently, in the majority of cases, newspaper reading makes no difference to agendas, and when it does make a difference, its effect is small, limited to only one issue, and only involves three of the most popular papers. If we conclude that these three papers do have an important effect on agendas, then we must logically conclude from the same evidence that seven other national newspapers have little or no influence on the other four issues.

Nevertheless, the Duffy and Rowden study is important because it offers useful evidence about agenda setting. It demonstrates that by far the most important determinants of individual agendas are not newspapers, but political identities and attitudes and a sprinkling of social variables. They also make the point that media agenda-setting powers may vary depending on the issue— different papers have different effects on different issues. In other words, media effects are contingent on other factors, among which partisanship, party identification, and individual values, attitudes, and opinions stand out. While it may come as no surprise that citizen political agendas are associated with voting patterns, political opinions, and social characteristics, the lack of a substantial and consistent newspaper influence may be unexpected and offers little support for the agenda-setting hypothesis. The following chapters identify other contingencies that augment this list. Meanwhile, this chapter turns from agenda setting to the closely related matter of election campaigns.

Campaign Effects in Britain, Sweden, and the United States

I know that only half of what we spend does any good.
I just wish I knew which half it was.
                    —*Anonymous election campaign manager*

Butler's account of 13 British general election campaigns from 1945 to 1987 concludes that election campaigns were like ritual dances that made no substantial difference to net voting outcomes.[54] They might have made a difference to individual changes in voting preference during the campaign, but if so, those switching their voting in different directions canceled each other out, leaving the net result pretty much the same. Nor did campaigns have much effect in the elections of 1997 and 2001.[55] The 1997 campaign was largely irrelevant to the election outcome, and, as King writes, for all the difference the campaigning made in 2001, it might as well not have happened.[56]

Much the same story was repeated in the general election of 2005. Noting that election outcomes are predicted well in advance of official campaign periods, Wlezien and Norris lay out the fundamental variables that mattered most in the election.[57] It was not the campaign but a healthy economy and the government's record on issues such as education and health. "Put simply, things in the country were going pretty well and most people did not want to change course, at least on these grounds alone."[58]

British election studies are not alone in finding small campaign effects. Summarizing the results of cross-national research in North America, Europe, and Australasia, Schmitt-Beck and Farrell write,

> Campaigning has its limits. The fact is that, for all the efforts a political actor like a party might put into a campaign, for all the resources it might bring to bear in selling itself, its candidates and its policies to the voters, if the voters are not buying then there is not much a campaign can do about it.[59]

Voters were not buying in the 2001 British election because the Conservatives were trying to sell the wrong thing. As Norris puts it, they "banged on about the Euro, asylum seekers, tax cuts and crime, in a dialogue of the deaf, while the public remained more concerned about schools and hospitals."[60] In contrast, Labour's record on basic economic issues was good. Prices, interest rates, and unemployment were low, taxes remained constant, and economic growth and retail sales were up. Like Clinton in his second term, the Labour government of 1997–2001 had presided over a period of peace and prosperity. All this sounds like the "mainsprings of American politics" that Zaller claims are the driving forces of US politics and the peace, prosperity, and probity that others find to be the foundations of presidential approval ratings in the United States.

Voting patterns are often predictable in advance of an election because the fundamentals that matter—partisanship and party identification, economic voting, social cleavages, and the evaluation of parties and candidates—are embedded months or years before the final campaign starts and, short of a major political earthquake, not much changed thereafter.[61] In December 2011, 45,000 Americans were asked whom they would vote for if the candidates in the forthcoming presidential election were Barack Obama and Mitt Romney. Obama had a lead of 4 percent. In the election 11 months later, Obama won by 4 percent.[62] The Hillary Clinton–Donald Trump election four years later saw the same fixity of long-term voting intentions, with only short-term fluctuations around them, despite the unprecedented nature of the Trump campaign. According to the *Los Angeles Times,* "Almost nothing has dramatically altered for any length of time to narrow the lead in polls held by the former secretary of State. . . . The reason: Voters have hardened, and mostly negative, views of both nominees and have stuck with their choice regardless of any new revelations."[63] As one observer writes, "Most of the things that journalists obsess over—the candidates' charismatic qualities or lack thereof, their smiles, their gaffes, the little scandals that explode—often don't mean a thing."[64]

Although they may have little or no effect on party voting, campaigns can do other things. A Swedish study found that the campaign did make a small, positive difference on voting turnout.[65] Distinguishing between news seekers and news avoiders, it concludes that campaigns help to mobilize news avoiders and so reduce the gap between the politically interested and uninterested. The difference between seekers and avoiders is the main driver of political activity in this instance, although campaigns can have a marginal impact of raising the voting turnout of news avoiders.

Evidence linking campaign effects with voter turnout is not new. In 1927, a young researcher at the University of Chicago named Harry Gosnell conducted a neat experiment showing how a registration campaign could be effective.[66] He sent half his sample of 6,000 people different sorts of encouragement to register and, being a good social scientist, he used the other half as a control group. At close of registration, three-quarters of the experimental group were registered but only two-thirds of the control group.

In spite of all the uncertainty about campaign effectiveness, politicians and newspapers pour vast amounts of money, energy, and time into them, paying for mountains of opinion poll data, focus group research, and costly advertising agencies to guide them.[67] Nevertheless, they can—and sometimes do—get their campaign strategies seriously wrong when they ride their own hobby horses up political cul-de-sacs.[68] The media, as Seymour-Ure observes, are always self-obsessed.[69] Politicians can be the same. After all, both are human beings who make mistakes, get stuck in groupthink, or simply get things wrong, just like the hedgehogs in Tetlock's study of expert political judgment (see Chapter 2).[70]

Voters also have a talent for forgetting, and campaign effects can be short-term and quickly buried by partisans.[71] At one point in 2012, Obama's support bounced around 2.8 percent, but that was reduced by half in the final weeks almost entirely by Romney supporters switching back to him after a short period on Obama's side. These voters discarded pro-Obama messages because they were not especially keen on them to start with.[72]

Moreover, the causal relations between the agendas of parties and media, on the one hand, and of the electorate, on the other, are open to interpretation. According to Gelman and King's theory of enlightened preferences, voting intentions are the product of economic conditions, party identification, ideology, and issue preferences, which they call fundamental variables.[73] Voters have their own material and ideal interests, and the job of party campaigns and the media reporting them is to enlighten voters about parties' and candidates' policies so that voters align their preferences with the party that best represents them—in which case, the media are less able to persuade voters than they are able to inform voters on whom to support.

Lenz proposes a theory rather different from Gelman and King's, based on repeated interviews with a panel of voters who developed a preference for George W. Bush or Al Gore according to their views about Bush's proposal to allow individuals to invest Social Security funds in the stock market.[74] It might at first appear that voters based their candidate preference on their own policy position about Social Security funds, but Lenz argues the opposite. His interview evidence suggests that voters start with a candidate preference, learn that candidate's policy positions, and then adopt those positions as their own. The Gelman-King and Lenz theories differ on what is cause and what is effect, but agree that media and election campaigns do not so much set agendas as make it possible for voters to align their own preexisting preferences with a candidate or a policy.

Campaign Effects, Political Knowledge, and Voter Mobilization

Campaigns have an effect beyond encouraging nonpolitical individuals to turn out to vote on election day. Political campaigns are times of heightened awareness of politics and of greater flow of information about party policies and differences. As a result, citizens are motivated and have the opportunity to learn from campaigns.[75] Research on the British election campaign in 2001 shows that the public's knowledge of issues rose on 8 out of 11 items after only brief exposure to information about the issues and that there was little decay in this knowledge over the next three weeks.[76] Campaign learning was greatest among the least well informed and, as a result, the knowledge gap between the most and least knowledgeable voters was closed a little. The British public was not well informed before the campaign, but the know-nothings and the know-littles did learn quite a lot and quite quickly. They learned from TV, party websites, and newspapers. This is consistent with evidence from the United States that finds election campaigns are information rich and educate citizens about politics.[77] It seems that voters learn about election issues from campaigns, even if these campaigns have little effect on their voting intentions.

Conclusions

The public demonstrates a widespread ability to reject or ignore media (and other) messages and does this in different ways and for different reasons. Some deny or reject the validity of a message; others accept the evidence but interpret it in a different and unexpected way; and still others accept the message but do not act accordingly. We see repeated examples of these attitudes in studies of how Americans reacted to news of the Vietnam War and the Clinton-Lewinsky affair, to newspaper endorsements in British elections and the political agendas of British media, and to election campaigns in both countries. In some cases, citizens are impervious to what the media say. Sometimes they pick and choose what they want to believe, and sometimes they believe something different or the opposite of what they are told.

Drawing attention to the way some people reject or ignore certain media messages should not obscure the fact that others receive and absorb messages that change their mind and behavior. The experimental work discussed in Chapter 2 finds individuals who accepted arguments and evidence they were initially opposed to, and a casual look at recent history shows that public opinion has shifted to some extent on ethnic and sexual equality, the rights of minorities, immigration, the environment and global warming, and open government and corruption. Whether and to what extent these shifts have occurred in response to media campaigns or other circumstances is a different matter.

Media agenda-setting powers can fail for two main reasons. First, journalists, politicians, and advertising gurus are human beings who can and do get it wrong, using bad data, misinterpreting good data, or simply failing to recognize what is in plain view (see Chapter 2 on expert advice). Like any other group in the population, they may listen only to the bees buzzing in their own bonnet. Second, the media agendas can fall on fertile and stony ground according to whether they resonate with audiences or not. If they do not, they are likely to be rejected or ignored, and if they do they may positively reinforce audience priorities. The former suggests an absence of media agenda-setting capacities and the latter a weak one. It seems odd, however, to talk about the agenda-setting powers of the media when they reinforce what is already there. Swimming with the tide is easy. Swimming against it is the real test of strength.

We see a third possibility in the 1997 British general election, when both the media agendas and the public agendas moved in the same direction in response to the same real-world events. Similarly, American journalists and some of their audience read the same writing on the wall as the Vietnam War developed.

That different people respond in different ways to the same message from the same source and in different ways to the same message from different sources testifies to the leakiness of the media system. It is a hit-or-miss affair because groups in the population relate in their own ways to the news. They avoid, deny, ignore, or accept the news, depending on the message and its source and on their own social and economic circumstances, party identification, ideology, and political interest and awareness. These individual characteristics rest, in turn, upon education, income, sex, age, and class, race, religion, and ethnicity. These variables appear time and time again in explanations of political attitudes and behavior, and they form the basis of the standard model of the social sciences. They also appear as control variables in most empirical studies of media effect, and for the most part they seem to outweigh media effects as influencers or determinants of public opinion and mass behavior. The variables of the standard model influence not onlywhat media messages people receive but also how they react to them in different ways to draw different conclusions.

The leakiness of the news media system also depends on the obtrusiveness or unobtrusiveness of issues. Media effects are likely to be smaller on opinions about obtrusive issues because the public is likely to have already formed a judgment about them.[78] Obtrusive issues resonate with the public because they deal with everyday experience and knowledge—taxes, prices, employment, incomes, health, education, security, pensions—and the public usually has its own views about them. Media effects may be larger on unobtrusive issues because they are new, technical, perceived as less important, or not so common in daily life, so public opinion about them is comparatively unformed.[79] Equally, audiences are less likely to take interest in unobtrusive issues and more likely to take notice of obtrusive ones but to have settled views about them. According to Campbell, "If there is one dependable law in the world of mass communications, it is those most likely to seek information are already the best informed."[80]

A pattern is beginning to emerge in which media effects can be, and not infrequently are, rather weak or nonexistent. This does not suggest that they are usually weak or nonexistent, even less that they always and inevitably are. However, the evidence does show that media effects are sometimes weak on major, nontrivial matters such as war, national elections, political agendas, and presidential impeachment. The pattern also suggests circumstances in which the effects are stronger or weaker. Personal and household concerns were the driving forces of the electorate's agendas in the British elections of 1987 to 2010 and in some European elections. Most Americans treated the Clinton-Lewinsky scandal not as a public and political matter but as a private and moral one, and their views and values were not much affected by what the media said. Distrust of the news media also played a large part in the public's rejection of what they thought was a media agenda to bring down Clinton. A similar distrust is expressed by readers of *The Sun,* which seems to have put circulation and profit before political influence, as other Murdoch papers and Fox News have done alongside the *Express.* If following the money is the first priority of a paper or TV channel, then political influence and agenda-setting may have to be sacrificed to delivering a message that readers want to hear.

Indications emerge that the news media are less important in the formation of public opinions than real-world events and circumstances, including peace, prosperity, and security. These are said to be the fundamental, driving forces of politics. Twenty years ago, Kuhn pointed out that media influence is "filtered through a prism shaped by personal experience, socialisation by the family and education and by sociological variables such as class, gender, ethnic status and age."[81] This chapter confirms his focus on sociological variables, and the next confirms the significance of his comment, not widely recognized at the time, about personal experience.

Notes

1. Zaller 2001.
2. Zaller 2001: 252.
3. A. Rusbridger, "Courage Under Fire," *The Guardian* (Manchester), July 10, 2006, http://www.theguardian.com/media/2006/jul/10/pressandpublishing.egypt.
4. There is nothing new about fake news. It was a feature of political life long before Hillsborough, McCarthy, the Committee on Government Operations, Goebbels's *Reichsministerium für Volksaufklärung und Propaganda,* the Zinoviev letter, and the nineteenth-century yellow press in the United States. It is as old as politics itself.
5. "Liverpool's 23-Year Boycott of The Sun Newspaper," BBC News, February 24, 2012, http://www.bbc.co.uk/news/uk-england-merseyside-17113382.
6. *New York Times,* September 28, 2016.
7. Schudson 1995: 6.
8. C. Lavin, "The First Law of Journalism: To Confirm . . . ," *Chicago Tribune,* May 19, 1996, http://articles.chicagotribune.com/1996-05-19/features/9605190041_1_alexander-cockburn-journalism-soren-kierkegaard.
9. Ranney 1983: 147–150; Meyrowitz 1995: 133; Fox, Van Sickel, and Steiger 2001; Sabato 2001; Barnett 2002.
10. Miller 1999: 728.
11. Newman 2002: 785. On Clinton's opinion poll ratings, see also L. Saad, "Clinton Coasting Comfortably Despite Controversies," Gallup, June 13, 1998, http://www.gallup.com/poll/4204/clinton-coasting-comfortably-despite-controversies.aspx; "Presidential Approval Ratings - Gallup Historical Statistics and Trends," https://news.gallup.com/poll/116677/Presidential-Approval-Ratings-Gallup-Historical-Statistics-Trends.aspx.
12. Delli Carpini and Williams 2001: 177.

13. An exception is Lawrence and Bennett 2001.

14. A. Kohut, "Most Foresee Embarrassment, Not Impeachment: Americans Unmoved by Prospect of Clinton, Lewinsky Testimony," August 4, 1998, http://assets .pewresearch.org/wp-content/uploads/sites/5/legacy-pdf/85.pdf. See also Miller 1999: 727.

15. Larson and Wagner-Pacifici 2001: 771n62.

16. "Voters Not So Angry, Not So Interested," Pew Research Center, June 15, 1992, http://people-press.org/1998/06/15, and "Americans Unmoved by Prospect of Clinton, Lewinsky Testimony," Pew Research Center, August 4, 1998, http://www.people-press .org/1998/08/04/.

17. "Poll: Too Much Lewinsky Coverage," *CNN All Politics,* January 29, 1998, http://edition.cnn.com/ALLPOLITICS/1998/01/29/poll/; F. Newport, "Clinton's Popularity Paradox," Gallup, January 31, 1998, http://www.gallup.com/poll/4264/clintons -popularity-parodox,aspx.

18. Pew Research Center, "Public Votes for Continuity and Change in 2000: Other Important Findings and Analyses," February 25, 1999, http://www.people-press.org/1999 /02/25/other-important-findings-and-analyses-32/.

19. "Poll: Too Much Lewinsky Coverage." See also Bell 2000.

20. Bennett 2002.

21. "Poll: Too Much Lewinsky Coverage"; "Pew's Poll Numbers: Lewinsky Testimony— a Yawn," Pew Research Center, http://assets.pewresearch.org/wp-content/uploads/sites /5/legacy-pdf/83.pdf; "Americans Unmoved by Prospect of Clinton, Lewinsky Testimony."

22. Miller 1999: 724. See also http://articles.cnn.com/1998-01-29/politics/poll-1bill -clinton-union-speech.

23. Carretta and Moreland 1982.

24. Carretta and Moreland 1982.

25. Miller 1999: 724.

26. Andolina and Wilcox 2000; Cronin and Genovese 1998. For a discussion of the public-private distinction and its importance in this case, see Lawrence and Bennett 2001: 431–437.

27. "Poll: Too Much Lewinsky Coverage."

28. Larson and Wagner-Pacifici 2001: 771–772.

29. Quoted in Enomoto and Baker 2005: 53.

30. Sonner and Wilcox 1999: 557.

31. Sonner and Wilcox 1999: 556.

32. "Americans Unmoved by Prospect of Clinton, Lewinsky Testimony."

33. Zaller 1998; Zaller 2001: 252–278.

34. Peace and prosperity are the two objectively measured fundamental determinants in Hibbs (2008).

35. See also Newman 2003 and Miller 1999.

36. E.-I. Dovere, "Tony Perkins: Trump Gets 'a Mulligan' on Life, Stormy Daniels," *Politico Magazine,* January 23, 2018, https://www.politico.com/magazine/story/2018/01 /23/tony-perkins-evangelicals-donald-trump-stormy-daniels-216498.

37. McCombs 2014: 47–51.

38. McCombs 2014: 2.

39. Walgrave and Van Aelst 2006: 92.

40. De Vreese (2007) also finds that agenda setting is conditional on other factors and is not true for all media or individuals.

41. Miller 1991.

42. Miller 1991: 139.

43. Miller 1991: 62.

44. Norris et al. 1999: 122–129.

45. Norris et al. 1999: 124–129. See also Seymour-Ure 1997: 598.

46. Harris, Fury, and Lock 2006.

47. McCombs 2014: 47–51.

48. Norris 2006.
49. Norris 2006: 209.
50. Moore and Ramsay 2015.
51. MacArthur and Worcester 1992.
52. Russell Neuman et al. 2014.
53. Duffy and Rowden 2005.
54. Butler 1995: 3.
55. King 1997; Butler and Kavanagh 1997: 243.
56. Bartle, Crewe, and Gosschalk 1998: xx; King 2001.
57. Wlezien and Norris 2005.
58. Wlezien and Norris 2005: 871.
59. Schmitt-Beck and Farrell 2002: 188.
60. Norris 2001: 573.
61. Campbell 2005: 81.
62. Sides and Vavreck 2014.
63. *Los Angeles Times,* October 31, 2016.
64. Tomasky 2016: 43.
65. Strömbäck 2017: 251.
66. Gosnell 1929.
67. Maarek 1995.
68. Norris 2001: 586.
69. Seymour-Ure 2002: 133.
70. Tetlock 2005.
71. Hill et al. 2013.
72. Bartels 2014.
73. Gelman and King 1993.
74. Lenz 2012.
75. Arceneaux 2006.
76. Norris and Sanders 2003.
77. Iyengar and Simon 2000: 156.
78. Zucker 1978.
79. Happer and Philo 2013.
80. Campbell 1966: 323.
81. Kuhn 1997: 280.

5

Personal Knowledge
and Experience

It is usually assumed that we are all largely, if not wholly, dependent on the news media for our knowledge of the wider world. The first sentence of one textbook states, "Empirical research has long confirmed that for most people the mass media are the major sources of information."[1] Similarly, the opening sentence of an article reads, "The news media represent the principal intermediary between real-world events and the public. Since people depend on the media for information about the course of public affairs . . ."[2] Or, as Kiewiet puts it, "Information about economic conditions must be obtained from newspapers and television."[3]

More recently, websites have been added to papers and television as a main source of information, and in the United Kingdom, it is said, people now get their election news from television and the Internet (that is, the web).[4] Likewise, the American Press Institute finds that most citizens access their news on a number of electronic devices from various digital media, although other sources are increasingly important, including the paid and volunteer staff of political parties using phones and canvassing neighborhoods on foot.[5]

However, there may be something wrong with the claim that most citizens depend on the media and political parties for their political information and opinion. In the previous chapter, we found that the election agendas of voters in Britain are more usually built around their own lives rather than around the agendas of the news media and political leaders. The American public also based its views about impeaching President Bill Clinton on what they thought was important in a president and on their own moral judgments, rather than on what the press and TV news told them. In 1997, readers of partisan papers in the United Kingdom voted or abstained according to their own understanding of economic and political circumstances, not the party line or endorsement of their chosen paper. Similarly, they set their own agendas in a series of British general elections rather than following those of the media.

The public appears to have access to other sources of news and opinion that provide them with their own means of drawing conclusions about what the media tell them. This may be because people live in their own world and draw their own conclusions from it. They pay taxes, use public health services, visit doctors, go to hospitals, come into contact with public agencies and bureaucrats, travel on public roads, use public transport, encounter homeless people on the streets, experience welfare and social services, walk past boarded-up shops, see police on patrol, pass through airport immigration control and security checks in public places, stroll in public parks, use public libraries, and have their garbage collected. Large numbers work in the public services, serve in the military, enroll children in school, live on pensions, work or not, and accept good or bad pay. They learn about interest rates and inflation from managing their domestic economies, and they learn about the state of the national economy from their work experiences of being laid off, made redundant, or securely employed. If they do not have firsthand experience of all these things, they often hear about them from friends, family, colleagues, and neighbors.

However, it does not follow that the information they gain from their personal experience is correct.[6] Their world may be untypical and limited, or they may misperceive it, misjudge it, or view it from a strange perspective. However, for the present discussion about media power what matters is whether they form opinions about political issues on the basis of what they see and hear around them in their own world rather than what the media tell them. Perhaps it is more accurate to say in some cases that their opinions determine what they see and hear around them. Either way, immediate, firsthand experience and knowledge of the world may play a role in the origins of public opinion and behavior.

This chapter explores the idea that encounters with daily life may have (1) a direct impact on individual political knowledge, attitudes, and beliefs that (2) override or moderate media messages and (3) have a broader effect on their judgments about the political system they live in. The chapter considers four studies. The first deals with how Americans use their experience of the real world to evaluate the performance of the national economy. The second shows how Russians use their experience of the world around them to evaluate what they see on television news. The third looks at how Swedes use their personal experience of public services to form their opinions about specific political services and broader ideological matters of government and politics. The fourth returns to the question of whether the American press caused the collapse of public support for the Vietnam War.

The Economy as a "Doorstep Issue"

According to MacKuen, Erikson, and Stimson, "The electorate develops its economic expectations from the economic forecasts available in the mass media."[7] Similarly, Soroka assumes that the population must get its economic information from the news and, as a result, "if media overrepresent negative economic trends, people will tend to have a view of the national economy that is somewhat more negative than is warranted."[8]

How else could they develop views about a remote and complex matter unless they have specialist knowledge of economics, backed by information and some personal experience of business and finance? Research by Haller and Norpoth shows how it is done in the United States. They call the economy a "doorstep issue," not in the sense that it is a random response to a doorstep opinion pollster but because the economy is like the doorsteps we cross when moving around in the normal course of a day—something we do all the time without noticing.[9]

Haller and Norpoth tested this hypothesis in the United States using a two-track research design combining individual cross-sectional data with aggregate, time-series trends, both involving a 40-year run of questions asked by the Survey of Consumers. The first question about economic trends asks, "Would you say that at the present time business conditions [in the country as a whole] are better or worse than a year ago?" This is not a pocketbook question about personal economic conditions, but a question about country-wide business conditions, an apparently remote and collective matter for most individuals. The second question is about exposure to economic news: "During the last few months, have you heard of any favorable or unfavorable changes in business conditions [in the country as a whole]?" This is a question not specifically about the economic news media but about information received from any quarter, including economic news gained from personal conversations. Forty years of survey figures show that barely half the public, on average, had heard any economic news in the last few months. As expected, those who were highly educated reported far higher levels of exposure to economic news than those who were less highly educated.

Haller and Norpoth's cross-sectional analysis is based on the monthly Survey of Consumers in each of the presidential election years 1980, 1984, and 1988—a total of 14,000 cases. First, they compared individual verdicts on whether the economy had improved or worsened over the previous year with what people heard about business conditions, and they show that, by and large, the two tend to move together. The correspondence between individual opinions and what people had heard was not perfect, but in all three years the two corresponded quite closely.

This suggests that individuals do indeed develop their views about the national economy based on what they hear about business trends—except that those without economic news tend to have the same views as those with it. Opinions about the performance of the economy tend to move in the same direction whether or not people had heard anything about business conditions. It is worth noting that those with no economic news did not make wild guesses about the economy, nor did they try to conceal ignorance with noncommittal "no change" responses.

Haller and Norpoth next turned to their second research track, an aggregate time-series study, and correlated the index of economic evaluations for each month from 1978 to 1990 with the opinions of those with economic news. The correlation between news and opinion is .82, and between month-to-month changes in news and opinion it is .66. When the same time series is run for people without news, it repeats almost exactly the same pattern. As a result, the correlation between the opinions of those with and without economic news is .91. Haller and Norpoth write, "What is most astonishing here, just as it was for the individual level analysis, is how well a large number of people manage to draw a picture of the economy without hearing news about it."[10]

Where do those without economic news get their opinions? The answer is that those with economic news blend what they hear with what they personally experience to form their judgment, but those without economic news rely rather more heavily on their own experience. Consequently, the fit between personal finances and economic opinions is closer for those without news, but those with news also use their own finances to form an opinion.

One possible explanation is that people without economic news get their opinions secondhand from those with it. Haller and Norpoth reject this explanation, pointing out that the opinions of those without economic news correspond closely to their own personal economic circumstances, which would not happen if they took their cues from others who do not necessarily share these circumstances.

Haller and Norpoth conclude,

> The picture of the economy in the minds of people without news is by no means a blank slate or an incoherent jumble. Across time (in monthly surveys from 1978 to 1990) as in election-year cross-sections (1980, 1984 and 1988), opinion of no news respondents closely matches the opinion of those respondents exposed to economic news. Respondents without news share the dominant opinion of those with news in each of those years: they just seem a little less sure . . . regardless of news exposure, the general public follows a path of economic opinion well marked by the signposts of the real economy.[11]

Other features of this work hold important lessons for media research. First, a great deal of economic news never reaches a target audience because half the population does not receive it. For them, the news had little or no direct impact. Second, about a quarter of those with economic news formed a view of the economy that was different from the news they received. Some groups accept the news they get, but others do not, and sometimes they are large minorities. News is a leaky system that does not always hit a target and is not always accepted when it does. And, third, those with economic news, and certainly those without it, base at least some of their judgment about the economy on their own experience of the real world rather than reports about it.

Television News in Russia

A rather different aspect of news media leakiness and real-world politics is found in Mickiewicz's in-depth focus group study of TV news audiences in Russia.[12] TV news in Russia is controlled by the Kremlin or its business friends. Since the demise of TV-6 and REN-TV, all three national TV channels (One, Two, and NTV) are partly or wholly owned by the state or energy companies close to it, and they have largely suppressed messages that are not actively supportive of them. Nevertheless, Russians are heavy users of TV news, which is by far the preferred media source of political information.[13] Since many Russians do not trust the TV news they get, they use personal knowledge and experience to interpret and recast it and also to fill in gaps when they believe they have not been given important information.

Given the Kremlin's near monopoly of TV news and the public's dependence on it, Kremlin politicians and media owners assume that whatever they say is swallowed by the general population, but this does not reckon with what Mickiewicz calls "audience power" to decode and interpret what it sees and hears. Russians do not passively absorb their TV news: they pass it through the filters of personal experience to weigh it, judge it, and compare it with other sources of information. The heuristics Russians use to process their news originate in the past with events that are much broader and deeper than the news they happen to be watching. As a result, there is a "dramatic mismatch" between the messages sent by Moscow and the viewing public's interpretation of them.[14]

Mickiewicz assembled 16 focus groups in four Russian cities and presented them with different, real-life accounts of a set of events, including news coverage opposed to the official state version as well as coverage by state-owned or -controlled TV stations. In the group discussions that followed, it was clear that Russians knew television was not a reliable and impartial source of news and that the Soviet years had taught them how to deal with it. As Mickiewicz puts it, "It is important in post-Soviet Russia to arm oneself beforehand against the agendas of [news media] owners and to be ready to apply mental correctives." This involves knowing and understanding the content, tone, and approach of TV channels and how the state channels present anodyne news that blurs, softens, prettifies, and minimizes bad news. Russians took it for granted that some "news" stories, especially the good-news ones, were planted as government propaganda. They were aware of the high level of corruption in Russia and assumed that much of the news was bought. They understood crises were concealed behind a welter of meaningless statistics and they could ignore or promptly forget them. They were aware that serious policy problems were presented as simple bureaucratic matters to be solved by committee or a new government ordinance. Participants complained about the lack of "good-news" stories on television while rejecting those they did see as unbelievable.

In election campaigns, Mickiewicz writes, TV news viewers expected character assassination of the opposition. They knew that television time was not fairly allocated and that the Kremlin, not the electorate, set the agenda and corruptly manipulated elections. Russian viewers used personal experience and shortcuts to extract meaning from limited and biased news sources. They followed campaigns on television, but because many of these did not relate to their own experience and they disliked the mudslinging and personal attacks, many ended up confused and aggressive, not pacified and contented as the elite intended.

Identifying the channel they were watching and knowing its bias allowed viewers to make allowances for what they saw and informed them about what correctives to make for its biased reporting. Russian TV news viewers are skilled at identifying news channels by their content, tone, and approach. They check the news of one channel against another to squeeze out whatever facts they can from the meager amount of reliable information available. When they were presented with a biased and one-sided account of a story, they evaluated the content to try to spot what was not said. Some even played the role of "news detectives," watching different news channels and reading different papers in an attempt to triangulate a more complete and believable picture. In doing this, they relied heavily on their personal experience and knowledge and that of others who were closer to the scene of a particular news item.

Most of the research on belief preservation and motivated reasoning (see Chapter 2) finds that individuals spend more time disconfirming evidence that does not fit with their own beliefs, while allowing the evidence they agree with to pass without much critical thought.[15] The Russian focus groups, however, were as active in decoding news they agreed with as they were with the news they disagreed with. This audience characteristic differs from results in the West.

Education made a difference. College graduates were more abstract and analytical in their treatment of TV news. They had longer memories and could connect events across time to form a general impression of what was occurring based on experience, though they did find it harder to judge news about foreign countries. Consequently, foreign news, of less interest overall to Russian viewers, was also less likely to be contested. This is consistent with the idea that people are less likely to attach firm opinions to unobtrusive issues, thus allowing more room for media influence. But, at the same time, news reports about these peripheral issues are less likely to attract audience attention.

Mickiewicz concludes her study of Russian TV news–viewing audiences with the following observation:

> The effort contributed by Russian viewers and their sophistication about information are impressive, and confound the assumptions of those who determine the news agenda. . . . Some years after the dissolution of the Soviet Union, our Russian focus group members had not lost their astonishing sophistication in expanding what the news stories had deliberately left out or, while there was still a diversity of views, what the opposition station had exaggerated beyond credibility.[16]

It may be that Russians are used to taking their state-controlled news with buckets of Black Sea salt and that citizens of the established democracies are more trusting of their media. That is open to doubt (see the following chapter), and both the Russian and the Western evidence about the Clinton-Lewinsky affair, agenda setting, and campaign effects suggests that people use their daily experience and values to make judgments about the news they get. They filter the news through their knowledge and experience of the real world before they accept, reject, or ignore it.

The Personal and the Political in Sweden

A Swedish study by Kumlin examined how individuals use their personal experiences of the welfare state to form political opinions and attitudes, not just about public services but also about government and politics in general.[17] This research asked a sample of citizens about their experiences and evaluations of public services and about the experiences of others they know. They were asked about public services they interacted with, as well as others they had not experienced directly, and how they had changed in the previous two or three years. They were also asked whether they and others were treated correctly, about the efficiency of the service, about their ability to influence the services, and whether they and others could get the services they had a right to. These responses were then correlated with a set of political attitudes covering approval of the government in office, satisfaction with democracy, trust in politicians, political ideology on a left-right scale, and beliefs about the proper size of the public sector.

Kumlin found that Swedes connected their personal experience of public services to their views about government and the overall functioning of the democratic system, and he concludes that "personal welfare state experiences have significant effects on political orientations."[18] Moreover, personal experience with public services has a bigger impact on political attitudes and ideology than the personal economic matters investigated in the large literature on economic voting. Kumlin writes,

> Citizens are not entirely dependent upon politicians, the mass media, or experts, for information relevant to political learning in adulthood. Far away from the hustle and bustle of elite politics and mass media attention, there are other opinion formation processes going on where political trust and ideology are gradually updated in the light of new independent personal observations of welfare state arrangements and public services.[19]

In Britain, personal experiences in the workplace and with public services are also associated with attitudes toward liberty and established authority. The authors of one study found that experience of discrimination—in the workplace and among women, young people, and those who are less well educated—raised commitment to liberty and equality.[20] Similarly, negative experiences with the police—not simply contact with the police—correlated with support for liberty and reduced confidence in the judicial system.

Conversely, in Britain the general public's interest in politics, partisan activism, addiction to current affairs programs on television, and participation in voluntary associations had no such associations. It would seem that everyday experiences in life and with state agencies have a smaller effect than bad experiences.

Personal experience with public services can also give meaning and importance to news reports about them. Quoting research by Mutz and Iyengar and Kinder, Kumlin observes that there is a mutually reinforcing effect between personal experiences of a particular kind and mass media coverage of the same topic. Reports about unemployment, for example, can politicize unemployed people by turning their personal experience and concerns into public and political ones. He notes, "The mutually strengthening interaction effects between the political impact of personal experiences and that of mass media coverage: both personal welfare state experiences as well as mass-mediated welfare state information become more influential when the two are similar to each other."[21] Personal knowledge and experience influence how people interpret the news, and the salience of a news report is heightened when individuals have direct experience of the issue.

Vietnam: A Victory for the Press and Television?

Vietnam is said to be the world's first television war.[22] It has often been claimed that the media lost the war for America by misreporting the news and creating antiwar sentiment among the public.[23] Robert Elegant's pithy statement sums up the view of many politicians, senior military officials, and journalists:

> For the first time in modern history, the outcome of a war was determined not on the battlefield but on the printed page and television screens—never before Vietnam had the collective policy of the media sought, by graphic and unremitting distortion, the victory of the enemies of the correspondents' own side.[24]

The assumption is that the news media must have been responsible because the vast majority of Americans had little or no firsthand experience or knowledge of the war: they did not fight in the paddy fields, fly helicopter gunships, or fire a weapon at the enemy, so it must have been television and newspaper reports that informed and shaped public opinion.

The argument is strongest when it claims that the Tet Offensive in January 1968 was the turning point in public opinion because it was systematically misreported in the American media. Among many others, Braestrup claimed that the offensive was presented quite wrongly as a defeat for the United States.[25] This false and defeatist reporting is said to have caused a steep decline in confidence of the US government and people and, eventually, the loss of the war.

Later research fails to find evidence for this thesis.[26] Many commentators have pointed out that even though the Tet Offensive was not the defeat the media claimed it to be, the news about it did not have the effect Baestrop, Elegant, and many others have claimed. In fact, the Tet Offensive initially stiffened hawkish opinion in the United States for about six weeks, after which a more dovish mood set in.[27] However, support for the war had started its long-term decline well before 1968, as both Zaller and Mueller show.[28] In fact, the decline set in as early as 1965. Mueller's study concludes that the Tet Offensive simply confirmed what many Americans were already coming to believe about the war.[29]

Neither does the evidence suggest a large media impact before or after the Offensive. An examination of American TV coverage shows it to be bland and uncritical until the Offensive in 1968, but even after that it rarely presented war scenes of battle, blood, and death that would disturb Middle America. Vietnam is described as "the first living room war," but from 1965 to 1970 American television rarely presented war footage of combat or fighting.[30] It was not gruesome war images of death and destruction that caused public opinion to change.

It is possible that reports of the Tet Offensive did influence public opinion, but not because it was presented as a defeat for the United States. The US military and government's public statements consistently underestimated Vietcong strength, on the grounds that divulging the true figures would create a political bombshell, making it clear that the enemy could wage a protracted war of attrition.[31] The Tet Offensive caused the American public to lose faith and trust in US leaders when people realized they had not been told the truth and that the Vietcong forces were far stronger than they had been told. According to Schudson, the Johnson administration lied repeatedly about the progress of the war, to the extent that the term "credibility gap" came into common parlance.[32] After being told for years that no such attack as the Tet Offensive was even possible, Middle America made up its own mind about whether their country could and should continue to fight.

Mueller found that changes in public support for both the Korean and the Vietnam War followed "remarkably similar" patterns.[33] In both cases, the most powerful single cause of declining support was the American casualty rate. This, again, might suggest TV broadcasts of body bags and military funerals dramatically influenced public opinion, until it is pointed out that American support for the Korean War followed exactly the same pattern of falling support as casualties rose. The Korean War was fought when barely a quarter of American households owned TV sets, yet support for the war fell to about a third of the population.[34] In any case, there was virtually no TV coverage of the Korean War, and television news played a minor role in informing even those citizens who owned a TV about the conflict.[35] Furthermore, despite TV news coverage of the Vietnam War, public support continued for considerably longer than for the Korean War and declined only when the number of American casualties in Vietnam surpassed the number of casualties in Korea.

A comparison of the Korean and Vietnam Wars suggests the influence of the news media on public opinion has been greatly exaggerated and was probably slight in both cases. Even this may exaggerate the case: according to Moss, the impact of the media on the outcome of the Vietnam War was "peripheral, minor, trivial, in fact, so inconsequential it is unmeasurable."[36] Mounting opposition to the conflicts was directly associated with the hard, real-world facts about war casualties, not with TV coverage or defeatist journalism.[37]

Public opinion of the Iraq war followed a similar pattern. In a study entitled "Reality Asserts Itself," Baum and Groeling found that public opinion was more malleable at the start when the public was less well informed about events and the "rally-around-the-flag" tendency was strong. But as information accumulated about the war, opinion shifted according to the reality of events, and the ability of elites and journalists to spin the news declined.[38] The liberal American media no more lost the wars in Korea, Vietnam, and Iraq for the United States than the yellow press of Pulitzer and Hearst pushed the country into the Spanish–American War or World War I.[39]

Conclusions

It is commonly assumed that because the great majority of citizens have little or no firsthand knowledge of political events they must rely heavily, perhaps entirely, on the news media to keep them informed. This gives the news media a huge influence over public opinion. Therefore, Bourdieu writes,

> Television enjoys a *de facto* monopoly on what goes into the heads of a significant part of the population and what they think . . . with their permanent access to public visibility . . . journalists can impose on the whole of society their vision of the world, their conception of problems, and their point of view.[40]

According to Habermas, the media are now powerful agents that create a society in which citizen-consumers passively absorb entertainment and information that has been approved by media corporations. Citizens no longer participate in the public sphere; they have become spectators of the media content that shapes public opinion.[41] The media, according to Iyengar, Peters, and Kinder, provide compelling descriptions of the world that the public cannot directly experience and hence can prime the public view of what is serious and important and what looms large in their evaluation of presidential performance.[42]

Claims like these are built on the dual assumptions that individuals rely heavily, if not completely, on the news media as sources of political information and opinion, and that they soak up whatever news and opinions are poured over them. Both assumptions are dubious insofar as citizens have their own everyday experiences of some public issues and services and use these and their own opinions and values to judge what news sources tell them.

Research on everyday life as a source of political information and opinion is rare, presumably because it is assumed to be of no importance. Therefore, this chapter must draw its conclusions with caution. The evidence is limited and needs corroborating, but it does suggest that citizens use their own daily contact with the world around them and their own opinions about it to form their judgments about political matters. Sometimes they do this with very little input from the mass media, either because they do not receive the message or because they reject it. Sometimes they do it in conjunction with the media, but even then, they pass the news they receive through the filter of their own experience.

Haller and Norpoth call the economy a "doorstep issue" because it is something that people come across all the time without noticing. Education, transportation, taxes, prices, inflation, unemployment, pensions, health and health services, public parks, police services, public regulation of businesses, housing, welfare, state pensions, banks and money market failures, the effectiveness of public bureaucracies and social services, public health, working conditions, and trash disposal may also be considered doorstep issues of daily life that citizens use to shape their judgments about politics and public policy.

The news media may have more influence over the public on foreign affairs and distant matters that citizens have no firsthand knowledge about, but even then, as public opinion about the Korean and Vietnam Wars indicates, this influence is secondary to other fundamental values. In the case of the wars in Asia in the 1950s and 1960s, public opinion seems to have been guided more by concern about mounting American casualties than by media news about the war. People may have depended on media reports for information about casualties, but what hawks and doves made of the figures depended not on the media but on their own values and predispositions. Similarly, many millions across the Western world had no direct knowledge of conditions in Iraq, weapons of mass destruction, or the likely consequences of regime change, but this did not prevent them protesting against the war. Furthermore, a substantial proportion of the population believed that weapons of mass destruction had been found, even used, in Iraq when the news was busy telling them the opposite, so here again the press had no impact on what people chose to believe.

There seem to be three pathways that link personal experience, news media messages, and public opinion. One goes directly from personal experience to public opinion formation, largely bypassing the media. For example, in the Haller and Norpoth study, those who had no economic news relied heavily on their household finances to form judgments about national economic performance. Another study concludes, "the importance of an issue in the actually received media coverage exerts only little influence on the assessment of issue importance of a respondent. Instead, personal factors, such as issue involvement, interpersonal communication, and the issue assessment of the network partners, exert a substantial impact."[43]

The second pathway involves a mix of media messages and personal experience in which news from the media is interpreted and tempered by personal encounters with the world. This is how Americans with economic news form opinions about national economic performance and how Russians interpret their TV news.

Third, Kumlin suggests a mutually reinforcing pathway whereby those with personal experience of an issue may attach greater importance to media reports about it. In other words, people may pay more attention to a news item that resonates with their experience, and in doing so they convert the matter from a personal and private concern to a public, political one. This possibility casts a different light on the notion that framing news as human interest stories has the effect of absolving politicians of responsibility for public problems.[44] For example, because human interest stories about unemployment in the media concentrate on the experience of a single individual, they often attribute the unemployment problem to the plight of that particular individual's alcoholism, drug abuse, fecklessness, or random bad luck, not with their being a victim of government economic policies. The third pathway, however, suggests that human interest stories may carry political weight of a special kind because other individuals with personal experience of the same issue are more likely to pay attention to them. And seeing others in the same boat may also encourage them to see the issue not as a personal and private one, but as a public one requiring collective action. The Me Too movement is an example of how a few individuals speaking out can mobilize large numbers with the same experience.

Behind this discussion lies a more general problem: it is a complicated matter to distinguish between what is out there in the real world that we perceive directly and what is passed to us through the filters and biases of the news media. Take a simple example: this morning I took my umbrella with me to work because the weather forecast said it would rain. Does this mean that the forecast caused my behavior because it persuaded me that it might rain? It is tempting to say so. How else would I have known about the threat of rain? But that assumption is not right, because sometimes I listen to the forecast and do not act on its predictions, and sometimes I carry an umbrella without having listened to the forecast. The choice to listen is mine. This morning I chose to listen and act, but then this was also because my knowledge and past experience told me that the forecast is generally correct nowadays and I can trust it. I also cast an eye on the black clouds overhead before deciding that the risk of a good soaking, as indicated by clouds and forecast, outweighed my highly developed capacity to lose umbrellas. And besides, this morning I also happened to have handy an umbrella that I've failed to lose, whereas on other occasions I have heard a bad weather forecast and then searched in vain for the one I must have left on a train the week before. The simple act of listening to the weather forecast, making note of it, and carrying an umbrella is the outcome of a complex mixture of weather news, personal experience, and individual choice. This makes it difficult to distinguish between the direct effects of real-world events and the indirect effects of news reports about them. The moral of the story is that attitudes and behavior that seem to be caused by the media may actually be the result of a complex interaction between media messages and individual responses to them based on individual life experience.

Let us return to the well-documented example of the American media and the Vietnam and Korean Wars. Was it the objective evidence of war that caused Americans to rethink their pro-war attitudes, or was it the way the media reported the war? No doubt some journalists reported it in a biased and sensational way, though that is a matter of opinion. What is not a matter of opinion is that Americans responded in similar ways to mounting casualty rates in both Korea and Vietnam, and yet the Korean War was waged without much media coverage and very little TV content. Second, politically aware hawks used antiwar news to reinforce their prowar attitudes about Vietnam, whereas politically aware doves used the news to reinforce their antiwar attitudes. Third, large numbers of Americans were involved directly or indirectly in the Vietnam War. Between 1964 and 1975, more than 9 million military personnel served on active duty, almost 3 million in uniform; 58,000 were killed, 75,000 were severely disabled, 23,000 were totally disabled, 1,600 were missing in action, 760 were prisoners of war, and almost 18,000 of those killed were married. Between 1964 and 1973, 2.2 million people were drafted for military service in the United States, Southeast Asia, West Germany, and elsewhere. Given these numbers, it is probably the case that many civilian Americans had personal connections of some kind (six degrees of separation) with someone fighting in the war in Vietnam. Like the national economy, the war was a doorstep issue.

The controversy about real-world versus mediated world as forces behind public opinion is a conundrum that may never be solved. It is difficult, perhaps impossible, to sort out the independent effects—in which case it is difficult to understand why it is so often assumed or confidently asserted that the media carry the weight of causal explanation. What is clear is that we cannot assume that the public relies on the news media for almost everything they know and feel about the political world. Nor should it be assumed that public opinions about events are a response to media reporting rather than a response to the events themselves. Opinions are more likely to result from a mix of what individuals experience for themselves and what the media tell them about the world.

Notes

1. Negrine 1989: 1. See also Mughan and Gunther 2000: 1.
2. Fraile and Iyengar 2014. See also Philo 2014: 1.
3. Kiewiet 1983: 22.
4. Oxford University, "Where Do People Get Their News?," Medium, May 30, 2017, https://medium.com/oxford-university/where-do-people-get-their-news-8e850a0dea03.
5. "How Americans Get Their News," American Press Institute, March 17, 2014, https://www.americanpressinstitute.org/publications/reports/survey-research/how-americans-news. See also "Where Do We Get Our News?," PBS *Frontline*, http://www.pbs.org/wgbh/pages/frontline/newswar/part3/stats.html. It is perhaps not surprising that news organizations find that most people get their news from news organizations. Nielsen 2012.
6. Howell and West 2009.
7. MacKuen, Erikson, and Stimson 1992.
8. Soroka 2012: 525.
9. Haller and Norpoth 1997.
10. Haller and Norpoth 1997: 565. See also Killick 2017.
11. Haller and Norpoth 1997: 572–573.

12. Mickiewicz 2008.

13. Mickiewicz 2008: 21, 28.

14. Mickiewicz 2008: 5.

15. Fine 2006: 106.

16. Mickiewicz 2008: 121, 205.

17. Kumlin 2004.

18. Kumlin 2004: 199.

19. Kumlin 2004: 205.

20. Miller, Timpson, and Lessnoff 1996: 330–363.

21. Kumlin 2004: 67.

22. National Archives, Pieces of History, "Vietnam: The First Television War," https://prologue.blogs.archives.gov/2018/01/25/vietnam-the-first-television-war/.

23. For an account of how politicians, military leaders, and journalists blamed the media for losing the war, see Carruthers 2000: 110–119.

24. Elegant 1981.

25. Braestrup 1977.

26. Hallin 1989; Moss 1998.

27. Mueller 1973: 107.

28. Zaller 1992: 202; Mueller 1973: 56.

29. Mueller 1973: 57.

30. Hallin 2006: 282; Hammond 1989: 238.

31. Dougan and Weiss 1983: 22.

32. Schudson 1995: 147; Hallin 1989: 12.

33. Mueller 1973: 65.

34. M. Stephens, "History of Television," *Grolier Encyclopedia*, http://www.nyu.edu/classes/stephens/History%20of%20Television%20page.htm. The American Century, "Number of TV Households in America 1950–1978," https://www.americancentury.omeka.wlu.edu/items/show/136.

35. Carruthers 2000: 108.

36. Moss 1998: 274.

37. Mueller 1973.

38. Baum and Groeling 2010.

39. Anderson, Downie, and Schudson 2016: 24–26.

40. Bourdieu 1998.

41. Habermas 1989: 85–92.

42. Iyengar, Peters, and Kinder 1982.

43. Roessler 1999: 666.

44. Iyengar 1994.

6

Political Talk

If people did not talk it would be futile to publish papers. . . . They would exercise no durable or profound influence; they would be like a vibrating string without a sounding board.

—Gabriel Tarde[1]

Because we spend a large part of ordinary life talking to others, this chapter naturally follows the previous one in dealing with an important part of everyday existence. People do not live in bubbles, isolated from others and their social surroundings. Their lives are rooted in overlapping networks of family, friends, neighbors, colleagues, and acquaintances. For many, life *is* this network of relationships. When we meet and talk, we sometimes exchange views about politics, express opinions, comment on information, check our views against others, and perhaps try to persuade or be persuaded by them. Some of us avoid politics, but on many occasions we touch on them among all the many subjects of conversation.[2] This is not to say that political discussion in social networks is systematic, focused, and organized. Mostly, it is casual and incidental, brief and haphazard, but it can affect how people react to the news and opinions they receive from the media.

Gabriel Tarde, a French sociologist, and Lord Bryce, a British academic and politician, both wrote 130 years ago about the importance of conversation in the formation of individual and public opinions and as a constraint on the influence of the press. Their accounts are strikingly similar, although they reached their conclusions independently. Tarde believed that newspapers provided a menu of ideas for talk in coffee shops and salons that was essential for the crystallization of individual opinions and their aggregation into public opinion. Bryce wrote that businessmen read the paper at breakfast and then refined or reformed their opinions by talking about the news with colleagues and friends in the smoking car of their commuter train. This politically engaged and informed group then passed its information and opinion on to the mass of less-informed citizens. Tarde wrote that the impact of the papers rested on their "compatibility" with the aims and principles of their readers, and likewise Bryce saw that to be acceptable newspapers had to meet the "predilections" of their readers, which were built around education, habits of mind, accepted ideas, and religious and social attachments.[3]

These theories languished for some 55 years before being discovered anew and independently by Lazarsfeld, Berelson, and Gaudet in *The People's Choice* and subsequently with explicit reference to Tarde this time by Berelson, Lazarsfeld, and McPhee in *Voting*. This led directly to the two-step flow of communication elaborated in Katz and Lazarsfeld's *Personal Influence* in 1955. Clark credits Tarde for the original idea of the two-step flow. That theory was incorporated into the mainstream of behavioral science, but its implications for media influences on politics were not much researched until the turn of the twentieth century. The 1990s saw a revival of the notion that conversation and word of mouth can play a decisive role in how the public interprets the news it receives, this time with the benefit of more survey data, sharper statistical tools for analysis, and a clearer understanding of "compatibilities" and "predilections." This work shows how apposite were the writings of Tarde and Bryce, more than a century after their publication.

This chapter begins with some general observations about discussion networks and political talk as influences on political attitudes and behavior in Western societies.[4] It then moves on to a closer look at four studies. The first is a quasi-experimental project that examines the importance of political discussion in an American city, Pittsburgh, which was deprived by strike action of its local papers for several months—an unusual situation. The second is an analysis of the impact of discussion circles, the media, and other political communications on voting behavior in the 1992 US presidential election. The third study is a cross-national comparative work on the impact of the media and discussion circles on voter preferences in the United States, United Kingdom, Spain, and West Germany. The fourth examines the ways in which discussion networks influence the way citizens receive political advertising.

The Political Significance of Discussion Networks

A 2016 survey in the United States found that about two-thirds (63 percent) of Americans say family and friends are an important way they get news, some of it by word of mouth, some by online messaging, and some offline.[5] One in 10 said family and friends were their most important source of news, especially those who paid less attention to broadcast news. Another survey found that the great majority of Americans (85 percent) preferred to share the news they got with others by word of mouth rather than by online messaging (15 percent).[6] Many American churchgoers also heard political news and views from the pulpit.[7]

Whereas family and friends form the majority of discussion circles, 91 percent of human resources executives in the United States say they have witnessed political discussions in the workplace, 45 percent rarely, but 18 percent often, and most of a congenial if passionate nature.[8] The field work for this survey was conducted eight months before the presidential election of 2016, not at the height of the campaign when political interest was high. The study also found that almost a quarter of companies sent their employees information about how the candidates' policies might impact their company—a channel of political communication not much investigated. According to a survey conducted by the American Press Institute, 65 percent of Americans discovered news by word of mouth, directly or by phone, and in spite of the interest in the new communications technologies, they get their news more often this way than by email, text messaging, online news, and social media.[9] Studies of online messaging should take such findings into account.

No one keeps count of how often they talk politics or whom they talk to, so the survey figures are approximate. There is, for example, some evidence that survey research tends to underreport informal political discussion.[10] Nevertheless, the evidence is that most people talk sometimes about politics and quite a few talk often. This corresponds with the idea that new technology, even if it spreads rapidly, usually changes social patterns slowly and is incorporated and fused with existing patterns to form a mixture of old and new.

Some of these figures might seem high, but they are not out of line with other findings. According to the 2005 World Values Survey, the great majority of people in Western democracies talk to their friends about politics every week. The figures range from 90 percent in Sweden and Switzerland to 67 percent in Spain and the United States, with 80 to 90 percent of people talking weekly about politics in most countries. More detailed data (Table 6.1) show that a large minority in most countries discuss politics "frequently" and most discuss them at least "occasionally," although between a quarter and a third say they never discuss them. These figures are similar to findings from other studies.[11]

Research on political discussion circles in the United States found that political talk covers controversial topics of abortion, taxing and spending, the Iraq war, and the clash of values and interests.[12] Also, people were able to engage freely in ordinary political conversation about national, international, state, and local affairs at home and at work, though less frequently in civic

Table 6.1 Frequency of Discussing Political Matters with Friends, 1989–1990

	Frequently (%)	Occasionally (%)	Never (%)
East Germany	50	42	7
Iceland	38	49	12
Denmark	24	55	21
West Germany	24	59	16
Slovenia	22	60	18
Canada	19	56	25
Norway	19	63	18
Austria	18	50	31
Sweden	18	61	21
Switzerland	18	68	14
Netherlands	15	59	25
UK	15	51	34
USA	15	57	28
Italy	13	45	42
France	12	53	34
Finland	10	71	18
Belgium	9	43	47
Japan	6	60	33
Average	17	54	28

Source: Inglehart, R., et al., (eds.). 2004. *World Values Survey: All Rounds—Country-Pooled Datafile*, Madrid: JD Systems Institute, http://www.worldvaluessurvey.org /WVSDocumentationWVL.jsp.

organizations, at worship, and in commercial spaces.[13] The workplace may be an important venue for crosscutting political discussions that result in greater political empathy and tolerance for the viewpoints of others.[14]

Political talk is common among friends and family. The 2014 British Election Study found that around four out of five respondents named at least one discussant, and two out of five named three, the most frequent being spouses, friends, and relatives.[15] A month before the 2016 European Union referendum in the United Kingdom, a survey asked, "Thinking about when you talk with friends and family, have you brought up the subject of the EU referendum when talking to any of the following people?" Six out of 10 (61 percent) said they had discussed the referendum with family, 54 percent with friends, 27 percent with colleagues, 18 percent with others in their social circle, 8 percent with others outside their social circle, and 21 percent had done none of these.[16] The EU referendum was an exceptional political event; in normal times, the number of people talking politics is probably lower. Even so, Ofcom reported that 21 percent of adults (age 16 years and older) typically got some news by word of mouth, a figure matched by another report that found 17 percent did so.[17] When looking for news information on the EU, 20 percent across all 27 member states said they turned to discussion with relatives, friends, and colleagues (compared to getting their news from television, 49 percent; the web, 33 percent; newspapers, 30 percent; and radio, 18 percent).[18]

Sometimes political discussion takes place among like-minded people, but more often it includes others with different social and political opinions.[19] Johnston and Pattie found that large numbers of people had politically diverse networks and encountered different opinions in their political discussions with friends and acquaintances.[20] Similarly, a Pew study found that most Americans talked about politics with people of varying political views, although this was less common among people with strong political opinions.[21] The more varied the range of political opinion in a country, the more political discussion there is.[22]

The political complexion of discussion circles makes a difference. Those involved in consensual discussion circles are likely to hold their views more strongly. Conservative voters in the United Kingdom who talk mainly to other Conservatives tend to be more conservative in their views, and socialists who talk mainly to other socialists tend to be more socialist, while those who talk more to supporters of a particular party are more likely to switch their vote to that party.[23] The causes and effects are not clear: Do homogeneous discussion circles reinforce the agreed opinions, or do people self-select similar others to talk to?

Talk is also associated with political behavior. Those involved in political discussion are more likely to participate in politics and have higher levels of civic competence.[24] For people who are not inclined to vote, the most effective motivation to do so is discussion with people they know personally.[25] As usual, it is difficult to sort out causes and effects, but there is evidence that the causal chain can run from talk to action, although often with the help of a predisposition to action. One study finds that the effects of civic talk among first-year students in a university dormitory resulted in civic participation in that year and that the effect was evident three years later.[26] Another study found that those who are well informed are less susceptible to judgments about political candidates formed in social networks and that the rate of decay of such judgments also depends on how well a person is informed.[27]

In short, discussion circles have consequences for political attitudes and behavior. As Johnston and Pattie conclude, "Political conversations do make a difference, therefore. They are mainly (though not exclusively) relatively local, they do lead to people changing their vote choice, and they can influence whether individuals change their opinions."[28] Huckfeldt and Sprague reach similar conclusions: "The political preferences of citizens have important consequences for the vote choices of other citizens who look to them as political discussants. . . . Vote preferences are socially structured, not only by the characteristics of the voter, but also by the characteristics and preferences of others with whom the voter discusses politics."[29]

Discussion Networks in the Presence and Absence of News Media

Given what is known about the significance of political discussion for the formation of political attitudes and voting behavior, it is possible that discussion may have important consequences for what news people receive and how they react to it.

Mondak's quasi-experimental research in Pittsburgh in 1992 provides evidence. An eight-month strike prevented the two local papers, the *Pittsburgh Press* and the *Pittsburgh Post-Gazette,* from being distributed.[30] Mondak compared residents in three congressional districts in Pittsburgh with three similar congressional districts in Cleveland that were not deprived of their local papers. Results suggest that the absence of a local press did not inhibit the quantity of general political knowledge about the presidential and Senate elections because there are many other sources of information about national-level politics, namely, television, radio, national papers, and other local papers. The absence of the two local papers did reduce the attention paid to the local congressional election and the quantity of discussion about it. At the same time, the absence of the local press made discussion more important in the voting decision.[31] As Mondak puts it, "Because the media context was so poor, Pittsburgh voters sought guidance from their discussion partners."[32] Political talk had a larger effect on congressional voting decisions in Pittsburgh than in Cleveland, from which Mondak concludes that the news media and personal discussion compete as influences on voting, "Provided that two people talk, the political predispositions of one may influence the electoral decisions of the other . . . social influence occurs because most voters cast a wide net when endeavouring to acquire political information. . . . Political discussion contributes to that information mix, with resulting influence on electoral choice."

His remark about casting a wide net also resonates with the conclusions of Chapters 5 and 11 in this book, and his remark that the news media and personal discussion compete as influences on voting resonates with what other chapters say about the ways that media effects are moderated by other influences. It does not, however, tell us much about how discussion moderates the impact of the media. This is examined in other research on the social calculus of voting.

The Social Calculus of Voting

Beck, Dalton, Greene, and Huckfeldt studied voting in the Clinton-Bush-Perot US presidential election campaign in 1992.[33] They observed that voters looked to their personal discussion circles and political and social organizations for opinions about political information and partisan messages they received from other sources, notably the mass media. The researchers set out to estimate the contributions made by each of these sources of information and opinion to voting decisions.

The research design involved five kinds of information. First, phone interviews were conducted with a sample of citizens in 39 representative counties. Second, from each respondent in this sample they collected a list of up to four people with whom participants discussed important matters, plus a fifth who was explicitly identified as a political discussant. Third, content analysis was carried out on a sample of 6,537 items of news, comments, and editorial opinion about the presidential campaign from 46 of the main newspapers published in the sample counties, paying particular attention to their evaluation of the three main presidential candidates. Fourth, they performed the same kind of analysis on the election content of the national television news programs. And finally, they surveyed the election activities of parties in the counties and asked individual respondents for information about the three organizations most important to them and which candidate, if any, these supported.

The purpose of the research was to estimate which of these five factors influenced voting decisions, holding constant the sociodemographic variables of race, education, income, religion, and gender, as well as party identification and political ideology and the contextual factor of the major party vote in each respondent's county.

About a third of respondents were in homogeneous partisan networks, but the others reported belonging to mixed discussion circles, although they were predominantly but not exclusively for either Bush or Clinton. The partisan nature of discussion networks was judged by respondents and by the candidate preferences of the five "snowballed" respondents in the network. Snowballing is a technique used for studying social networks and consists of asking a primary respondent to nominate others in their social circle, who are then approached as secondary respondents in the survey. As with a small snowball that is rolled along the ground in the snow, the method picks up a growing number of members of the social network and, hence, more information about it. The partisan leanings of TV and newspaper election coverage was assessed using the content analysis of election coverage and was judged on the whole to be mostly evenly balanced. Such bias as did emerge was pro-Clinton but was small and, where it did occur, both the electronic and the print media sent out mixed messages that were partly favorable and partly unfavorable for each candidate.

The hypothesis that party identification is the most powerful predictor of the vote is confirmed by a set of highly significant regression coefficients. Consistent with most of the evidence on political attitudes and behavior, and with the argument of Chapter 3 in this book, how people vote is heavily determined by preexisting attitudes toward political parties and their candidates. Political ideology is also associated with voting to a statistically significant degree, but not as strongly as party identification.

Next in importance in the social calculus of voting are individuals' political discussion networks. Both the perceived and the actual party political leaning of the network make a statistically significant difference to the voting decision. The close association between discussion networks and votes cast is impressive given that each respondent was asked to identify four members of their network with whom they discussed "important matters," not necessarily politics, and a fifth person with whom only the presidential election was discussed.

Newspapers and television have an impact on voting, but a weak and mixed one. Media bias was measured in five different ways: by two subjective estimates of respondents (perceived paper bias and perceived TV bias) and by three objective measures (actual news bias, actual editorial bias, and actual TV bias as judged by content analysis). Of these five factors, only actual editorial and perceived TV bias had a significant effect on voting, but only in some regressions. Because the actual Clinton bias of newspapers was weak, voters had no clear or strong impression of it. For TV bias, perceptions rather than actual bias mattered for two of the three measures of party voting, albeit not strongly. Even here, the results were puzzling and counterintuitive because the greater the perceived bias in favor of Clinton, the larger the Bush vote. The authors suggest that this was not because of anything related to the 1992 campaign or the media coverage of it, but a result of a hostile media effect in which Bush voters perceived a Clinton bias. It may also be another example of the boomerang or negative reinforcement effect, whereby those with strong partisan opinions use counterinformation to strengthen their political views, even when the bias against their opinions is perceived, not actual.

None of the other variables, with the possible exception of income (not education), had a strong or persistent association with voting. However, the study suggests that political parties and other organizations may have a small effect on the voting behavior of those with low political awareness, including those who did not vote. Party campaigning seems to have little impact on people who are politically aware and those with a party identification and ideology, which is consistent with the conclusions of Chapters 3 and 4 in this book.

Beck and his colleagues draw the following conclusions: "Organizations and personal discussants serve as more consequential carriers of partisan messages than the media. . . . The powerful effect of personal networks is one of the most significant findings of this study."[34] These conclusions are supported by an experimental study of the effects on political attitudes of discussions between those who watched partisan television and those who did not.[35] The authors found that discussion not only influenced the attitudes of viewers and nonviewers but its effects were stronger than the direct effects of watching the news. They conclude that this result underlines the powerful influence of discussion with the result that the impact of partisan television may spread well beyond those who watch it. It does not follow from this that the indirect impact of partisan television is stronger than that of nonpartisan news. Nonpartisan news also provoked discussion, and because its audiences are larger, its direct and indirect effects are spread more widely. The fact that television can affect those who do not watch it may help explain why public service television has a "rainmaker effect" on viewers who prefer commercial channels. This is discussed in Chapter 9.

Political Communication, Personal Communication, and the Filter Hypothesis

Does the research carried out by Beck and his colleagues in the United States apply to other Western countries? Schmitt-Beck's research covering Britain, Spain, West Germany, and the United States suggests that it does.[36] He found that citizens may receive political cues from their discussions with others about media messages and that these can act as filters that determine how people receive and interpret news media content. "Political conversation is more than just an alternative channel for receiving political information, supplementing the mass media. It also fulfils a crucial 'meta-communicative' function by telling them whether or not media messages are valid, and whether or not they should therefore be accepted."[37]

Schmitt-Beck's study examined the associations between voter preferences and three groups of variables that might influence them. The first group is a broad array of social and attitudinal factors that influence political predispositions, including class, values, party identification, and religion—in other words, the standard model. The second group consists of mass media exposure to newspapers, news magazines, TV news, and talk shows. The third group covers the personal environment of individuals, especially their political discussion networks.

While sizable proportions of partisans with strong political attachments engage only with like-minded others, in none of the countries did they exceed 50 percent of the total sample. In Britain, 34.3 percent engaged only with like-minded others, 50 percent in Spain, 37.2 percent in the United States, and 38.3 percent in West Germany. The chances of individuals voting for a particular political party were high if they were exposed to media messages supporting that party *and* they engaged in discussion circles that supported the same party. The chances of voting for that party were lower if they were exposed to the same media messages *but* they were involved in mixed political discussion. The influence of the media was stronger when media messages reinforced personal political discussion and weaker when they opposed personal discussion. This generalization applies to almost all the various partisan combinations of media and political discussion in the four countries.

Schmitt-Beck concludes that at a time when party loyalties, affiliations, and identifications were in decline, the role of the mass media and personal discussion networks in shaping party preferences and voting behavior may well have been increasing. However, the effect of media messages was also contingent upon the nature of discussion networks. Media messages are reinforced if discussion circles uniformly agree with them, but are likely to be rejected if they do not, or they are likely to be devalued if discussion circles are of mixed opinion.

On the Limits of Persuasion

Most studies of discussion networks and politics examine how these factors moderate the impact of the news media, but political advertising is a different matter because its partisanship is obvious, direct, and designed to persuade. How, if at all, does political talk among family, friends, and acquaintances affect susceptibility to the persuasive attempts of political advertising? Neiheisel and Niebler investigated this question by studying how the composition of voter discussion networks conditioned the persuasive effects of televised campaign advertising in the 2008 US presidential election.[38]

They distinguished between political advertising that reflected the preferences of individuals and dissonant advertising that did not. They also distinguished between partisan disagreement and general disagreement, which is more frequent and intense, in discussion networks.[39] Individuals may be reinforced by the advertising they are exposed to and by their discussion networks, but they may also be cross-pressured by advertising and their discussion networks. In addition, some individuals are not involved in political discussion circles.

Using waves 9 and 10 (September and October) of the American National Election Study, and employing a large number of social, economic, and political control variables (the standard model), their work presents clear evidence of reinforcement effects. Individuals located in politically homogeneous discussion networks were more likely to strengthen their candidate preference when they were presented with political advertising consistent with their preferences. The more they were exposed to such advertising, the stronger the reinforcement. However, individuals in networks marked by general disagreement did not show this reinforcement effect. Even medium levels of disagreement were enough to wipe it out.

The effects of dissonant messages are different. We might expect them to carry more weight in the absence of consistent cues from a homogeneous discussion network, but this is not the case. Individuals in networks marked by high disagreement are more likely to stick to and even strengthen their initial voting preference in the face of opposition advertising. General disagreement in a discussion network not only limits the capacity of political advertising to influence voter choices, but also increases the boomerang effect of negative reinforcement.

We might also expect those who are not involved in a discussion circle of political conversation to be more strongly influenced by political advertising, given their lack of information and opinion from conversation partners. Once again, this is not the case. They do not react to campaign influences to any significant degree, although, strangely, consonant advertising makes them *less* certain of their candidate preference.

Last, Neiheisel and Niebler found no evidence that partisan disagreement in discussion networks had any moderating effect on the capacity of political advertising to influence voting preferences. General disagreement does the moderating work, but in ways that are unexpected and consistent with the minimal effects theory of negative reinforcement. This mixed set of results may help explain the limited effects of election campaigns, as discussed in Chapter 3. If so, the moral of the story seems to be that political advertisers should be careful about how they spend their money, because much less than half of advertisements may be effective and the rest may have no impact—or the opposite effect of the one intended.

Conclusions

The experiences of daily life have an influence on which news items people pay attention to and how they interpret the news that touches upon their experience. Talking to others is an important part of life, and it may also play a part in influencing the effects of the news media and political advertising on voter behavior. The influence of the news media on political attitudes depends on whether political talk reinforces, neutralizes, or opposes media messages, and some research finds that the influence of political talk on voting behavior is much stronger than that of the media. This finding also applies to political advertising relayed to voters by the news media.

This conclusion is consistent with the word of mouth communication theory discussed in Lazarsfeld, Berelson, and Gaudet's *The People's Choice,* and Katz and Lazarsfeld's *Personal Influence,* with two significant differences. First, the composition of discussion circles and whether or not media messages agree with their outlook are key; individuals and groups may accept, reject, or ignore media messages on the basis of these factors—what Tarde and Bryce call predilections and compatibilities. Second, opinion leaders and followers seem to have a weaker effect on politics than conversations between group members, whether they are leaders or followers.

Political talk may work in three ways. It may have a direct influence on political attitudes and behavior that is separate and independent of the news media. Second, it may have an indirect, moderating effect whereby media messages are passed through the filter of political talk, which magnifies, reduces, or wipes out media effects. Third, media messages may be transmitted to the general public in two or more steps. For example, information may pass from the media to opinion leaders, who discuss it and then pass it on in their own form and with more discussion to opinion followers. The direct effect was explored by Beck and his colleagues in the United States, and the indirect effect was the focus of Schmitt-Beck's comparative work. These processes are not incompatible and may work alongside each other.

There are many unanswered questions about how political conversation interacts with the news. Is it affected by the intensity and duration of media messages, by the intensity, duration, and agreement/disagreement within groups? If strong partisans demonstrate a boomerang effect when confronted by news that is inconsistent with their opinions, do they also demonstrate the same effect when confronted by the contrary opinions of the people they talk to? Does this depend on whether issues are obtrusive and unobtrusive? Does the strength of discussion network effects increase when political trust and trust in the media decline but social trust remains strong?

What emerges from the evidence, however, is that individuals are not dependent on the news media for their political information and opinions. They accumulate both evidence and argument about political matters through direct contact with social, political, and economic factors of the world around them during the course of their daily life and from talking to others. If, as some research finds, political talk has a more powerful effect than the news media in shaping political opinions, the explanation may simply be that firsthand experience and face to face talk have a more immediate and more profound influence than the secondhand messages of the news media. Or, as Mutz puts it, personal communication may have greater normative social influence than impersonal communication.[40] Bennett, Flickinger, and Rhine are correct in saying that "discussing politics enhances citizens' knowledge of public affairs, even net of other variables known to affect political knowledge. Students of political behaviour and those interested in strengthening democracy need to treat political discussions as an important form of political participation."[41]

Notes

1. Gabriel Tarde, quoted in Clark 1969.
2. Eliasoph 1998; Huckfeldt 2014.

3. On Tarde and Bryce, see Clark 1969; Katz 1999, 2006; Vermeule 2011; DeFleur 1998.

4. The literature usually refers to discussion networks or discussion circles, but this seems to imply a structure and organization like those of reading circles that meet regularly in small numbers to discuss a book. Political talk is not organized or restricted in this way.

5. A. Mitchell, E. Shearer, J. Gottfried, and M. Barthel, "The Modern News Consumer," Pew Research Center, July 7, 2016, http://www.journalism.org/2016/07/07/the -modern-news-consumer/; A. Mitchell, E. Shearer, J. Gottfried, and M. Barthel, "1. Pathways to News," Pew Research Center, July 7, 2016, http://www.journalism.org/2016/07 /07/pathways-to-news/.

6. A. Mitchell, E. Shearer, J. Gottfried, and M. Barthel, "4. Social Engagement," Pew Research Center, July 7, 2016, http://www.journalism.org/2016/07/07/social-engagement/.

7. "Many Americans Hear Politics from the Pulpit," Pew Research Center, August 8, 2016, http://www.pewforum.org/2016/08/08/many-americans-hear-politics-from-the-pulpit/.

8. "Politics in the Office Survey: 94% Are Talking Politics at Work; Unlike Candidates, Keeping It Civil," Challenger, Gray, and Christmas, https://www.challengergray .com/press/press-releases/politics-office-survey-94-are-talking-politics-work-unlike -candidates-keeping.

9. "How Americans Get Their News," American Press Institute, March 17, 2014, https://www.americanpressinstitute.org/publications/reports/survey-research/how -americans-get-news/.

10. Walsh 2004; Eliasoph 1998.

11. Bennett, Flickinger, and Rhine 2000; Gibson 2001.

12. Delli Carpini, Cook, and Jacobs, "Public Deliberations."

13. Wyatt, Katz, and Kim 2000.

14. Mutz and Mondak 2006.

15. M. X. Delli-Carpini, F. L. Cook, and L. R. Jacobs. 2004. "Public Deliberations, Discursive Participation and Citizen Engagement: A Review of the Empirical Literature." *Annual Review of Political Science* 7, no. 1:315–344. http://www.britishelectionstudy .com/bes-resources/are-we-influenced-by-how-our-friends-vote/#.Vzmr7r6SYRZ.

16. T. Helm, "Tory EU Referendum Voters Are Switching to Remain, Says Poll," *The Guardian* (Manchester), May 21, 2016, http://www.theguardian.com/politics/2016/may /21/tory-eu-referendum-voters-switching-remain-opinium-observer-poll.

17. Ofcom 2015a: Table 5.44 (at https://www.ofcom.org.uk/__data/assets/pdf_file /0022/20668/cmr_uk_2015.pdf).

18. European Commission, Directorate-General Communication "Research and Speechwriting" Unit. 2012. *Media Use in the European Union*. Standard Eurobarometer 78. Autumn 2012. http://ec.europa.eu/public_opinion/archives/eb/eb78/eb78_media_en.pdf.

19. MacKuen 1990; Klofstad, McClurg, and Rolfe 2009; Huckfeldt, Mendes, and Osborn 2004; A. Mitchell, J. Gottfried, J. Kiley, and K. E. Matsa, "Section 3: Talking Politics: Leaders vs. Listeners and the Views People Hear," Pew Research Center, October 21, 2014, http://www.journalism.org/2014/10/21/section-3-talking-politics-leaders-vs -listeners-and-the-views-people-hear/; E. Fieldhouse, "Are We Influenced by How Our Friends Vote?," British Election Study, October 12, 2014, http://www.britishelectionstudy .com/bes-resources/are-we-influenced-by-how-our-friends-vote/#.Vzmr7r6SYRZ.

20. Johnston and Pattie 2006: 127, 132.

21. Mitchell et al., "Section 3: Talking Politics."

22. Anderson and Paskeviciute 2005.

23. Pattie and Johnston 1999; Johnston and Pattie 2006: 141.

24. Kenny 1998; La Due Lake and Huckfeldt 1998; McClurg 2003, 2004; Campbell and Wolbrecht 2006; Klofstad 2007; Zhang et al. 2010; Calhoun 1988.

25. Hillygus 2005: 62.

26. Klofstad 2007, 2009.

27. Huckfeldt, Pietryka, and Reilly 2014.

28. Johnston and Pattie 2006: 143.
29. Huckfeldt and Sprague 1995: 189. See also Mondak 1995.
30. Mondak 1995: 83.
31. See also De Vreese and Boomgaarden 2006.
32. Mondak 1995: 80.
33. Beck et al. 2002.
34. Beck et al. 2002: 69.
35. Druckman, Levendusky, and McLain 2018.
36. Schmitt-Beck 2003.
37. Schmitt-Beck 2003: 235.
38. Neiheisel and Niebler 2016.
39. Klofstad, Sokhey, and McClurg 2013.
40. Mutz 1998: xvi.
41. Bennett, Flickinger, and Rhine 2000.

7

Trust and Distrust

Audience scepticism has been particularly ignored when it comes to news media effects.

—*Y. Tsfati,* "Does Audience Skepticism of the
Media Matter in Agenda Setting?"[1]

An established finding of communications research is that trusted news is more likely to persuade.[2] Previous chapters in this book show that distrust of journalists was one reason why many Americans rejected the media agenda against Bill Clinton. Russians are deeply distrustful of their TV news, so they reinterpret it to reach their own conclusions. *The Sun*'s lack of influence over its readers' voting behavior coincides with it being the least trusted national daily paper in the United Kingdom.

This chapter returns to take a closer look at audience trust and distrust of the media as a source of media influence or lack of it. The first section presents evidence about trust in the Western media; the second distills some general patterns of this evidence. The following section considers the causes and consequences of low trust in the media, especially the hostile media effect and why individuals do not necessarily abandon news media they do not trust. The chapter then examines how trust and the need for individuals to understand politics interact to influence the processes of priming, framing, and agenda setting. The final section suggests ways in which audience trust of the media moderates their influence, either alone or interacting with other individual characteristics.

Mixed Patterns of Low and Declining Trust in the Media

Distrust of newspapers is nothing new.[3] But it is more acute and widespread now. According to a Gallup poll in September 2015, trust in the media in the United States was at a historical low, with 7 percent professing "a great deal of trust and confidence" in the press to report the news fully, accurately, and fairly; 33 percent trusted the press a "fair amount," 36 percent trusted the press "not very much," and 24 percent trusted the press not at all.[4] Gallup, ABC/Facebook, Harris, and Pew People-Press polls all reported widespread distrust of news sources, including the Internet.[5]

Comparable figures for the United Kingdom are found in the Edelman Trust Barometer, in which 38 percent of the general population said they had trust in the media. An Ipsos MORI poll from 1983 to 2017 asked participants whether they trusted eight professional and occupational groups to tell the truth and found that journalists were consistently ranked in the bottom two positions, with 62–75 percent distrusting them.[6] These figures are confirmed by YouGov data for 2003 to 2018 comparing trust in 16 occupational groups to tell the truth (Table 7.1).

Media distrust in the United States and United Kingdom is not exceptional. The Edelman Trust Barometer for 2018 shows that the media are distrusted more than they are trusted in 22 of 28 countries, including 11 Western democracies (Figure 7.1). Across the European Union (EU), 54 percent tend not to trust the press.[7] Other international surveys find similarly low levels of trust.[8]

Table 7.1 Trust in Professional, Political, and Journalist Groups
              to Tell the Truth, 2003 and 2018, United Kingdom

Group	2003 (%)	2018 (%)
Family doctors	93	84
School teachers	88	75
Local police officers	82	71
Judges	68	68
Senior police officers	72	59
BBC news journalists	81	51
ITV news journalists	82	42
Broadsheet journalists	65	42
My local member of Parliament	44	33
Leading Labour politicians	25	23
Leading Liberal Democrat politicians	36	23
Leading Conservative politicians	20	19
Midmarket journalists	36	15
Estate agents	16	14
People running large companies	20	14
Tabloid journalists (Red-Tops)	14	6

Source: Political Trackers/Survey Results/YouGov, https://today.yougov.com/topics /overview/survey-results.

Note: Broadsheet papers are the *Times, Telegraph, Guardian, Independent*, and *Financial Times*; midmarket papers are the *Mail* and *Express*; and tabloid papers are *The Sun* and *Mirror*.

Figure 7.1 Trust in the Western Media, 2018 (percentage)

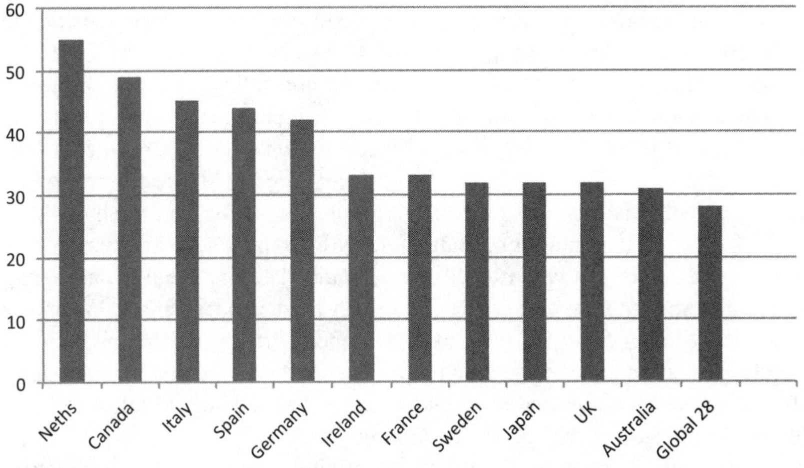

Source: *2018 Edelman Trust Barometer Global Report* (Edelman, January 21, 2018), https://www.edelman.com/trust-barometer.

Four Patterns of Media Trust

Because survey results vary—sometimes substantially, according to methods, sampling frames, time, place, and questions asked—we can gain only a general impression about media trust internationally. Nevertheless, four general patterns emerge from survey results. First, media trust is declining. A recent Gallup poll (September 2016) reported American trust and confidence in the mass media had dropped even lower than in 2015, with only 32 percent saying they had a great deal or fair amount of trust in the media.[9] The decline in trust was spread fairly equally across age groups but was much steeper for Republicans than for Democrats, a finding replicated by a Pew Research Center poll.[10] Another Pew survey found increasing numbers of people believing that the press reports news inaccurately, tends to favor one side, and is open to influence by powerful people and organizations.[11]

Trust in truth telling of occupational groups in the United Kingdom (Table 7.1) fell from 2003 to 2018, but the drop was particularly steep for journalists working for the BBC, commercial television (ITV), and broadsheet newspapers. It was less dramatic for midmarket newspapers and the tabloids, but trust in the tabloids was so low (14 percent) there was not much room for further decline.[12] In 2012, British confidence in the media fell to a seven-year low, with 33 percent trusting the press and 66 percent distrusting it.[13]

Second, trust and confidence are lower for some types of media than others. In 2017, across the European Union, the Standard Eurobarometer Survey found that radio was the most trusted medium (59 percent), television the next (50 percent), and newspapers third (46 percent), followed by the Internet (36 percent) and social media (21 percent and falling).[14] Although Internet use has increased by leaps and bounds in recent years, distrust is also growing, and in all 33 countries surveyed, distrusters of social media outnumbered trusters.[15] The Reuters Institute of Digital Media Survey of 37 countries found that the news media were trusted most of the time by 44 percent of their total population, compared with 51 percent who trusted "my media" and 23 percent who trusted social media. The European Broadcasting Union Media Intelligence Service found that trust in social media news has been hit by fake news.[16] In the United Kingdom, trust in social media news was 12 percent in 2018, compared with 54 percent who trusted "News I use," and 42 percent who trusted news in general.[17] In the United States, the corresponding figures were 13, 34, and 50 percent.[18]

Third, the averages across the EU as a whole conceal substantial variations among countries. In 2011, for example, 80 percent of Swedes trusted radio media, putting it above television and newspapers, but in Turkey only 24 percent did so, which put radio well below television and the Internet. In Finland and Sweden, three-quarters of the population trusted television, but in Greece barely more than one in five did. And in Finland and Slovakia, almost two-thirds trusted the press, compared with only 18 percent in the United Kingdom. In Spain and France, the press, often a poor third in the trust tables in other countries, was more highly regarded than television. Television outranked radio in Belgium.[19] Fewer than 1 in 12 in the United Kingdom place much reliance on Facebook and Twitter as sources of information, compared with almost 3 out of 4 who relied on BBC news (Figure 7.2).

Fourth, these averages conceal large variations among media of the same kind. As Figure 7.2 demonstrates, trust in British journalists to tell the truth ranges from 48 percent for the broadsheets to 18 percent for the midmarket papers to 10 percent for the tabloid papers. Another UK survey of members of Parliament and "opinion formers" found that 7 percent trusted *The Sun* to report fairly and accurately compared with 80 percent who said the same for BBC News.[20] Individuals also trust the media in their own ways, expressing more trust in "my media" than in "the media."[21]

Generalizations about trust in "the media," therefore, can be misleading because they conceal big differences among countries, among media types, among media of the same type, and among individual users. Nevertheless, trust in the media is generally low and declining, and because the trustworthiness of a source of information is an important factor in its influence, it follows that the influence of the media may be low and declining. Consistent with this, evidence from the United States shows that

Figure 7.2 Trust in UK Media Outlets, 2012 (percentage that trusts completely/somewhat)

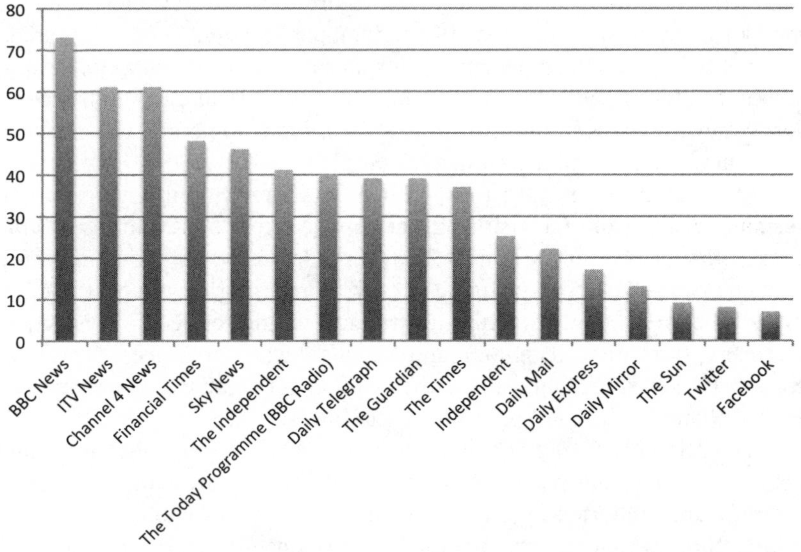

Source: A. Pugh, "Poll Suggests The Sun Is Least Trusted Newspaper," *Press Gazette*, September 12, 2012, http://www.pressgazette.co.uk/poll-suggests-sun-least-trusted-newspaper.

Notes: Figures are responses to the question, "To what extent, if at all, do you trust each of the following media outlets to report fairly and accurately?" Answers ranged from *trust completely, trust somewhat, neither trust nor distrust, distrust somewhat,* to *distrust completely.*

distrust of the news media results in voters discounting campaign communications and relying more on their own preformed partisan opinions.[22] Evidence discussed in previous chapters shows this is also true in the United Kingdom in relation to election agendas and campaigns.

Public Service and Commercial News

Possibly a fifth pattern of media trust emerges from differences in levels of trust between public service media and their commercial counterparts. This is a tentative suggestion, partly because of lack of evidence and partly because public service and commercial television overlap and influence each other in modern mixed systems. Mixed systems, unlike purely commercial ones, often use public interest regulation of both public service and commercial media with the aim of producing impartial, reliable, and comprehensive news. Mixed systems may encourage a degree of backdoor commercialization of the public service because of a need to maintain audience share in competition with the commercial sector.

Nevertheless, there are differences between commercial and public service broadcasting in mixed media systems. One of these involves trust in their news programs. In Table 7.1 and Figure 7.2, BBC TV news tops the media trust ratings in the United Kingdom, ahead of the main commercial channel (ITV) and 26 percentage points ahead of commercial Sky News. A survey conducted by Kantar Media shows the BBC heading the trust scores for 28 news sources in the United Kingdom, including other TV channels, radio, newspapers, and digital natives on the web.[23]

More evidence is found in the Times Mirror Survey, which asked respondents to score television and newspapers for "believability" (Table 7.2). Although the survey is now 20 years old, it is worth quoting because it is one of the few cross-national surveys comparing newspapers and TV news. The three countries with the strongest public service TV systems— Germany, the United Kingdom, and Canada—have the highest scores for trust in TV news, while three countries with larger commercial sectors—the United States, Italy, and Spain—have the lowest.

The data in Table 7.2 are no more than suggestive, given that only eight countries were included and the percentage differences are sometimes small, but they are supported by a BBC/Reuters/Media Centre poll: Trust in the Media 2006, which reported unprompted responses to questions about the most trusted news source.[24] In Germany, it was public radio and television, with ARD as the most common response (22 percent). In Britain, BBC News was the most frequent unprompted response (32 percent), which was at least three times higher than the scores for the commercial channels of Fox News, CNN, and ABC in the United States. Evidence of higher trust in public service broadcasting is certainly not conclusive, but it is consistent

Table 7.2 Ratings of Media Believability in Eight Countries (percentage)

	TV News	Newspapers
Germany	90	84
United Kingdom	85	53
Canada	81	71
Mexico	75	74
France	74	68
United States	73	68
Italy	67	63
Spain	64	60
Average	76.1	67.6

Sources: Times Mirror Center for the People and the Press, March 16, 1994; "Mixed Message About Press Freedom on Both Sides of Atlantic," Pew Research Center, March 16, 1994, http://people-press.org/report/19940316/mixed-message-about-press-freedom -on-both-sides-of-atlantic.

with evidence discussed in the next chapter that considers public and commercial media systems in greater depth. Meanwhile, this chapter turns to the question of what explains low trust in the media and its implications for its influence on public opinion and behavior.

What Explains Low Trust in the Media?

The data in Table 7.3, drawn from six surveys in the United Kingdom and United States between 2005 and 2012, indicate why media trust is low and declining in those countries. In both cases, most people—sometimes large majorities—believe the media are open to influence by powerful individuals and organizations, are biased, tend to lie, are too critical, report inaccurately, contain too much bad news, and are subject to government interference. Large minorities believe there is too much foreign influence. Much the same set of reasons for distrust emerged from a study of 10 diverse countries (Table 7.4), where many believed that the media suffered too much foreign influence and governmental interference, published too many bad stories, and employed journalists who were too critical of government and business leaders and yet not able to report freely. Because the grass is always greener, the international media were trusted more than their own. Another survey found that large majorities believed that the news was not reported accurately, did not present all sides of the story, and failed to strike the right balance between freedom of speech and respect for cultures.[25]

This long and serious list of complaints strikes at the heart of impartial, comprehensive, and trustworthy news reporting. In addition, a dismal view of the news media in the United Kingdom has been further strengthened by a long series of controversies, including misreporting, checkbook journalism, abuse of individual privacy and rights, sensationalism, phone tapping, and scandals involving journalists and media personalities. Successive British governments from Margaret Thatcher to Tony Blair have clashed with the media over its reporting of death in Gibraltar ("Death on the Rock"), the extreme right wing of the Conservative Party ("Maggie's Militant Tendency"), the Falklands War (giving the enemy "the oxygen of publicity"), Northern Ireland (the "Real IRA"), and Iraq's weapons of mass destruction ("sexed up dossier"). These aggressive spats may have undermined trust in the news.

Whatever the truth of these assertions, there are good reasons for not blaming the media alone for public distrust. First, trust and confidence in the press and the media were low a decade before the modern round of scandals and complaints against them. Asked in 1985 about their respect for a dozen groups in British public life, not a single respondent in the survey gave newspaper proprietors the most respect and 17 percent gave them the least, less than any other groups except trade unions.[26] Nevertheless, as Tables 7.5 and

Table 7.3 Evaluations of the News Media in the United States and United Kingdom

Beliefs	Percentage
Often influenced by powerful people and organizations (US)	80
Tend to favor one side (US)	77
Sometimes/frequently lie (US)	74
Tell lies sometimes/frequently/always (UK)	73
Try to cover up mistakes (US)	72
Out of touch with average Americans (US)	70
Report celebrities too much/too critically (UK)	70
Report politicians too much/too critically (UK)	69
Too many bad news stories (US)	68
Often inaccurate (UK)	66
Don't care about people (US)	63
Too many bad news stories (UK)	63
Dependent on powerful people and organizations (UK)	59
Government interferes too much (UK)	58
Often inaccurate (US)	56
Dumbed down in recent years (UK)	55
Government interferes too much (US)	52
Too much foreign influence (UK)	48
National media too liberal (US)	45
Immoral (US)	42
Too much foreign influence (US)	42
Hurt democracy (US)	42
Tell the truth some of the time/hardly ever (UK)	40

Sources: This table is compiled from the following sources published between 2006 and 2011: http://www.pollingreport.com/media.htm; "Over Half of Americans Say They Tend Not to Trust the Press," Harris Interactive, Harris Poll no. 24, March 6, 2008; "Internet News Audience Highly Critical of News Organizations," Pew Research Center, August 9, 2007, http://people-press.org/report/348/internet-news-audience-highly-critical -of-news-organizations; YouGov, Trust in the media, October 24–27, 2011, https://yougov.co .uk/topics/politics/articles-reports/2011/11/14/trust-media; BBC/Reuters/Media Center Poll: Trust in the Media, May 3, 2006, news.bbc.co.uk/2/shared/bsp/hi/pdfs/02_05_06mediatrust .pdf; BBC/Reuters/Media Center Poll: Trust in the Media, "Media More Trusted Than Governments" poll, http://news.bbc.co.uk/2/shared/bsp/hi/pdfs/02_05_06mediatrust.pdf; J. Ray, "Majority of Britons Distrusted Media Before Hacking Scandal," Gallup, July 27, 2011, http:// www.gallup.com/poll/148679/Majority-Britons-Distrusted-Media-Hacking-Scandal.aspx.

7.6 show, although trust in the media is low, it is no lower than for some other major institutions, and its decline in recent years follows the same pattern found in many countries and across a wide array of institutions and occupational groups.[27] The average trust score for all institutions in 38 nations in the Edelman survey is 51 percent and for the media, 52 percent. The press often gets a better score than trade unions and national parliaments.

More detailed country polls confirm this comparative picture. A Gallup poll in June 2013 found that Americans displayed little confidence in TV

Table 7.4 Attitudes Toward the Media (percentage)

	Brazil	Egypt	Germany	India	Indonesia	Nigeria	Russia	S. Korea	UK	USA
Reports news accurately	51	73	58	76	92	76	54	64	51	51
Reports all sides of story	49	59	41	69	88	63	64	48	32	29
Too much foreign influence	77	48	34	58	53	46	30	71	48	42
Government interferes too much	64	49	32	56	59	75	49	71	58	52
Too many bad news stories	80	59	62	55	44	30	58	69	63	68
Journalists able to report freely	48	41	33	42	69	47	25	33	45	38
Too critical of government/ business leaders	62	52	24	51	68	56	16	58	48	48
Trust international media more than national	30	43	19	35	20	41	9	33	47	55
Stopped using media sources because lost trust	44	40	15	28	17	27	10	39	29	32

Source: BBC/Reuters/Media Center Poll: Trust in the Media, "Media More Trusted Than Governments" poll, May 3, 2006, news.bbc.co.uk/2/shared/bsp/hi/pdfs/02_05_06mediatrust.pdf and http://www.globescan.com/news_archives/bbcreut.html.

news and newspapers but still marginally more than in big business, organized labor, and Congress.[28] In fact, television and radio ratings are often higher than those for government, business, and trade union organizations, although they are well below ratings of military, judiciary, medical, and educational institutions. Similarly, the latest Harris Interactive poll of confidence in the leaders of 16 institutions placed the press almost at the bottom of the table (11 percent had a great deal of confidence) but still above Wall Street and Congress (7 percent and 6 percent, respectively) and level with law firms, but far below the military (57 percent) and small businesses (50 percent).[29]

If low and declining trust is a general pattern found across a wide array of social institutions in many countries, then media-specific and single-country explanations cannot alone explain low and declining trust in journalism. These may explain part of but not the whole story, or even a major part of it.

A second look at Tables 7.5 and 7.6 suggests that complaints similar to those brought against the media are also leveled against politicians, businesses, law enforcement, civil servants, and public figures. They, too, are thought by some to be economical with the truth, biased and self-seeking,

Table 7.5 Trust in Media, Business, Government, and Nongovernmental Organizations, 2012 (percentage of population)

	Media	Business	Government	NGOs	All Institutions
Netherlands	61	65	61	59	61
Italy	57	62	31	74	56
Canada	54	56	56	66	58
Poland	48	46	28	55	44
Spain	46	32	20	51	37
USA	45	50	43	58	49
Australia	43	57	47	65	53
Germany	42	34	33	48	39
France	41	28	31	60	40
Sweden	38	54	62	41	49
UK	37	38	38	54	41
Japan	36	47	25	30	34
Ireland	35	43	35	53	41
Russia	33	41	26	28	49
World total (n = 38)	52	53	43	58	51

Source: "2012 Edelman Trust Barometer," Edelman, January 23, 2012, https://www.edelman.com/research/2012-edelman-trust-barometer.

Table 7.6 Trust in Selected National Institutions (percentage of population)

	Army 2010	Police 2010	Radio 2011	Television 2011	Justice/ Legal System 2011	Press 2011	National Parliament
Belgium	67	65	70	72	36	60	46
Denmark	76	89	73	68	84	50	64
Germany	70	77	66	59	60	50	46
Spain	67	68	50	41	44	41	11
France	71	62	60	42	45	51	42
Italy	65	58	39	40	42	34	8
Netherlands	71	73	70	66	65	60	49
Australia	72	78	68	72	71	59	48
Finland	91	91	78	76	77	64	59
Sweden	63	82	80	73	73	45	70
UK	85	71	54	53	50	18	23
European Union (32 countries)	70	64	57	53	47	43	28

Source: European Commission, Directorate-General Communication "Research and Speechwriting" Unit. 2012. *Media Use in the European Union.* Standard Eurobarometer 78. Autumn 2012. http://ec.europa.eu/public_opinion/archives/eb/eb78/eb78_media_en.pdf.

Note: Press = newspapers.

unprofessional, corrupt, out of touch, trying to cover up their mistakes and misdeeds, uncaring about people, and in the pockets of powerful interests. They also have been widely reported (by the press) to have been involved in scandals, lying, breaches of trust, illegal actions, incompetence, pursuit of self-interest, and transgressions of good democratic practice. In other words, there is not much difference between the media and its journalists and the top people in many other institutions. In which case, explanations of declining trust in the media must be placed in a wider context of declining trust in many central institutions across Western society as a whole. Explaining this broad and general trend is beyond the scope of this book, but we can look more closely at a well-researched trust effect that applies to the media, namely, the hostile media effect.

The Hostile Media Effect and the Hostile World Effect

Trust in the media is associated with the hostile media effect, or the tendency of those with strong beliefs to regard news reports to be biased against their views, even if others and impartial content analysis find the news reports to be unbiased. A study of the 1992 US presidential election found that many Republicans believed the papers favored Bill Clinton, but Democrats reading those papers believed the papers supported Bush.[30] In neither case was there a correspondence between what readers believed and what the papers actually said, as shown by content analysis. In the United States, 81 percent of those with consistent liberal opinions distrusted Fox News, but 72 percent trusted National Public Radio, compared with the 88 percent of the consistent conservatives who trusted Fox News and distrusted NPR.[31]

At first sight, the hostile media effect might seem to be a convincing media-specific explanation of low trust in the media. On second viewing, though, this also appears to be a mistake. Just as declining trust in the media is part of a general trend of declining trust in many institutions, so also the hostile media effect is part of a bigger picture—the hostile world effect. A long list of hostilities may contribute to a person's attitude about the world: the claim that the tax system is biased against them; that the law discriminates against their perfectly reasonable behavior while others get away with flagrant misdeeds; that while they are generally honest and law-abiding, others are no better than they should be; that the welfare systems treat them unfairly; that they get a parking or speeding ticket while others get away with it. Some people insist that they are victims and others are exploiters; that they are hardworking and loyal while others are slackers and selfish; that they are in the right, others in the wrong; that immigrants and minorities are privileged while they suffer; that their talents are overlooked while the less able are rewarded; and that, in the words of Tom

Waits, "everywhere I go it rains on me." These are variations on the theme of the hostile media effect, and they all boil down to variants on the complaint that the referee's poor decisions cost my team the Saturday game— "we was robbed." The hostile media effect exists and helps in understanding the causes of low trust in the media, but it is part of a much broader hostile world effect.[32]

Why Do People Read Papers They Do Not Trust?

If media distrust is high and rising, why do people bother with them? Paradoxically, low trust in the news media may not result in avoidance of them. As we saw in the previous chapter, Russians have little faith in their TV news but continue to watch it. Why? Tsfati and Cappella found a low correlation between trust and consumption of the news media, which led them to ask, "Why do people watch news they do not trust?"[33] The answer, they say, is that people watch TV news for a host of reasons. One they call "the need for cognition (TNC)," which is a curiosity about the world and a wish to understand it—a need to know, think, and discuss. Tsfati and Cappella found that those with a high need for cognition were relatively unaffected by their low trust in the news media and consumed comparatively large doses of it. In fact, news consumption increased when higher distrust was combined with high cognitive needs. Conversely, low trust plus low cognitive needs resulted in low attention to news media. Once again, we see how the relationship between the news media and their audiences is influenced by moderating factors—in this case by an interaction producing unexpected results. And once again, the news media form a leaky system in which different people with different combinations of characteristics consume it or not for different reasons, and probably to different effect.

Tsfati and Cappella's conclusion answers a puzzle about why people read *The Sun* when they place so little trust in it. They say they like the paper because it is cheap and cheerful, it can be scanned in a 10-minute tea break, it is fun and funny and does not take itself seriously, and they recognize it is not really a newspaper at all. The following quotations (presented here in their original, unpunctuated form) make the point:

- "It's better if you don't actually look at *the Sun* in the same way as a 'Newspaper'"
- "I read it for a laugh, some of the things they consider news are ridiculous."
- "The Sun isn't about the news. It's a tea-break comic. You get a pair of tlts, some cartoons, a crossword, two sodukos, you can catch up on the sport and, a brief bit of news, all on page two. Then when

you've finished with it you can give it to the Misses so she can catch up on the moronic show buss' gossip."

- ". . . i find it entertaining. Granted its not a great newspaper for actual news and often gets it wrong but its the newspaper my family bought when i was growing up so Ive just sort of stuck with it. Its popular amongst working class people because it is easy to read and lots of images."

- "I like it because it is a light hearted look at the news...The Sun mixes showbiz with news and real life and is an entertaining read. You can pick it up and put it down whenever you have a spare 5mins throughout the day. i rarely get time to see the news on TV so surely it is better than knowing no news at all??!! As for Page 3 I just ignore that one!!" [Page 3 of *The Sun* in those days was devoted to a photo of a topless woman.]

- "It's because they're easy to read and you don't have to think very hard. Also they can be perused in ten minutes during lunch hour."

- "Cheap and cheerful rather than expensive and boring."

These comments seem to confirm the theory that low trust and low need for cognition produce a low demand for hard news. But interestingly, and contrary to their image of being politically ignorant, uninterested, and unaware, some readers of *The Sun* display a degree of political knowledge and sophistication in justifying their choice of paper.

- "The *Mail* has a lot more news (it has a lot more WORDS). It has a very specific, identifiable 'pitch,' focusing heavily on the fears of their readers (immigration, crime) and making them feel that some-one is on their side. [In my opinion] this comes at the cost of a lot of vindictive lies and exaggerations, but there we are."

- "The Daily Mail is different to them [the *Sun and* Mirror] though. It's not seen as 'low-brow' like The Sun/Mirror/Star but [in my opinion], the Mail is infinitely more reprehensible."

- "It [the *Sun]* is a rubbish paper, but it's not as hateful as the *Daily Mail*. The Torygraph [*Daily Telegraph*] does have a slightly better standard of journalism than the Daily Fascist [the *Mail*], but that's hardly difficult."

- "The Sun is an awful paper but the *Mail* is worse. Its 'robust right-wing views' are just reactionary scaremongering and pointless hatred. All newspapers have an agenda, but tabloids are more likely to simply lie to you."[34]

These remarks show low trust in *The Sun*, which helps to explain why its readers failed to follow its political lead in recent general elections. As

Gunther points out, "It is what audiences do with news, as well as what news people do with news, that accounts for judgements of trust in the mass media."[35]

Trust, Priming, and Agenda Setting

The idea that newspaper effects on readers depend on trust, among other things, is examined in another American study by Miller and Krosnick, which examines the three-cornered relationship between trust, priming, and agenda setting.[36] Priming, they write, is a mental process that increases the accessibility of a subject in an individual's mind—it refers to the ease with which information and opinion come to mind when the same or similar subjects arise. As Iyengar, Peters, and Kinder write, "The standards citizens use to judge a president may be substantially determined by which stories newscasts choose to cover and, consequently, which considerations are made generally accessible."[37] Or, to quote McCombs again, agenda setting occurs when "citizen students'" views on a matter reflect what they have been taught over and over again in the recent past by their "teachers," that is, the media.[38] According to Miller and Krosnick, the accessibility hypothesis has an important implication:

> Thus, the theory of media priming views people as victims of their own minds—if a political issue is activated in people's memories by media attention to it, they presumably use the concept when asked to make political judgements—not by conscious *choice*, but merely because information about the issue appears automatically and effortlessly in consciousness.[39]

The accessibility hypothesis is also said to apply to agenda setting: the political agenda is what people think about because it consists of political topics that have been repeated by the news media in the recent past. Miller and Krosnick, however, suggest a different process. They reason that people who trust a given news source are likely to be influenced by its account of what is important, because if a trusted source treats a topic as important, then it is probably important for them. However, they go on to state that trust alone is not enough. To be able to follow the media agenda, it is also necessary to understand the news and its significance and to store its content and implications so that they can be retrieved and used later. Trust combined with a lack of understanding does not facilitate priming or agenda setting, because that combination is likely to leave people at sea, unable to make much sense of the waves, tides, whirlpools, and crosscurrents of the news.

Miller and Krosnick try to unravel the associations of trust, knowledge, and understanding, on the one hand, and the news media's priming and agenda setting, on the other. They have found little evidence to support the accessibility hypothesis. Instead, a combination of trust and political knowledge facilitates priming because prior knowledge helps people absorb and understand the news they are exposed to, and trust versus distrust makes the news media more persuasive. Agenda setting of the media is strongest among the most trustful and knowledgeable.

Miller and Krosnick write that most accounts in the research literature assume that priming amounts to the manipulation of citizens without their awareness or consent, because it causes them to unconsciously follow what they have been primed to think about by the news media. Their studies suggest, however, that people are not unknowing victims of the reflex actions of the mind. Those who trust their news sources are more likely to show the media effects of priming, framing, and agenda setting—not because they are ignorant and confused but, on the contrary, because their knowledge and understanding enable them to decide which news sources to trust and then to note what they are saying.

This conclusion is supported by a study of the influence of the economic content of British national newspapers on changes in the public's political and economic attitudes during the first Blair government of 1997–2001. This study found that broadsheets, but not the tabloids, have an influence, although broadsheet influence is modest and confined to particular sections of the population.[40] It is, perhaps, no coincidence that people who are better informed and educated read the broadsheets and trust their newspapers more than tabloid readers trust theirs. Broadsheets may exercise a modest influence, because informed readers pick them for their politics and for their reliable news.

Research confirms the existence of such agenda reasoning and finds that it is associated with a specific form of media trust known as "gatekeeping trust," which is the belief that a particular medium reports genuinely important news items accurately.[41] Gatekeeping trust is an important moderator of agenda-setting effects, and it is the product of political knowledge and conscious judgment about "my media" in contrast with "the media." Once again, we see how different media have different effects on people with different personal characteristics and decisionmaking methods.

Further evidence of this interaction between the news media and their audiences is found in a study of media effects on voting and protest behavior.[42] The study found that political trust, confidence in the political system, and political knowledge act differently as intermediaries between media exposure and these two forms of political behavior. Statistical tests suggest that the media have the effect of increasing political knowledge, but the correlation between exposure to the news and protest behavior is not causal. Exposure to political news is associated with protest behavior only if it is also associated with confidence in the political system—the feeling that the system will respond to those who protest. The authors conclude that it is important to disentangle forms of political behavior when searching for media effects, and their study also shows that it is necessary to disentangle interaction effects of personal characteristics.

Conclusions

Nyhan and Reifler state that "a vast literature in psychology and political science has shown that statements are frequently more persuasive when they come from sources that are perceived as knowledgeable, trustworthy or highly credible."[43] Because there is plentiful evidence that trust in the media is comparatively low and declining, the media's persuasive powers may also be low and declining. At the same time, trust varies substantially from one medium to another: it is often comparatively high for radio news, public broadcasting systems, and newspapers of record, and much lower for tabloid papers, Internet news, and social media.

In any case, trust alone does not explain how individuals use and are affected by the news media. Individuals who distrust the media do not necessarily avoid them. On the contrary, those who are motivated to know about and understand politics are likely to be heavy consumers of the news, even if they have low trust in it, whereas those who are both distrustful and unmotivated are news avoiders. Similarly, trust alone is not necessarily associated with agenda setting and priming. Those who have good knowledge, awareness, and understanding of politics and who trust a news source are more likely to take cues from it. This is not consistent with the accessibility hypothesis of agenda setting, priming, and framing, which assumes that what people think about, and how they think about it, is the product of an unconscious reflex reaction prompted by repeated media messages in the recent past. In contrast, research finds that people who choose to trust some, but not other, sources of news take shortcuts in making judgments by following the agenda of sources they trust. It is no coincidence that the most trusted media are generally the most trustworthy: the news broadcast by the BBC, PBS, SVT, and ARD, for example, and by newspapers of record.

At this point, it is possible to start joining up some of the dots in Chapters 2 through 6. These chapters have shown that different news media have different effects on different people. Some pay little attention to the news; some flatly reject what they are told in the mainstream news media; some are selective of what they believe and disbelieve; the beliefs of some are positively reinforced, but others' are negatively reinforced; some accept the news they receive and change their attitudes and behavior; some accept the news but do not change their behavior. Because the same message from the same medium can provoke different reactions in individuals, and because the same message from different media can provoke different reactions in the same person, we can conclude that reactions to the news depend on individuals rather than the medium or its content.

It is not possible to predict news media effects by simply examining media content. There is little doubt that some news is low quality, biased, and superficial, but we cannot assume that such content will necessarily have adverse effects on media consumers. Individuals can reject, ignore, or accept what they read in the papers, and the least reliable news sources may have the smallest impact, if any.

Part of the difficulty in pinning down media effects on audiences is the interaction between the media and their audiences, but another problem is that different combinations of individual audience characteristics also produce different media effects—a second level of interaction. For example, low trust combined with a need to understand and be informed about politics (the need for cognition) results in high news media consumption, whereas low trust and low interest result in low consumption. Similarly, different combinations of trust and political understanding have different implications for agenda setting. Those who know about and understand politics and who have a news source they trust are more inclined to follow that source's agenda, whereas those who have low trust and good political understanding are less likely to do so. The interactions between trust in the media, partisanship, political awareness, understanding, and knowledge play important parts in conditioning news media effects.

In some circumstances, a different set of causes and effects operates. Rather than the media shaping public opinion or public opinion shaping media content, both may respond to the same stimuli. The American public and the media seem to have reacted in the same way to the seemingly hopeless cause of the Vietnam War. In the United Kingdom in 1997, some newspapers and many voters reacted in the same way to the political and economic climate of the time. It was the real-world state of the US economy that caused the financial press, those with economic news, and those without economic news to develop similar judgments about the state of the economy.

It is difficult to sort out which of these are causal relations, but one thing is clear: if the media rub against the grain of public opinion, they are discounted and ignored. We see this in experimental psychology studies of belief preservation, the Clinton-Lewinsky case, agenda setting in British elections, Russian reactions to state-controlled TV news, and the way that aware hawks reacted to the anti–Vietnam War messages of the American media.

What drives public opinion and behavior is not the media but individual variables of the standard model of social science—mainly, education, class, income, age, sex, ethnicity, and religion and, where politics are concerned, partisanship, party identification, and political understanding and knowledge. Compared with the influence of these variables, media effects are usually, but not always, weak, patchy, or insignificant. This accords closely with the fact that most social scientists turn to these individual variables when they seek to explain public opinion and behavior in general.

Notes

1. Tsfati 2003.
2. Hovland, Janis, and Kelley 1953; McGuire 1986; McGraw and Hubbard 1996; Eagly and Chaiken 1993; Lupia and McCubbins 1998; Miller and Krosnick 2000; Mickiewicz 2008: 183–190; Nyhan and Reifler 2012: 14.
3. Sternheimer 2003: 7; Anderson, Downie, and Schudson 2016: 57.
4. R. Riffkin, "Americans' Trust in Media Remains at Historical Low," Gallup, September 28, 2015, http://www.gallup.com/poll/185927/americans-trust-media-remains-historical-low.aspx?g_source=trust percent20in percent20mass percent20media percent202015&g_medium=search&g_campaign=tiles.
5. E. Mendes, "In U.S., Trust in Media Recovers Slightly from All-Time Low," Gallup, September 19, 2013, http://www.gallup.com/poll/164459/trust-media-recovers-slightly-time-low.aspx; "Internet News Audience Highly Critical of News Organizations," Pew Research Center, August 9, 2007, http://www.people-press.org/2007/08/09/internet-news-audience-highly-critical-of-news-organizations/; Harris Poll, New York, February 14, 2012, https://theharrispoll.com/new-york-n-y-february-14-2012-looking-back-to-the-1950s-the-way-americans-got-their-news-was-pretty-simple-it-was-either-their-local-newspaper-or-one-of-the-three-nightly-newscasts-today/; "Press Widely Criticized, but Trusted More Than Other Information Sources, "Pew Research Center, September 22, 2011, http://www.people-press.org/2011/09/22/press-widely-criticized-but-trusted-more-than-other-institutions/; "Gallup Poll, Sept. 5–8, 2013," PollingReport.com, http://www.pollingreport.com/media.htm.
6. "Trust in Professions: Long-Term Trends," Ipsos MORI, November 29, 2017, https://www.ipsos.com/ipsos-mori/en-uk/trust-professions-long-term-trends?view=wide.
7. European Commission, Directorate-General Communication "Research and Speech-writing" Unit. 2012. *Media Use in the European Union.* Standard Eurobarometer 78. Autumn 2012. http://ec.europa.eu/public_opinion/archives/eb/eb78/eb78_media_en.pdf.
8. Gallup World Poll 2010; Financial Times/Harris Poll 2011.
9. A. Swift, "Americans' Trust in Mass Media Sinks to New Low," Gallup, September 14, 2016, http://www.gallup.com/poll/195542/americans-trust-mass-media-sinks-new-low.aspx?g_source=Politics&g_medium=newsfeed&g_campaign=tiles.
10. J. Ericsen and J. Gottfried, "Partisans Disagree on News Media's Best, Worst Traits," Fact Tank, September 29, 2016, http://www.pewresearch.org/fact-tank/2016/09/29/news-media-best-worst-traits/.
11. "Press Widely Criticized, but Trusted More Than Other Information Sources."
12. Broadsheet papers are *The Times, Telegraph, Guardian, Independent,* and *Financial Times;* "mid-market" refers to *The Mail* and *Express;* and "tabloid" to *The Sun* and *Mirror.*
13. L. Morales, "Snapshot: Britons Less Trusting of Media," Gallup, December 7, 2012, http://www.gallup.com/poll/159110/snapshot-britons-less-trusting-media.aspx.
14. European Commission 2012.
15. J. McKenna, "Which European Country Has the Most Trusted Media?" World Economic Forum, June 2, 2017, https://www.weforum.org/agenda/2017/06/which-european-country-has-the-most-trusted-media/.
16. European Broadcasting Union, Media Intelligence Unit, February 27, 2018, "Trust in Traditional Media Increases Across Europe"; https://www.ebu.ch/news/2018/02/trust-in-traditional-media-increases-across-europe.
17. Newman et al. 2018: 63.
18. Newman et al. 2018: 112.
19. European Commission 2011.

20. Populus and Open Road, "Power, Principles and the Press," 2015, www.theopen -road.com/wp-content/uploads/2012/09/power-principles-and-the-press-open-road-and -populus1.pdf.

21. "'My' Media Versus 'the' Media: Trust in News Depends on Which News Media You Mean," American Press Institute, May 24, 2017, https://www.americanpressinstitute.org /publications/reports/survey-research/my-media-vs-the-media/; Newman et al. 2018: 10.

22. Ladd 2010.

23. "Public Perceptions of the Impartiality and Trustworthiness of the BBC," BBC, June 2015, http://downloads.bbc.co.uk/aboutthebbc/insidethebbc/howwework/reports/pdf /bbc_report_trust_and_impartiality_jun_2015.pdf.

24. Globe Scan, "BBC/Reuters/Media Center Poll: Trust in the Media," http://news .bbc.co.uk/1/shared/bsp/hi/pdfs/02_05_06mediatrust.pdf.

25. Globe Scan, "BBC/Reuters/Media Center Poll: Trust in the Media." See also "News Media Rated Highest for Covering Important Issues, Lowest for Reporting on Politics Fairly," Pew Research Center, January 11, 2018, http://www.pewglobal.org/interactives /media-habits-map/.

26. Heald and Wybrow 1986: 281. The press and trade unions were at the bottom of the confidence in institutions table in 10 European countries in 1981. See also Harding, Phillips, and Fogarty 1986: 95.

27. 2015 Edelman Trust Barometer, "Trust in Institutions Drops to Level of Great Recession," January 19, 2015.

28. "Confidence in Institutions," Gallup, http://www.gallup.com/poll/1597/confidence -institutions.aspx. See also C. Funk and B. Kennedy, "Public Confidence in Scientists Has Remained Stable for Decades," Pew Research Center, April 6, 2017, http://www.pewresearch .org/fact-tank/2017/04/06/public-confidence-in-scientists-has-remained-stable-for-decades/.

29. "Confidence in Congress and Supreme Court Drops to Lowest Level in Many Years," Harris Poll, May 18, 2011, https://theharrispoll.com/new-york-n-y-may-18-2011 -the-harris-poll-has-been-measuring-the-confidence-of-the-american-public-in-the-leaders -of-major-institutions-since-1966-in-most-years-only-a-few-institutions-experience/.

30. Dalton, Beck, and Huckfeldt 1998: 120.

31. A. Mitchell, J. Gottfried, J. Kiley, and K. E. Matsa, "Appendix C: Trust and Distrust of News Sources by Ideological Group," Pew Research Center, October 21, 2014, http://www.journalism.org/2014/10/21/appendix-c-trust-and-distrust-of-news-sources-by -ideological-group/.

32. Bennett et al. 1999.

33. Tsfati and Cappella 2005.

34. These quotations appear in https://uk.answers.yahoo.com/question/index?qid =20080922041717AAWT53F. The quotations are reproduced in their original form, punctuation, and spelling.

35. Gunther 1992: 163.

36. Miller and Krosnick 2000.

37. Iyengar, Peters, and Kinder 1982.

38. McCombs 2014: 47.

39. Miller and Krosnick 2000: 302. Italics in the original.

40. Gavin and Sanders 2003.

41. Pingree and Stoycheff 2013.

42. Corrigall-Brown and Wilkes 2014.

43. Nyhan and Reifler 2012: 14.

8

Diffuse and Subconscious Media Effects

The media help legitimate the hegemonic ideological system with images and themes that propagate private enterprise, personal affluence, individual acquisitiveness, consumerism, superpatriotism, imperialism, racial stereotyping, and sexism.

—*M. Parenti,* Make-Believe Media:
The Politics of Entertainment[1]

Previous chapters have examined media effects on public opinion about scandal in the White House, the Vietnam and Korean Wars, national economic performance, national elections, political agendas, political advertising, and public services. These are headline-hitting, obtrusive, and relatively specific matters, some of them highly controversial, much discussed, and touching on individual values, political identity, and personal experience. It appears that it may be difficult for the media to exercise much influence over salient issues of this kind.

However, underlying moods, feelings, and unconscious dispositions are a different matter. They are the wallpaper and elevator music of existence, taken for granted or accepted unthinkingly as inevitable parts of the natural order. They involve diffuse and tacit understandings about such matters as civic cooperation and duty, political efficacy, trust, cynicism, tolerance, democratic values, and political understanding. They concern things that most people are less aware of, and it may be that media effects on such low salience matters are strong, precisely because they are exercised below the level of public consciousness.[2]

There are many such claims about media effects of this kind. Because they concentrate on bad news about disasters, death and destruction, crime, corruption, and catastrophe, the media are said to have a "mean world effect" that creates an underlying mood of political cynicism, distrust, and insecurity. Attack journalism, negative campaigning, political conflict, and incivility in political life may contribute to this effect because it is said that bad news undermines trust and a civic culture of peaceful cooperation, respect, empathy, and participation. The mean world effect may also be fueled by the crime, horror, disaster, and violence of films and TV dramas. Sensationalism, superficiality, and sound-bite journalism are said to result in lack of political understanding and apathy. For some, it is not the content of TV programs that is crucial; rather, it is the *form* of the medium that means it is unable to do anything other than entertain and amuse its audiences, no matter its best intentions to inform and educate.[3] For others, television, advertising, and glossy magazines encourage individualism and materialism while undermining a sense of community and civic duty.

According to the "bread and circuses" argument, the entertainment media distract the population from serious political matters and political engagement. Soap operas, films, sit-coms, quiz and reality shows divert attention from news and political discussion and encourage a self-centered lack of social responsibility in a "wannabe" world of fame, wealth, youth, and beauty. In these ways the entertainment media and advertising industry may work subtly and silently to create a public mood that erodes democratic practices and citizenship norms—effects that might be exaggerated by the growth of infotainment and "reality news."[4]

These claims must be taken seriously because support for media malaise is found in a large literature written by a wide variety of distinguished experts and commentators, and because some evidence suggests that the entertainment media are associated with the various manifestations of media malaise.[5] This chapter, therefore, considers the under-the-radar effects of the mass media, especially the entertainment media. First it considers Norris's virtuous circle hypothesis in what is probably the most wide-ranging study of political communications in modern democracies. Second, it examines in-depth studies of the associations of radio, newspapers, and television, on the one hand, and political attitudes and knowledge, on the other. After that, it turns to a Belgian study of the associations between 15 different types of TV programs and civic engagement. The fourth section presents experimental research from the United States that shows how incivility in televised political debates causes low political trust, and the last part of the chapter examines the idea that citizens now participate less in political and community activity because they are too busy watching television.

The Virtuous Circle

Norris's *Virtuous Circle* is an important book for understanding the unconscious effects of the media. It deals directly with the strong version of media malaise theory, which argues that political communications in modern society undermine diffuse confidence in the political system and create widespread political disillusionment with its practices, politicians, and institutions. Her study uses cross-sectional data to establish patterns of association, and time-series and experimental data to identify causes and effects. She examines data from different surveys covering different years, different media systems, and different political systems. The countries covered include 10 Western European countries, the G8, and the United Kingdom and United States. She bases her conclusions about the effects of TV and radio news, newspapers, and party communications on a wide-ranging battery of measures of political attitudes and behavior. Together, these cover the field, leaving few gaps of any importance. Last, she uses education, age, gender, and income as control variables and dummy variables for 10 European states to estimate country effects.[6]

The result is a large set of regressions, most of which yield little evidence to suggest that the media have an adverse effect on support for democratic government and politics. Across 10 nations covered by the European Election Studies of 1989 and 1994, citizens who paid close attention to election campaigns in the news media were most positive about the political system at every level, including support for democracy as the best form of government, confidence in national government, and confidence in the European Union and its performance. Individual attention to the news media was not associated with trust or distrust in foreign nationals, with attitudes toward Europe as a community, or with support or lack of support for political leaders. Norris writes, "At no stage across this battery of indicators did we find any evidence that media attention was significantly associated with political cynicism."[7]

This conclusion is based on cross-sectional survey data, so to disentangle the complex relations between media use and political attitudes, Norris turned to time-series panel data collected by the 1997 British Election Study (BES), which interviewed the same people four times during the 12 months leading up to the election. It found that as election day approached, more people voiced the opinion that politicians were responsive to public concerns. Those who were most attentive to the news were consistently more likely to hold this opinion, but those who were the least attentive changed their attitudes by the same amount and in the same direction, which suggests that attitude change was independent of media use.

The panel data show, as previous research does, that attention to the news declined slightly in the last month of the campaign, while political trust increased during this period. This might be taken as support for the malaise theory in which the media are responsible for distrust and that paying less attention to them would result in stable or rising trust. However, the figures also show that the most and least trusting people followed different patterns of media use. Newspaper reading declined slightly more among those with lower political trust, but television news viewing fell more among those with higher trust. At the same time, political trust followed the same upward trend for all groups, irrespective of changes in their media use. In other words, people used the media in different ways, and changes in their trust levels did not correspond to changes in their news media attention. Norris concludes that the most plausible interpretation of the mixed patterns is a "virtuous circle" in which the most knowledgeable and trusting people pay the most attention to the news media, which reinforces their knowledge and trust.

Although the United States is often thought to be an exceptional case among Western nations, the evidence shows US media consumers follow similar patterns to those in Europe. Exposure to the news media is positively associated with most indicators of political knowledge, attitudes, and behavior, although in most cases the association is not strong. The single exception was a correspondence between entertainment television and lower levels of political participation. We return to this finding later in the chapter.

The wealth of data in *The Virtuous Circle* suggests three general observations about the news media and politics on both sides of the Atlantic. First, media variables invariably show a weak and often insignificant association with measures of diffuse political support. When they are statistically significant, the coefficients are usually small but positive. As Norris states, "The association between use of the news media and civic engagement often was only modest"; consequently, "There is little support for either the optimistic belief that the media can generate civic engagement or the pessimistic view that they can dampen it down."[8]

Second, social and economic control variables—education, gender, age, and income—are usually substantial and statistically significant. They constitute the powerful forces most strongly associated with political attitudes and behavior, although their strength varies from one regression to another. Income has the biggest effect on national trust, age counts most for leadership support and voting turnout, and education is most closely associated with knowledge about party leaders in the United States. In all cases, one or more of these measures is more powerful than any media variable.

Third, the evidence comparing 10 countries in Western Europe shows that the relationships between the news media and the political attitudes and behavior of citizens vary substantially from one country to another. Put another way, whether the media have a larger or smaller effect, and whether this is positive for democracy or negative, depends upon the country. This is an important finding, but "country" in this context is a black box with unknown contents. Consequently, we have little idea of what particular country features cause media effects to vary, though we do know these relate to the country as a whole, not the characteristics of individual members of its population. One possible cause is discussed in the next chapter, which deals with the difference between public service and commercial media systems. Meanwhile, this chapter continues with an account of how British television and newspapers are associated with some underlying political attitudes.

Mobilization and Malaise

A study of media use based on a British Social Attitudes (BSA) survey measures TV watching and newspaper reading and estimates their associations with political knowledge and a set of political attitudes that capture aspects of political malaise.[9] The attitude measures are political trust, political cynicism, democratic satisfaction, and subjective political efficacy (the feeling that an individual can exercise influence on political affairs). These are often said to be influenced by the mean world effect of bad news and the social capital–eroding powers of television. The survey does not ask about radio listening, which may have been an omission, although 63 percent of participants claim that television is their main source of news compared with 23 percent and 14 percent who say the same of newspapers and radio, respectively.[10]

The BSA questionnaire asks respondents how many hours of general television and TV news they watch and how much attention they pay to political and economic news items. It does not go into detail about specific types of programs, but audience figures show that those who watch the most television tend to focus heavily on entertainment television (for example, soap operas, films, comedies, sports, and reality and game shows) rather than news, current affairs, and educational programs. The survey asks respondents to specify which newspapers they read regularly (at least three times a week), making it possible to compare readers of the broadsheets (about 10 percent of the population age 18 years and older) with tabloid readers (54 percent). Regular newspaper readers (60 percent) can be compared with a control group of people who did not read any newspaper regularly (40 percent). Fewer than 3 percent of the population does not own a television, and the size of this group is too small to use as a reliable control for TV viewers, so the study uses the number of hours of television watched per week as a measure of TV exposure instead.

The BSA includes a battery of 20 questions about political knowledge and attitudes. This is a formidable set of questions, but it also overloads statistical analysis to an impossible extent. The solution is a standard form of data-reduction exercise (principal component analysis), which shows that the 20 measures cluster into six main groups (components), namely knowledge about party preferences on four main policy issues; political interest and understanding; internal political efficacy; political trust; political cynicism; and democratic satisfaction. Using these six groups as the measures of political attitudes and behavior, rather than the 20 separate items, makes the analysis simpler and more comprehensible. Because both political attitudes and media use are closely intertwined with age, education, income, political identification, and occupational status, these were used as control variables to isolate the role of the media.

The results show that newspaper audiences are different from TV audiences. Other things being equal, broadsheet readers are significantly better informed about politics, are more trusting politically, and claim higher levels of political understanding than others. The "better informed" part of this statement is confirmed by a 27-nation study of political knowledge in Europe and another in Spain, so it is a general European pattern, not a specifically UK one.[11] Tabloid readers are little different from non–newspaper readers in these respects and show few signs of media malaise.

Those who watch a lot of television are less well informed about politics (according to the factual test of knowledge) and rate themselves lower on political interest and efficacy. However, the regression coefficients are only weakly significant and substantively small. Those who watch a lot of TV news, in contrast, are better informed and claim higher levels of understanding and efficacy, and their satisfaction with democracy score is higher.[12]

In short, there is little evidence that attention to newspapers and TV news is associated with indicators of media malaise.[13] On the contrary, the reverse is true of those who read a broadsheet paper and watch a lot of TV news, whereas those who read a tabloid regularly are little different from those who do not read a paper regularly.[14] Some evidence indicates that those who watch a lot of television exhibit some aspects of media malaise, but the data are weak and patchy and, like *The Virtuous Circle* study, do not provide clear support for malaise theory.

The overall effects of the different media vary. Only 10 percent of the population regularly reads a broadsheet paper, so newspapers' strong and positive influences on political knowledge and attitudes are limited to a small section of the population. More than half the population (55 percent) claim to watch TV news seven days a week, so its weaker and positive effects are widely but more thinly spread. It is possible that self-rated TV news viewing figures are inflated, perhaps greatly inflated by some groups in the population (see Chapter 11). Nevertheless, those who claim to watch a lot of TV news are also better informed according to an objective measure of political knowledge, which suggests that TV news does indeed inform and educate viewers.

Whereas some people turn on their television to watch the news, probably a much larger number watch the news because their television is on—

they fall into the news rather than seeking it out. This helps to resolve some of the problems of cause and effect that result from self-selection. Unlike the readers of broadsheet papers, who choose their paper, many in the large and heterogeneous audiences for TV news are not self-selected because they watch the news as a consequence of their TV habit. In their case, associations between the media and measures of trust, knowledge, subjective efficacy, political understanding, and satisfaction with democracy are not likely to be an artifact of self-selection but (for most individuals) an inadvertent by-product of unselective television watching.

This, in turn, is consistent with Norris's virtuous circle effect. Those who also watch a lot of TV news are better informed and express higher levels of self-rated understanding, subjective efficacy, and confidence in democracy and lower levels of political cynicism. The virtuous circle effect is also demonstrated by going through the same procedure for the broadsheet readers. In their case, those who watch a lot of TV news are as well or better informed and generally as positive about democratic politics, or more so, than those who watch less news. Once again, there are some indications of political malaise among the consumers of TV news, but few are statistically significant and even these are substantively weak. One possible explanation for this is that readers of *The Sun* watch more television news than readers of *The Guardian*, which helps improve their political knowledge, raise their level of political understanding, and counterbalance the politics of their paper.

The results tell us something about the idea that the "medium is the message" and about Postman's theory that the very form of television means that it can do little but entertain because it consists of a colorful "peek-a-boo" world of constantly shifting moving images.[15] The evidence from the British study is that, as Postman claims, we learn more about politics from reading a good newspaper than we do from watching TV news, but it does not confirm his argument that television can do nothing but amuse us. On the contrary, irrespective of whether they read a tabloid or broadsheet or no newspaper regularly, those who watch a lot of TV news are better informed than those who watch little TV news. Those who get their news from either papers or television, or both, know more about politics and have more positive attitudes toward politics than do those who avoid the news. Whether it is newspapers or television, the medium is not the message; the message is the message whatever medium communicates it.[16] Postman is right about the printed word, wrong about TV news.

Having said all this, it is nevertheless the case, once again, that the overall effects of newspapers or television, whether negative or positive, are comparatively small. Access to cable and satellite television, ownership and use of home video recorders, and cinema attendance have no measurable effects at all, although that may have changed since the study was done in 1999. The powerful variables in this study of political knowledge and attitudes are not media measures but, first and foremost, education, which produces the strongest and most consistently significant effect, followed by political identification. Income and gender are also important. Each of these four are all more powerful than the media variables. Once again, we find that the media play a comparatively small part in the explanation and understanding of mass political attitudes. Their role is not always negligible, but comparatively weak when set against the more influential social and political forces of education, political identity, income, and gender.

It might be argued that the BSA survey does not tap the correct variables or delve into the subtle and indirect effects of media influence, but if the news media are as powerful as often claimed, it is reasonable to expect that something would show up in the BSA survey's 20 political measures. Newspaper and TV news are associated with political knowledge in this study, so why does it not find associations with political attitudes if there are any? It might also be argued that the modern media are so ubiquitous in society that everyone is more or less subject to their strong influences to the same degree, in which case the study will not pick up media effects. There is no way of testing this proposition in the Western world, where television saturates society. Nevertheless, a few consistent differences are found between people who regularly read a newspaper and those who do not, between those who watch a lot of television and those who do not, and between those who watch a lot of TV news and those who do not, so it is possible to pin down some media effects, even if television is ubiquitous.

An obvious deficiency of the research is that it is based on a cross-sectional survey that can establish correlations, not causation. Other studies can explore causes and effects, however. In addition to the *Virtuous Circle* study, a Swedish study fills in this gap by using a three-wave panel study of voters in an election campaign in 2006.[17] It examined the associations and interactions among three related variables: interest in politics, interest in the news generally, and attention paid to particular TV channels, newspapers, and public service radio. The study found strong and consistent three-way causal and reciprocal relations among the three measures. The strength of the causal relations varies a little, but they are all positive and mutually reinforcing, so the authors conclude that their evidence supports the theory that the media mobilize people rather than creating media malaise.

A study that analyzes several panel studies of the 2000 US presidential election concludes that media effects on political trust, both positive and negative, depend on both the type of media—newspapers, television—and the trust levels of individuals.[18] The fact that there are both positive and negative effects depending on the medium and the trust placed in it is, of course, a central argument of this book. This study also found that the news media made no difference to low-trusting individuals but improved the trust levels of those with higher trust, which is the main thrust of Norris's virtuous circle.

A final problem with research that concentrates on the effects of the news is that most people give most of their time to the entertainment content of the media rather than to its news and current affairs programs. Perhaps it is the entertainment content that is responsible for media malaise. But there again, there are many kinds of TV popular entertainment programs—sports, music, comedy, soap operas, educational, reality shows, talk shows, game shows, art and literature, cartoons, home improvement, gardening, cooking, dance, and a wide variety of film genres covering action, romance, mystery, crime, horror, disaster, and drama.[19] Quite possibly some of these have consequences for political attitudes and behavior, and others do not. The next section of the chapter considers this suggestion.

Soaps and Insecurity

Hooghe's Belgian study is one of the few to examine the effects of a wide variety of TV content. He examines the associations between the amount of time that TV viewers spend with 15 kinds of TV programs, on the one hand, and three sets of indicators of their social capital, on the other.[20] To reduce the amount of data, he analyzed the time audiences spent with the 15 types of content to produce three clear clusters of TV viewers. The first group (soaps) spent the most time on soap operas and, to a lesser extent, comedy shows, quizzes, dating programs, and hospital series. The second group (movies) watched movies, crime series, cartoons, and science fiction. The third group (news) favored news and current affairs, talk shows, and classical music. The survey measured the total time people spent watching television and identified the station—public or commercial—they enjoyed watching the most. In this way, the study covered five measures of TV viewing: the amount of time spent watching different kinds of television, the most-watched channel, and the time spent with three broad types of programming (soaps, movies, and news). Gender, age, education, income, marital status, children in the family, religion, length of residence, and membership in voluntary associations were control variables.

The study found that those who spent a lot of time watching television usually watched soaps and movies on commercial channels. In fact, most Belgians spent time with soaps and movies on commercial channels, so there is a strong negative association between watching the news and watching commercial television. This is consistent with research showing that TV audiences divide roughly into those who watch comparatively little television and concentrate more on public service channels and news and those who watch a lot of television, mainly entertainment on commercial channels.[21]

Hooghe then measured the associations between television watching and three sets of independent variables that served as indicators of social capital. The first he calls "individualism," which is the reverse of reciprocity between citizens, a prime characteristic of social capital. He found that the more time people spent watching television and the more time they spent watching soaps, the more likely they were to favor individualistic norms that are incompatible with reciprocity. The second social capital measure was political powerlessness (labeled subjective competence in some studies). The data show that the more people watched television, the more powerless they felt, but the more news they watched, the less powerless they felt. The third measure of social capital was "insecurity in daily life," which served as an indicator of the mean world effect. Total hours of TV watching correlated significantly and positively with this variable, but it is not entertainment television in general that undermines civic attitudes and diffuse political support. Rather, it is the soap opera factor alone that was associated with heightened feelings of insecurity. Movies, crime series, cartoons, and science fiction did not have this effect, and neither did the news factor.

The role of soaps in this respect is strange. It might reasonably be expected that the violence of horror, crime, and disaster movies, mixed in with bad news, would generate feelings of insecurity, as Gerbner and his colleagues suggest.[22] But this is apparently not the case—in Belgium, at least. This, however, raises the question of what it is about soap operas, comedies, quizzes, dating shows, and hospital series that explains their link with insecurity. It is not immediately obvious that the homely domestic dramas of daily life that constitute the stock in trade of soap operas can account for the mean world effect, even if family rows, conflict, bad behavior, and meanness are important parts of them.

Hooghe suggests two possible explanations. Either spending a lot of time watching television at home isolates people from community life and a lack of real-life experience, which somehow fuels fears of rising violence. Or, the cause-and-effect relationship is reversed, and a fear of violence and of a mean world induces people to retreat to the escapism of soaps and comedies in the safety of their own living room. There are reasons for believing that the second explanation is more plausible. It is consistent with results from the large amount of research showing audiences self-select their TV diet and suggests that those who do not view the world as a particularly mean, dangerous, or violent place are not frightened off by horror, crime, and violent movies. It also avoids the need for rather tortuous and implausible explanations of why soaps, comedies, quizzes, and dating programs are indeed responsible for feelings of threat, fear, and personal insecurity. The statistical link between the two is another example of correlation, not explanation or causation: rather than soap operas and the like causing feelings of insecurity, it is more likely that feelings of insecurity lead people to favor the domestic dramas of soap operas. And rather than movies, crime series, and bad news causing feelings of personal insecurity, it is the people who are more insecure who enjoy this kind of television.

A final point should be made. Although media variables in the Belgian study are sometimes associated with measures of social capital, the strength of these associations is substantively small, even when the associations are statistically significant, something often noted in other chapters in this book. The variables that pop up repeatedly in studies of mass attitudes and behavior—gender, age, religion, and family circumstances—are the driving forces behind political attitudes, not how much television people watch or the kinds of programs they prefer. Television plays a small role—usually a more positive than negative one—in shaping aspects of social capital, but a much weaker one than the stronger forces of the standard model of the social sciences.

Televised Incivility and Political Distrust

An impressive experimental study of one possible cause of the mean world effect investigated the impact of televised incivility on trust.[23] The authors observe that much political debate on television is extreme, confrontational, and coarse, involving rancorous conflict, invective, bickering, and incivility. They also point out that although there is a widespread belief that television is associated with low trust, there is rather little evidence to support the claim. To shine empirical light on the subject, the authors formulated the hypothesis that uncivil conflict between politicians on television causes the public to have negative reactions to politicians and government. They further suggest that this effect results from gut-level emotional reactions to the violations of social norms, rather than from cognitive awareness of excessive conflict.

The researchers devised three laboratory experiments to test these hypotheses. Actors were hired to play the roles of politicians engaged in civil and uncivil debate. In both cases, they expressed exactly the same opinions, using the same arguments in the same scripted words, but in the civil exchange they went to extremes to be polite, saying such things as, "I'm really glad Bob raised the issue of . . ." and "I don't disagree at all with your points, Bob, but . . ." In the uncivil exchanges, they raised their voice, never apologized for interrupting, and used comments such as, "You're really missing the point here, Neil, . . ." and "What Bob is completely overlooking is . . ." They also used nonverbal cues such as rolling their eyes and ruefully shaking their heads to suggest lack of respect.

The experimental design was sophisticated and carefully thought out. It involved control groups, holding constant important variables while changing one at a time, taking account of possible self-selection bias, using interview and questionnaire data as well as measurements of physiological reactions, and scheduling follow-up interviews a month after the experiment to examine for long-term effects. The authors conclude that their experiments show that "uncivil political discourse has detrimental effects on political trust," and not just trust in politicians, but also trust in Congress and the institutions of government. Television, they write, is likely to exacerbate the effects of incivility more than the printed word because it thrives on drama and presents a uniquely intimate perspective.

Television may well have more of an impact than the printed word in this particular respect, but uncivil behavior in American politics is not new or a special feature of the television age.[24] Variously termed *mean, nasty, bitter,* and *hateful,* politics has risen and fallen in the United States over the past 200 years, following patterns of polarized politics, national crises, critical elections, and major social and economic change such as the Civil War, the New Deal, the Cold War, and McCarthyism.[25]

It can be argued that the effects of televised incivility are limited in some circumstances. Individuals may take a more favorable view of incivility if a politician they support is arguing a case they agree with against a politician and opinions they oppose. Righteous anger may be understandable and excusable if it is used against the unrighteous. Partisans may display confirmation bias by approving the bad behavior of the good guys and rejecting exactly the same behavior of the bad guys. Aggressive rhetoric appeals to aggressive individuals, so once again it is the interaction between the message and its audience that determines the effect.[26]

Some research finds that incivility in workplace political discussion is not the norm. A study of human resource executives in the United States found that 91 percent had witnessed political talk at work, though this occurred rarely in almost half the cases.[27] Almost two-thirds of the executives reported that the discussion was respectful and congenial. Human resource staff might differ from most other workplace groups, but the results of this study do suggest that incivility among politicians does not necessarily contaminate citizen political talk. As before, it is necessary to ask who is and who is not led to behave in this way, and why.

More important, however, are the words and images that come to mind when negative feelings about politics and politicians are discussed: lying, sex scandals, "sexed-up dossiers" to justify war, corruption, self-interest, economic failure and crisis, tax hikes, unemployment, illegal expense claims in the Palace of Westminster, uncaring and inept responses to natural disasters, the Bay of Pigs, Iran-Contra, Watergate, government surveillance, torture, water-boarding, "read my lips," false statements, repeated failures answering interview questions, unkept promises, weasel words, self-serving policies, government failure, and incompetence. Any one or a combination of these could account for much more than uncivil behavior as a possible cause of low and declining trust in politics and politicians. If uncivil behavior has an impact, it likely is because seeing senior politicians behaving badly gives license to others predisposed to behave badly to do the same.

Low and declining political trust is pervasive, across many occupations and professions, including police officers, civil servants, government officials, journalists, bankers, businesspeople, and even religious leaders (see Chapter 7). Many of these citizens do not make appearances in the public arena, but when they do they usually behave with the utmost civility, or else they are represented by soft-spoken and silver-tongued public relations staff trained in the gentle arts of persuasion.

In short, none of this is to deny the experimental evidence that uncivil behavior may play a part in causing distrust but only to suggest that the part of incivility may be small, even if it involves more objectionable behavior than the rolling of eyes and the rueful shaking of heads.

Stealing Time

There is another and possibly much more important way in which television might affect mass behavior. Instead of engendering an apolitical or antipolitical mood in its audiences, it may simply steal the time that people used to devote to political activity in the good old days. In 2013, citizens of the European Union on average spent 3 hours 56 minutes a day watching television, with a high of 5 hours 40 minutes in Romania and a low of 2 hours 27 minutes in Luxembourg.[28] Perhaps the biggest effect of television is that it takes people out of the community and isolates them in their living rooms.

A Dutch study compared hours of TV watching and newspaper reading with political and voluntary activity.[29] As in most other Western countries, the Netherlands experienced a great expansion of television from the 1950s to the 1990s, when the number of sets increased from zero to millions and the hours of broadcasting and number of channels available rose steadily. During this time, however, average hours spent on voluntary and political activity rose, although some forms and types of activity increased while others declined. Political parties suffered a substantial membership loss, but direct political action increased, especially in the form of petitions, action groups, and demonstrations.

The same Dutch study followed up with a time diary–keeping study in the 1980s and 1990s in which individuals recorded what they were doing at intervals throughout the day, which provided information about how individuals used their time and how time use has changed over the years. The study shows that the relationship between hours of TV watching and political activity and other voluntary activity is complicated by many other considerations, particularly life-cycle commitments to work, family, and education and the amount of free time associated with these.[30] The growth of television in the 1950s and 1960s also happens to coincide with the introduction of household time- and labor-saving devices and with the postwar economic boom that made a greater variety of leisure-time activities affordable. There was also a shift in patterns of journey to work, and both work and leisure travel were affected by the spread of car ownership. The Dutch study also found generational differences among those brought up before and during the TV age.

Consequently, there is no simple relationship between watching television and social and political involvement. For example, between 1980 and 1995 in the Netherlands, TV viewing time rose among well-educated people who were brought up without televisions and less-well-educated people brought up with them. Voluntary activity increased in the first group by 0.6 hours a week and stayed constant in the second group. This and similar cases in the diary-keeping study led the authors to conclude that there is no clear evidence that a greedy television has gobbled up the hours previously devoted to participation in the community.

This conclusion is supported by a study across the border in Belgium that also investigated the theory that television has crowded out participation in voluntary activities.[31] About a fifth of the participants watched less than an hour of television a day and, contrary to the idea that less television meant more participation, these people were *less* likely to participate in voluntary activities. This may seem strange, but a closer look shows them to be professional, well-educated, high-income individuals in double-income households who work long hours and have children living at home. People with high levels of education and income are usually well informed and engaged with political affairs, but in this case they have little time for television and voluntary activity because work and family life crowd out both.

It is likely that the association between watching television and the use of any other medium varies according to time, place, and subgroup characteristics. The most important message in the Dutch and Belgian studies is that work, family, and economic and social changes are significant determinants of media use and political attitudes and behavior. The two studies show how causes and effects in media studies can be easily misunderstood and that making a direct link between hours watching television and lack of political interest and activity is far too simple and often simply wrong.

Conclusions
This chapter examines evidence of whether the media have a covert, under-the-radar effect of undermining democratic attitudes and behavior. Media-

induced mean world and bad news effects are often believed to cause political alienation and apathy and to undermine democratic support, although
audiences are largely unaware of these effects. The theory claims that horror, crime, and disaster films create fear, insecurity, and anxiety in the public. Advertising encourages materialism, self-centeredness, and pursuit of
personal success, and puts a premium on youth, beauty, and celebrity at the
expense of community values, civic duty, and the public good. Do the
covert and implicit messages of the news, entertainment, and advertising
media help create a public mood of distrust, fear, and cynicism that cor-
rodes democracy and its institutions?

Research finds some evidence for this, but more frequently media
effects—especially media news effects, when they reach a level of statistical significance—are *positively* associated with a wide range of democratic
and civic behavior, including trust in the populations of other countries (in
the EU), support for democracy as an ideal form of government, support for
government performance and institutions, support for national government,
political trust, voting turnout, trust in government, campaign activism, subjective political efficacy, self-rated understanding of politics, low cynicism, and a belief that democracy is working well. Even those who fall
into TV news, who have been said to suffer most from media malaise,
show higher levels of political knowledge and more positive attitudes
toward politics and democracy.[32] Contrary to the theory that television
news can do little other than amuse and entertain us, the evidence consistently shows that it informs and educates us about politics. This does not
mean that it always or inevitably does this, but it is generally so. The result
is that there is not just a virtuous circle of the news media affecting audience members who are more politically involved and knowledgeable and
who seek out political information and opinion. There is also a virtuous
effect on those who are not motivated to seek out news but who read a
paper for something to do during the lunch break or watch the evening
news because the television is already turned on.

Some evidence demonstrates that it is not TV news but entertainment
television that does the democratic damage, but here again the findings are
weak and patchy, possibly because "entertainment" covers a multitude of
virtues and vices, ranging from educational documentaries, classical con-
certs, and Shakespeare plays to horror movies, violent crime shows, and
disaster films. People who watch a lot of television mainly watch entertainment television on commercial channels and so are exposed to large
quantities of advertising. Unfortunately, there is not much research on what
kind of entertainment television has what kind of effect on what kinds of
audiences, but one study that examined a wide range of entertainment content found that soap operas (and other innocuous-seeming programs) were
statistically associated with feelings of social insecurity. We might wonder

what it is about soaps that might induce insecurity, or reverse cause and effect and ask, instead, whether people who have feelings of insecurity are likely to stay at home watching the comforting domestic dramas of soap operas. We have little information to sort out this chicken-and-egg problem, meaning that caution, not firm opinion, is required.

If we question causal relations between soap operas and insecurity, then we better be consistent and question causal relations between TV news and political information. Do people who are politically aware and informed self-select to watch a lot of TV news to keep abreast of events, or do people who happen to watch a lot of TV news pick up their political information and opinion from it? The virtuous circle theory proposes that it is a bit of both but also shows that, holding constant political awareness and interest, those who watch TV news whatever their level of political engagement tend to know and understand more about politics. Causal analysis of time-series data confirms this. Those who attend to the political media during election campaigns end up better informed and less disillusioned by politics. In short, controlling for the type of newspaper read, the amount of TV entertainment watched, and the level of political interest and awareness (as well as a clutch of other social and economic variables), those who watch more TV news are better informed than those who watch less, and they generally, not always, express opinions showing that they have not succumbed to media malaise.

That said, this chapter adds further weight to the conclusion that media effects, even when they are statistically significant, are generally small and outweighed by other more powerful variables such as age, income, education, gender, political interest, and party identification. Moreover, generally media effects are mixed, with positive, negative, and neutral influences on democratic attitudes and behavior, so generalizations about media effects are rarely substantiated. Different media with a different content have different effects on different people.

In a nutshell, the news media do exert some effects on the diffuse and implicit features of political support, but these effects are usually weak and patchy and they often have more positive consequences for democracy than negative ones. The background characteristics of audiences, rather than media exposure, are the main determinants of what citizens think and do about politics: age, sex, education, income, ethnicity, and political interest and awareness count for much more than which newspaper they read or what kind of TV programs they watch.

Notes

1. Parenti 1992.
2. See, for example, Russo and Chaxel 2010.

3. Postman 1985.

4. Bennett 2005a, 2005b.

5. Holtz-Bacha 1990; Bennett et al. 1999; Putnam 2000; Norris 2000: 22–46; Durante, Pinotti, and Tesei 2014.

6. Norris 2000. See also Norris 1996.

7. Norris 2000: 246–247.

8. Norris 2000: 314, 277.

9. Newton 1999.

10. The BSA also contains information about access to cable and satellite television, ownership and use of home video recorders, and cinema attendance, which were tried in various ways and combinations in the regression equations on political knowledge and attitudes. In the great majority of cases, they were insignificant. Measures of different kinds of electronic media use were also tried in the regressions, but two simple measures—the number of hours of television watched and the number of times per week TV news was watched—were invariably the most powerful.

11. Fraile and Iyengar 2014; Fraile 2011.

12. See also Prior 2005.

13. See also Leshner and McKean 1997.

14. Evidence of higher levels of political knowledge among those who read newspapers and watch TV news is also found by Dimitrova et al. (2014).

15. Postman 1985.

16. See also Norris and Sanders 2003.

17. Strömbäck and Shehata 2010.

18. Avery 2009.

19. Holbert 2005.

20. Hooghe 2002.

21. Schmitt-Beck and Wolsing 2010; Aarts and Semetko 2003.

22. Gerbner et al. 1986.

23. Mutz and Reeves 2005. See also Berry and Sobieraj 2014.

24. Herbst 2010; Shea and Fiorina 2012.

25. Shea and Sproveri 2012.

26. Kalmoe, Gubler, and Wood 2018.

27. "Politics in the Office Survey: 94% Are Talking Politics at Work; Unlike Candidates, Keeping It Civil," Challenger, Gray & Christmas, https://www.challengergray.com/press/press-releases/politics-office-survey-94-are-talking-politics-work-unlike-candidates-keeping.

28. "Average Daily Time Spent Watching TV per Capita in Europe in 2016, by Country (in Minutes)," Statista, http://www.statista.com/statistics/361551/time-spent-watching-tv-europe.

29. De Hart and Dekker 1999.

30. See also Alesina and Giuliano (2011) on the importance of family for political activity.

31. Hooghe 2002.

32. The original work on media malaise and falling into the news was done by Robinson (1975, 1976).

9

Public Service and Commercial Television

Today the unique contribution of public broadcasting is no longer in doubt and well-known examples, such as the BBC, are universally acclaimed: public service plays an irreplaceable role in providing citizens with information, education and entertainment free of commercial, State or political influences.

—*World Radio and Television Council,*
Public Broadcasting: Why? How?[1]

In the second half of the twentieth century, when mass surveys came on stream, political science focused on survey data about how individuals used and were influenced by the media. Because there were few cross-national surveys, most of this work was done within countries that took their media systems as given, concentrating on individual consumers and overlooking institutional arrangements.[2] Toward the end of the century, large-scale cross-national surveys started to appear, making it possible to compare countries and consider the nature and effects of different media systems. Institutions were brought back in, and both consumer and producer sides of the equation entered the picture. Studying one without the other is likely to produce only partial explanations, if not misleading ones. Therefore, the last chapters of this book consider the media producers and consumers, especially the interaction between the two.

Cross-national research on media systems is still in its early years, but differences between public service and commercial broadcasting have been studied in Europe, which because of the number and variety of its countries, has been labeled "God's natural laboratory." This chapter concentrates on the main features and effects of public service and commercial broadcasting in Europe, with occasional reference to the small public service sector in the United States.

The chapter starts with an account of public service and commercial media and the fusion of the two in mixed systems. These differ in the quantity, quality, and timing of their news programs. An early, pathbreaking study of how newspaper reading and TV-watching habits of the populations of seven countries are associated with the public's knowledge of politics is then summarized. The chapter goes on to consider later research covering a broader range of countries and a wider assortment of political attitudes and behavior and examines how public service news media are associated with levels of social trust and the theory that it can have a rainmaker effect on total country populations, including individuals who do not watch much public service television. The next section examines how public service and commercial television relate to social capital, and then how they relate to public opinion about immigration. The last, brief part of the chapter summarizes national studies of media systems and their links with democracy.

The chapter concentrates on terrestrial TV channels. Although their audiences are declining in the digital era, they are still a main source of news, whether accessed with old or new technology. (The extent to which consumers use new electronic technology is considered in Chapter 10.) Nor does this chapter consider the role of public service radio because little is known about it, even though it is often highly trusted, still widely used, and takes the lion's share of the national market in some countries. Radio is the Cinderella of news media research.[3]

Public Service, Commercial, and Mixed Media Systems

Starting with the United Kingdom's Television Act of 1954, most Western democracies deregulated and commercialized their media, but not to the same degree. Some opted for wholesale commercialization; others maintained public services to run in tandem with commercial ones. Most Western democracies now have mixed public-private systems, and mix them in different proportions, ranging from 70 percent of national audiences in Denmark to 12.5 percent in Greece and 3 percent in the United States.

The mix means there is no clear distinction between public and private. Some public service media are allowed to raise commercial income to supplement their public funds, and some must do so to remain viable. Because audience figures are still important, they may also have introduced a degree of backdoor commercialism in their operations. Although public service broadcasting is supposed to be wholly independent of governments and other political and business interests, this ideal has been achieved to varying degrees in different countries. Some public channels are genuinely free of political and commercial constraints, but others struggle, not always successfully, to maintain their political independence.

On the other side of the coin, some commercial TV and radio stations are subject to public service regulations designed to produce accurate, comprehensive, and impartial news and to provide equitable broadcasting time for parties at election time. Other commercial channels have accepted public service responsibilities.[4] This mixture and fusion of public and commercial mean that the distinction is a matter of degree but is an important one that has persisted into the twenty-first century.[5]

Public, private, and mixed systems are different, in turn, from those under direct state control. Some new democracies and post-communist states have largely or completely privatized their media as a reaction to their old state propaganda machines, but in others the state continues to control or influence news broadcasting. This makes it important to distinguish between public service and state broadcasting. There are notable differences between them.

News Quantity, Quality, and Timing

Notwithstanding the blurring and partial convergence of public and commercial news broadcasting systems, public service news in Europe is generally thought to be more professional and politically neutral than other news sources and to adhere to higher standards of journalism.[6] The public service stations also broadcast more news. Between 1971 and 1996, the total number of hours a week that public service television devoted to news and current affairs almost tripled from 1,168 to 3,042 in Organisation for Economic Co-operation and Development (OECD) countries. In part, this resulted from an increase in the number of news channels.[7] And it takes no account of possible changes in news content from hard to soft, and from in-depth to brief news headlines, photo opportunities, and sound bites. Neither does it take account of how much use the general public makes of increased opportunities to access news (on this, see Chapter 11). Also, the larger number of channels and lengthening of broadcasting hours brought a large increase in hours devoted to entertainment television, from 1,505 to 6,020, which might affect the public's news diet (also discussed in Chapter 11).

A cross-national comparison of public service, mixed, and commercial TV systems shows that the hours devoted to news and current affairs fall, and those for entertainment increase as one moves from "pure" public service to mixed, and from mixed to commercial systems (see Table 9.1). Between a quarter and a third of broadcasting hours are devoted to news and current affairs in the public service systems compared with a spread of 14 to 27 percent of broadcasting time in commercial countries.

Public TV channels continue to provide more news, more hard news, and more international news.[8] A Council of Europe report covering 38 countries in 2013 finds that although public services make up 14 percent of all TV channels, they produce 30 percent of the news programming.[9]

Table 9.1 News/Current Affairs and Entertainment TV Programs as Percentages of Broadcasting Hours in Public, Mixed, and Commercial TV Systems

System	Country	News and Current Affairs	Entertainment
Public	Austria	28	44
	Denmark	25	54
	Hungary	34	30
	Average	29	43
Mixed	Finland	30	48
	France	13	47
	Germany	36	56
	Italy	28	43
	Ireland	14	60
	Norway	24	52
	Poland	33	35
	Spain	21	63
	Sweden	7	48
	UK	37	33
	Average	25	48
Commercial	Belgium	19	53
	Czech Republic	27	39
	Greece	27	56
	Netherlands	27	46
	Portugal	14	61
	Switzerland	16	40
	Turkey	22	45
	USA	19	36
	Average	21	47

Source: Norris 2000: 107–108.

Their news programs report more hard news about events, issues, and substantive policy debates compared with commercial news, which contains more soft news about personalities, election races, and games of political strategy.[10] The same is true of the publicly subsidized newspapers in Sweden, Norway, and France, which provide more original, in-depth, and balanced news coverage than their commercial counterparts, especially those more heavily dependent on advertising.[11]

Public service news programs are also more likely to be longer and broadcast more frequently and in peak viewing hours in the early evening and late evening.[12] A study comparing the United States with five European countries over a 20-year period from 1987 to 2007 finds that the commercial system in America offers the smallest diet of news and analysis.[13] In competition for advertising revenues, and hence for audience numbers, commercial channels tend to reserve prime-time viewing hours for their most popular entertainment programs. They usually have fewer and shorter news broadcasts and air them at less popular times. Public service countries provide a greater and richer volume of news with multiple opportunities to access it.[14] And, not least, public service news in Europe has a widespread reputation of being accurate, comprehensive, balanced, and fair.[15] Indeed, some observers have described the BBC's election coverage as "fairness run wild" and list thorny problems that different forms of balance and impartiality bring with them.[16]

The public service systems in Western Europe vary in their financing, organization, and duties, but in the United Kingdom, Sweden, the Netherlands, Germany, Denmark, Italy, France, and Spain they are the main and most trusted single source of news.[17] And in seven out of eight countries studied in one survey, public service channels were named as the main source of news, the exception being the United States where the Public Broadcasting Service has a very small audience share.[18] The question is, what effects, if any, do the differences between commercial and public services have on the attitudes and behavior of the general public?

Political Knowledge

Dimock and Popkin's study of the United States, Canada, Britain, France, Germany, Italy, and Spain was the first comparative survey of citizen political knowledge.[19] It is difficult to compare knowledge about national politics where there are differences between, for example, prime ministerial and presidential systems, or between unitary and federal governments. Therefore, the survey asks five questions about significant international political events and leaders that have the same meaning across nations.[20]

The US public is the least well informed, whereas the German public is the best.[21] More than half of the Americans (58 percent) answered none or only one of the five questions correctly, compared with 58 percent of the Germans who answered four or five correctly. Neither age nor sex explains the national differences. Among both college- and the non-college-educated participants, the Americans are the worst informed of the seven nations. In all countries, men know more than women about international politics, but Italian and German women know more than American men.

Dimock and Popkin's evidence shows that it is not the amount of daily exposure to the news (in minutes) that is important for political knowledge, because newspapers are more important for the acquisition of political knowledge than television, as we saw in the previous chapter. In six of the seven countries (not Canada), those who say they get most of their news from the papers are significantly more knowledgeable than those who relied more on television. And in six of the countries, reading a newspaper makes a statistically significant contribution to political knowledge. The importance of newspapers shows up clearly in the comparison of Germany and the United States. The Germans spend 10 fewer minutes a day than Americans with the news media altogether, but their superior political knowledge results from the fact that more of them (79 percent of Germans compared with 49 percent of Americans) read a paper the day before they were interviewed. Germany is the only country where more time is given to the newspaper than TV news.

Although the newspaper effect is stronger, TV news viewing makes a difference. When demographic variables and newspaper reading are held constant, regular TV news viewers are better informed in two countries—the United Kingdom and Germany, where high-quality public service TV news is available.[22] In comparison, the effect of regular TV news watching in the United States is not only statistically insignificant but also the lowest of the seven countries. In spite of high education levels, the US population is doubly disadvantaged by the news content of most of its papers and most of its TV news. Germans are twice advantaged because they have not only a set of high-quality newspapers, but also high-quality public service TV news with significant audience shares.

Quality newspapers and public service news are not the only influences on levels of public knowledge of politics, as we have seen in previous chapters, but they have a measurable effect. Dimock and Popkin conclude by saying,

> Relying on a newspaper may be more active and efficacious than viewing TV, as evidenced by the fact that relying on newspapers leads to more information than relying on television; there is clear evidence, however, that television can do better than it does in America. What viewers get from TV is not determined by inherent limitations on the ability of people to absorb information they see and hear. The differences between NBC and the BBC matter.[23]

Knowledge and the Knowledge Gap

Dimock and Popkin's early research has been confirmed by more than a dozen publications over the past 15 years. They show that populations with public service broadcasting find it easier to access hard, high-quality news about national and international affairs. Starting with Aarts and Semetko's pathbreaking study of media and political involvement in the Netherlands, a growing wave of research shows that watching TV news, whether commercial or public service or both, generally has a positive association with political knowledge.[24] This contrasts with some studies that find little or no association between news media exposure and political knowledge, but it may be no coincidence that many of them are based on research in the United States, where, as Dimock and Popkin found, neither newspapers nor television add much to levels of information.[25]

In Europe, public service TV news has stronger associations with knowledge than does commercial news. For example, one study concluded that

> public service TV news matters and contributes more to an informed electorate than commercial TV news. . . . Altogether, these results support the growing number of studies that on the aggregate level suggest that the public service–based systems sustain a higher level of political knowledge than market-based systems.[26]

Four main reasons account for this. First, and already discussed, is the comparatively high levels of trust in public service news. The second is the quantity, quality, and timing of their news programs. Third, it is likely that more politically aware and better-informed citizens are attracted to public service news rather than the commercial channels and that exposure to public service news then adds still more to their understanding and knowledge. And, fourth, some less-aware and less-well-informed people may fall into public service news, so learn about politics inadvertently as a by-product of their TV-watching habits.

However, as before, these explanations raise the tricky problem of causes and effects. Time-series studies help to sort this problem by tracking before and after events and controlling for self-selection effects. Some of these studies track political knowledge and news media exposure and content, and most of them find that exposure to public service news results in increased levels of knowledge. For example, a four-wave panel study of the Swedish national election in 2010 found that those who watched public service channels learned more and that this political knowledge growth occurred among public service viewers independently of their political motivation and news attention.[27] The public service effect was even stronger among those with little political interest. Similarly, Fraile and Iyengar's study of the 27 member states of the European Union used a technique known as propensity score matching to compare individuals with the same political motivation and ability but different news sources. Both broadsheets and public service news have a strong positive effect on political knowledge.[28]

Citizens in countries with a large public service audience are more likely to fall into the news because more of it is broadcast during peak viewing hours.[29] The learning process is also stronger when the source of information is trusted. In contrast, it used to be thought that falling into the news caused political distrust, apathy, and confusion—another example of the bad news and mean world effects—but later research shows that on the contrary, falling into the news adds to the knowledge, understanding, and confidence of those who are less politically aware and active.[30]

Norris documents the virtuous circle effect of the news media in which politically aware and informed people seek out the news from different sources, which then feeds them more knowledge and raises their political awareness and knowledge.[31] In addition, there is a virtuous circle effect that boosts the political knowledge of less-aware and -informed people who fall into the news. In sum, the political knowledge and awareness benefits for those who jump into the news also apply to those who fall into it, and falling into the news is a feature of public service TV channels with large audiences.

This virtuous circle results in a further narrowing of the knowledge gap between the best- and worst-informed citizens. TV audiences can be divided into two broad groups. The larger group is less well educated and less politically informed and aware and tends to watch more television, particularly entertainment programs on commercial channels. A smaller group is better educated, more informed, and more aware and tends to watch less television but more news on public service channels.[32] The larger group becomes better informed and aware when it falls into public service news. The result is a smaller knowledge gap in countries with public service broadcasting.[33]

Scholars disagree about how much the virtuous circle narrows the knowledge gap, and for whom it works best, and why. In one study, the strongest effect was on those with the least political interest, but a different study found that the effect worked *only* on this group.[34] Fraile and Iyengar's comparative study of the 27 EU member states, however, found no evidence that public service television reduces the knowledge gap.[35] Their research confirms that broadsheet newspapers have a stronger effect on increasing knowledge than TV news and tabloid papers, but only the broadsheets have the capacity to reduce the knowledge gap.[36]

The explanation for these differences may be that not all public services are the same.[37] Soroka et al. suggest that the effect depends on audience share, the proportion of income derived from the public purse, and independence from the political influence of the state and the government.[38] Following the conclusions of Chapter 7 in this book, it may also be that the more independent of government and commercial interests the public services are, the greater the public trust in their news programs and the more influential they are likely to be. At the same time, some commercial TV channels are regulated by public service requirements to produce news that is impartial, fair, and reliable, so in this respect, their effects may not differ much from the public service stations—in which case a crucial difference may be the extent to which commercial TV and radio stations are subject to public service regulations requiring their news programs be accurate, fair, and balanced.[39] This in turn may influence the extent to which they are trusted by the public. Perhaps more sensitive measures of these variations would reveal more about public service and commercial services, rather than simply dividing the media system into three broad categories of public service, mixed, and commercial.

Commercial and Entertainment Television

Some research suggests that the commercial media produce the mean world and videomalaise effects, but research results are often weak and mixed and do not add up to strong support for the claim.[40] This may be, in part, because some studies measure the number of hours of television watched, while others measure the amount of time spent specifically with the news. Or perhaps the effects of commercial television vary according to the size of its audience and the quantity and quality of its news. The larger the commercial sector's audience share, the bigger its impact is likely to be, but equally, the fiercer the market competition, the more likely it is that entertainment is given priority over news and the less likely it is that the news will be delivered during peak hours. The more closely aligned TV broadcasting systems are with economic and political interests, the less trusted they are (see the discussion on Russian TV news in Chapter 5).

De Vreese and Boomgaarden remark that effects of commercial news can vary depending on viewer attitudes and behaviors.[41] They find commercial news has a positive influence on political knowledge and voting turnout, though a smaller one than public service news, and suggest that what may matter is not a comparison of public versus commercial, but the content of the news, whichever the channel, and whether it is broadcast during prime-time viewing hours. As things presently stand, public services make a major contribution to the amount and quality of news available to the public and a smaller difference to levels of public political knowledge, positive attitudes toward democracy, and a smaller knowledge gap. How long this will last remains to be seen, given political and commercial pressures to commercialize broadcasting of all kinds.

The Rainmaker Effect

Most research on media effects, and most of that quoted in the previous section of this chapter, deals with direct effects of the media, but the media may also have an indirect influence. Direct effects occur when individuals access the media themselves. Indirect effects occur when the media influence the general context and culture of a country, which then affects all citizens, irrespective of their media use. Putnam, Pharr, and Dalton refer to this as the "rainmaker effect" because, just as the gentle rain from heaven falls upon the just and unjust alike, so also a general climate of trust or distrust may affect all members of a society, whatever their personal inclinations and media habits.[42] Direct effects are measured in both national and cross-national studies. Indirect effects must be studied by examining cross-national data that take account of how national media systems influence national cultures.

Schmitt-Beck and Wolsing studied direct and indirect media effects on social trust in 25 European countries.[43] Social trust is the single best indicator of social capital, which, as media malaise theory claims, is being undermined, especially by television. Schmitt-Beck and Wolsing observe that evidence for this claim is weak and inconclusive. Some studies find a relationship between TV viewing and low social trust, some do not, and others find that it is entertainment television that does the damage.[44] The authors also point out that this research concentrates on direct effects, so they set out, instead, to understand how national patterns of TV watching in different countries have direct and indirect influences on social trust on national populations as well as their individual members.

They found that TV effects were not just produced by how many hours people spent in front of the flickering screen—it was also important to know which TV channels and programs they favored. Because commercial channels prioritize light entertainment and public channels broadcast more hard news and programs promoting social understanding and integration, Schmitt-Beck and Wolsing hypothesized that public service television was less likely to undermine social trust than commercial television. Following the rainmaker theory, they also hypothesized that the influence of public service channels extended to the population as a whole, including those who mainly watched commercial channels.

To test their hypotheses, Schmitt-Beck and Wolsing used the European Social Survey (ESS) for 2002 and 2004 to judge the robustness of the results at different times. This survey measures TV viewing hours per week and trust levels in 25 European countries. Controlling for a large set of individual social and demographic characteristics, and for the GDP and age of democracy of a country, the researchers found that individual levels of TV watching had little influence on individual trust. What was statistically significant were the TV viewing habits of a country's total population. On average, irrespective of individual TV viewing habits, those who lived in countries where a lot of television was watched were less trusting socially than those in countries whose population watched less.

The overall effect of watching a lot of television, however, was also dependent on the kind of television viewed—public service or commercial. Regardless of the TV channels they preferred, those who lived in countries with a strong public service system were more trusting than those in countries with commercial systems. Moreover, the trust effect was found among individuals in public service countries irrespective of which TV channels they personally favored, hence the rainmaker effect that affects all citizens whatever their TV habits. The rainmaker effect is virtually identical in both the 2002 and 2004 ESS surveys. Schmitt-Beck and Wolsing conclude,

> Social trust is not necessarily lower among Europeans who are avid consumers of TV than among TV avoiders; rather trust is lower for members

of societies where average TV usage is higher. . . . The more of a society's TV time is devoted to watching programs on public instead of private channels, the more trusting its members are, regardless of their own personal TV habits.[45]

Public Service and Opinion About Immigration

Further evidence of direct and indirect effects of public service and commercial television is found in two Belgian studies. Using data collected by six European Social Surveys across 15 to 25 European countries between 2003 and 2013, Jacobs, Hooghe, and de Vroome examined the links between television and anti-immigrant attitudes.[46] By means of multilevel analysis, they studied TV effects at both the individual and country levels. This enabled them to test the conclusions of Schmitt-Beck and Wolsing about individual direct effects and country-level indirect effects of television.

The results of the study show that anti-immigrant views were most closely associated with the social and economic characteristics of individuals. Older adults had more negative views, and those with higher levels of education and who were more satisfied with their income and life in general had more favorable views toward immigrants. These characteristics were the main drivers of opinion about immigrants, but television also played a small role. Those who watched a lot of commercial television held more negative views about immigrants compared with those who watched public service stations.

There is also evidence of TV effects at the country level. Country populations that watch a lot of television are not more likely to hold anti-immigrant views, and neither are those who watch a lot of commercial television. But individuals in countries with large audiences of public service television are significantly less likely to hold anti-immigrant opinions. These results corroborate those of Schmitt-Beck and Wolsing. In other words, as far as social trust and feelings about immigrants are concerned, public service television seems to have an indirect, rainmaker effect.

Another Belgian study confirms the public service media effects on attitudes toward immigrants.[47] Content analysis of news programs from 2003 to 2013 showed that TV news is consistently negative—with bad news messages—but the commercial news is more so, with rather more negative and sensational references to fear, anger, and conflict. Over the 10-year period, public service news was more balanced and presented more hard information than commercial news programming.

Using panel data drawn from Belgian Election Surveys of 2009 and 2013, the study then shows that TV viewing habits and opinions on immigration changed very little in this period. Controlling for a long list of variables (sex, age, education, religion, economic position, left-right ideology, political interest, and television and other news consumption), the study found that individuals who preferred public service television expressed greater tolerance toward asylum seekers and immigration and saw immigrants as less of a cultural threat. They were also less likely to want to close national borders to asylum seekers. These opinions were most closely associated with education, left-right ideology, and political interest, and consistently weaker with the measures related to TV viewing in the study.

Because this study was based on panel data that covered the same individuals in 2009 and again in 2013, it enabled the authors to be certain that the hypothesized causes in 2009 preceded the hypothesized effects in 2013. The study found a causal path from watching public service news to lower levels of prejudice against asylum seekers. The authors accept a number of limitations on their study and the tentative nature of their conclusions, but they suggest that public service television plays a role, though a small one, in setting social norms of tolerance toward immigration. Their results are consistent with those of Hooghe and Jacobs; Jacobs, Hooghe, and de Vroome; and Schmitt-Beck and Wolsing.

Democracy and the Media

Gunther and Mughan's collection of essays on the media and democracy in Spain, Russia, Hungary, Chile, Italy, the United States, Japan, the Netherlands, the United Kingdom, and Germany reaches a clear conclusion about the relative merits and deficiencies of commercial and public service television in those countries.[48] The conventional wisdom is that a vibrant open and competitive marketplace of ideas is the best way of reconciling the power of the mass media with the needs of democracy. However, the essays in their book reach a different conclusion.

The British case of public service television and regulation of commercial TV news and election broadcasting shows how attention to the mass media encourages civic engagement, compared with the tendency in the United States for the mass media to cause low turnout and political cynicism.[49] Kaase shows how the introduction of commercial television in Germany in 1981 had a "surprisingly large" effect only a few years later in reducing by a substantial fraction the TV audience for the high-quality political information provided by the public networks.[50]

Gunther and Mughan conclude from the 10 nation studies that, contrary to conventional wisdom, public sector broadcasting enhances the quality of democracy more than its commercial market-driven counterpart. The public services cover more news and more policy-relevant information, and are more scrupulous in respecting journalistic impartiality toward parties, politicians, and politics in general.[51]

Conclusions

Cross-national research on public service and commercial television is still at an early stage, but a fair weight of evidence shows a positive link between viewing public service television and increased political knowledge and positive political attitudes and behavior. Public service news programs are generally longer, broadcast more frequently, contain more hard and international news, are more impartial, and more often broadcast during peak viewing hours. As a result, it is easier to access richer, more informative, and more trustworthy news in European countries with public service TV.

Public service television is not the same in all countries, however, and its social and political benefits may depend on the size of its audience, its degree of independence from government, the proportion of its income that comes from public funds, and whether it broadcasts its main news programs at peak viewing hours. Where public service broadcasting has these characteristics, more people fall into the news and learn from it as a by-product of their TV viewing habits. Contrary to results from earlier work, there is no evidence that those who fall into the news suffer from political confusion, alienation, or cynicism. On the contrary, they generally accumulate knowledge and maintain positive political attitudes.

There is a double virtuous circle: news seekers in Western countries can always find reliable hard news that informs and aids an understanding of politics. People who are less politically aware or politically interested come to know and understand more about politics if watching the news is a daily habit, and they are more likely to fall into high-quality news if they live in a country with a large public service sector. Consequently, public service television reduces the knowledge gap between the politically best- and worst-informed citizens, though this effect may largely or entirely be limited to the least politically involved sectors of the population and may vary to the extent the public service reaches those sections of the population.

The rainmaker effect of public service broadcasting extends its influence beyond viewers who happen to prefer public channels to commercial ones. The larger a country's audience for public service television, the higher its population's social trust and the more tolerant their attitudes toward immigrants and asylum seekers. The effects of public service television touch the entire population, even those who prefer commercial channels, whatever their personal characteristics and inclinations, and help sustain a civilized, tolerant, and trusting culture.

Public service news may be important for another reason. As discussed earlier in Chapter 2, the ideas and information people pick up first tend to be preserved, even when they are later shown to be wrong. Public service channels are more likely to deliver news that is accurate, comprehensive, and impartial, so citizens are less likely to acquire information that is inaccurate, biased, or difficult or impossible to correct.

Some evidence, inconsistent and weak though it is, suggests that commercial television, especially entertainment content, is associated with some aspects of media malaise. The reason for the inconclusive results may be that, like public service television, not all commercial systems are the same. Broadcasting in some countries is wholly commercial; in others public and commercial broadcasting are mixed in different proportions. Some countries regulate terrestrial (also known as "broadcast" and "over-the-air") TV news in the public interest; others leave it to the market in the same way that newspapers may print what they like within the limits of the law. News programs on commercial channels that are required to follow public service rules about providing balanced, impartial, and accurate news tend to be more reliable than those not regulated in this way. Postman, a perceptive writer on the media, stated bluntly, "The effect [of commercial television] on political life will be devastating."[52] Subsequent research shows this is an exaggeration and that although commercial television does little to improve viewers' knowledge, awareness, and understanding of politics, neither does it do anything like devastating harm.

Four general points emerge from recent research on media systems. First, compared with effects of other variables, media effects are mostly small, even when they are statistically significant. Usually, the variables of the standard model of the social sciences (class, education, income, age, sex, political interest, partisanship, and party identification) are more closely associated with mass political attitudes and behavior than are media effects. Curran et al. conclude,

> But although cross-national differences in the organization of the media, and how and when news is reported, are significant influences on levels of public knowledge, they are less important than deep-seated societal factors . . . [and] gender and education are strong predictors of knowledge, more so than media exposure. But what is very much more important . . . is interest in politics.[53]

Second, media content rather than the medium itself matters. Contrary to the idea that television can do nothing but entertain, there is strong evidence that television can educate and inform as well. The amount and quality of the news content is what influences society—not the medium communicating it. The message, not the medium, is the message.

Third, public service television is usually found in countries that are well-established democracies with a wealthy, egalitarian, homogeneous, well-educated population and with high levels of social trust and low levels of corruption. Although research tries to control for such country-level characteristics, it is possible that the benefits attributed to public service broadcasting are actually the product of the wider social, political, and economic characteristics of the societies in which public service broadcasting remains strong—in which case, the wider characteristics may be responsible for both the existence of the public services and the democratic benefits they seem to produce. Large-scale, cross-national, multilevel analysis, preferably over a period of time, will provide the most convincing evidence to unravel these complex interrelationships.

Finally, research about media systems is still young. It is clear that public service and commercial systems differ between and within themselves, and it is clear that their differences are associated with variations in the political knowledge, attitudes, and behavior of their audiences. But the precise nature of these associations is not yet known, and neither are the causal relations between them. Given the pace of commercialization that is making public service broadcasting an endangered species, these matters will have to be researched before it is too late.

Notes

1. World Radio and Television Council 2011.

2. Hallin and Mancini (2004) is a significant exception in this period.

3. With some exceptions, mostly dated.

4. Boulton 1998: 203.

5. Papathanassopoulos and Negrine 2011.

6. Humphreys 1996: 116–122; Cushion 2012.

7. Norris 2000: 104–105.

8. Curran et al. 2009; Schmitt-Beck and Wolsing 2010; Nikoltchev 2007; Aarts and Semetko 2003; De Vreese and Boomgaarden 2006; Aalberg et al. 2013; Tóka and Popescu 2009; Fraile and Iyengar 2014; Wonneberger, Schoenbach, and van Meurs, n.d.; Dimitrova and Strömbäck 2012; De Vreese et al. 2006.

9. Council of Europe 2013: 7.

10. Aalberg et al. 2013; Curran et al. 2014.

11. Strömbäck and Dimitrova 2006; Skogerbø 1997; Benson and Hallin 2007; Benson 2010.

12. Brants and Siune 1998; Aarts and Semetko 2003.

13. Aalberg, Van Aelst, and Curran 2010.

14. Esser et al. 2012.

15. On the BBC, see, for example, Goddard, Scammell, and Semetko 1998: 172.

16. Blumler, Gurevitch, and Nossiter 1995: 75–76; Semetko 1996.

17. K. E. Matsa, "Across Western Europe, Public News Media Are Widely Used and Trusted Sources of News," Pew Research Center, June 8, 2018, http://www.pewresearch .org/fact-tank/2018/06/08/western-europe-public-news-media-widely-used-and-trusted/.

18. A. Mitchell, E. Shearer, K. Simmons, K. E. Matsa, L. Silver, C. Johnson, M. Walker, and K. Taylor, "2. Southern European Countries More Fragmented in News Sources, but for Nearly All Countries, Top Main Source Is Public, Not Private," Pew Research Center, May 14, 2018, http://www.journalism.org/2018/05/14/southern-european -countries-more-fragmented-in-news-sources-but-for-nearly-all-countries-top-main -source-is-public-not-private/.

19. Dimock and Popkin 1997.

20. Questions were asked about the name of the president of Russia (Yeltsin), the country threatening to withdraw from the nuclear nonproliferation treaty (North Korea), who Boutros Boutros Ghali was (UN Secretary General), the ethnic group that had conquered much of Bosnia and surrounded Sarajevo (Serbians), and the name of the group that Israel had reached a peace accord with (the PLO).

21. This was also the finding of Bennett et al. (1996).
22. See also Norris et al. 1999: 72.
23. Dimock and Popkin 1997: 223.
24. Curran et al. 2009; Curran et al. 2014; Aarts and Semetko 2003; Aarts, Fladmoe, and Strömbäck 2012; De Vreese and Boomgaarden 2006; Tóka and Popescu 2009; Aalberg, Van Aelst, and Curran 2010; Newton 1999; Norris 1996, 2000; Strömbäck and Shehata 2010; Soroka et al. 2013; Shah, McLeod, and Yoon 2001; Shehata et al. 2015; Leshner and McKean 1997; Strombäck 2017.
25. Price and Zaller 1993: 148–152; Delli Carpini and Keeter 1997; Drew and Weaver 2006.
26. Iyengar et al. 2010.
27. Shehata et al. 2015.
28. Fraile and Iyengar 2014.
29. Blumler (1970: 79–87) made this point almost 50 years ago.
30. Newton 1999.
31. Norris 2000.
32. Aarts and Semetko 2003; Hooghe 2002; Newton 1999.
33. Aalberg and Curran 2012; Aalberg, van Aelst, and Curran 2010; Curran et al. 2009; Soroka et al. 2013; Shehata et al. 2015.
34. Shehata et al. 2015; Popescu and Toka n.d.; Shehata and Strömbäck 2011.
35. Fraile and Iyengar 2014.
36. Newton 1999; Norris 2000; Dimock and Popkin 1997; Leshner and McKean 1997.
37. See, for example, Esser et al. 2012; Soroka et al. 2013.
38. Soroka et al. 2013. A longer but similar list is provided in a report by Benson and Powers (2011).
39. In 1987, the Federal Communications Commission of the United States eliminated its "fairness doctrine" requiring those holding broadcasting licenses to be honest, fair, and equitable in their treatment of important public issues, but it retains its equal time rule for competing political candidates, though with exceptions.
40. Aarts, Fladmoe, and Strömbäck 2012; De Vreese and Boomgaarden 2006; Holtz-Bacha and Norris 2000. Media malaise is probably a better term than videomalaise to capture all the claimed adverse effects of the media, whether caused by television, newspapers, radio, or the web.
41. De Vreese and Boomgaarden 2006.
42. Putnam, Pharr, and Dalton 2000: 26. See also Newton and Norris 2000.
43. Schmitt-Beck and Wolsing 2010: 479.
44. See, among others, Putnam 1995: 679; Brehm and Rahn 1997; Shah 1998; Norris 2000; Hooghe 2002; Freitag 2003; Shah, McLeod, and Yoon 2001; Lee, Cappella, and Southwell 2003; Holtz-Bacha 1990.
45. Schmitt-Beck and Wolsing 2010.
46. Jacobs, Hooghe, and de Vroome 2017.
47. Jacobs, Meeusen, and d'Haenens 2016.
48. Gunther and Mughan 2000.
49. Semetko 2000: 373–374.
50. Kaase 2000: 384–391.
51. Gunther and Mughan 2000: 442.
52. Postman 1985: 50.
53. Curran et al. 2009: 21.

10

Hyperpluralism in the Digital Age

Despite the fact that in the majority of discussions about media owner-ship *and media* pluralism *the terms are often elided, the two concepts are not necessarily identical.*

—D. Ward, O. C. Fueg, and A. D'Armo,
A Mapping Study of Media Concentration
and Ownership in Ten European Countries[1]

When considering the structure and content of the modern news media, two crucial features should be taken into account. The first is the increasing centralization of ownership and control of legacy and digital media by a few multinational, multimedia conglomerate corporations, many with major interests in other commercial activities. Second, the reverse development of the digital media has multiplied the amount and variety of news available and made much of it easier, quicker, and cheaper to access. Both have consequences for media pluralism and, it is widely claimed, powerful consequences for the ways in which the media can shape and influence political life. This and the following chapters review the evidence for these claims. But first we must take a closer look at the pluralist theory of the media, which has been a cornerstone of the media's role in developed democracies for over a century and a half.

The central idea of pluralism is that there should be many different and competing sources of news that reflect an array of political opinions, giving each a voice in the political system. In this way, truth will emerge from the competition of ideas, the power of the press will not be concentrated in a few hands, and different political groups will be represented in the political debate. The public will be supplied with a diversity of news and opinions and citizens will be able to make up their own minds about political issues.

Competition among many news sources minimizes the power of the press and maximizes the power of citizens; a monopoly or oligopoly of news sources maximizes the power of the media and minimizes that of citizens, as every autocrat knows. Therefore, the purpose of this chapter is to estimate the degree of news media pluralism in two countries—the United States and the United Kingdom—in order to understand an important constraint on the media's political influence. The increasing concentration of ownership and control of the old media—television, radio, and print—has been a subject of research for many decades, but to the best of the author's knowledge there has been no systematic attempt to map the huge expansion and diversification of the new electronic media and their consequences for a pluralist news media. This chapter attempts to fill the gap. First, however, it is necessary to consider the problems of pluralist theory and their implications for democracy.

Problems of Pluralist Theory

Though it has a distinguished heritage and is widely accepted, classic pluralist theory of the media as formulated in the nineteenth century has problems. First, a marketplace of ideas does not guarantee that truth will emerge.[2] On the contrary, market theory tells us that free competition will, sooner or later, result in adjustments between supply and demand so that shops and restaurants, for example, will provide what consumers want and are willing to pay for, even if it's junk food. They will provide healthy food if people want and are willing to pay for it. Similarly, a competitive market for news will provide high-quality or junk news according to demand. The danger lies in Gresham's law: that the bad drives out the good. This problem is found most obviously in the pages of the poorest-quality papers, tabloid television, hate radio, and on many websites.[3]

Second, pluralist theory assumes that a plurality of independent producers is the best or only way to cover a plurality of political opinions and news content. This is questionable. A single source of news may be internally pluralist in its content in the sense that it is impartial and reliable and provides a comprehensive coverage of events. Equally, many producers may have the same political bias. The point is made by Ward:

> Despite the fact that in the majority of discussions about media *ownership* and media *pluralism* the terms are often elided, the two concepts are not necessarily identical. A concentration of media ownership can provide a plural and diverse range of programmes as is evident for instance in the monopolies granted to public sector broadcasters in the pre 1980s period. Likewise, a very plural competitive market with a number of different actors can produce a very narrow range of programmes.[4]

A similar point is made by Hesmondhalgh in his commentary on McChesney, who warned about increasing concentration of ownership and control of the media, and Compaine, who made the case for free-market competition.

> But both McChesney and Compaine fail to provide an adequate assessment of the contemporary media. Both deal poorly with crucial issues of content—of what the media actually put out. And both are reductive in seeing the shape of the media as the result of economic factors.[5]

Ward and Hesmondhalgh are right to stress the importance of content and internal pluralism, which is why Western democracies place great value in internally pluralist television news produced by public service and commercial channels and in newspapers with a record of trustworthiness. In addition, as Hesmondhalgh notes, the distinction between the organization of a media system and the pluralism of its news coverage shifts attention from the ownership and control of the media—by no means unimportant—to the content of the news media. What is most important for democracy and its citizens is the quality of news reporting, not who owns or controls the news organizations, and pluralist content can be produced by market pluralism or internal pluralism or a mixture of both. Classic pluralist theory is wrong to assume that a fragmented and competitive news market is the only or the best way to achieve pluralist news content.

The third problem with pluralist media theory is that it takes little or no account of the news-consuming behavior of the public. Like classic free-market economics, which assumes that consumers have full knowledge of the market, pluralist media theory assumes that attentive citizens will gather news from a variety of sources to get a broad picture of what is going on and make up their own minds about it. The real world is not like this. Most people have neither the time nor the interest to acquire a full and rounded understanding of politics. They may habitually tune in to two or three news sources, but few systematically compare and contrast information from an array of sources to get a comprehensive understanding of all points of view. Most use heuristics, shortcuts, cues, and gut rationality to form opinions and reach decisions, and an efficient way of doing this is to rely heavily on one or two trusted sources of news. The flaw in the pluralist heaven, to misquote E. E. Schattschneider, is not so much that the heavenly chorus sings with a strong upper-class accent but that many in the audience listen only intermittently, and then only with one ear.

These observations suggest that a complete pluralist theory of the media has at least three elements: pluralism of news sources, pluralism of news content, and pluralist behavior of news consumers. Each is independent of the others. A pluralism of news producers does not guarantee a pluralism of news content any more than a single producer necessarily lacks it. And neither pluralist producers nor pluralist content guarantees pluralist news-gathering behavior of citizens. On the contrary, some fear that the fragmentation of the media in the information-rich digital age enables individuals to avoid the news altogether or select only those sources that share their own political views.

The next chapter considers the pluralism of news audiences—the demand side of the equation. This chapter deals with news suppliers and the extent to which the news media system is pluralist in number, and with the diversity and quality of news content. Regarding news producers, it is common to distinguish between the old media (terrestrial television, radio, and printed newspapers, magazines, and journals) and the new media (desktop publishing, cable and satellite television, local and community radio, and the web).

This distinction between the old and new media introduces another problem. It is confusing and misleading, because the two are inseparably fused. The technology of the new media is used extensively by the old media. Indeed, the reputed oldest newspaper in the world, Sweden's official gazette, *Post-och Inrikes Tidningar,* first appeared in 1645 and since 2007 has been available only in electronic form, although its purpose and content remain much the same as in its first edition. In the same way, large numbers of newspapers and "old" TV channels and radio stations use new technology to reach their audiences. The old media are often known as *legacy* platforms, and the new, as *digital* media. These are better terms than *old* and *new* because they do not confuse content with the technology used to communicate it.

The new technology does not add to pluralist content if it is simply a new way of delivering old media content—old wine in new bottles.[6] However, it can add to news pluralism in two ways. First, the number of digital natives producing news content that was not and could not be delivered with the old technology has increased exponentially, and they add hugely to the amount and diversity of political news and opinion available. Second, the new technology makes it easier, quicker, and cheaper to access news from different sources. In the United States, those with the most communication gadgets are no more or less likely to use the old media, but they report that it is easier and more enjoyable to get news than before.[7]

Mapping News Media Systems

To estimate the degree of media pluralism or lack of it, this chapter maps the outlines of the British and US systems and their political content, distinguishing between new technology and new content and taking account of market diversity and internal pluralism. The chapter deals only with the United States and the United Kingdom because these two countries are as well documented as any in the Western world and because they are all that can be managed within the space of a single chapter. This involves marshaling evidence about the numbers and variety of mass and specialist news producers and estimating the diversity of the news and opinion they produce. (See Appendices 10.1 and 10.2.)

Such a mapping exercise should not be complicated in theory, but turns out to be difficult and imprecise in practice. The ownership and control of the old mass media are well documented in public records, their news content has been studied by means of content analysis, and a lot is known about their audiences. Much less is known about the digital media because they are owned and controlled by a mixture of a few giant companies and by tens of millions of small organizations and private individuals who are too numerous to count. The giants are secretive and protect their commercially valuable information and its political uses, and it is virtually impossible to keep up with the rapidly increasing numbers and turnover of a long, long tail of digital natives. The result is not just a lack of evidence about the digital media, but an almost complete lack of evidence about their effects.

Even the basic information we do have can be confusing because of different definitions. Simple data on the number of TV channels in the United Kingdom and United States are difficult to pin down because published figures deal variously with stations, channels, and number of licenses, and they can include or exclude cable, time-shift, and high-definition (HD) versions or cover only free-to-view channels.

Radio is another problem. There were an estimated 44,000 radio stations in the world in 2010; that figure is the latest available, and increasing numbers and high turnover make it difficult to keep up with developments since then. We do not know how many radio stations are available on the net, where they are accessible to people in Britain and the United States, although partial lists and links can be found on various websites. Even the Federal Communications Commission cannot say exactly how many active radio stations there are in the United States, although it issues a list of stations that have been silent for at least two months. Some figures do not take account of the silent stations, and others include booster and translator stations, which increase the availability of radio signals but do not diversify content. Nevertheless, in round numbers there are approximately 15,500 radio stations in the United States and 676 Ofcom-licensed radio stations in the United Kingdom. We have approximate figures for how many of these are available on the net, and it is also known that the total audiences for these radio stations are enormous—270 million a week in the United States and 49.2 million in Britain. The British listen to radio an average of 20.8 hours a week.[8]

On the other hand, the news content, if any, of radio is difficult or impossible to gauge. The website Tunin.com lists about a thousand news and talk radio stations around the globe that are accessible on the net, but there is little systematic information about the news or analysis of content of the other 43,000. Some, probably a small minority, are dedicated news and talk stations, but others broadcast news a few times a day; some have one-minute news headlines on the hour, and others have no news at all. There is also the problem that some, perhaps many, radio stations (and TV channels) do not have the means of producing their own news, so they get it from another source, usually from a parent or partner company or a news agency. According to one source, the news content of almost all commercial radio stations in the United Kingdom is provided by Sky News.[9] Once again, this adds to listeners' ease in accessing the news from an increasing number of outlets, but it does not add to the diversity of the news.

Most parts of the media system suffer from the same sorts of data problems. Trying to estimate the contours of the system is like using the naked eye to count the number of stars in a cloudy night sky. Nevertheless, even before Galileo's telescope, the ancient world had guessed there was a vast number of stars. Similarly, though we cannot count the individual entities of the global news media system with much accuracy, we know there is a vast collection of them.

Details of the news media system of the United Kingdom and the United States are presented in the appendices of this book for those who want to trawl through the mass of facts, figures, and sources. For those who want to get to the bottom line quickly, they are summarized in this chapter, but it should be noted, as one source puts it, that "The digital revolution is full of contradictions and exceptions."[10]

The Structure and Content of the News Media in the United Kingdom

Despite difficulties with the evidence, we can draw a few conclusions about the news media in Britain. First, the mass news markets of television, radio, and print media—the legacy media—seem at first to be anything but pluralist, and the same appears to be true of the major players of the digital media.[11] Increasingly, the legacy media are being absorbed into large multimedia corporations that are part of even larger multinational conglomerates with far-reaching financial interests. At the same time, the news content of the legacy media is decreasing, audiences are shrinking, journalist numbers are falling, and news budgets are dwindling.[12] These trends have done a great deal to undermine news media pluralism—to the extent that a parliamentary report warned 11 years ago that market forces were producing media bias and the suppression of information. Market forces have probably intensified since then.[13]

Such concerns are serious, but they must be considered alongside two other developments—the existence of internally pluralist news sources and the exponential growth of electronic sources of news and opinion that increase the means of accessing news.

Pluralist News Markets and Internal Pluralism

Many studies draw attention to the lack of pluralism in the British media system that results from the concentrated ownership and control of the newspaper industry and the BBC taking a very large share of TV and radio audiences.[14] However, even though the mainstream media are concentrated in a few hands, a closer look at news content suggests a rather different picture. Like other public service broadcasters in Europe (see Chapter 9), BBC Radio and TV devote more time to foreign and hard news than commercial TV channels and radio stations. The public channels broadcast more news and more hard news at more popular hours, devoting 11 percent of peak-time TV hours on its five main channels to news and 4 percent to current affairs; the figures for its daytime TV are 13 percent and 2 percent, respectively.[15] BBC World News broadcasts on television and radio throughout the day in 28 different languages, reaching a weekly audience of 376 million around the world in 2018.[16] BBC Radio 4 broadcasts in-depth news in the morning, at midday, in the early evening, and in the late evening, and it has 56 national and regional stations for diverse audiences, all with regular news and current affairs programs and broadcasts in English, Welsh, Gaelic, and Asian languages.

Though criticized by some, the BBC is widely believed to produce comprehensive, balanced, and impartial news, as far as this is possible, which gives it an important place in the country's news system. It is the most highly trusted source of political news in the country (see Chapter 7) and plays a role of special importance at times of national emergency. On July 7, 2005, when London was hit by terrorist bombs, the BBC website received around one billion hits, serving about 5.5 terabytes of data, with up to 40,000 page requests per second at peak times.[17] In times of national crisis the population turns to the BBC for trustworthy news. The BBC is one of the few organizations in the United Kingdom able to maintain coverage of global events.[18]

ITV and Channel 4 are subject to the same public service requirements of producing accurate, comprehensive, and impartial journalism and are also trusted news sources that are well regarded. Like the BBC, ITV and Channel 4 contribute significantly to the pluralism of the British media system in two important ways: they cover national and international events with hard news that is as reliable as any other news source, more so than most; and by most standards, they produce a balanced and impartial account of diverse opinions. Channel 4 was launched as an alternative to mainstream TV channels with a special mission to serve tastes and interests not generally catered to by other UK broadcasters, including ethnic, language, regional, and sexual minorities.[19] Its programs include respected peak-time news programs, political documentaries and analysis, and political comedy.

It is misleading to measure pluralism by the yardsticks of concentrated ownership and audience figures alone. The BBC and NewsCorp's newspapers, especially *The Sun,* are alike in having large audience shares, but they are poles apart in terms of quality, quantity, and internal pluralism. Counted as a single organization, the BBC contributes little to news pluralism, but treating it as an internally pluralist organization composed of many subsidiary units is an entirely different matter. And to the BBC's contribution to the national (and international) media system must be added the public service–regulated news and current affairs programs of ITV and Channel 4.

The same sort of case can be made for newspapers, for example in Mutz and Martin's study of selective exposure to dissimilar political views expressed in newspapers and personal discussions—a study that compares Britain and the United States.[20] The study points out that British newspaper readers will not get dissimilar political views by reading a partisan national newspaper, but overlooks the fact that most readers of the partisan tabloid press do not trust it, and a majority of the population get their news from TV and radio, and both the BBC and commercial terrestrial television are more pluralist and trustworthy.

The Long Digital Tail

The second consideration alongside the growing concentration of ownership and control of the mainstream media is the long, long tail of news and opinion sources generated in recent times by new electronic and digital technology, or with its help. It is true that there is growing consolidation of the larger organizations in the digital world, but there is also a rapidly growing number and diversity—a long tail—of websites, each with a small number of pages and users. Diversity and pluralism are decreasing among the big organizations but increasing among the small ones.

Once again, radio illustrates the diverging trends of ownership and content. On the one hand, a few organizations each control a large number of radio stations, although the biggest of these, the BBC, caters to diverse groups of listeners. On the other, more small radio stations are being created, although there is a turnover of these. Every county and city in Britain has its own radio station, as do many large and small towns and a great many smaller communities. BBC Radio broadcasts in 27 languages, and there are another dozen news and talk stations, a dozen more for minority ethnic groups, plus local stations for military bases, motor racing circuits, prisons, universities, schools, and hospitals. According to the commercial sector organization Radio Centre, 334 commercial stations reach an audience of 35 million each week with 3,000 hours of public service content and an average of 22 three-minute news bulletins daily. But the document says nothing about the news content or news sources used.[21] The Office of Communications (Ofcom) presents a succinct account of the overall local media landscapes that come within its purview in the United Kingdom, noting the heterogeneity of regional, local, and community-level operators, some small, some large, run by commercial and public organizations, media trusts, local government, and individuals, with few providers operating across more than one platform.[22]

And then there is the web. No one knows how many websites (unique hostnames) there are, but a decent estimate is around 1.5 billion worldwide, of which only around 200 million are believed to be active, with the rest mainly dormant, parked, or reserved names. Most of the 200 million have little or no political content defined—even in a broad way—but even a small percentage of them probably adds up to a large absolute number. Even if only one-half of 1 percent is primarily political in content, this amounts to one million websites. Many of the most popular news websites are those of the legacy TV channels, radio stations, newspapers, and magazines, which add little to news pluralism but make it easier, cheaper, and quicker to access their news.[23] There are also hundreds of digital natives that do add substantially to news pluralism—blogs, the webpage equivalents of political pamphlets and leaflets, newsletters, chat rooms and discussion forums, videos, have-your-say facilities, and digital native newspapers that are increasing in number every day. These add up to a sum that is nontrivial in absolute numbers and that caters to the interests of the United Kingdom's ethnic, religious, age, local, regional, community, occupational, voluntary, and recreational groups. Some material is not free to access, but a large amount is, and although much of it has small or tiny audiences, the point of this chapter is to register its existence, not how much citizens make use of it. That is for the next chapter.

That said, the transformations brought about by the new technologies are not quite as complete as they might be and, perhaps, were thought to be only a short time ago. First, as with the legacy media, a few huge businesses are consolidating their hold over large and important parts of the digital system. It is also the case that most of the most popular news websites are not digital natives, but online versions of legacy national newspapers and TV stations.[24] In March 2015, 10 of the United Kingdom's top news websites had a total digital audience of 150 million unique visitors, of which two digital natives, *BuzzFeed* and *Huffington Post,* accounted for 18 million, or 12 percent of the total. The other eight were legacy platforms consisting of seven national newspapers, plus the BBC.

Moreover, digital native news sites rely a lot on legacy media news. The *Huffington Post* includes original content but also aggregates news from other sources, especially the legacy media, and relies heavily on Associated Press. Facebook's trending topics site was claimed to be a *vox pop* account of what people on the street were talking about, but it is now "curated" by editors who decide what is trending and what is not and who "deactivate" material that is not supported by at least 3 of 10 legacy news sources that include Fox News, *The Guardian,* and the BBC.[25] Curating is also used to deactivate fake news, foreign interference in elections and referendums, and abusive, threatening, offensive, and illegal material posted on websites, but how much is done and how successful it is in achieving its goals are not known.

It should not be assumed that hard copy and web versions of old newspapers are the same. *The Guardian*'s websites, like the sites of the *New York Times* and *Der Spiegel,* often carry longer and more detailed versions of their hard copy news as well as blogs, analysis, readers' comments, and other material that does not appear in the printed editions. The BBC has a huge amount of material on its websites that is not broadcast on TV or the radio. Many of the legacy sites of TV channels, radio stations, and newspapers provide breaking news throughout the day plus real-time accounts of events. To this extent the extra website material does enhance pluralism of content.

Despite more control, hierarchy, and curating of the giants, plus some legal restraints, mountains of material about virtually every political party and group, political issue and event are available on the Internet from almost every part of the globe, together with opinion about them from almost every conceivable political standpoint. A complaint about the Internet is that it has failed to deliver the unorthodox, innovative, critical political content that it was predicted to offer in its early years. This is true of some parts of the web, but not others. One list of the top 10 political blogs in the United Kingdom describes them variously as "anti-establishment," "feisty," "independent," "mischievous," "waspish," "de-bunking," and "robust"—all part of the style of blogs in general and what early commentators hoped for.[26]

USA: News Media Structure and Content

In many ways the media systems of the United Kingdom and the United States are different. The US system is much larger, has a proportionately larger capital value and turnover, is far more commercial, and includes a public broadcasting sector that is a fraction of the size of the BBC. It is more decentralized geographically, with regional and local media playing a greater role. Cable TV is more important and more partisan. At the same time, the systems in the two countries are similar in their increasing concentration of ownership and control of some sectors but large, diverse, and growing numbers of producers in others. For this reason, the discussion of the US market is briefer than that of the UK media, not because it is any less important or interesting but because, with a few significant exceptions discussed below, there is little need to rehearse the details all over again. They are in Appendix 10.2 for those who want them.

Perhaps the most common concern about the emergence of a few giant multinational multimedia corporations is that the mass media news outlets they control are likely to be systematically biased in the interests of their corporate owners, and increasingly constrained by the economic interests of the advertisers on whom they depend.[27] Actual practice seems to be different. One study of coverage of a presidential election found that, compared with many of the national British papers, American newspapers are fairly neutral in their campaign reports.[28] They generally provide a balanced evaluation of issues and events, and where there is partisan bias, it is demonstrably small and mixed with competing partisan messages. Most newspapers were careful to separate news and editorial opinions. The same study found that network TV news was even more balanced and impartial. A content analysis of 1,156 TV election reports shows that all channels presented a balance of favorable and unfavorable stories about the candidates.[29] This conclusion applies to news about the presidential election, which was the subject of the study, and does not necessarily apply to other political matters.

Prior's summary of studies of American news media content draws the same conclusion. "Most large US media outlets," he writes, "are politically centrist and provide a balance of competing viewpoints," although smaller, more specialized and opinion-focused media in the form of blogs, talk radio, cable news, and websites show greater bias and one-sidedness.[30] D'Alessio and Allen's meta-analysis of media coverage of presidential elections in the United States from 1948 to 2008 also found "no evidence of a unilateral, monolithic bias, at least in presidential election news coverage."[31] Rather, there is what Schudson calls a muddled and multidimensional picture of the world.[32]

The result is that significant parts of the commercial mass media in the United States—both newspapers and the three main network TV channels—exhibit a degree of internal pluralism not dissimilar to that of the BBC and ITV in Britain. In other words, the news produced by commercial businesses is not necessarily politically biased in party political and election terms, although this does not preclude the possibility that it may be biased in other ways. This raises the underresearched questions: Why are some commercial news media politically biased while others are not? What are the implications of this for studies of the increasing concentration of ownership and control of the news by multinational multimedia corporations? And what are the implications of the assumption that a free-market commercial system is the best way of producing news media pluralism?

These are big questions that cannot be tackled here, but it is worth mentioning one possible answer. In the final analysis, the owners of the commercial media may come down in favor of their own particular economic interests rather than those of the large business sector of which they are a part. For example, Chapter 3 describes how Murdoch's *Sun* newspaper in the United Kingdom switched its party support in 1997 because it followed the changing voting patterns of its readers rather than taking the risk of alienating them and losing circulation. When the political mood of its readers swung back to the Conservatives in 2010, so too did *The Sun*. For the same reason, Murdoch's English paper opposed independence at the time of the Scottish referendum campaign, but his Scottish one favored it. In the United States, Fox News gave a lot of air time to vote-losing Republican candidates who were favored by the Fox audience and reflected the audience's own views back to them. "Follow the money" explains the political position of the Murdoch news media in these cases.

Local papers in the United States may be under pressure to be impartial in their reporting of presidential campaigns because the circulation figures essential for their economic viability demand they attract readers from all sections of political opinion in a relatively small market. In comparison, the national market for daily papers in the United Kingdom (about 8.8 million) is large enough for newspapers to target particular rather than general audiences, and hence they can afford to be partisan or sectional in their appeal, and may profit from it. The same may be true of national cable news channels, TV programs, and websites in the United States.[33] None of this suggests that economic self-interest is the sole motive behind the impartial and balanced journalism of internal pluralism, but it can be a constraint for the commercial media.

Although the evidence supports the notion that US national TV networks and local papers are more internally pluralist than is often claimed, there is also evidence that the web is less politically pluralist than early predictions claimed it would be. First, as in Britain, some of the most heavily used news websites in the United States are those of the legacy media, not the digital natives. These sites increase the reach and accessibility of the news but do not add much to its pluralist content. There are all sorts of problems in estimating the number of website readers, and figures must be treated with caution.[34] Nevertheless, in the United States in 2018, 12 of the 15 most popular online news sites were those of legacy newspapers and TV stations, which had 60 percent of the estimated total number of unique monthly visitors.[35] However, the top three news sites were digital natives (Yahoo!, Google, and *Huffington Post*), with 40 percent of the total number of unique monthly visitors. More than half (55 percent) of *New York Times* regular readers, 48 percent of regular *USA Today* readers, and 44 percent of *Wall Street Journal* readers said they use a digital edition.[36] The *New York Times* had close to 1.4 million digital-only subscriptions in 2016, and the *Wall Street Journal* had close to 1.3

million in 2017. The top 10 newspapers in 2013 registered a total daily digital circulation in excess of three million.[37]

News from legacy sources also figures largely in the social websites. For example, a Pew survey in 2011 reported that 27 percent of American adults said they regularly or sometimes get news or news headlines through social network sites, but 72 percent of them also said this is the same news they would get elsewhere.[38] There is also a tendency for the new digital natives to draw heavily on the content of the legacy news. The *Huffington Post,* Drudge Report, and Facebook have all taken to using the mainstream media that they were once believed to be replacing.[39] Consequently, some of the most popular news websites in the United States do not add much in the way of news pluralism, and some of the digital natives contribute less to critical independent thinking that was once thought to be the hallmark of the web. A recent review comments that their results are dishearteningly modest compared with media such as the *New York Times, Washington Post,* and *The Guardian.*[40] According to the same author, one of the largest digital native news sites and the leader of their second wave of innovators, *BuzzFeed,* is in danger of being known mainly for its pictures of cats.[41] As Fenton puts it, "It is easy to wax lyrical about the *potential* of a digital age to change news for the better. For now the reality appears somewhat different."[42]

This conforms to previous patterns of technological innovation. In their early stages, there tends to be a large number of small, competing producers, but over time the industry coalesces around a small number of large and dominant organizations. Likewise, each initial stage of media innovation—for radio, TV, digital—has provoked a wave of optimism about a new, competitive era of communications to be replaced by later stages of market consolidation and control, none more so than in the electronic era.[43] Predicted benefits have been pared down by a handful of digital empires built by the "move fast and break things" Internet billionaires, who are similar in some ways to the old robber barons and media moguls of the industrial era.[44] The result is that the digital media are less open, competitive, and pluralist now than many hoped they would be only a few years ago.

Nevertheless, as in other countries, digital technology has transfigured the entire broad- and narrowcasting system in the United States and is opening up vast amounts of international news sources. It is estimated that there are 270 foreign TV news channels available on the Internet in the United States, and the number of foreign newspapers and radio stations runs into the thousands.[45] Another source lists 74 round-the-clock news channels in the United States, with another 49 available from around the world.[46] In some cases, this includes the legacy news media, with the *New York Times, Mail Online, Washington Post, Guardian, Wall*

Street Journal, USA Today, Los Angeles Times, and NBC and BBC in the top fifteen.[47] English-language political blogs alone number around 4,800. The extent of news media pluralism in the United States is detailed in Appendix 10.2 at the end of the chapter.

Conclusions

This chapter starts from the observation that classic pluralist theory of the news media assumes that only a varied and large number—usually unspecified—of producers will provide a comprehensive account of the news and opinion about it. This overlooks the possibility that many producers may deliver news of the same narrow and biased nature, while a single producer may be internally pluralist and deliver a comparatively balanced, accurate, and comprehensive account of news and opinion. Internal pluralism is the value placed on newspapers of record and on public service TV and radio news. It is necessary, therefore, to make a clear distinction between the organization of media systems and the news content they produce.

Internally pluralist news organizations can be commercial or public sector ones. This undermines the idea that the commercial sector is inevitably biased toward the political right, and the idea that only a free-market system can deliver pluralist news content. Most people are not news junkies and do not habitually scan different news sources to compare their accounts of news and opinion but, instead, rely on one or two main sources of news, which puts a premium on popular news media that are internally pluralist.

Another clear distinction should be drawn between the new digital means of communication and the content delivered by it. The new technology can be used to convey anything that can be converted to digital form, whether it is produced by the legacy media or digital natives. A great many of the legacy TV channels, radio stations, newspapers, and magazines use the new technology. In fact, in the United Kingdom and United States, the most popular news websites are those of the legacy media. Hence the terms "new media" and "old media" can be confusing if they suggest that the two are separate and different from each other. From a pluralist theory perspective, reading the morning paper on the web rather than in hard copy does nothing to increase news diversity if both contain the same content, which is not always the case. Nevertheless, the new technology may be a pluralist asset insofar as it makes it easier, quicker, and cheaper to both produce and access news from different sources.

With these distinctions in mind, this chapter has set out to map the pluralist organization and content of the news media in the United Kingdom and the United States. It quickly becomes clear that remarkably little is known about large parts of the two national systems, although they are probably as well documented as any in the Western world. Despite a sometimes severe lack of information, two general conclusions emerge with a reasonable degree of certainty. First, ownership and control of the legacy mass media, including the news media, are increasingly concentrated in a few multinational multimedia conglomerates. This is well documented, and a clear trend of consolidation in some parts of the new digital media is also beginning to appear. Yet it cannot be assumed that the United Kingdom or the United States lacks a healthy measure of legacy news pluralism, because some of their largest news sources are internally pluralist.

In the United Kingdom, licensing laws require ITV and Channel 4 to deliver balanced, accurate, and impartial news, and the BBC follows voluntarily. All three are guided by professional standards of reporting and all three have news and current affairs programs that are noted for their hard national and international news that is balanced and reliable. There are also four national newspapers of record, although they have relatively small circulations. In the United States, content analysis shows the three national TV networks, a few national newspapers, and many local newspapers to be reasonably nonpartisan and neutral in their reporting of national politics, at least during election campaigns. In some countries, the neutrality, accuracy, and balance of TV and radio news are the result of state regulation in the public interest; in others they seem to result partly from market conditions and partly from professional standards and integrity. Nevertheless, and in accordance with the hostile media effect, these news sources are criticized by the left in politics for being right-wing and by the right for being too liberal and left-wing.

Because internally pluralist news sources in the United Kingdom and United States are both public and commercial, we cannot assume that the commercial media are always and necessarily biased in news reporting, and neither should we assume that a competitive commercial market is the only or best way of engineering a pluralist news system. It seems the figures on concentration of ownership and control do not tell us much about content pluralism of the news media. In Denmark, the public sector accounts for 60 percent of the TV market, which means that the country has a far better, more reliable, and more impartial source of news than the highly commercial system of Italy.

The second conclusion about media pluralism concerns the number and variety of digital news sources. Precise numbers are not known and perhaps never will be, but the total number of free online TV channels, radio stations, newspapers, magazines, political blogs, and associated political websites runs into the tens of thousands, perhaps the hundreds of thousands, even taking into account rapid turnover, ghost sites, dormant sites, and reserved addresses. Most TV channels and radio stations and many newspapers and magazines are available on the Internet. Many have little or no political content, and some of those that do address politics have paywalls, but even so web news sources number in the tens of thousands and cover just about every country and language in the world and virtually every political event and topic from almost every political viewpoint.

The modern news system is pluralist to a degree undreamed of in the past. Pluralist theory emerged in the mid-nineteenth century when there were a few dozen producers of comparatively expensive newspapers, magazines, and political tracts and pamphlets, most with limited audiences. Newspapers used to be the main or only source of news for a vast majority of the public in the United Kingdom, but they were expensive to produce, heavily taxed, and cumbersome to distribute. The *Times,* with daily sales of some 40,000 in 1850, controlled 80 percent of the national market.[48] Even now, when sales have fallen consistently over the past 50 years, in the United Kingdom more than 7 million people buy a national daily paper, most of which have online editions that tally some half a million visitors a day. The United Kingdom has another 1,500 regional newspapers, some with circulations in the hundreds of thousands, approximately half with online editions. And to these have been added online radio and TV news, plus political webpages that are uncountable but extraordinarily diverse in content and origin. Not all of these are free to access, but costs for producers and consumers are lower by far in real terms than the cost of the *Times* in 1850. If it is true that pluralist news media systems minimize the power of producers and maximize the power of consumers, then consumers have never had it so good or been so powerful.

This conclusion is subject to a qualification of huge importance. It refers to the number and variety of news sources that are available, not to the number or variety that are actually used by the average citizen. As the folk saying goes, you can lead a horse to water but you can't make it drink, and the fact that we now have a hyperpluralist news media system does not mean that citizens take advantage of it. The news diets of British and American citizens are the subject of the next chapter.

Appendix 10.1: UK Media Organization and Political Content

Reliable, up-to-date figures for some aspects of the news media system are hard to come by, and there are many gaps and unknowns, particularly where the web is concerned, but also for parts of the legacy media. Some of the available figures have to be treated with caution, partly because of different definitions and partly because they include or exclude different things. For example, the numbers for TV channels may include or exclude high definition (HD) and time-shift versions of the same programs, and the numbers for radio stations may or may not include booster, translator, and dormant stations. There is a fairly precise figure for the number of websites in the world, but it usually includes parked, dormant, and reserved addresses. We can only guess at the political content of the web, however politics may be defined. The following data are the best that could be found across a large number of sources, but some are estimates or guesstimates.

Television

In 2016, Ofcom issued a total of 1,293 national TV licenses, most of them for cable (1,038) and digital terrestrial stations (206).[49] The BBC has 9 national TV services, not including HD versions, and 15 regional windows, plus the Red Button service for extra programs and features. Its commercial subsidiary BBC WorldWide operates another 13 channels and co-owns with other broadcasters 3 stations operating in the United Kingdom and abroad. According to one website, there are more than 480 digital terrestrial, satellite, cable, and International Protocol TV stations in the United Kingdom, including 20 or so dedicated to news that originates from abroad (China, India, Nigeria, United States, Qatar), but this list does not include Internet sources of news.[50]

Five TV channels account for just over three-quarters of national audiences, with BBC1 and ITV1 taking about a third and a fifth, respectively, of the daily total TV audience.[51] The two main national TV stations of the BBC had a combined audience share of 36.5 percent, and one commercial group, ITV plc, controls 11 TV channels with 19.6 percent of the audience. Two companies control many of the most popular cable channels.

As cross-media ownership rules have been relaxed, a few companies have taken major interests in two or three markets, notably Newscorp (newspapers, TV, and radio), the *Daily Mail,* General Trust (national and regional newspapers, radio), and Granada (radio, TV, and publishing).[52]

A few popular TV channels are important because they are where the great majority of the population gets its news, but a rather different picture emerges from the TV channels dedicated to news. The MAVISE database of the European Audiovisual Observatory identifies 347 TV channels in the world dedicated to news, of which 214 are located in Europe. The numbers do not include local, business, or parliamentary channels.[53] According to the MAVISE data, 620 international, national, and regional TV channels in Europe were available in the United Kingdom in 2013 (some of them time-shift channels or HD duplicates), of which 25 are dedicated to news and business. This does not include "generalist" channels that may also broadcast the news regularly. The 20 or so dedicated news channels from outside Europe include Al Jazeera, Bloomberg, CCTV (China), CNBC Europe, eNCA Africa, EuroNews, Fox News, France24, RT (Moscow), NDTV (Delhi), NHK (Japan), and CNN. The UK market is notable for the number of Arabic, Asian, Chinese, Indian, and Pakistani channels it produces.[54]

The BBC has the largest and most comprehensive news coverage of the TV stations in Britain. Besides its national mainstream channels with their regular news programs, it operates 15 regional windows, which have larger-than-average audiences for their regional news programs than the national ones. The regional programs are broadcast twice a day plus a weekly current affairs program. Their license contracts require them to "engage with the local democratic process" and "facilitate civic understanding and fair and well-informed debate through coverage of local news and current affairs programmes."[55] BBC Scotland, BBC Wales, and BBC Northern Ireland have their own news slots, and BBC News is a rolling 24-hour television news network shared with BBC World News. Parliament has its own special BBC channel, covering the two Houses and its Select Committees; the Scottish Parliament and the Assemblies of London, Northern Ireland, and Wales; the European Parliament; and the annual conferences of the main political parties and the Trades Union Congress (TUC). The BBC also contributes to the Welsh-language S4C; partners with Alba, a part-time channel in Scottish Gaelic; and has a wholly owned commercial subsidiary (BBC Worldwide) company with channels in the United States, Canada, the Nordic countries, and Japan and broadcasts in Arabic, Persian, and Hindi.

The second-largest television network, ITV, is a network of regional services that also broadcasts news and other programs across the whole network. It has national and regional news with large audiences and a variety of local and national news programs. Like the BBC, it does not editorialize or carry political advertising and is required by its license to produce full, impartial, and accurate news. It carries the same party political broadcasts and election broadcasts as the BBC under strict regulations.

Channel 4 was launched as an alternative to mainstream TV channels with a special mission to serve tastes and interests not generally catered to by other UK broadcasters, including ethnic, language, and sexual minorities.[56] Its programs include a daily peak-time news program of 30 minutes, political documentaries and analysis, and political comedy.

Over 40 domestic TV channels cater specifically to minority ethnic and linguistic groups, including Afro-Caribbeans, Arabs, Bangladeshis, Chinese, Greeks, Indians, Poles, Hungarians, Romanians, Kurds, and many Asian stations.[57]

There are also specialist TV news channels devoted to local government, business and finance, the health services, and the armed forces. More than 20 other TV channels are dedicated to news, including Sky News, Star News, Al Jazeera, Bloomberg, CCTV (Chinese), CNBC Europe, eNCA Africa, EuroNews, Fox News, France24, RT (Moscow), NDTV (Delhi), NHK (Japan), and CNN.

Print

One source lists 23 daily papers in the United Kingdom, 13 Sunday papers, 10 non-English-language titles, 80 regional dailies, and 690 regional weeklies.[58] Of the approximately 1,300 regional and local papers in the United Kingdom, 91 are paid daily and Sunday editions, 491 paid weeklies, and 420 free weeklies.[59]

About 15 million people buy a paper every day, mostly one of the 11 national titles. Three companies control 70 percent of their daily sales, and five account for 92 percent of daily and 80 percent of Sunday circulation. Four companies have 448 regional and local titles and a readership of more than 20 million, but there are another 130 publishers in the market.[60] Ownership concentration and regional monopolies are increasing.[61] Many local areas have no paper, and one paper has a monopoly in a third of them.[62] As newspaper sales, budgets, and advertising revenues decline, the press relies increasingly on a handful of news agencies.

More than 8,000 magazines are published in the United Kingdom, including business, professional and occupational titles, consumer magazines, newspaper supplements, and academic journals. The 400 members of the Periodical Publishers Association control about 2,300 magazines and 80 percent of market turnover.[63]

Besides the national and regional press, there is a long tail of local and community papers. Scotland has 150 and there are between 50 and 60 Welsh-language papers. Northern Ireland has six daily papers, including one in Gaelic, and 50 local papers. Many of these are not controlled by the conglomerates. The UK as a whole has papers for Catholics, Jews, Protestants, Muslims, Baptists, Christian Scientists, and Zoroastrians as well as for children, seniors, and students. The Commission for Racial Equality lists 103 ethnic minority newspapers and periodicals published in 12 languages for more than 25 different ethnic, national, or religious groups in the United Kingdom.

British political magazines cover politics of the left, right, center, nationalist, and green persuasions, and there are others for satire, political ideas, the homeless population, the study of parapolitics, and most of the regions and continents of the globe. These include *New Left Review, New Statesman, The Week, Private Eye, Prospect, Spiked, Spectator, Red Pepper, The Internationalist, Liberal, The Irish Democrat, The Socialist, Solidarity, Big Issue, Morning Star, Socialist Appeal, Peace News, Socialist Worker,* and *Weekly Worker.* One source lists 180 political magazines from all over the world, though they are mainly English-language publications.[64]

Radio

In 2015, a total of 676 radio licenses were issued by Ofcom to UK radio stations, covering analogue FM and ASM (316), community (265), digital, and multiplex.[65] The BBC has 46 national and regional stations across the United Kingdom and Channel Islands. In addition, there are 325 local commercial stations and 270 community stations, most for local areas and some for military bases, motor racing circuits and prisons, and a further 28 day-restricted services.[66] Schools and universities operate over 70 stations, and there are 200 under the umbrella of the Hospital Broadcasting Association.

Some commercial stations share their programming, so the number of content options is less than the number of stations.[67] Nevertheless, like television and print, there is concentrated ownership and control in the commercial radio market, where seven financial groups control 86 percent of the market, and the two largest (Bauer and Global) account for 32 percent (37 million) of all listening hours.[68] This does not apply to the 270 stations of the community sector that are run by independent bodies.

Most radio stations do not broadcast much news or comment, but the association for commercial radio stations states that each of its 348 members provides an average of 22 three-minute news bulletins a day, with a concentration during breakfast peak-time listening hours.[69] Three-minute bulletins are no more than headlines and news flashes, but local commercial radio claims an audience of 35 million a week.

The BBC has 57 national and regional stations serving diverse audiences and broadcasting in Welsh, Gaelic, and Asian languages, and all broadcasting regular news and current affairs programs.[70] BBC World Service broadcasts news and analysis in 27 languages, and Radio 4, Radio 5 Live, the Asian Network, and Bloomberg Live Radio have long news and discussion programs. There are another dozen or so other news and talk stations with regular coverage of news and current affairs.

Local radio stations cover every county and large city in the country, many towns, large and small, and many local communities. There are also radio stations for universities, the military, hospitals, commercial businesses, sports, immigrants, comedy, people who are blind and partially sighted, and, of course, the radio industry itself. At any given time, there are 10 to 20 radio stations for ethnic language and religious groups, including multilingual news stations, although there is constant change and turnover.[71]

Ofcom presents a succinct account of the local media landscape in Britain, noting the heterogeneity of its regional, local, and community-level operators, some small, some large, run by commercial and public organizations, media trusts, local government, and individuals, with few providers operating across more than one platform.[72]

Web

Reliable figures for the net are most difficult to find. The numbers are often huge and some are matters of speculation and impressions. Parts of the system are large, highly decentralized, independent, and privately owned, and there is no central collection of data. Turnover is sometimes rapid, and in some cases the evidence is fragmented and minimal.

One thing is certain, however. The web makes available an enormous amount of news and opinion from every part of the globe and covers just about every political viewpoint. More than 20 dedicated news channels are available on TV in the United Kingdom, and many more are streamed over the Internet. The website Tunein.com lists almost a thousand news and talk radio stations available from all over the world. The number of print newspapers in the world that publish online is so large as to be virtually uncountable, but one source shows that the United Kingdom alone has about 880 daily and weekly papers online.[73] Another 90 percent of commercial radio stations stream online.[74]

News aggregator sites that digest and link the reader to other news sources include Expatica, Dods: Politics Home, Spiked, Yahoo!, NewsNow, and Google News. Some of the larger news websites are heavily dependent on aggregated news from other sources. And then there is the incalculably huge number and constantly changing variety of websites and blogs that cover just about every political viewpoint under the sun. Like the TV, radio, and print markets, important parts of the web are beginning to cluster around a few giant companies such as Wikipedia, AOL, Yahoo!, Google, and Facebook. But this leaves an extremely long tail of small, specialist, independent webpages written by small organizations or individuals.

As well as the 20 British daily and Sunday papers available on the web, there are 25 domestic news websites. Specialist news websites include Orange News, BBC, Reuters, The Week, The Voice, AOL UK, and *Huffington Post*'s UK edition. News aggregators include Expatica, ePolitix, Dods: Politics Home, Spiked, Yahoo!, NewsNow, The Week, and Google News. It is difficult to obtain an accurate number of online newspapers in the world, partly because there are so many, turnover is high, and the number is increasing, but they come from every country in the world and run into the tens of thousands.[75] To give an impression, Ireland, Scotland, and Wales contribute 370 to the global total and Iceland another 25.[76] The same problem applies to global online TV channels, but one source lists 75 English-language news channels (excluding the BBC's) and another 135 in other languages.[77]

Nine of the 10 most popular news websites are not digital natives but online versions of legacy national daily newspapers and the BBC. In March 2015, 10 of the United Kingdom's top news websites had a total digital audience of 150 million unique visitors, of which two digital natives, *BuzzFeed* and *Huffington Post,* accounted for 18 million, or 12 percent of the total. The other eight were legacy platforms consisting of seven old media newspapers plus the BBC. Yahoo! is a digital native, but, like many news aggregators, much of its news content is sourced from the legacy media.[78]

One complaint about the Internet is that it has failed to deliver the unorthodox, innovative, critical political content that was predicted for it in the early years. However, one list of the top 10 political blogs in the United Kingdom describes them variously as "anti-establishment," "feisty," "independent," "mischievous," "waspish," "de-bunking," and "robust"—all part of the style of blogs in general.[79]

Appendix 10.2: US Media Organization and Political Content

The Federal Communications Commission (FCC) issued 31,445 broadcasting licenses in 2016, but more than 10,000 were for translator and booster licenses. These increase the accessibility of news for consumers, but they do not add to its diversity. Of the remaining 20,000 FCC licenses, 15,491 were for AM and FM radio stations and 1,782 for TV stations. Of the radio licenses, 26.4 percent were for FM educational stations and the rest commercial. Of the TV licenses, 17 percent were for educational and the rest for commercial stations. Another 3,800 licenses were issued for small, low-power, and local TV stations run mainly by local groups, churches, communities, and small businesses or individuals.[80] It is not known how much political news and commentary these stations produce, but it seems reasonable to suppose that most have rather little and a small minority a lot. Most are music stations that may or may not broadcast news headlines at intervals. In this respect, local TV and radio in the United Kingdom and United States are probably rather alike.

TV

There are three main national TV news networks, 35 news TV channels (which also stream live on the Internet[81]), plus 10 national and 5 local cable news channels. In addition, another 350 public TV stations broadcast regular news and current affairs programs, as do 15 local news TV stations run mainly by government, community, and public affairs bodies.[82] As in the United Kingdom, local and regional TV is more important than that of the national networks, with 82 percent of the population getting some or a lot of news from local TV; 76 percent getting it from national organizations; 77 percent from friends, family, and acquaintances; and 34 percent from social media.[83] Of approximately 3,000 mainly domestic TV channels, the average American pays for a bundle of 180 channels but actually watches only 16 to 20 of them.[84] Fourteen networks broadcast in Spanish; the Public Broadcasting Service (PBS) and 28 others broadcast in English and Spanish. There are about 38 religious channels.

PBS does not approach the BBC in its number of channels and stations and their audience shares, but it has a network of 350 TV stations that serves all 50 states. Like the BBC, it is renowned for the quality of its programs, especially *PBS NewsHour*. In 2016, PBS was rated for the 13th consecutive year as the most trustworthy institution among all nationally known organizations.[85] Yet, its 4 million unique visitors to its news program in January 2015 compares with NBC's 56 million.[86]

Much news content is syndicated throughout the TV system, often by different outlets of the same organization, but sometimes by different organizations sharing the same source, usually a news agency. The effects are the same as that of radio translators and boosters—they increase news saturation, but not its pluralist diversity. We know little about how much news is syndicated within and between TV channels or radio stations. Although syndicated news does nothing for the diversity of news, it may be of benefit if, as some studies find, local TV news in the United States is internally diverse and relatively bias free. However, in 2018 the Sinclair Broadcast Group forced its 200 local TV stations to read the same Trumpian report about the dangerous spread of fake news.[87] At this point, warnings about centralized bias in the commercial news media are well taken.

Radio

Figures for the number of radio stations in the United States range from 10,322 to about 15,470.[88] Even the FCC has no precise way of keeping up-to-date. But whatever the particular number, there are an awful lot. Texas is listed as having 1,072; California, 970; Florida, 648; and even Wyoming, the least populated state, has 187.[89] These are divided into commercial and noncommercial stations, with three commercial companies—Cumulus, Clear Channel Communications, and CBS—owning almost 1,500 stations.

This leaves a large and growing number of independent radio stations serving specialist, niche markets. The FCC issued 4,096 licenses for educational radio stations in 2016. These are independent and locally owned and run, particularly low-power FM stations that are inexpensive to operate. National Public Radio (NPR) is not a radio station and does not own any, but the programs it produces can be heard on 860 stations across the country.[90] These include two daily news programs, extended coverage of special events and elections, and breaking news. Nine hundred NPR member stations and 28 national cable and satellite news channels broadcast in English and Spanish.[91] About two-thirds of the radio stations are affiliated with colleges and universities, some working jointly with public stations.

Although most of the growing numbers of news and talk radio stations are devoted to sports, weather, and local affairs, many of them have news headlines on the hour and other short news bulletins. Seventy-five stations broadcast morning news programs.[92]

One source states that 883 US stations broadcast in a total of 35 foreign languages, and another lists 61 broadcasting to Asians, 938 Christian stations, 473 for college students, 109 ethnic stations, and 61 dedicated to business news.[93] Figures for news-only radio stations vary greatly from a reliable Nielsen figure of 31, to 616 for news and talk, to over a thousand, which are also likely to be for news and talk.[94] News and talk is a popular form of radio, second only to country music.[95] In addition, thousands of foreign radio stations are available online covering virtually every country in the world—including North Korea. There are, for example, 70 country and subnational stations streaming from Europe, special stations for Albania, the Vatican, the Azores, and the Shetland Isles among them.

Print

The print media in the United States are in decline, but one source reports a total of 17,256 print publishing establishments in 2016, with 7,264 for newspapers, 6,486 for periodicals, 2,622 for books, 786 for directory and mail list publications, and 814 for other.[96] In 2007, there were 400 publishers of online books, 91 for self-publishing, 44 for audiobooks, and 18 for Kindle. Whereas the sales of mainstream political journals and magazines in hard copy (e.g., *Time, Economist, New Yorker, Atlantic*) are falling, the number of self-published print and e-books has risen from 85,000 in 2008 to almost 787,000 in 2016, and the sales of on-demand titles produced by reprint houses and self-publishing companies have increased from just under a million in 2009 to almost 2.8 million in 2010.[97] Up-to-date figures for books published in the United States are hard to come by, but in 2013 the total was approximately 305,000 new titles. Sales in 2015 topped 650 million, and for e-books it was more than 200 million. Once again, only a small minority of all books and periodicals, including journals and magazines, are concerned with politics, but the absolute numbers are not insubstantial.

The number of newspapers in the United States is shrinking, but there are still around 1,500 dailies and over 3,300 papers of other kinds. Estimated circulation was 31 million on weekdays and 34 million on Sundays in 2018, both down about 10 percent from the previous year. Six companies own 228 titles with a combined weekly circulation averaging 141 million in 2018.[98] Average unique visitors to the top 50 newspaper websites leveled out from the previous year at 11.5 million a month. A few companies such as Gannet, Lee Enterprises, and MediaNews each own upward of 50 local and regional titles with daily circulations in the millions.[99] The total number of newspaper newsroom employees declined from 71,640 in 2004 to 39,210 in 2016.[100] As in the United Kingdom, the number of cities with competing papers has shrunk considerably. In 2001, only 21 had "true competition among daily newspapers." Of the 6,500 periodicals, four companies owned 80 best-selling titles, with sales of $73 million.[101]

At the same time the specialist market has expanded exponentially, with at least 127 papers for Christian readers, 75 for Jewish readers, 149 for Hispanic readers, 149 for African American readers, and 193 for military members.[102] There are 6,579 community weekly papers (both subscriber and free).[103] Declining newspaper sales have led specialist ethnic publications into magazine and newsletter production in hard copy and electronic forms. Two websites list 154 and 99 "alternative" newspapers and weeklies.[104] Another lists 44 news and political magazines published, variously described as left-leaning, left, leftist, progressive left, liberal, right-wing, conservative, traditional conservative, neo-conservative, libertarian, alternative, cerebral, muckraking, and in-depth. There is also a news aggregator magazine, *Utne Reader,* that reprints a combination of new ideas and fresh perspectives from 2,000 other media sources.[105]

Digital

As in other countries, digital technology has transformed the communications system of the United States from top to bottom. Digital technology has opened up an entirely new national and international array of news sources. One company offers 270 international (i.e., from outside the United States) channels broadcasting in 26 languages.[106] According to one source, quoting the US State Department, there are currently nearly 800 media outlets from 113 countries operating in the United States, and many people in Washington, DC, are now said to turn to Al Jazeera, Deutsche Welle, France 24, Euronews, and China Central Television to get their foreign news.[107] Washington is not Slippery Rock or Lake Wobegon, but the point is that these TV stations are there if residents of Slippery Rock and Lake Wobegon want to use them.

In addition, thousands of foreign radio stations are available online covering most countries and regions of the world. One website offers links to dozens of TV channels, radio stations, and podcasts covering world and regional news, business and finance, and general news.[108]

The web provides its own special difficulties for research, with its explosion and turnover of sites, its ghost sites, parked and dormant sites, bought Twitter followers, and fake links, clicks, and followers.[109] Nevertheless, domestic and foreign TV news channels, radio stations, and newspapers run into the thousands, probably tens of thousands. One estimate has blogs of all kinds increasing from 4.3 million in 2004 to around 133 million by 2008, with about 120,000 added each day.[110] Only a small minority of these are political, but even so the weblog portal BlogCatalog lists approximately 4,800 political blogs, not all American.[111]

Notes

1. Ward, Fueg, and D'Armo 2004.
2. Quiggin 2012.
3. See, for example, D'Ancona 2017: 67.
4. Ward 2005: 3. Italics in the original.
5. Hesmondhalgh 2001.
6. A similar point about newspapers and radio was made by Paul Lazarsfeld in 1942, when he observed, "Radio has certainly provided a number of new enjoyments. In the communication of ideas and information however, where it can be compared to reading, it has, by and large, not created a new situation but only diversified the ways people interested in these communications can get more of them." I am grateful to Samuel Popkin for drawing my attention to this quotation.
7. "How Americans Get Their News," American Press Institute, March 17, 2014, https://www.americanpressinstitute.org/publications/reports/survey-research/how-americans-get-news/.
8. "Nielsen Audio: Radio—Streaming—Podcast—Measurement," Nielsen, http://www.nielsen.com/audio; "Q1 RAJAR Figures 2017," Mostly Media, May 24, 2017, http://www.mostlymedia.co.uk/q1-rajar-figures-2017/; "All Radio Listening" (infographic), Rajar, Quarter 1, 2018, https://www.rajar.co.uk/docs/news/RAJAR_DataRelease_InfographicQ12018.pdf. As usual with media statistics, estimated audience sizes vary from one source to another, but they all attest to radio's popularity.
9. Media Reform Coalition, *The Elephant in the Room: New Report on UK Media Ownership* (London: Media Reform Coalition, April 24, 2014), http://www.mediareform.org.uk/media-ownership/the-elephant-in-the-room.
10. Newman et al. 2018: 10.
11. Wu 2011.
12. Jones 2009; Underwood 2001.
13. House of Lords Select Committee on Communications 2008: 32. See also Smith and Tambini 2012: 36.
14. See, for example, Curran and Seaton 2010; Ward, Fueg, and D'Armo 2004; Doyle 2002; Doyle and Vick 2005; K. Voltmer, *Structures of Diversity of Press and Broadcasting Systems: The Institutional Context of Public Communication in Western Democracies* (Berlin: WZB, 2000), http://edoc.vifapol.de/opus/volltexte/2009/1965/pdf/iii00_201.pdf.
15. Ofcom 2011: 127.
16. "BBC's Global Audience Rises to 376 m," June 22, 2018, https://www.bbc.co.uk/mediacentre/latestnews/2018/bbc-global-audience.
17. "Statistics on BBC Webservers 7th July 2005," BBC, https://web.archive.org/web/20060221090846/http://www.bbc.co.uk:80/feedback/07July_Statistics.shtml.
18. Moore 2010.
19. Channel 4 Television, *Channel Four Television Corporation 2011 Report on Compliance with the General Equality Duty* (London: Channel 4 Television, January 2012), http://www.channel4.com/media/documents/corporate/Channel_4_Equality_Duty_Compliance_Report_2011.pdf.
20. Mutz and Martin 2001.
21. Radio Centre, *Action Stations* (London: Radio Centre, 2013), https://www.radiocentre.org/files/action_stations_web.pdf.
22. Ofcom 2009: 22.

23. Hindman 2009.

24. R. Edmonds, "New Research Finds 92 Percent of Time Spent on News Consumption Is Still on Legacy Platforms," Poynter, May 13, 2013, https://www.poynter.org/news/new-research-finds-92-percent-time-spent-news-consumption-still-legacy-platforms.

25. M. Nunez, "Want to Know What Facebook Really Thinks of Journalists? Here's What Happened When It Hired Some," Gizmodo, May 3, 2016; A. Hern, "Facebooks News Saga Reminds Us Humans Are Biased by Design," *The Guardian* (Manchester), May 13, 2016, https://www.theguardian.com/technology/2016/may/13/newsfeed-saga-unmasks-the-human-face-of-facebook.

26. T. Helm, "The 10 Best Political Blogs," *The Guardian* (Manchester), March 20, 2010, http://www.guardian.co.uk/culture/2010/mar/21/10-best-political-blogs.

27. See, for example, Bagdikian 2004; McChesney 1999; Curran and Seaton 2010; Ward 2005; Doyle 2002, 2007: 142; "Who Owns the UK Media?" Media Reform Coalition, October 2015, http://www.mediareform.org.uk/who-owns-the-uk-media; F. O'Grady, "Media Ownership: Power and Influence in the Hands of the Few," National Union of Journalists, April 23, 2014, https://www.nuj.org.uk/news/media-ownership-power-and-influence-belongs-to-few/; Schlosberg 2016; Gerbner, Mowlana, and Schiller 2018; "Resources," Columbia Journalism Review, https://www.cjr.org/resources; Media Reform Coalition, *Elephant in the Room*; Miller 2002.

28. Dalton, Beck, and Huckfeldt 1998; Beck et al. 2002.

29. Beck et al. 2002: 62; Dalton, Beck, and Huckfeldt 1998: 123.

30. Prior 2013: 103–104.

31. D'Alessio and Allen 2000: 103.

32. Schudson 1995: 185.

33. Bennett and Iyengar 2008: 723.

34. On the difficulties of researching the political content of the Internet, see D. Karpf, "Social Science Research Methods in Internet Time," working paper, Rutgers University School of Communication and Information, New Brunswick, NJ, http://sciencepolicy.colorado.edu/students/envs_5720/karpf_2012.pdf; "Digital Circulation Figures Are an Absolute Mess," Poynter, May 5, 2014, http://www.poynter.org/2014/digital-circulation-figures-are-an-absolute-mess/250218/.

35. "Top 15 Most Popular News Websites May 2018," eBiz, May 2018, http://www.ebizmba.com/articles/news-websites.

36. "In Changing News Landscape, Even Television Is Vulnerable," Pew Research Center, September 27, 2012, http://www.people-press.org/2012/09/27/in-changing-news-landscape-even-television-is-vulnerable/.

37. Z. Fox, "Top 10 U.S. Newspapers Ranked by Digital Circulation," Mashable, August 6, 2013, https://mashable.com/2013/08/06/newspapers-digital-subscriptions/?europe=true.

38. "Press Widely Criticized, but Trusted More Than Other Information Sources," Pew Research Center, September 22, 2011, http://www.people-press.org/2011/09/22/press-widely-criticized-but-trusted-more-than-other-institutions/.

39. Nunez, "Want to Know What Facebook Really Thinks of Journalists?"; Hern, "Facebook's News Saga Reminds Us Humans Are Biased by Design."

40. Massing 2015.

41. Massing 2015, 2016.

42. Fenton 2010: 565. Italics in the original.

43. Wu 2011.

44. Taplin 2017; "The paidContent 50: The Most Successful Digital Media Companies in the U.S.," Gigaom, January 31, 2011, https://gigaom.com/2011/01/31/the-most-successful-digital-companies. The "move fast and break things" people are also known as the "disruptive innovators."

45. "International News Channels," Wikipedia, last updated November 15, 2018, https://en.wikipedia.org/wiki/International_news_channels.

46. "Top 15 Most Popular News Websites," Ebiz/MBA, January 2019, http://www.ebizmba.com/articles/news-websites.

47. "List of Newspapers in the United Kingdom by Circulation: 20th Century," Infogalactic, last updated May 9, 2016, https://infogalactic.com/info/List_of_newspapers_in_the_United_Kingdom_by_circulation#20th_century.

48. "Look Up TV Broadcast Licensees," Ofcom, August 6, 2018, http://licensing.ofcom.org.uk/tv-broadcast-licences/current-licensees/.

49. "List of Television Stations in the United Kingdom," Wikipedia, last updated December 9, 2018, https://en.wikipedia.org/wiki/List_of_television_stations_in_the_United_Kingdom#NBCUniversal_International_Networks.

50. J. Plunkett, "BBC1 and Channel 5 Increase Their Audience Share in 2012," *The Guardian* (Manchester), January 10, 2013, http://www.theguardian.com/media/2013/jan/10/bbc1-channel-5-increase-audience-share.

51. The empirical details in this paragraph are taken from Ward 2005: 197–217.

52. MAVISE Database, http://mavise.obs.coe.int.

53. One provider offers a package of 20—FilmOn (https://www.filmon.com/group/news-tv).

54. Kevin 2015: 3.

55. *Channel Four Television Corporation 2011 Report on Compliance with the General Equality Duty.*

56. Georgiou n.d.

57. "UK Media Directory," Hold the Front Page, http://www.holdthefrontpage.co.uk/directory/.

58. Media Reform Coalition, *Elephant in the Room.*

59. "Regional UK Newspaper Groups & Companies," http://www.wrx.zen.co.uk/regions2.htm.

60. "UK Regional Newspapers," Magforum, http://www.magforum.com/papers/regional.htm.

61. Media Reform Coalition, *Elephant in the Room*; http://www.mediareform.org.uk/wp-content/uploads/2015/10/Who_owns_the_UK_media-report_plus_appendix1.pdf.

62. T. Quinn, "News Magazines: 'I See a Whale,'" Magforum, http://www.magforum.com/news_magazines.htm.

63. "List of Political Magazines," Wikipedia, last updated November 25, 2018, https://en.wikipedia.org/wiki/List_of_political_magazines.

64. http://licensing.ofcom.org.uk/.

65. "Community Radio Stations," Ofcom, http://www.ofcom.org.uk/static/radiolicensing/html/radio-stations/community/community-main.htm.

66. "Who Owns Which British Radio Station?," Media.Info, https://media.info/uk/radio/stations/by-owner.

67. Media Reform Coalition, *Who Owns the UK Media?* (London: Media Reform Coalition, n.d.), http://www.mediareform.org.uk/wp-content/uploads/2015/10/Who_owns_the_UK_media-report_plus_appendix1.pdf.

68. Radio Centre n.d.: 38.

69. BBC Sounds, Stations, http://www.bbc.co.uk/sounds/stations.

70. Georgiou n.d.

71. Ofcom 2009: 22.

72. "Newspaper Websites," Hold the Front Page, https://www.holdthefrontpage.co.uk/directory/newspaperwebsites/; http://www.wrx.zen.co.uk/soupress.htm.

73. Radio Centre, *Action Stations.*

74. See, for example, the listing of broadcast media in the US Central Intelligence Agency's *World Factbook*: https://www.cia.gov/library/publications/the-world-factbook/fields/2213.html.

75. "Icelandic Newspapers," OnlineNewspapers.com, http://www.onlinenewspapers.com/iceland.htm. This does not include *The Onion, Weekly World News, Anti-pedia, Private*

Eye, News Thump, News That Matters Not, The Spoof, and *Le Canard Enchaîné* and a few other similar publications.

76. "Most Watched TV Channels," wwiTV.com, https://wwitv.com/portal.htm.

77. Media Reform Coalition, *Elephant in the Room.*

78. Helm, "The 10 Best Political Blogs."

79. https://www.fcc.gov/edocs/search-results?t=advanced&titleText=broadcast%20station%20totals.

80. "Most Watched TV Channels," wwiTV.com.

81. "PBS Member Stations," PBS, http://www.pbs.org/about/about-pbs/stations/; "About PBS," PBS, http://www.pbs.org/about/about-pbs/overview/; "Most Watched TV Channels," wwiTV.com.

82. A. Mitchell, E. Shearer, J. Gottfried, and M. Barthel, "2. Trust and Accuracy," Pew Research Center, July 7, 2016, http://www.journalism.org/2016/07/07/trust-and-accuracy/.

83. J. Bachman, "The Ugly Numbers Behind Unbundled Cable TV," Bloomberg, December 6, 2013, http://www.businessweek.com/articles/2013-12-06/the-ugly-numbers-behind-unbundled-cable-tv.

84. PBS, *Today's PBS: Trusted, Valued, Essential 2017* (Arlington, VA: PBS, 2017), http://bento.cdn.pbs.org/hostedbento-prod/filer_public/value-pbs/Infographics/PBS2017TrustBroch_R10_singlepgs.pdf.

85. Pew Research Center, *State of the News Media, 2015* (Washington, DC: Pew Research Center, 2015), http://www.journalism.org/2015/04/29/public-broadcasting-fact-sheet-2015/.

86. J. Fortin and J. E. Bromwich, "Sinclair Made Dozens of Local News Anchors Recite the Same Script," *New York Times,* April 2, 2018, https://www.nytimes.com/2018/04/02/business/media/sinclair-news-anchors-script.html.

87. "Find Radio Stations by US State," Radio-Locator, http://www.radio-locator.com/cgi-bin/page?page=states; J. Waits, "Number of Radio Stations in the U.S. Grows This Quarter According to FCC," Radio Survivor, October 14, 2015, http://www.radiosurvivor.com/2015/10/14/number-of-radio-stations-in-the-u-s-grows-this-quarter-according-to-fcc/; "United States Press, Media, TV, Radio, Newspapers," Press Reference, http://www.pressreference.com/Sw-Ur/United-States.html.

88. "Find Radio Stations by US State," Radio-Locator.

89. "How NPR Works," NPR, https://web.archive.org/web/20100901113039; http://www.npr.org/about/nprworks.html.

90. "About PBS: Overview," PBS, http://www.pbs.org/about/about-pbs/overview/.

91. "America's Morning News," Tune In, http://tunein.com/radio/options/Americas-Morning-News-p201228/.

92. J. Keen, "Foreign-Language Radio Stations Provide Connection to Home," *USA Today,* June 16, 2011, http://usatoday30.usatoday.com/news/nation/2011-06-15-Foreign-language-radio-immigrants_n.htm. Most of the foreign-language radio stations are in Spanish, but around 150 of them are in other languages.

93. Pew Research Center, *State of the News Media, 2015*; USA News Radio; "Audio and Podcasting Fact Sheet," Pew Research Center, July 16, 2017, http://assets.pewresearch.org/wp-content/uploads/sites/13/2018/07/11183646/State-of-the-News-Media_2017-Archive.pdf; http://www.internet-radio.com/stations/talk/page30.

94. "Talk Radio Stations," Internet Radio, http://www.internet-radio.com/stations/talk/page30; "News/Talk Radio Stations," NewsLink, http://www.newslink.org/rneradi.html; "America's Morning News," Tune In.

95. "Economic Census: Industry Snapshots," US Census Bureau; Statista, https://www.statista.com/statistics/184543/establishments-in-us-print-publishing-by-sector-2007/; number of establishments in print publishing in the United States from 2007 to 2016, by sector, https://www.statista.com/statistics/184543/establishments-in-us-print-publishing-by-sector-2007; https://www.census.gov/econ/snapshots/index.php. Establishments are "a single physical location where business is conducted or where services

or industrial operations are performed," so these figures take no account of ownership and control.

96. "Number of Self-Published Books in the United States from 2008 to 2017, by Format," Statista, https://www.statista.com/statistics/249036/number-of-self-published -books-in-the-us-by-format/.

97. "2015 U.S. Book Industry Year-End Review," Nielsen, May 31, 2016, http://www .nielsen.com/us/en/insights/reports/2016/2015-us-book-industry-year-end-review.html.

98. "Newspapers Fact Sheet," Pew Research Center, June 13, 2018, http://www .journalism.org/fact-sheet/newspapers/.

99. "Newspapers Face a Challenging Calculus," Pew Research Center, February 26, 2009, stateofthemedia.org/media-ownership/newspapers/.

100. "Newspapers Fact Sheet," Pew Research Center, June 13, 2018, http://www .journalism.org/fact-sheet/newspapers/.

101. "United States Press, Media, TV, Radio, Newspapers," Press Reference.

102. "United States Press, Media, TV, Radio, Newspapers," Press Reference.

103. "United States Newspapers," 50States.com, http://www.50states.com/news /#.UybuP4VXu7g.

104. "Alternative News Media," Easy Media List, http://www.easymedialist .com/usa/alternative-newsweeklies.html; "Alternative Newspapers in United States," W3Newspapers, https://www.w3newspapers.com/usa/alternative/.

105. "News and Political Magazines," World-Newspapers.com, http://www.world -newspapers.com/news-magazine.html.

106. "International Channels," MyDish Dish Network, https://www.mydish.com /upgrades/international.

107. H. Rizvi, "Media: Foreign News Channels Drawing U.S. Viewers," Inter Press Service, January 29, 2010, http://www.ipsnews.net/2010/01/media-foreign-news-channels -drawing-us-viewers/.

108. "NPR Politics Podcast," Tune In, https://tunein.com/podcasts/Political-News /NPR-Politics-Podcast-p812883/?topicId=123025404.

109. The difficulties of researching the political content of the Internet are discussed by David Karpf ("Social Science Research Methods in Internet Time," working paper, Rutgers University School of Communication and Information, New Brunswick, NJ, http://sciencepolicy.colorado.edu/students/envs_5720/karpf_2012.pdf).

110. Davis 2009: 4.

111. BlogCatalog, http://www.blogcatalog.com/.

11

Audience Pluralism

There are serious dangers in a system in which individuals bypass general-interest intermediaries and restrict themselves to opinions and topics of their own choosing. In particular, I will emphasize the risks posed by any situation in which thousands or perhaps millions or even tens of millions of people are mainly listening to louder echoes of their own voices.
—C. R. Sunstein, Republic.com 2.0[1]

Media's greatest potential lies in its impersonal exposure of audiences to cross-cutting views, an essential form of communication in a highly pluralistic society. In order to sustain this benefit, however, news media must be structured so as to limit the public's capacity for selective exposure.
—D. C. Mutz and P. S. Martin,
*"Facilitating Communication Across Lines
of Political Difference: The Role of Mass Media"*[2]

The vast and diverse array of news media sources in Britain and the United States matters nothing if the average citizen does not make use of it. Therefore, the present chapter turns to the consumer demand side of pluralist media theory and to the vital but under-researched question of what use citizens make of the varied sources of news available to them. For a long time, the concern was mainly about how growing centralization of ownership and control of the media was providing too little choice and too much bias in the news, but the fragmented and diverse digital system provokes a different set of fears. The new system makes it possible for some people to avoid broadcast news altogether, but at the same time it is easier for others to confine themselves to news sources that reflect their own opinions and bias back to them, thus polarizing voters in isolated political camps. And although social websites could involve the younger generation in politics, there is also the possibility that they may do the opposite by focusing on social life, sports, music, and entertainment to the exclusion of the political.[3] On top of this, there is concern about the incivility of these sites and the way they have been used to try to manipulate elections and spread fake news.

This chapter is concerned with the use citizens make of the vast array of news sources available to them and to what extent they get a reasonably balanced diet of reliable and impartial news. Although these questions seem to be central to the idea of well-informed citizens and are a central but implicit part of pluralist theory, the news diets of the general population have not been much studied. A notable exception is the Fox News effect in the United States. There is also speculation about the impact of social websites, fake news, blogs, and chat rooms on political attitudes and behavior, but little systematic empirical research on the individuals who are exposed to them. Plausible speculation usually stops well short of trying to investigate and demonstrate effects.

It is unrealistic to expect most individuals to compare routinely the contents of a wide variety of different news media; indeed, the assumption that they will is a serious shortcoming of classic pluralist theory, but if the standard model of the social sciences applies to news attention, there is likely to be a normal distribution of news diets in the adult population. That is, the distribution of news diets across the general population is likely to repeat the bell curve of political activity, engagement, interest, and knowledge. News avoiders are likely to form a relatively small proportion at one end of the continuum, with another small percentage of news junkies at the other. The majority in the middle are likely to use one or two primary sources and, perhaps, occasionally additional ones. A growing percentage may be living in echo chambers of their own making. It should not be forgotten, however, that the news media are not the only source of news, nor are they necessarily the most influential.

Being a relatively new topic, research on audience pluralism has a number of pitfalls to deal with. Three stand out: lack of evidence; the over- and underreporting of news media attention; and the meaning of the word *news*. The chapter must start with these before moving on to substantive matters.

Problems of Research

Lack of Evidence
Some known unknowns about the structure and content of the pluralist media are listed in the previous chapter, but there are also large gaps in our knowledge of popular news consumption. Rather little is known about the news-gathering habits of the general public. How much attention do people pay to the political pages of their paper, if they read one, or to TV news, if

they watch it? Local and regional newspaper and radio stations are popular, but how much national and international news do they broadcast? Given the rising costs of news gathering and reporting, there is increasing reliance on syndicated news content that comes from one or a few sources that are used by a large number of outlets. For this reason, the Office of Communication (Ofcom) in the United Kingdom distinguishes between wholesale and retail news outlets, the wholesale measure being the better measure of news pluralism.[4] Another problem is that the content of the estimated 4,200 English-language political blogs is largely unresearched, with a few exceptions—as are the political contents of more than 200 social websites and their impact on their estimated 2.6 billion users.[5] Given the current concern, lack of information about social websites is a major difficulty for research.

Media technology and patterns of its use are changing rapidly, so research is often a step or two behind what is actually happening on the street.[6] In any case, it is more difficult to pin down the political effects of the new technology compared with the legacy media. For example, populist journalism has attracted research interest recently, but we know little about its impact.[7] Similarly, a good deal of evidence has been collected recently about who makes most use of digital news and about the amount and dissemination of fake news, but there is little research on their actual influence. According to one survey specialist, we know "surprisingly little about how people get news via social media, and how social media platforms might shape news consumption. Much of the current discussion is driven more by worry than by evidence."[8]

The size of the problem is indicated in Facebook's *Community Standards Enforcement Report* of May 2018, which revealed, for the first time, some numbers about Facebook's quality controls. Between January and March of that year, the company removed 583 million fake accounts, 837 million pieces of spam, 21 million pieces of adult nudity and sexual activity, 35 million pieces with violent content, and 25 million pieces of hate speech.[9] It suspended 200 apps suspected of data misuse.[10] It was also revealed that Russian propaganda had reached 126 million Facebook users, published more than 131,000 messages on Twitter, and uploaded over 1,000 videos on YouTube.[11] How much of this kind of material is available on an estimated 200 other social sites, not to mention other webpages, is unknown. Recent attempts to remove offensive and illegal material seem to be hit or miss, done in a great hurry, with clear and inconsistent criteria, and with poorly trained, low-paid staff in developing countries.

Over- and Underreporting

Markus Prior compared the results of survey-based self-reported exposure to national network news in the United States with Nielsen Media Research ratings based on "people meters." These are attached to the TV sets of a random sample of 5,000 US households and record who is watching what channel and program, so avoiding the worst problems of participant memory error and overestimates in self-reported data. Prior compared the Nielsen ratings with the National Annenberg Election Survey (NAES) of 2004, which asks random samples of US residents aged 18 years and older, "How many days in the past week did you watch national network news on TV?" specifying ABC, CBS, NBC, Fox News, and UPN News as answer choices.[12]

Nielsen ratings recorded between 30 million and 35 million watching the weekday evening news. The survey figure was between 85 million and 110 million, showing overreporting in the NAES on a huge scale. The 18- to 34-year-olds overreport by a factor of eight or more, but even the figures for older age groups are twice the Nielsen ratings. Prior concludes that there must be doubt about studies of media effects based on self-reported survey data.

Another Nielsen survey found that there is systematic underreporting of TV viewing in general because, it is suggested, this is a familiar activity that is taken for granted.[13] By the same token, it may be that use of new technology is overestimated and, because of social expectations, so also is the amount of attention paid to the political news.

The Meaning of News

One American survey asked respondents what type of news they followed "very closely."[14] The weather came top (52 percent), followed by crime (28 percent), sports (26 percent), and health (23 percent). Local government came in a poor sixth (21 percent) and politics/Washington news seventh (17 percent). International affairs was 10th (14 percent). Local, national, and international politics added together summed to the same figure as the weather's, 52 percent. Nonpolitical topics of news outnumber political ones by a factor of four. Similar results have been found in the United Kingdom, where weather and crime were the most popular news topics, and clearly nonpolitical topics were generally most popular.[15] Political scientists may assume that *news* means "news about politics," but most respondents to surveys seem to think differently. As one report on online news consumption and supply observed, "There is no consistent or comprehensive definition of news. It is not a homogeneous thing and what counts as news in online consumption may not fit even a loose definition."[16] Unfortunately, it is rare to find research that specifies what kind of news is being considered.

These three problems—lack of evidence, over- and underreporting of news media attention, and meaning of the word *news*—put serious difficulties in the way of a reliable attempt to map out audience pluralism. Nevertheless, some information allows for a rough-and-ready account of how many and what kinds of news sources are used by what kinds of people with what kinds of frequency. The rest of the chapter is given to this task. As in the previous chapter, this one focuses on the United Kingdom and the United States, for reasons of space and because they have some research to call upon.

Audience Pluralism: The United Kingdom

Recent evidence about the number and variety of news sources accessed by adults in the United Kingdom is provided by Ofcom's *News Consumption in the UK: 2016* report.[17] Covering television, radio, newspapers, and the web, and a sample of 2,894 UK people over the age of 16 years, the survey found that an average of 3.8 individual news sources are used across the four platforms. The figure varied little in the 2013–2016 period, and not much across demographic groups and geographical regions. The number 3.8 is composed of 42 percent using four or more sources, 14 percent using three, 21 percent using two, and 20 percent using only one. Most of those who used only one relied on the BBC. If a measure of attention to the news is based on a combination of the news sources used and the frequency of their use, then the BBC accounts for 42 percent of the total, compared with the next largest, ITN, with 11 percent.

The Ofcom report shows that the more news outlets an individual uses, the more likely they are to receive news from different wholesalers, which is the better measure of pluralist consumption (Table 11.1). In other words, the figure of 3.8 in the previous paragraph is a reasonable approximation, if slight overestimation, of the independent news sources accessed by the average citizen.

More detailed figures for audience pluralism are provided in a report commissioned by Ofcom from Kantar Media in 2012.[18] The Ofcom and Kantar figures are not exactly comparable because of different question

Table 11.1 Wholesale and Retail News Sources, United Kingdom, 2015 (percentage of total population)

News Providers	Wholesale	Retail
1	32	30
2	27	25
3	18	16
4	11	11
5	6	7
6	2	4
7	1	3
8+	0	2
9+	0	1

Source: Ofcom 2015a: Figures 2.4 and 2.5.

wording and the priming of respondents. Another research problem, therefore, is the lack of a consistent set of measures or methods for estimating
news consumption across all the media. The Kantar survey encouraged
respondents to think of a wide range of news topics and separated out political from other types of news. Hence its figures for political news are lower
than the general category of "news" in the Ofcom survey but are more
likely to be accurate so far as political news is concerned. The Kantar study
shows how individuals combine the four main platforms of television,
radio, newspaper, and the Internet for their news (Table 11.2). On average,
cross-media consumption covers almost 3.1 wholesale platforms (3.3 at the
retail level), 14 percent using only one, 25 percent using two, 26 percent
using three, and 36 percent using four or more (Table 11.2). Most of those
using only one source tuned into the BBC, and the most common combination was television, radio, and a newspaper. This means that a large
majority combine an internally pluralist source of news with at least one
other internally pluralist or partisan source. On average, they accessed 2.0
web news sites and 1.4 radio programs. BBC TV and radio figure very
largely in this list, the BBC being the largest provider of news in the United
Kingdom, with 80 percent of the adult population tuning in to its news and
current affairs coverage each week on television, radio, and the Internet.[19]
This reduces the retail measure of pluralism but adds an important internally pluralist source to it.

A third study of news-gathering habits, also commissioned by Ofcom
from Kantar, looked in greater detail at how consumers combined different
wholesale news providers to get their news (Table 11.3). Considering television, radio, newspaper, and the Internet, the most common combination
of the 14 possibilities was radio, television, and newspapers (18 percent),

Table 11.2 **Number of Wholesale News Sources Used, UK Population, 2012**

Number of Wholesale News Providers	Percentage of Population
1	14
2	25
3	26
4	18
5	10
6	5
7	2
8	1
Average	3.1

Source: *Annex 4: News Consumption in the UK* (London: Ofcom, June 29, 2012),
https://www.ofcom.org.uk/data/assets/pdf_file/0018/55602/annex4.pdf.

Table 11.3 Platform Combinations Used Nowadays, United Kingdom

Television	Newspapers	Radio	Internet	Percentage
X	X	X	O	18
X	X	O	O	14
X	X	X	X	12
X	O	X	O	11
X	O	O	O	10
X	O	X	X	10
X	O	O	X	8
X	X	O	X	7
O	O	O	X	2
O	O	O	X	2
O	X	O	O	1
O	O	X	O	1
O	O	X	X	1
O	X	X	X	1
O	O	O	O	
One platform only				14
2 platforms				36
3 platforms				29
4 platforms				12
Average				2.4

Source: Kantar Media, *Measuring News Consumption and Attitudes* (London: Ofcom, June 29, 2012), 44, http://stakeholders.ofcom.org.uk/binaries/consultations/measuring -plurality/statement/Annex5.pdf.

Note: The combinations are based on the question, "Which of the following do you use for news nowadays?"

followed by television and newspapers (14 percent), and radio, newspaper, and the Internet (12 percent). There is a fair spread of combinations, showing that none dominates and no large block of individuals gets their news in the same way. The news media are fragmented and so are their audiences. There is no such thing as "the media," only different and various collections of mediums, and no such thing as "the news audience," only different and various types of audiences.

A fourth approach to the news diets of the British population involved an analysis of access to multiple news sources online.[20] This survey estimated the overlapping unique audiences for each pair of the seven largest single sources of digital news in the United Kingdom, namely, the BBC, *Mail, Guardian, Telegraph, Sun, Independent,* and *Times.* The figures show the proportion of visitors to one site visiting another. The data were gathered by the automatic tracking method of the Nielsen UKOM/Nielsen home and work panel, so avoiding the problems of self-reported data, but this analysis deals only with desktop and laptop computer users. BBC News had the greatest amount of crossover traffic with other news sites, probably because it is the largest and most trusted single source of news. But there is also a greater amount of overlap than might be expected between sites of a different political color. For example, 45 percent of *Guardian* readers also visited the *Telegraph* site, and 49 percent of *Telegraph* readers visited the *Guardian* site. More than half of *Sun* readers saw the BBC, more than half visited *Mail* webpages, and more than a third visited *The Guardian*'s and *The Telegraph*'s. Half of *Independent* readers overlap with *The Telegraph*.

The Ofcom report concludes, "In general, there was a high level of overlap between different sources of news online; perhaps surprisingly, in the case of titles which have traditionally adopted opposing political views."[21] Many individuals are making use of quick and easy access to competing news websites, especially those without a paywall. In this respect, the web has made it easier to have a pluralist news diet rather than creating self-made echo chambers of political opinion.

Media Consumption: Diary Keeping, Interviews, and Focus Groups

A fifth study of British news audiences by Couldry, Livingstone, and Markham is built on qualitative and quantitative data gathered from a small diary-keeping study of 37 people plus a cross-sectional telephone survey of 1,017 adults aged 18 and older in the United Kingdom.[22] These were augmented by interviews and focus groups conducted with the diarists.

The diaries show that levels of media use varied considerably, but the pattern for each individual remained consistent over time, suggesting ingrained habits. With one exception, all watched TV news, nearly all listened to the radio, and 6 out of 10 (62 percent) read a newspaper regularly. Only four diarists (11 percent) claimed to read their paper thoroughly, and only two said they read more than one paper for comparisons. Of the 21 active Internet users, only one used it as the main source of news and opinion, but another 8 (22 percent) used it alongside television, radio, or a newspaper. However, the survey was carried out in 2005, and the spread of the new technology since then has multiplied web users.

The telephone survey of UK adults produced results broadly consistent with the diary evidence. A majority said they used the traditional news sources of television, radio, and newspapers at least three times a week. Television was the major source, watched by almost 90 percent three times a week, followed by radio news (71 percent), a national paper (61 percent), a local paper (56 percent); a quarter went online.

The survey found four main clusters of news media users:

1. The traditional cluster (14 percent of the sample) had the highest level of news exposure and was more likely to seek out news across all media except local papers.

2. The issue cluster (30 percent of the sample) followed special topics of interest (mainly the environment and health, crime and poverty) and used different news sources to check their accounts of these issues.
3. The celebrity cluster (14 percent of the sample) spent an average amount of time with the media and with the news but was heavily engaged in celebrity news about actors, musicians, models, and others.
4. The low-interest cluster (14 percent of the sample) had lower media consumption in general, and its news consumption was lower still.

In sum, these British studies are not strictly comparable because they all use different methods, definitions, and measures, but they all reach roughly similar conclusions. A small minority of approximately 15 percent of the adult population accesses little or no news. For the rest, the most popular source of news is the television, followed by radio, newspapers, and the Internet, although the most popular news webpages are those of TV terrestrial channels, especially the BBC, and the national newspapers. On average, individuals regularly access between three and four different sources of news, but men and some minorities access an average of four, with small groups tapping in to six or more and another minority avoiding the news. In other words, the shape of the distribution is much the same as most other measures of political attitudes and behavior. There are indications of a surprisingly large amount of crossover between different sources of news with opposing political messages.

With these broad conclusions in mind, we turn to the American evidence to see how it compares with the British.

Audience Pluralism: The United States
A Pew Research Center study of the news-gathering habits of the American public during the 2016 presidential election concludes, "Even as U.S. adults find one type of source most helpful, the majority still get election news in a given week from multiple different source types."[23] Of those who learned about the presidential election in the previous week, 9 percent depended on one stream of information, but almost half (45 percent) used five or more, mostly local and cable television (57 and 54 percent, respectively). Just as Haller and Norpoth describe the state of the national economy as a doorstep issue that is hard to avoid (see Chapter 5), so also the Pew Center describes the 2016 American election as a "news event that's hard to miss."[24] Perhaps that campaign was atypical of everyday politics because it was the most important single national election and because of the presence of Donald Trump, and yet the previous campaign appears to have been no different. About the 2012 election the Pew Center comments, "The numbers portray a diverse landscape in which no platform dominates

as the place for politics, and the vast majority of Americans say they regularly rely on multiple platforms to get political information. Just six percent said they turn regularly to just one platform."[25] A similar volume of crosscutting political messages is found among social website users, many of whom get news from two or more sites, and most of whom also get news from local, network, and cable television as well as news websites, radio, and hard-copy papers.[26]

The conclusions of the Pew studies are matched by those of an American Press Institute survey, which found that

> when it comes to who does the reporting, Americans don't tend to rely on a single source . . . the majority of Americans across generations now combine a mix of sources and technologies to get their news each week. . . . Furthermore, people access different reporting sources on a regular basis. When asked about their use of eight different reporting sources in the last week, Americans report using an average of between four and five sources.[27]

These studies are based on self-reported data and make no distinction between wholesale and retail outlets, but a Nielsen study that took these into account shows that more than half the American population watched more than one form of television news, with 90 percent of network news viewers also watching local news and 82 percent of local news viewers watching network news.[28] Cable news viewers—a comparatively small proportion of the total adult population—are also heavy consumers of local and network news. Three-quarters of them watch some network news, 82 percent watch some local news, and half watch all three. A quarter of those watching cable news watch only Fox News, 23 percent only CNN, and 15 percent only MSNBC, but more than a third watch two or more cable channels. Even so, 44 percent of Fox watchers also tune in to CNN, and 28 percent watch MSNBC.

The Nielsen, Pew, and American Press Institute studies come to much the same conclusions—most people use different news platforms and different news sources, and there is a fair amount of crossover traffic between news sites with a different slant. Within this broad picture of news-gathering behavior in the United States there are some differences among subgroups in the population, as there are in the United Kingdom. A Pew survey from 2008 found four main news consumers in the United States:[29]

- *Traditionalists.* Constituting almost half the adult population (45 percent), the traditionalists spend an average amount of time with the news, relying heavily on the television but using radio and newspapers an average amount. Few have home computers, fewer are linked to the Internet, and very few (7 percent) use the Internet for news. Less than half of the traditionalists (45 percent) reported using two or more main news mediums, and their political knowledge is lower than average.

- *Integrators.* Integrators make up the 23 percent of the adult population who are most interested in the news and spend the most time
with it. Two-thirds (66 percent) had watched TV news the day before
their survey interview, 46 percent had heard radio news, and 36 percent had read a paper. One in seven (14 percent) reported gathering
news online. Integrators had higher-than-average political knowledge,
and 70 percent claimed to use two or more main news sources.
- *Net newsers.* Net newsers made up 13 percent of the population. Typically, they were young, male, well educated, high income, and online
at work. A high percentage (75 percent) reported getting news online
in a typical day, and they had average newspaper and radio exposure,
though lower-than-average TV news use. Twice as many (17 percent)
were likely to read a paper online rather than in print (8 percent),
although 10 percent read both. In a typical week net newsers used
several different sources of online news, 26 percent regularly reading blogs, 30 percent watching the news, 19 percent listening to
radio, and 40 percent receiving news by email. These numbers add to
more than 100 percent because respondents are asked to name all
their news sources, and net newsers use three or four of them, combining them in different ways. Overall, they spent more time with the
news than the average person, they had a higher level of political
knowledge, and they were most likely to be news grazers.
- *The disengaged.* The disengaged made up 14 percent of the population. They had the lowest levels of education, income, and political
interest and knowledge. They spent the least amount of time with
each of the four main types of news media and showed little interest
in them. Fewer than one in five (18 percent) claimed to use two or
more news sources.

Much ink has been spilled about the capacity of digital technology to
transform the news system and so to change radically, for better or for
worse, the political attitudes and behavior of the public, with consequences
for democracy as a whole. In some ways, the new technology has transformed social patterns, but the typologies of news diets produced by British
and American research suggest, rather, that there has been a slow process of
adoption whereby some ways of delivering news have been added to the old.
This suggests modification rather than transformation of the old system.
Both the production and consumption of news have followed the pattern of
most technological innovation, with old producers stealing the clothes of the
innovators, and consumers sticking to their accustomed behavior but gradually augmenting it, not replacing it, with elements of the new.

This contrasts with the predictions of digital optimists and digital pessimists. The former believed that digital news media would reach parts of

the younger generation that the legacy media could not. The latter feared that the creation of echo chambers of opinion would foster extremism and political polarization. Neither theory finds much support in the evidence. More recently, the concern has been the spread of fake news and attempts to use big data and social websites to influence election and referendum results. The next section of the chapter examines these matters.

The Political Effects of the Digital Media

The New News Media

Ofcom data for 2016 show that the most common uses of digital devices are banking, buying goods and services, social networking, watching television and videos, and sending email. These outrank news, mostly by a large margin.[30] On average, people put the new technology to 3.6 different uses, of which 0.43 (12 percent) was for gathering general news. This probably overestimates the amount of political news accessed, given that most people seem to interpret "general news" to include all kinds of nonpolitical news, especially weather, sports, celebrity gossip, and family events. It is also likely to underestimate the nonpolitical uses because the Ofcom survey did not mention pornography, which is believed to account for a significant amount of Internet traffic.[31] Besides, the political news accessed via the new technology is overwhelmingly that of the old news media, not the digital natives. This suggests that the digital age has had much less political impact to date than optimists and pessimists predicted.

There is a tendency to exaggerate the importance of digital media and social networks, claiming that they have become major, even dominant forms of political communication. These claims often overlook what is included under the heading of news and what the original source of the digital news content is and even inflates their importance. A closer look suggests that Facebook and other social media play a significant supporting role in news consumption, but not a dominant one, and this more modest claim does not take into account what counts as news and where it comes from.[32]

About 6 percent of the UK adult population claim to use their smartphone to browse daily for "news and information," though once again, what kind of news from which sources is not clear.[33] Nevertheless, incidental exposure to news on social websites is not uncommon in the United Kingdom and adds to the diversity of news consumption—in much the same way that some individuals fall into TV news because the television is on rather than deliberately turning it on to watch the news.[34] At the same time, government, academic, lobbying, and nonprofit websites, which do not depend on advertising and which offer hard news, also attract a comparatively large number of searches. Therefore, overall the picture suggests that digital devices are not used much to access political news, but there are exceptions and the possibility of by-product learning.

In the United States, almost half the American population (46 percent) prefers to watch the news rather than read it (35 percent) or listen to it (17 percent).[35] Cable news audiences have increased until recently, and network news audiences continue to decline, but when questions are asked specifically about using the Internet to gather political rather than general news, the survey results do not offer much support for the idea that the new media have expanded political interest and activity. On the basis of surveys repeated over the years, in 2016 the Pew Research Center concluded that "despite the dramatic changes witnessed over the last decade, the digital news era is still very much in its adolescence."[36] Similarly, Isin and Ruppert comment that although the Internet has radically changed the meaning of citizenship—because of corporate and state surveillance—it has not changed politics radically, or at least it hadn't by 2013.[37] This is confirmed by another American study that provided free Internet access to those who did not already have it. The results raise doubt about whether the Internet benefits political interest, efficacy, and knowledge, even two and a half years after access was provided.[38] Similarly, a panel study of the 2010 Swedish election found that the digital media had very limited effects on political knowledge and participation compared with the control variables of gender, education, political interest, and offline participation.[39] General news had a weak positive effect on political knowledge but no impact on participation, whereas party and social websites showed the reverse pattern. The study concludes that the digital media have no general effects but that different types may have different effects. In this respect, the new media are the same as the legacy media, with weak but different effects according to the source and content of messages.

In the United States and United Kingdom, young people make the heaviest use of smartphones, tablets, and computers, especially to access social media websites, but in the United Kingdom the 18–24 age group is less likely than the 25- to 54-year-old age group to use them for news.[40] In the United States, in 2012 there were few people under 30 years old who went online for election news, and the most common sources of campaign information for this group were TV news and political comedy.[41]

The digital media have had a huge impact in some respects, but little in others. They have transformed the means of delivering political news by making it easier, cheaper, and faster to produce and consume, and by turning out an incomparably larger and more diverse volume of political information and opinion than ever before. Email and especially texting have been used effectively to organize protests and demonstrations.[42] But what is not clear is whether the digital media have had much of an impact in the

Western world, so far, in expanding the numbers interested in political news or whether they have much of an effect on political attitudes and behavior. As Hamilton says in *All the News That's Fit to Sell,* when Americans search for news on the Internet, they look for items that are entertaining or personally useful rather than broader news about general social and political matters.[43] In other words, it's business pretty much as usual.

Politics and Social Websites

Compared with older people, younger people in both the United States and the United Kingdom are more likely to use social websites, but they are less interested in politics, no more likely to be engaged with news on social media than the older age groups, and less likely to use the old news media. Their level of engagement with social media news declines as the input effort required of the individual increases.[44] In the United States, those who followed leads on Facebook came across only a sixth of the news stories seen by those who went directly online for news, and Facebook users spent only a quarter of the time with those stories.[45] This group makes use of quick and easy "touch-of-a-button" technology, but tends not to follow up with action, so it has been called the "slacktivists."

Trust in the social media in the United States is generally low, even among those who get news from them, and it has declined further as a result of fake news.[46] In the United Kingdom, Facebook and Twitter are considered less reliable, trustworthy, and accurate than most other sources of news.[47] The Reuters survey of 2018 found that only 12 percent of users trust the news on social websites.[48]

This evidence helps to explain why those who make heaviest use of digital devices and social websites are not particularly interested in their political content or in that of other news media either. The survey figures differ greatly according to whether respondents are asked about news in general or specifically about political news. Only 6 percent of participants claimed to have learned about the 2012 presidential campaign from Facebook, 3 percent from YouTube, and 2 percent from Twitter.[49] This despite Obama's heavy use of direct digital messaging in his campaign.[50] Four years later, it was widely believed that social websites played an important part in the 2016 US presidential election, but a careful study of social media as a main source of news shows social sites ranked fifth behind cable, network, and local TV news.[51]

Although a Pew study found that 20 percent of participants said they have changed their mind about a political issue or candidate as a result of something they saw on a social website, it also pointed out that 80 percent said they had not been influenced this way.[52] The 20 percent figure is substantial but raises questions about causes and effects, and although a great deal has been written about social media and the 2016 presidential election, little has addressed the tricky problem of demonstrating empirically that social media made a difference to the outcome. Fairly typical of journalism on the subject is an article in a specialist publication titled "Here's How Facebook *Actually* Won Trump the Presidency" that actually has no evidence to support the claim and actually does not even try to provide it.[53] Similarly, a British webpage titled "Why It's Facebook Wot Won It"— apparently unaware that *The Sun* did no such thing—actually has no evidence about Facebook effects on the 2016 election.[54] Clickbait like this is now common, but meanwhile, according to a study by Brabham, social networks in the United States are more often used to share photos of children and meals rather than joining politically charged hashtag trends.[55]

Neither has the political importance and influence of social websites been established in Britain. The most extensive and in-depth study, subtitled "How Social Media Shape Collective Action," disarmingly admits that it cannot prove that political action is mobilized by social sites rather than by other factors and points out (as does Chapter 2 in this book) that such forms of mass behavior have occurred in the past, long before there was electronic communication or any other kind of mass communication. Lacking evidence, the study opts for "a plausible set of relationships."[56]

Another publication titled "Why Social Media May Have Won the 2017 General Election" states that "social media platforms emerge as important players in this election." The study includes no evidence to support this claim, but the argument and assumption behind it is that 2017 was a surprising result for Corbyn and Labour. The party concentrated effort on mobilizing the youth vote and attracted a large amount of support with social media, left-wing blogs, and videos using popular musicians and rappers to generate publicity. Some of this campaign material, it is said, reached even larger audiences than the daily sales of some tabloid papers, which prompted speculation about the "youthquake" vote being mobilized by Labour via social media. This study also disarmingly admits that "it will be a long time before we can really assess their influence in 2017, and some things we will never know."[57] It, too, rests on "a plausible set of relationships."

Plausible, that is, until it was shown later that there was no youthquake in the 2017 election.[58] Turnout among younger voters was actually slightly lower than in the previous election, and their support for Labour was no different. In other words, social media, left-wing blogs, and videos are perfectly plausible explanations for something that did not happen. The history of speculation about media effects has many such examples.

This is not to say that one section of Facebook users did not use that network for political purposes, but the incomplete evidence we have suggests that—to employ Bennett's terms[59]—the politically engaged are a smaller group than the disengaged, perhaps substantially smaller. But then, political spectators have always heavily outweighed activists.

How Young Americans Navigate the News Landscape

An insight into how young Americans use the multiplicity of news sources available is provided in a 2016 Knight Foundation focus group study of 52 teenagers and young adults aged 14 to 24 years.[60] The study found that, for the most part, young Americans do not follow the news so much as it follows them. They fall into it, which suggests, as do other studies, that they are not interested enough to seek it out, but they come across it when using digital media for other purposes.[61] What is interesting is how they then process the news and the similarities they share with the way Russians view their TV news (as recounted in Chapter 5). Both audiences are distrustful of the news and assume most sources are biased or unreliable. Young Americans are also aware of the algorithms used by the media to tailor news and other information to the tastes of their audiences.

The Knight Foundation research found that young Americans often tried to compensate for their lack of trust in biased news by checking reports from different sources, mostly checking television but also video evidence and the reports of citizen journalists. They distinguished between "my news" and "other news." Like Russian news audiences, young Americans thought it necessary to know where the information came from to make up their mind about it. Some who find the news depressing tried to avoid it, but others thought it was something they should know about. Some used aggregator sites to check different sources and to get a different view of American politics—another example of how the ease of accessing digital news enables individuals to compensate for low media trust by cross-checking different reports. In this way, low trust combined with easy access may encourage pluralist news-gathering habits. Equally, the reverse process may be occurring, in which the ease of accessing different accounts of the same political event—for example, one with fake news and another debunking it—may be contributing to declining trust, but this cannot explain why there is such a big difference between trust in the social sites and in other news sources, or between particular news sources, such as the BBC and the *Washington Post,* on the one hand, and *The Sun* and Fox News, on the other.

Political Polarization

Partisan, radical, and extremist news sources make it easier for some to isolate themselves from the national political discourse and from opinions that confront their own, so helping to polarize the electorate.[62] Probably the most important of these polarizing new sources are cable news channels, digital native websites, hate radio, political blogs and podcasts, and some material on YouTube.

Perhaps the first thing to note about them is even if they are widely recognized, they are rarely used. Almost half (45 percent) of Americans have heard of Breitbart, but only 7 percent claim to use it weekly. In Britain, 19 percent know about Breitbart, but 2 percent claim to use it, and the equivalent figures in Germany are 17 percent and 1 percent.[63] The 15 left and right partisan news sources on the web in these three countries average a regular weekly audience of 2.8 percent of their populations. Like the Yeti and fake news, many have heard about them, but few claim to have encountered them.

Prior subjects the polarization thesis to close, careful, and thorough study.[64] He observes that research is seriously hampered by lack of information, but there are reasons why a close link between the partisan news sources of the new media and political polarization is open to doubt. First, most Americans are politically moderate and partisanship has not increased much in recent decades, although there is evidence of increased partisanship in a small minority. Second, partisan political messages may have different effects on different people, and in any case, persuasion does not happen easily—as Chapter 2 in this book shows.[65] Third, as noted above, though there is evidence that some partisans select news media that reflect their own opinions, most get their news from two or three different sources, including nonpartisan ones or partisan ones of a different color. The majority of people have a mixed news diet, including nonpartisan and internally pluralist sources. Fourth, audiences for partisan cable news programs are small, at around 10 to 15 percent of the voting-age population. Whereas heavy users of Fox News are more selective and less pluralist in their habits, they constitute only about 5 percent of the adult population. Fifth, according to self-reported evidence, more than 50 percent of Americans "regularly" or "sometimes" watch Fox News, but according to Nielsen ratings, a large majority tune out of all cable news. Last, there is the problem of cause and effect: Has cable television polarized the electorate, as far as there has been polarization, or have cable channels caught up with such polarization as there was before they came into existence? Prior concludes that "most Americans remain politically moderate or indifferent and their news exposure reveals non-ideological patterns insofar as audience overlap between cable news channels of different ideological flavours is quite high."

Subsequent Pew research confirms the finding that most Americans do not live in self-made news bubbles.[66] Most rely on various sources of news, although those with consistently conservative or liberal views (that is, those with consistent ideological views on the left or on the right) at the ends of the political spectrum get their news in ways that are distinct from each other and from the majority in the political center. Consistent conservatives are aware of fewer news outlets, and Fox is the only trusted source for 72 percent of them. Almost half of them concentrate their news attention on Fox News, although only a small minority use it exclusively. They are also more likely to see political opinions on Facebook that confirm their views and more likely to report that their friends share the same opinions. It would seem that the narrower news focus of the conservatives is part of the mental set of conservative Americans and not something created by Fox News.

Consistent liberals are aware of more news sources and use a wider range of them, including National Public Radio and the *New York Times.* They trust a larger number of news sources and are more likely than conservatives to see views inconsistent with their own on their social media, although they are more likely to block others for political reasons.

Pew data in Table 11.4 present more detail. It shows the wide range of news sources available in the United States and how widely many cast their nets in search of news. Most consistent conservatives and liberals are not politically isolated, although small numbers are. The majority come across dissenting views, though less often than the larger number of moderates and centrists. Between a quarter and a fifth of the consistent conservatives turn to network news in a given week, and smaller numbers use the *Wall Street Journal,* the BBC, CNN, and aggregator sites. Liberals rely more heavily on PBS and NPR as well as CNN, NBC, the BBC, and the *New York Times,* and they also use a longer tail of more specialized news outlets. Although only a quarter (25 percent) of respondents with mixed ideological views said most of their close friends share their political views, that was true for roughly half (52 percent) of consistent liberals and two-thirds (66 percent) of consistent conservatives. However, nearly half the consistent conservatives and nearly a third of the consistent liberals said they sometimes disagreed with their closest political discussion partners.

A study of Donald Trump and Hillary Clinton supporters in 2016 reveals a similar pattern in which Trump supporters selected a narrower range of right-wing news compared with the more mainstream and left/liberal sources favored by Clinton supporters. Most Americans, including those who use social websites and partisan cable news, continue to access the traditional media that uphold professional standards of reporting, and many use them to cross-reference what social websites and cable channels tell them.[67] In general, it seems, there is not a great difference in this respect between Republicans and Democrats in the United States, but there are differences between those on the wings of their parties.[68] The evidence suggests that those on the right are less eclectic in their news gathering than those on the liberal and left side of politics.

The potential for a self-selected echo chamber effect is probably greater for the web, because it carries a higher proportion of polarized news reporting than the mainstream media and makes it easier and cheaper to access and share that news. American research, however, casts doubt on this idea. One study found that "echo chambers and filter bubbles are undoubtedly real for some, but we also find that—on average—users of social media, aggregators, and search engines experience *more* diversity than non-users."[69] Another found that the growth of polarized politics in

Table 11.4 Where Americans Got Their News About Government and Politics in the Past Week, 2014

Consistent Conservatives		Consistent Liberals		Mixed Ideological Views	
	%		%		%
Fox News	84	NPR	53	CNN	49
Sean Hannity Show	45	CNN	52	ABC News	42
Rush Limbaugh Show	43	MSNBC	38	NBC News	40
Glenn Beck Program	34	PBS	37	Fox News	39
TheBlaze	29	NBC News	37	CBS News	32
ABC News	26	BBC	34	MSNBC	25
CBS News	22	Daily Show	34	USA Today	11
NBC News	21	New York Times	33	PBS	12
CNN	20	ABC News	33	Google News	26
Drudge Report	20	CBS News	30	New York Times	8
Yahoo! News	17	Huffington Post	29	BBC	12
Breitbart	16	Colbert Report	26	Wall Street Journal	7
Wall Street Journal	16	Google News	18	Washington Post	4
Google News	13	Washington Post	17	Yahoo! News	27
MSNBC	13	Yahoo! News	16	NPR	12
USA Today	11	USA Today	13	Huffington Post	8
BBC	10	Wall Street Journal	12	New Yorker	1
Huffington Post	10	Al Jazeera America	12	Colbert Report	6
NPR	8	Politico	12	Daily Show	7
PBS	7	New Yorker	10	Bloomberg	3
Washington Post	6	Mother Jones[a]	10	The Economist	2
New York Times	5	Fox News	10	Sean Hannity Show	3
Bloomberg	5	The Guardian	9	Rush Limbaugh Show	3
Politico	4	Slate	9	Glenn Beck Program	2
The Economist	2	Daily Kos[a]	9	Drudge Report	2
Al Jazeera America	2	Ed Schultz Show[a]	8	The Guardian	2
Daily Kos[a]	1	BuzzFeed	8	Al Jazeera America	2
Daily Show	1	The Economist	7	TheBlaze	1
The Guardian	1	ThinkProgress[a]	6	Breitbart	1
Ed Schultz Show[a]	1	Bloomberg	5	Politico	2
Colbert Report	1	Glenn Beck Program	1	BuzzFeed	3
Mother Jones[a]	0	Breitbart	1	Mother Jones[a]	1
ThinkProgress[a]	0	Sean Hannity Show	1	Slate	1
New Yorker	0	TheBlaze	1	Daily Kos[a]	0
BuzzFeed	0	Drudge Report	1	Ed Schultz Show[a]	0
				ThinkProgress[a]	0

Source: "Where News Audiences Fit on the Political Spectrum," Pew Research Center, October 21, 2014, http://www.journalism.org/interactives/media-polarization.

Note: a. Denotes a sample size too small to analyze audience profiles.

recent years is strongest in the 75-year-plus group, which also happens to be the group that is least engaged with the Internet and its social websites.[70] A third discovered that individuals who seek ideologically consistent sites, even the ideologues among them, did not avoid news sites that challenged their political opinions. On the contrary, they were more likely to use them.[71] This is consistent with a study that found that ideological segregation of online news consumption was low in absolute terms, significantly lower than the segregation of face-to-face discussion circles.[72] An extreme example concerned visitors to stormfront.org, a site for "White Nationalists . . . the voice of the new, embattled *White* minority!" Over a four-week period, they were twice as likely to visit nytimes.com as those who called up Yahoo! News.[73] It would be interesting to know whether they do this out of general political interest or whether it is part of a focused reality check.

This group of studies relied on the reported behavior of respondents, but other research reports on the actual web browsing histories of 50,000 Americans who regularly read online news. It concentrated on the sharing activity of web users because it shows that individuals have read a piece they think is interesting or important enough to pass on to others. It found that polarizing opinion pieces are shared, but they constituted only 6 percent of the total amount of web material dealing with international and national news, and they accounted for only 2 percent of all the news actually accessed. The authors conclude that although web material does increase ideological segregation, the magnitude of its effects is small.[74]

Prior's suggestion that the new media have caught up with preexisting polarization rather than creating or strengthening it is supported by the experimental work of Arceneaux and Johnson.[75] They found that those who watched cable news in the United States were already polarized in their political opinions and that the news they received had little effect on their political behavior. On the contrary, like the partisans in experimental psychology research and the hawks in Zaller's study of the impact of Vietnam War news (see Chapters 2 and 3), more balanced and internally pluralist news had the countereffect of negatively reinforcing their preexisting polarized ideas. This suggests that cable news has not polarized America, but that partisan news has caught up with demand and satisfied it.

Another experimental study found that the overall influence of partisan news was reduced because of lack of trust in it.[76] Many US conservatives trust Fox News, but larger numbers do not, with the result that Fox News is one of the few news sources in the country with a negative net trust score. Its effects are limited to the extent that it has little impact on the majority of voters, who do not believe it is trustworthy.[77] In France, Germany, Switzerland, and the United Kingdom, it seems that the populist press has the effect of reinforcing the opinions of those already inclined toward populist ideas and reinforces the views of those opposed to them.[78]

Fake News

This brings us to a recent wave of fake news. The concern about fake news is well merited, and research on its production and dissemination is important, but also of concern is that we have almost no information about its impact, or if indeed there is any impact.[79] If the evidence and argument about television and newspapers in the previous chapters of this book are to be believed, and if these results apply to the digital media, which they seem to, the answer about the impact of fake news may be that it is "small to negligible." That remains to be investigated with reliable studies of media impacts, but meanwhile some circumstantial evidence supports this assertion.

First, there seems to be a disjunction between what people express concern about and what they actually come across themselves. The Reuters study of social media in 37 countries found that 58 percent of participants expressed worries about made-up news but struggled to find examples they have seen. What they meant by "fake news" also included poor journalism, political bias, and clickbait headlines that aimed to attract attention by exaggeration, drama, scandal, and sensationalism, all of which are characteristics of fake news but are not exclusive to it.[80]

The authors of one thorough study were careful to point out that their research did not set out to assess how fake news affected the 2016 US presidential election and that their work had limitations.[81] Based on an online survey of the web browsing of 1,200 people, and a database of 156 news-related stories, it used Facebook sharing of election news reports to estimate the number of fake stories read by American adults. Observing that relatively few Americans trust Facebook or use it as their main source of news, and allowing for a placebo effect on those who claimed to have seen and believed fake news stories—that is, stories invented by the researchers in order to assess the reliability of responses to actual fake news stories—the authors conclude that each American saw and remembered 1.14 fake news stories, perhaps more. They allow for the fact that education, age, total media consumption, and party identification (the standard model again) were associated with accurate identification of fake and real stories. Taking this into account, they estimated that the fake news stories in their database would have changed vote shares in the election by an order of hundredths of a percentage point.

Also emphasizing the limitations of their study and stressing that fake news poses serious problems for democracy, Nelson and Taneja found that the fake news audience during the 2016 US presidential election was a small subset of the net's heaviest users.[82] The audience size for average real news sites was about 28 million unique visitors, while that for an average fake news site was about 675,000. The audience for all the fake news sites together was smaller than that for most real news sites separately. Moreover, fake news sites suffer from the law of double jeopardy, because not only are their audiences small, but they are also disloyal. Whereas the majority of Internet news audiences stick to their preferred site of mainstream legacy media, the minority who visit the fake news sites flip between a more politically diverse range of less popular sites and also use the mainstream sites. In addition, they spend less time with each of these varied news sites than with real news on the mainstream pages. This is helpful, interesting, and relevant but throws no light on fake news effects on voting behavior

Explaining News Consumption

Eight factors seem to shape news consumption in Britain and the United States:[83]

1. The daily cycle of news gathering follows the normal patterns of daily life—listening to breakfast radio in the morning and while driving to and from work, reading a newspaper during the lunch break or on mass transport and in the evening at home, watching evening news and late-night political comedy, grazing news on the web at work. Different social groups find various combinations of these fit their daily routine.
2. News media are chosen for the kinds of news and opinion they carry: newspapers are useful for current news and opinion; Sunday papers for longer articles of analysis and opinion; television for news summaries and comment, breaking news, and political comedy; radio mainly for multitasking and breaking news; the Internet for particular items of interest, breaking news, and news grazing, often at work; other websites for political blogs, citizen journalism, videos, and digital editions of newspapers and TV news.
3. Pluralist habits also depend on work and education. The better-educated and higher-income groups with office computers tend to graze the news on the net; others rely more heavily on legacy media. In general, the older age groups get more news and are more likely to access the traditional sources of television, newspapers, and radio, but whether this is a life cycle or generational effect is not clear.[84]
4. People focus on the news more closely when important events are taking place—referendums, wars, terrorist attacks, and elections. Television is heavily used for filmed coverage of dramatic events. Americans turned on the network news when they heard about the Kennedy assassinations and 9/11. In 2012, 85 percent followed the presidential debates on television only, 3 percent followed on computers or mobile phones only, and 11 percent followed them live by dual screening on television and computer or mobile phone. The British turned in huge

numbers to BBC News (television and web) for information about the London bombings in 2005.

5. Those with higher levels of education and office jobs tend to graze electronically delivered news and watch late-night political talk and comedy shows on television. People who are less well educated and without work experience on a computer are more likely to rely on the old media.

6. Older generations are more interested in the news and tend to concentrate on the old media. Younger generations are less interested and tend get digital news on a screen.

7. Those with a special political interest such as the environment, health, or poverty tend to scan different media for coverage of their topic and use aggregator sites. They cover more news sources than average.

8. Pluralism is a function of political interest, a need to know about politics, and enjoyment following the news, but news from one medium or another about major issues and events is hard to avoid altogether, even for news avoiders.

These observations are subject to the qualification that they cover the communications channels of television, newspapers, radio, and the web and that reliable information about the political content of some media, even major ones, is hard to come by. These observations do not take into account magazines, monthly journals, blogs, political leaflets, and circulars from candidates and political campaigns or the news acquired in daily life (Chapter 5) and discussion circles (Chapter 6). To this extent, figures based on the news media alone are likely to underestimate pluralist behavior and exaggerate the role of the media. Assuming that the news media are the main or only source of political information and opinion for the great majority of the population is a mistake.

Conclusions

Pluralist theory of the media hinges on a close, three-cornered relationship of pluralism of news sources, pluralism of news content, and pluralism of news audiences. It relies on competition among many news sources that produce political information and comment from a range of different political perspectives that citizens then use to inform themselves about competing opinions to draw their own conclusions. All three are necessary conditions for news pluralism in modern society, but none has been systematically and thoroughly studied in depth, least of all the news-gathering habits of citizens.

That said, and recognizing that the evidence is patchy, noncomparable, and often problematic, British and American research points toward similar general conclusions about pluralist audiences, suggesting there are three broad groups in the population. About 15 percent pay little or no attention to media news, although some political events and issues are difficult to avoid—even for this group. At the other extreme, between a fifth and a third regularly use three or four main news sources—a combination of television, radio, newspapers, and the web—and a few others occasionally. Those with a special interest in a particular political issue tend to refer to a variety of reports about it. The third and largest group in the middle (approximately 30 to 40 percent) keep up with the news from two or three main sources in a typical day, and a few other sources more sporadically. A small percentage, approximately 5 to 8 percent, rely heavily on only one news source, which may be partisan or internally pluralist—Fox News in the United States and the BBC in the United Kingdom, for example.

It might be argued with good reason that the hyperpluralism of modern media systems is largely irrelevant where mass audience pluralism is concerned. The existence of hundreds of thousands of news sources is of little consequence when the great majority of people use two or three mainstream news sources, mainly newspapers, radio, and television, in their legacy and digital forms. These are what count most in estimating the news diet of the great majority of citizens, which means that special attention should be paid to the mainstream media. Two questions are important here. First, to what extent are the mainstream media internally pluralist, and second, to what extent does the public have a cross-media news diet that provides a mix of political opinion—what Ofcom calls news wholesalers? There is not much research to provide answers to these questions, but what there is finds that most citizens mix their news from different wholesale sources with different political views, including internally pluralist ones that provide balanced and reliable news. To this extent, the great majority of citizens access relatively few sources of news, but these sources are mainly internally pluralist and are provided by different news wholesalers.

A small minority live in echo chambers that reflect their own opinions back to them, but most who regularly tune in to partisan news also tap into other sources. Overall, most people demonstrate a moderate degree of news-gathering pluralism, just as most demonstrate a moderate degree of political interest, knowledge, and engagement. Once again, little is special about media audiences: the distribution of news-gathering habits is much the same as the distribution of political attitudes and behavior and is best explained in terms of the standard model of objective demographic factors of democratic and subjective political inclinations, such as political interest and awareness.

Television, newspapers, and radio are still the most important sources of news for most individuals, although the legacy forms of these media are declining as their audiences (and revenues) are declining. However, the most popular news sites on the web are those of the legacy newspapers and TV stations, not the digital natives. The main digital natives are also heavily dependent on the old media for news content. This is not surprising because providing the news is expensive, time-consuming, and labor-intensive and requires skilled labor, so many news providers piggyback on the old news media. But because opinion is cheap, the supply of opinion on the web is abundant.

By and large, the new technology has not yet increased the political interest of the younger generation. Almost the entire group subscribes to a social network, but a minority put it to political use, and they are mostly politically active anyway, and, like the politically aware sections of older generations, they also make good use of the legacy news media. Most age groups use the digital media for the nonpolitical purposes of shopping, banking, music listening, social networking, texting and emailing, gathering health information, watching films and videos, and playing games. Compared with these, few use the digital media for gathering news, and even then, though we cannot be sure, the term *news* seems to involve mainly the weather, sports, friends and family, health, and celebrity gossip, with political news coming well down the list of priorities.

The new media have not polarized the electorate. Americans who confine their news to a single cable channel—notably, Fox News—form a small minority of the American population, and many of those who watch Fox News or other partisan sources also access other news sources. Consistent conservatives have a narrower news diet than consistent liberals, but most of them use a variety of partisan and nonpartisan sources. In the United Kingdom, most of those who concentrate heavily on one news source use BBC TV and radio or ITV news, so they get a more pluralist account of the news than Fox News provides.

In short, the best hopes and worst fears about the new communications systems have so far failed to materialize. Many of the younger generation, who are the heaviest users of the social websites, continue to be as nonpolitical as they ever were. The politically engaged—whether old, young, or middle aged—who make most use of the old news media, have added the new media to their repertoire, though often they use the new media to access legacy media content. In this respect, digital sources have augmented rather than replaced the old ones, resulting in slow adaptation, not rapid transformation. The new media have radically changed how some members of the public get their news, but they have not greatly changed what news people get or which kinds of people typically get it. As the Pew Research Center puts it, "Despite the dramatic changes witnessed over the last decade, the digital news era is still very much in its adolescence."[85]

Pluralist news-gathering habits of the general population seem to be driven by three main sets of factors: the political interest and awareness of individuals; the opportunities and constraints of daily routines; and the particular capacities of different media. Each news source has its special uses and is employed at different points in daily routines.

Because most people are not ideologues or partisans, they tune in to a mixture of news but mainly use the old mainstream sources of radio, newspapers, and television that have a pluralist approach to the reporting of politics. In the United States, these sources include local papers and radio stations, national newspapers of record, network news, and the news it syndicates to local stations, plus (for a minority) NPR and PBS. In the United Kingdom, BBC TV and radio are preeminent, followed by ITV and, perhaps surprisingly, local and regional papers. They are a practical alternative to the pluralist ideal in which every citizen regularly gets a full and varied account of the news from a wide variety of sources.

The digital media have also introduced three potentially important features into the modern news media system. By making it easier, quicker, and cheaper to produce and access different news sources, they have made it easier, quicker, and cheaper for citizens to diversify their news diet. Second, and as a consequence, individuals can and do cross-check news about items of interest with different news sources, usually turning to trusted mainstream media to check webpages and other news reports they do not trust. Third, individuals mix and match their news sources in their own ways, so there is no large bloc of citizens all receiving the same news from the same mass media sources. Although the mainstream news media are still important, the fragmentation of the news media system means that individuals bundle different combinations of news sources. If there ever was a public sphere of political discourse, it has been undermined not by the multinational multimedia conglomerates, as the Frankfurt school suggests, but by a cacophony of myriad TV channels, radio stations, desktop publications, political websites, blogs, videos, citizen reporters, news aggregators, fact checkers, and short-lived viral phenomena. The consequences for mass attitudes and behavior and for political integration and stability have yet to be clearly established or, in some cases, studied at all.

It bears repeating that although the news media are an especially important source of information and opinion in any democracy, they are not the only source. Chapters 5 and 6 in this book show that individuals pick up knowledge of politics and public policies from their own experience of daily life and from their discussions with others. These have a strong influence on the news that individuals pay attention to and how they react to it. The firsthand immediacy of personal experience may give it a special role, which may explain why some studies find experience and discussions to be more influential in the formation of public opinion than broadcast and narrowcast news by whatever means. It is true that an understanding of news media effects requires comparisons across platforms.[86] It is no less true that such research should take careful note of other sources of news, notably the moderating effects of personal experience and political conversation.

And last, it must be emphasized that, in spite of its importance for an understanding of what news citizens get and from what sources, research on audience pluralism is in its early infancy, so the conclusions of this chapter must be treated with special caution. What seems to be clear is that audience pluralism is an important research topic that requires more attention.

Notes

1. Sunstein 2009.
2. Mutz and Martin 2001.
3. Prior 2005.
4. http://stakeholders.ofcom.org.uk/binaries/research/tv-research/news/News_Report _2013.pdf; https://www.ofcom.org.uk/research-and-data/tv-radio-and-on-demand/news -media/news-consumption (accessed via "News Consumption in the UK").
5. "Social Media Statistics & Facts," Statista, https://www.statista.com/topics/1164/social -networks/; "How Many Social Networking Websites Are There?," HowManyAreThere?, August 1, 2011, http://www.howmanyarethere.net/how-many-social-networking-websites -are-there/.
6. Bennett 2013.
7. Aalberg and de Vreese 2017: 3.
8. R. Fletcher, "Is Social Media Use Associated with More or Less Diverse News Use?," Rasmus Kleis Nielsen, November 25, 2016, https://rasmuskleisnielsen.net/2016 /11/25/is-social-media-use-associated-with-more-or-less-diverse-news-use/.
9. G. Rosen, "Facebook Publishes Enforcement Numbers for the First Time," Facebook Newsroom, May 15, 2018, https://newsroom.fb.com/news/2018/05/enforcement-numbers/.
10. "Facebook Suspends 200 Apps over Data Misuse (Update)," Phys.org, May 14, 2018, https://phys.org/news/2018-05-facebook-apps-misuse.html; M. Isaac and D. Wakabayashi, "Russian Influence Reached 126 Million Through Facebook Alone," *New York Times,* October 30, 2017, https://www.nytimes.com/2017/10/30/technology/facebook -google-russia.html.
11. Isaac and Wakabayashi, "Russian Influence Reached 126 Million Through Facebook Alone."
12. Prior 2009a, 2009b.
13. Whiting 2009.
14. "Section 3: News Attitudes and Habits," Pew Research Center, September 27, 2012, http://www.people-press.org/2012/09/27/section-3-news-attitudes-and-habits-2/.
15. Kantar Media, *Measuring News Consumption and Attitudes* (London: Ofcom, June 29, 2012), https://www.ofcom.org.uk/__data/assets/pdf_file/0031/54679/annex5.pdf.
16. Measuring Online News Consumption and Supply: A report for Ofcom 2014: 55, Measuring-online-news pdg – Adobe Acrobat Reader DC (accessed via https://webarchive .nationalarchives.gov.uk/.../internet/Measuring-online-news.pdf).
17. *News Consumption in the UK: 2016* (London: Ofcom, June 29, 2017), https:// www.ofcom.org.uk/__data/assets/pdf_file/0017/103625/news-consumption-uk-2016.pdf.
18. *Annex 4: News Consumption in the UK* (London: Ofcom, June 29, 2012), https:// www.ofcom.org.uk/__data/assets/pdf_file/0018/55602/annex4.pdf.
19. *BBC Annual Report and Accounts 2014/15* (London: BBC, 2015), http://downloads .bbc.co.uk/annualreport/pdf/2014-15/bbc-annualreport-201415.pdf.
20. *Communications Market Report 2012* (London: Ofcom, July 18, 2012), 278, Figure 4.59, https://www.ofcom.org.uk/__data/assets/pdf_file/0013/20218/cmr_uk_2012.pdf.

21. *Communications Market Report 2012*, 278.

22. Couldry, Livingstone, and Markham 2016.

23. J. Gottfried, E. Shearer, M. Barthel, and A. Mitchell, "The 2016 Presidential Campaign—a News Event That's Hard to Miss," Pew Research Center, February 4, 2016, http://www.journalism.org/2016/02/04/the-2016-presidential-campaign-a-news -event-thats-hard-to-miss/.

24. Gottfried et al., "The 2016 Presidential Campaign—a News Event That's Hard to Miss."

25. Pew Research Center Journalism and Media Staff, "Internet Gains Most as Campaign News Source but Cable TV Still Leads," Pew Research Center, October 25, 2012, http://www.journalism.org/2012/10/25/social-media-doubles-remains-limited/. For reasons of space, this chapter has to concentrate on the United States and United Kingdom, but it is worth noting that Swedish citizens also mix and match their news sources in much the same way as Americans and British do (Strömbäck, Falasca, and Kruikemeier 2018).

26. E. Shearer and J. Gottfried, "News Use Across Social Media Platforms 2017," Pew Research Center, September 7, 2017, http://www.journalism.org/2017/09/07/news -use-across-social-media-platforms-2017/.

27. "How Americans Get Their News," American Press Institute, March 17, 2014, https://www.americanpressinstitute.org/publications/reports/survey-research/how-americans -get-news/. This study was conducted in January and February 2014—outside the rather special conditions of presidential election campaigns.

28. M. Jurkowitz and A. Mitchell, "How Americans Get TV News at Home," Pew Research Center, October 11, 2013, http://www.journalism.org/2013/10/11/how-americans -get-tv-news-at-home/.

29. Pew Research Center, "Audience Segments in a Changing News Environment: Key News Audiences Now Blend Online and Traditional Sources," August 17, 2008, www.pewresearch.org/wp-content/uploads/sites/4/legacy-pdf/444.pdf.

30. *Communications Market Report 2016*.

31. M. Castleman, "Dueling Statistics: How Much of the Internet Is Porn?," *Psychology Today*, November 3, 2016, https://www.psychologytoday.com/blog/all-about -sex/201611/dueling-statistics-how-much-the-internet-is-porn.

32. For a close examination of the data, see W. Oremus, "How Many People Really Get Their News from Facebook?," *Slate*, December 20, 2016, https://www.slate.com/articles /technology/technology/2016/12/how_many_people_really_get_their_news_from_facebook .html?via=gdpr-consent.

33. Ofcom 2011: 76.

34. R. Fletcher, "Social Media and Incidental Exposure," *Digital News Report*, http:// www.digitalnewsreport.org/survey/2017/social-media-incidental-exposure-2017/.

35. A. Mitchell, E. Shearer, J. Gottfried, and M. Barthel, "1. Pathways to News," Pew Research Center, July 7, 2016, http://www.journalism.org/2016/07/07/pathways-to-news/.

36. A. Mitchell, E. Shearer, J. Gottfried, and M. Barthel, "The Modern News Consumer," Pew Research Center, July 7, 2016, http://www.journalism.org/2016/07/07/the -modern-news-consumer/.

37. Isin and Ruppert 2015: 7.

38. Richey and Zhu 2015.

39. Dimitrova et al. 2014.

40. Ofcom 2011: 76.

41. "Section 1: Campaign Interest and News Sources," Pew Research Center, February 7, 2012, http://www.people-press.org/2012/02/07/section-1-campaign-interest-and-news-sources/.

42. Bennett, Segerberg, and Walker 2014.

43. Hamilton 2004: 205.

44. Mitchell et al., "The Modern News Consumer"; "Section 1: Campaign Interest and News Sources," Pew Research Center; Kantar Media, *Measuring News Consumption and Attitudes*.

45. Bennett 2016: 3.

46. "Edelman Trust Barometer 2018—UK Findings," Edelman, January 22, 2018, https://www.edelman.co.uk/magazine/posts/edelman-trust-barometer-2018/; N. Newman, "Overview and Key Findings of the 2017 Report," *Digital News Report,* http://www.digitalnewsreport.org/survey/2017/overview-key-findings-2017/.

47. Kantar Media, *Measuring News Consumption and Attitudes*, sections 3, 5, 8.

48. Newman et al. 2018.

49. Pew Research Center 2012: 8–10.

50. Pew Research Center Journalism and Media Staff, "How the Presidential Candidates Use the Web and Social Media," Pew Research Center, August 15, 2012, http://www.journalism.org/2012/08/15/how-presidential-candidates-use-web-and-social-media/.

51. Allcott and Gentzkow 2017.

52. M. Anderson, "Social Media Causes Some Users to Rethink Their Views on an Issue," Pew Research Center, November 7, 2016, http://www.pewresearch.org/fact-tank/2016/11/07/social-media-causes-some-users-to-rethink-their-views-on-an-issue/.

53. I. Lapowsky, "Here's How Facebook *Actually* Won Trump the Presidency," *Wired,* November 15, 2016, https://www.wired.com/2016/11/facebook-won-trump-election-not-just-fake-news. Italics in the original. Younger age groups are variously described as 18–29.

54. G. Kenningham, "Why It's Facebook Wot Won It," Campaign, June 8, 2017, https://www.campaignlive.co.uk/article/why-its-facebook-wot-won/1435935#lh7k5oi MDUz1qzTM.99.

55. D. C. Brabham, "Studying Normal, Everyday Social Media," Social Media + Society, May 11, 2015, http://journals.sagepub.com/doi/10.1177/2056305115580484.

56. Margetts et al. 2016: 20.

57. Margetts 2017: 387.

58. C. Prosser, E. Fieldhouse, J. Green, J. Mellon, and G. Evans, "The Myth of the 2017 Youthquake Election," British Election Study, January 29, 2018, http://www.britishelectionstudy.com/bes-impact/the-myth-of-the-2017-youthquake-election/.

59. Bennett 2008: 2.

60. M. Madden, A. Lenhart, and C. Fontaine, *How Youth Navigate the News Landscape* (Miami, FL: Knight Foundation, February 2017), https://kf-site-production.s3.amazonaws.com/publications/pdfs/000/000/230/original/Youth_News.pdf.

61. Other work suggests that the volume of online political activity is heavily dependent on offline activity, but nevertheless, online activity adds a small but significant increment to offline activity—see Kahne and Bowyer (2018).

62. Sunstein 2007, 2009: 7.

63. Newman et al. 2018: 21.

64. Prior 2013. See also the earlier studies of Iyengar and Hahn 2009; DellaVigna and Kaplan 2006; Morris 2005.

65. The statement "persuasion does not happen easily" seems to be a reference to cognitive bias, belief preservation, and motivated reasoning discussed in Chapter 2.

66. A. Mitchell, J. Gottfried, J. Kiley, and K. E. Matsa, "Political Polarization and Media Habits," Pew Research Center, October 21, 2014, http://www.journalism.org/2014/10/21/political-polarization-media-habits/. See also A. Mitchell, J. Gottfried, J. Kiley, and K. E. Matsa, "Section 1: Media Sources: Distinct Favorites Emerge on the Left and Right," Pew Research Center, October 21, 2014, http://www.journalism.org/2014/10/21/section-1-media-sources-distinct-favorites-emerge-on-the-left-and-right/.

67. Y. Benkler, R. Faris, H. Roberts, and E. Zuckerman, "Study: Breitbart-Led Right-Wing Media Ecosystem Altered Broader Media Agenda," *Columbia Journalism Review,* March 3, 2017, http://www.cjr.org/analysis/breitbart-media-trump-harvard-study.php.

68. Media Insight Project, "Partisanship and the Media: How Personal Politics Affect Where People Go, What They Trust, and Whether They Pay," American Press Institute,

July 13, 2017, https://www.americanpressinstitute.org/publications/reports/survey-research /partisanship-and-media/.

69. N. Newman, "Overview and Key Findings of the 2017 Report," *Digital News Report,* http://www.digitalnewsreport.org/survey/2017/overview-key-findings-2017/. See also E. Shearer and J. Gottfried, "News Use Across Social Media Platforms 2017," Pew Research Center, September 7, 2017, http://www.journalism.org/2017/09/07/news-use -across-social-media-platforms-2017/.

70. Flaxman, Goel, and Rao 2013.

71. Garrett, Carnahan, and Lynch 2013.

72. Gentzkow, Shapiro, and Sinkinson 2011a.

73. Gentzkow, Shapiro, and Sinkinson 2011b: 1823.

74. Flaxman, Goel, and Rao 2013.

75. Arceneaux and Johnson 2013.

76. Baum and Groeling 2010.

77. Hopkins and Ladd 2014. It is also worth noting that examination of Fox and NBC's reporting of US involvement in the Iraq and Afghanistan wars shows rather little difference between the two so far as their "bad news content" is concerned. (See Aday 2010.)

78. Müller et al. 2017.

79. On the production and dissemination of fake news, see, for example, Woolley and Howard 2017; Guilbeault and Woolley 2016; McNair 2017; Brundage et al. 2018; Bounegru et al. 2018; Shao et al. 2017; Marwick and Lewis 2017. This is a good and significant body of empirical research, but its purpose is not to research fake news effects.

80. Newman et al. 2018: 20.

81. Allcott and Gentzkow 2017.

82. Nelson and Taneja 2018.

83. See, for example, *Annex 4: News Consumption in the UK* (London: Ofcom, June 29, 2012), https://www.ofcom.org.uk/__data/assets/pdf_file/0018/55602/annex4.pdf; "The Personal News Cycle: How Americans Choose to Get Their News," American Press Institute, March 17, 2014, https://www.americanpressinstitute.org/publications /reports/survey-research/personal-news-cycle/.

84. See, for example, A. Kohut, "Pew Surveys of Audience Habits Suggest Perilous Future for News," Poynter, October 4, 2013, https://www.poynter.org/newsletters/2013 /pew-surveys-of-audience-habits-suggest-perilous-future-for-news/.

85. A. Mitchell, E. Shearer, J. Gottfried, and M. Barthel, "The Modern News Consumer," Pew Research Center, July 7, 2016, http://www.journalism.org/2016/07/07/the -modern-news-consumer/.

86. Bode and Vagra 2018.

12

Explaining Media
Political Effects

*What must astonish people with casual beliefs in the vast power of the
media is how difficult it is to measure media influence.*
—M. Schudson, The Power of News[1]

More than 30 years ago, Yale psychologist W. J. McGuire, a specialist in
persuasion, advertising, and mass communications, opened an essay on
media impacts with the following:

> That myths can persist despite conflicting evidence is demonstrated by the
> robustness of the belief that television and other mass media have sizeable
> impacts on the public's thoughts, feelings and action even though most
> empirical studies indicate small to negligible effects.[2]

The myth persists, at least as far as the news and politics are concerned.
Observation of the everyday shows that large proportions of the population
reject some media messages, even if they are amply supported by the best
possible evidence and repeated regularly over long periods of time. No less
common, large numbers of people believe things that find little or no support
at all in the mainstream media. It is also clear that individuals can respond
in different ways to the same message from the same medium and that the
same person can react in different ways to the same message from different
sources. An example in recent years is the willingness of sections of the
British and American populations to believe or reject fake news, which
alerts us to the possibility that the effects of the news media depend as much
on the characteristics of their audiences as on the content of the message.
Numerous studies of political attitudes and behavior show that when things
such as education, income, sex, religion, political interest, and party identification are taken into account, media impacts on the thoughts, feelings, and

219

actions of the public are generally reduced to low or insignificant levels. This suggests that media effects on mass political attitudes and behavior depend heavily on the personal characteristics and fundamental beliefs of people in the audience—their material and ideal interests. This chapter of the book gathers together the evidence and argument for this conclusion, but because the evidence does not lead to the conclusion that media effects are always and everywhere weak and insubstantial, the chapter also explores the circumstances in which their influence may be stronger than usual.

Because both producers and consumers of news can contribute to media effects, the key to understanding these effects is how producers and consumers interact—especially how people process and interpret the news they receive. This chapter summarizes the most salient points about the interactions, based on the large amount of detailed evidence provided in previous chapters.

Three preliminary warnings are necessary. First, it is difficult to pin down media effects with any certainty, given the close reciprocal relations between the media and their audiences. Second, there are large gaps in our knowledge about the media and their audiences and the effects of one on the other. Evidence about the digital media is especially lacking. Third, to isolate media effects, it is necessary to untangle a complex set of causes and effects that are, themselves, closely interrelated. Good research tries to do this by making allowances for the possible effects of factors other than the media, and the many different kinds of media and content, and by comparing people who are exposed to possible media effects with a control group of those who are not. The problem is whether the right variables have been controlled and whether the measures available capture them fully. There is often some statistical leakage somewhere. Given these three caveats, any conclusions about media effects, including those that follow, must be treated with caution.

To break down the problem into its constituent parts, the chapter is divided into two main parts that deal with the consumer and the producer sides of the equation, although media effects cannot be understood without considering the interactions of the two.

News Consumers

Belief Preservation
Experimental psychology has accumulated an impressive body of research over the past 60 years, showing that individuals can preserve beliefs that run counter to the evidence available, sometimes in the face of all known facts, logic, and argument. Indeed, attempts to correct misinformation and first impressions can result in a boomerang effect—reinforcement of the misinformation in which false beliefs are strengthened by finding new arguments to support them, shifting the goalposts, and even inventing evidence

and rejecting a weighty accumulation of scientific research. This large volume of experimental research suggests that individuals are capable of holding fast to opinions whatever the media, or other sources of information, say, and hence the power of the press may be both less and more complicated than is commonly supposed.

The power of belief preservation in the face of opposing evidence reported in the media is demonstrated in the real world every day. Consider those who believe that weapons of mass destruction were discovered in Iraq, that Barack Obama was not born an American, that leaving the European Union would release £350 million a week for the National Health Service (NHS), that the Holocaust never happened, that conspiracies have been responsible for an endless list of events—from the death of President John Kennedy and the first moon landing to the idea that the Clintons are involved in a massive pedophile ring organized out of a pizzeria in Washington, and that Donald Trump was denied a majority of the popular poll in 2016 by three million illegal votes.

The ability of citizens to stick to their opinions is also found in the United Kingdom among people who do not follow the politics, party endorsement, and agendas of the newspaper they read. In the United States, the majority of Americans rejected the media campaign to impeach President Bill Clinton, and large numbers ignored their newspaper's endorsement of Hillary Clinton and opposition to Trump in the 2016 election. Many in the United States believe that the press makes up stories about President Trump, but others believe that itself is fake news. Belief preservation is not limited to a small percentage of extremists and true believers—it is widespread throughout society.

Beliefs Without Mainstream Media Support
Besides rejecting media messages they do receive, large percentages of the public also demonstrate a capacity to believe things for which there is little or no support in the mainstream media. This may apply less to politics than to other areas of life, but it still has an impact on some issues of government and public policy. There are an estimated 90 million creationists in the United States, and many of them campaign to change school curricula; have strong views about marriage, abortion, ethnicity, religious freedom, and the validity of science; and they are typically associated with strong political opinions and voting patterns.

Avoiders, Deniers, Ignorers, and Accepters
It seems that people respond in four main ways to political news. Some avoid it as much as possible. This group seems to number somewhere between 10 and 20 percent of the US and UK populations, and although they are not much affected by the news, they probably cannot escape it totally, especially because there are sources of political information other than the media.

The second group, deniers, is made up of those who reject what they see, hear, and read in the news. In Zaller's classic study (discussed in Chapter 3), politically engaged hawks rejected the mainstream media's anti–Vietnam War message. In the British general elections of 1987, 1997, 2001, 2005, and 2015, the British public as a whole rejected media agendas in favor of their own bread-and-butter concerns of everyday life. Americans in the tens of millions rejected the media agenda to impeach Bill Clinton over the affair with Monica Lewinsky, just as tens of millions rejected their newspaper's endorsement of Hillary Clinton and voted for Trump in 2016. Chapters 3, 4, and 5 of this book contain other examples where significant proportions of the population rejected the news they received. This does not mean that everyone always protects their beliefs, only that many individuals display a capacity to do so when news they receive is inconsistent with their own worldview.

A third response to the news is to accept the evidence and argument about a given matter but ignore it. There is often a thin line between denying and ignoring, but an example of ignorers is the cigarette smokers in the Western world who know about the health dangers and the risk, but continue with the habit nonetheless. Similarly, the media pour out warnings about unhealthy diets, lack of exercise, alcohol and drug abuse, but mounting numbers continue to do themselves harm. It is one thing to ignore news about things that do not affect you, but another to ignore news and thereby endanger yourself. If it comes to a contest between what the news is reporting and individual beliefs, needs, and habits, the latter usually win.

The fourth way of responding to the news is to accept it and act upon it. Accepters may initially have strong beliefs about an issue, but then change their opinions (at least in the short run) when presented with contrary evidence. There are many examples of mass attitude change in response to an accumulation of media and other reports. Large numbers of people have given up smoking, taken up exercise, stopped excessive sunbathing, and adopted a healthier diet in response to advice repeated endlessly in the mass media (among many sources of information) over the past decades. Beliefs about climate change, same-sex marriage, the environment, feminism, the welfare state, and immigration have also changed. It cannot be assumed that the news media are entirely responsible for these developments, but the point is that people do change their minds and the news media may help them to do so.

An individual can react to the news in all four ways depending on the news source, the subject matter, and their own values and beliefs. This makes it unwise to generalize about media effects as if they were uniform. Instead, we should be asking who avoids, rejects, ignores, or agrees with which messages from which sources and why.

Beliefs of Conviction and Convenience

Beliefs range in strength from the true beliefs of convinced partisans to beliefs of convenience. The former can be unshakeable, sometimes in the face of compelling evidence and logic to the contrary. The latter are more superficial and appear to be convenient smoke screens used to hide more deep-seated beliefs of conviction, disappearing like yesterday's snow when they are no longer needed, but leaving true convictions intact.

For some, fake news seems to involve a willing suspension of disbelief. The belief that £350 million a week for the NHS that Brexit campaigners claimed would be available if the United Kingdom left the EU was dropped within hours of the referendum result being announced, but few Brexiteers seemed to care about that. In the United States, some saw the plan for a wall along the Mexican border not as a real project but as a symbol of "America First" nationalism. In general, the more strongly held a belief, the less the media influence, and vice versa.

The Strong Social Forces of the Standard Model

The accumulation of 60 years of research has found that the fundamental variables of education, social and economic status, income, age, sex, ethnicity, and religion are most usually associated with a wide range and variety of mass attitudes and behavior. These, and variables closely associated with them, form what might be called the standard model of the behavioral sciences. They are measures invariably used as controls to test the power of other variables, and one or a combination of them usually wins the contest. Media effects are no different when tested against the standard model insofar as their effects are usually weak and patchy when standard model variables are taken into consideration. Partisanship, party identification, trust, and political interest also enter into the mix of the standard model where political attitudes and behavior are concerned.

We can see the standard model going about its usual work in the previous chapters. It usually plays a major role in explaining how much attention people pay to the news, what newspaper and TV news channel they choose, how much television and what kinds of programs they watch, how much they learn from the news, whether they prefer commercial or public service television, and what news media they trust. President Clinton's approval ratings were unaffected by the sustained impeachment agenda of the press because what counted was party identification, distrust of the media, and the priority citizens placed on peace, prosperity, and political moderation. The last three, and variations on them, have explained presidential approval since polling began, and it was no great surprise that they, rather than the media campaign for impeachment, explain Clinton's approval ratings during the year-long Clinton-Lewinsky scandal and afterward. Similarly, it was not *The Sun* or any other newspaper that won the 1992 and 1997 British elections but "the economy, stupid," aided and abetted by party identification.

Even when the standard model is not directly involved, media effects do not necessarily take their place. It was not the *New York Times* or network news that caused a proportion of Americans to change their mind about the

Vietnam War, as many have claimed, but the harsh reality of mounting military casualties and body bags and the way that politically aware doves and Democrats reacted to them. An antiwar mood developed in the United States for the same reasons and in the same way during the Korean War, a war that had a fraction of the news coverage that Vietnam had. British voters pay little heed to media election agendas when these fail to resonate with their everyday concerns about public services and household finances. The fact that Trump had barely any newspaper endorsements in 2016 did not prevent 59 million Americans from voting for him for reasons to do with voter age, ethnicity, education, household finances, and location plus some attitudes that rarely find approval in the mainstream media.

The media conform to standard social and economic patterns in other respects as well. They respond to consumer preferences just as supermarkets do. The new digital media have followed the usual pattern of response to rapid technological change, with a rapid turnover of many small producers in the first phase, followed by a period of consolidation and centralization around a few main players. Consumers have also responded to new communications technology as they have to other technological innovations—not by switching wholesale to the new, but by mixing elements of the old and the new. The result has been the typical pattern of adaption, not transformation of the industry, in part because the legacy media quickly took up digital means of communication; stealing the clothes of the opposition is an age-old political and business practice.

In suffering loss of public trust, the media are no different from many other major social institutions. Media specialists tend to explain this in terms of media-specific causes, but these cannot be the main explanations and certainly not the only ones, given that many institutions in many Western countries have the same problem. Media factors may play a part, but the underlying dynamic is society-wide. Similarly, the hostile media effect, which appears at first sight to be a special feature related to the media, turns out to be part and parcel of the much broader hostile world effect in which individuals feel themselves to be embattled, hard done by, ignored, and unjustly treated.

In all these respects, there is little that is unique or special about the media. They often follow the normal producer and consumer trends and patterns of other institutions. In particular, they often have no special powers or influence over political opinion and behavior. These, as behavioral science has found, remain the province of population demographics and their associated political values, identities, and attitudes.

This raises a point about a feature of contemporary political science. Media research is full of observations and findings about the direct and indirect influences of the media on voting, agenda setting, priming, framing, and a broad-ranging assortment of political attitudes and behavior. Nevertheless, most other work on these subjects has little to say about media effects. Take just two examples. A recent thorough, detailed, and comprehensive account of turnout and party voting in British elections manages to provide a robust explanation of them without so much as a mention of television, newspapers, radio, and the web.[3] Similarly, a book on elections, democracy, party identity, and voting choices in the United States has no more than three fleeting references to the mass media.[4] The disconnect between media studies and general political science explanations of the same political phenomena is striking and suggests that something is missing or wrong somewhere.

Personal Experience and Reality Checks

Although it is commonly assumed that the media are the main or only source of political news and opinion, this is not the case. Individuals garner all sorts of political knowledge and experience in their daily lives, coming into contact with, among other things, education, health services, social services, taxes, street people, the cost of living, pensions, boarded-up shops and buildings, housing issues, police and fire services, public transport, roads, the banking system, commercial and professional practices, and public bureaucracies. The topic is underresearched, but there are indications that citizens use their first- and secondhand experience to form judgments about specific public policy issues and about government and democracy in general.

The public also has a view on a wide range of moral and ethical issues that relate to politics—minority rights, political ethics, same-sex marriage, crime and punishment, equality, pornography, immigration, political asylum, commercial practices, drugs, abortion, nuclear energy and weapons, the environment, feminism, conduct in public life (and the private lives of people in public life), court sentences, war, and sexual abuse. They do not need media advice on such matters and many forcefully reject it, using their own eyes and ears instead.

Even though the two lists of practical and moral political matters just presented are long, they leave out many issues that are remote from everyday life and do not involve widely held moral standards. These include aspects of foreign policy; a wide array of scientific, medical, technical, educational, and economic matters; and the detailed administrative workings of government and public services. The media may have much greater influence over public opinion on such issues because the public has little personal experience with them and the ethical issues they involve. Nevertheless, this has not stopped people from making judgments about the wars in Iraq and Afghanistan, national economic performance, genetically modified food, global warming, wind farms, fracking, and the intractable complexities of Brexit.

Personal experience seems to act as a sort of reality check on some types of news and opinion. It was not "*The Sun* wot won it" for Labour in

1997, but the impact of real-world economic and political conditions on Conservative and Labour identifiers. Russians use their own experience and knowledge to recast their TV news. British voters ignored media election agendas in 1987, 1997, 2001, 2005, and 2015 because they did not correspond to the agendas of their own lives based on their personal finances and views about the importance they attached to the issues of housing, education, health, employment, and taxation. This is why models of voting that successfully predict British election outcomes take little notice of media influence, concentrating instead on economic expectations, wars, taxes, public services, and leadership ratings. Swings in American public opinion about the Korean and Vietnam Wars closely followed the number of casualties and body bags. Citizens often ignore what the news and political pundits tell them on such matters and use their beliefs and values to make political judgments instead.

Nevertheless, it is perfectly possible for people to be realists on some issues but not on others. Individuals may have responded to real-world developments about the Vietnam War or base their judgments about the national economy on their domestic finances, but, at the same time, they may reject evidence for gun control, the death penalty, and evolution. They can also realistically perceive the real world around them but draw very different conclusions about their experience. This makes it all the more difficult to predict how any given individual will respond to any given media message.

However, to claim that what is "out there" in the real world can sometimes be an important reality check on news reports raises the conundrum about how to distinguish between actual events and how they are presented in the news. The two are always and inevitably intertwined and virtually inseparable. Lies, propaganda, fake news, and the devious arts of spin doctors aside, the best journalism must always select what news to report and what facts and opinion to report, using language that is likely to be value loaded to some degree. How then can we possibly tell whether citizens base their politics on what is out there in the real world or on journalism's distorted and biased representation of it?

Some argue that it is impossible to distinguish between the real world and the reported world and that our perceptions of politics are always and inevitably colored by the reported world. Perhaps so, but there is still a problem. If it is impossible to distinguish between the real world and the reported world, how can we conclude, as many do, that our perceptions of politics are determined by the reported world, not the real one? The only conclusion must be that we should suspend judgment on something that is a philosophical puzzle, or at least be less certain about the power of the media to shape our view of the world. Meanwhile, there is good evidence that the public does base at least some of its political judgments and decisions on personal experience of the world and subjective moral standards.

Personal Discussions

Political talk and chat among family, friends, neighbors, and colleagues are integral to daily life and the personal experience discussed in the previous section and, not surprisingly, political conversation is also an influence that moderates media effects. Although some people avoid politics, most adults talk about them fairly regularly, if in a sporadic, disorganized, or fleeting manner. Some of this is restricted to talk with like-minded others, but usually it involves at least one person with different political opinions. American research finds that political talk has a stronger effect on voting patterns than the news media, and a comparative study of three European countries and the United States finds that discussion groups not only inform their participants, but also help them evaluate the importance and veracity of media messages. It seems that discussion moderates the effect of the news by strengthening, weakening, or counteracting it. Exactly how or why it does this is not yet clear, but it is probable that media messages that are consistent with the views of a group are likely to be enhanced, whereas messages that are resisted by the group are diminished. Mixed discussion groups are more likely to have mixed or no effect. In other words, group discussion is a significant part of the process whereby individuals come to acquire political information and opinion, pick out what is important in the news media, and then reject, ignore, or accept messages.

If the moderating influence of discussion is not taken into account, there may be an illusion of media power in which it, alone, is assumed to be the driving force behind political opinions. If moderating influences are taken into account, we can see that it is not the media alone, but the way media messages interact with discussion groups, that magnifies, minimizes, or changes their effects.

Trust

Trust is a precondition of willingness to believe information and accept opinion. That levels of trust in the media in many Western countries are low and declining suggests that the media may also have low and declining credibility and influence. However, the issue is not so simple. First, different media prompt different levels of trust among different sections of the population in different countries. By and large, the most trusted are also the most trustworthy, as far as this is possible in the real world of journalism. In the United States, the *New York Times* and PBS are the most trusted media sources, and in the United Kingdom it is the *Financial Times, The Economist, The Guardian,* and the BBC. The political content of the Internet and the tabloid press in Britain are the least trusted sources of news. At the same time, people tend to trust "my media," but not "other media," with the result that some groups trust one news source (for example, Fox News in the United States) while others distrust it. This makes it difficult to generalize about "trust in the media" and its implications for media effects.

Trust plays a crucial part in agenda setting, priming, and framing. Agenda-setting theory assumes that individuals accept what they have been told in the news and store it accurately in their memories—both questionable assumptions in light of the evidence that individuals often reject or ignore media messages, and that memory is often unreliable. More convincing is the evidence that individuals choose to trust certain sources of news ("my media") and use them as shortcuts to form political opinions. Agenda setting, in this case, is not a mindless process of citizens absorbing and recalling what they have been told, but a conscious decision based on calculations of which news sources are to be believed.

Commercial newspapers in the Western world seem to be faced with a trade-off between trustworthiness and market share. Either they can produce serious news and analysis, in which case they are likely to have more influence over a smaller audience that trusts them, or they can produce lightweight, racy, soft news, or very little political news at all, in which case they are likely to exercise little, if any, influence on a larger audience. *The Sun* in the United Kingdom, for example, outsells all other British national daily papers, but it is the least trusted of them. This may explain why most research has failed to find much evidence that *The Sun* influences the way its readers vote.

News Producers

Consumer and producer sides of the media equation are closely interdependent, not the least because consumers self-select the media they favor, and the commercial media, like any other businesses, must satisfy the demands of their consumers. The same is true of public service media to some extent, if they are to keep their market share of audience. Minority media, especially those on the web, which do not have to make a profit or even cover their costs, can produce what they like within the law, so there is a huge number and great diversity of news sources, mostly opinion rather than information, that appeal to small audiences. But the mainstream commercial media of television, newspapers, and radio are bound by the golden chains of the market, which allow some leeway, but media that test the strength of the chains have to pay a price.

This section of the chapter summarizes what is known (and not known) about news producers. It focuses on the differences between newspapers and television; old and new media; public service and commercial media; and news and entertainment programs. Each has somewhat different implications for public political knowledge, attitudes, and behavior. This section has little to say about radio because we know little about its political content or effects. The new digital media get a lot of attention of the plausible explanation kind, but, in general, we know little about their political content and less about their impact on users. For all the concern about Russian attempts to influence American voters and the EU referendum in the United Kingdom, we have no information (as yet) about how successful these attempts were.

Myriad News Sources

There are few exact or reliable figures for the total number of news outlets available in either the United Kingdom or the United States. We often have to rely on approximations, estimations, guesstimations, and shots in the dark. But, as the appendices in this book show, there are so many news outlets that even allowances for large margins of error let us conclude that news sources of all kinds and types run into the hundreds of thousands. They come from every quarter of the globe, in just about every language on earth, and represent just about every conceivable political subject and opinion, from anarchism and the African National Congress to Zionism and Zimbabwe. The result is the most pluralist news system the world has ever seen.

Newspapers and Television

Taking into account the social, economic, and political nature of their audiences (that is, the standard model), there is little evidence that either television or newspapers contribute toward a mean world effect on politics. On the contrary, other things being equal, those who follow the news most closely, on television, in the newspapers, or both, are generally better informed, more likely to participate in politics, and more supportive of democracy and its institutions.

Generally, newspaper readers know more about politics than those who rely on TV news, so it seems that Postman is right to claim that the printed word is better at educating and informing citizens, possibly because it requires more focused attention on the part of the audience.[5] On the other hand, TV news does more than merely amuse us. It, too, informs and, consequently, there is little evidence that the medium is the message as far as politics is concerned. The content of tabloid television and tabloid newspapers has much the same political effects on consumers, and the effects are different from those of quality papers and TV news channels. The message is the message, not the medium.

Commercial Media and Entertainment Television

There is some evidence that watching a lot of television, especially entertainment content, has an adverse political effect on viewers, but the effect is patchy and weak. However, the problem is the usual one of unraveling the complex interactions between audiences and the media. Less educated and low-income groups tend to watch a lot of television and favor entertainment programs on commercial channels. But independently of their TV habits, they are likely to be less well informed and less interested in politics and to express negative views about government and democracy, so the question is, what do the media contribute, in addition to their low interest and negative views? When the variables of the standard model are taken into account, the answer is usually "rather little."

Research on the effects of entertainment television may also be inconclusive because there are many different kinds, ranging from documentaries, classical music, and Shakespeare, to horror films, crime series, sitcoms, and soap operas. One of the few studies that unpacks the complicated, three-cornered associations of audience characteristics, kinds of TV programs, and political attitudes is a Belgian project (as discussed in Chapter 8) that failed to confirm the suggestion that either TV news and current affairs or films and crime series have any adverse effect on political attitudes. Instead, the study found that watching soap operas, comedy shows, quiz shows, and dating programs was statistically associated with feelings of personal insecurity, but not with two other attitude measures. Although the association is statistically significant, it is not strong. Even so, it presents a puzzle. Do the homely dramas of soap operas and humor of sitcoms engender feelings of fear and insecurity in their audiences? Or, given what we know about how individuals select what they watch on television, is it more likely that those who are fearful and insecure turn to the reassuring comfort of soaps and sitcoms, leaving those who are confident and unthreatened free to enjoy horror, violence, crime, and disaster movies?

Perhaps the most striking thing about research on TV effects is that, holding other factors constant, it generally finds that regular attention to the news is associated with political knowledge and a wide array of positive political attitudes and behaviors. On the other hand, watching a lot of television, which usually means watching a lot of entertainment television on commercial channels, is not usually associated, positively or negatively, with either political knowledge or attitudes. There is a little evidence of adverse effects and the effects, if any, of commercial and entertainment television are usually small.

Public Service and Commercial Media

In most Western European countries, the TV market is shared in varying proportions between public service and commercial channels, and evidence showing consistent differences between the two is accumulating. Public service channels usually carry more news and more hard news, and broadcast it more frequently and at peak viewing hours. In some countries, they have a formal responsibility to appeal to all sections of the population and to be a national unifying influence, not a divisive one.[6] The public trusts them more highly than most other sources of news.

Other things being equal, watching public service television is associated with higher levels of political knowledge, a smaller knowledge gap between well-informed and poorly informed audience members, civic attitudes of cooperation and engagement, political empowerment, social trust, confidence in political institutions, political participation, and voting turnout. The effects of public broadcasting are not limited to its audiences but extend to those who prefer commercial TV channels as well. That is, regardless of which TV channels they prefer, viewers in countries with a strong public service media are more trusting than those who live where commercial systems dominate. This rainmaker effect of public service media has been observed across 25 countries in Europe, although it is not clear what lies behind the phenomenon or what is cause and what is effect. Perhaps those who watch public service news also discuss it more with others and spread its influence beyond the circle of watchers. Or perhaps more cohesive, trusting, and egalitarian societies have preserved a larger public service element in their media system, and the public services, in turn, reinforce social inclusiveness and political unity.

Not all public services are the same. Countries mix public and commercial television and radio in different proportions; there are no pure public systems and few pure commercial ones to allow for clear-cut comparisons. Each country has its own rules and regulations for its public broadcasters, and these vary according to their share of the national market, degree of real independence from state and government, and degree of independence from commercial income. Similarly, commercial systems are constrained to different degrees by state regulations that require them to broadcast news that is accurate, comprehensive, and impartial. Consequently, the effects of public and commercial television vary in breadth and strength from one country to another. It has been suggested that the larger their audience share, the more public service stations are protected from commercial pressures, and the greater their independence from government and the state, the greater their beneficial effects are likely to be for democracy.

Public broadcasting is a democratic asset for other reasons as well. In established democracies, politically interested individuals have plenty of news sources to tap into, but for others, public television and radio are easily accessible, single sources of trustworthy news. If public service news is their only or main port of call, then at least these people are getting information from a reasonably reliable and impartial source. And if it is true, as psychologists claim, that first opinions tend to stick in the memory, then it is important to have news that gets it right to start with.

Having said all this, the effects of public service media on their audiences are generally small. Though statistically significant, they are overshadowed by the social and economic characteristics of their audiences—the standard model again. Nevertheless, a dozen or so studies covering most of Europe have found that public service media have a consistently positive effect on democratic attitudes and behavior.

Digital Communications

The term *new media* is confusing. It obscures the distinction between the new digital means of communication—the technology—and the content that it carries. The content may be produced by the old (legacy) media or by new (digital native) media. Digital natives provide new content and use new technology, and the old legacy media have also taken up the new technology with alacrity; they put "old wine in new bottles," and their consumers run into the millions every day. The new technology has vastly increased the amount and variety of news and opinion available in the world and has made it easier, quicker, and cheaper to produce and access this news. But although the new technology has transformed the ways in which increasing numbers of people get their news, it has not necessarily changed or expanded the range and variety of the news they get. The most popular sources of news on the Internet in the United States and United Kingdom are produced by the legacy media (established newspapers and TV channels).

Neither has the new technology managed to increase the political interest and involvement of the younger generations most at ease with digital devices. These have mainly been put to political use by those who were already politically aware, and they, like the older age groups, use it in conjunction with the legacy media, not to replace them. There is no evidence that the new media have been widely used by people with strong opinions to cocoon themselves in an ideological echo chamber of their own making. This is true of only a small minority in the United States, but most people do not limit their news diet to one or two ideologically congenial sources.

We have little evidence about the impact of the web on the political attitudes and behavior of the population. We know which demographic groups go online most frequently, and we know that, for the most part, this does not involve politics, because they use the Internet mainly for other purposes. Most who say they get news online are usually getting news about the weather, sports, health, music, consumer information, family, and celebrities. Political news is far behind these priorities, although some may be exposed to political news as a by-product of pursuing their other interests. This is to be expected given that the standard model has long recognized that most people are not deeply involved in politics, especially young people. Political activists use the new means of communication to organize their activities, but the majority of people continue to gather most of their news from the legacy media, often using the new technology to do so and adding in a few digital natives to the mix. The web in general, and social websites in particular, are not generally trusted sources of political information. The new technology has spread far and fast, but its political impact is still comparatively small. This may change, but meanwhile, the plausible speculations of digital pessimists have not been realized; nor have the plausible speculations of the digital optimists.

The web does, however, make it easier to produce and access news, with the consequence that some individuals with political interest use it to cross-check information against different sources. The web facilitates the pluralist gathering of political information.

Pluralism and Political Bias

Pluralist theory of the news media argues that a plurality of news sources providing a range of information and opinion is important for democratic politics, because it ensures that media power is not concentrated in only a few hands, and because it maximizes the power of citizens to make up their own minds on the basis of their knowledge of different accounts of events and issues. In this way, truth will emerge from the free competition between ideas.

Pluralist theory has a long and venerable history, but it runs into three main problems. First, truth does not necessarily emerge from the free competition of ideas. In a competitive market, the producers of news deliver what consumers want and are able and willing to pay for, and if there is a demand for misinformation, fake and biased news, and opinion that confirms popular prejudice, then that is what the market produces. A free market has nothing to do with truth emerging, only the adjustment of supply and demand for news of different kinds.

The second problem is that it cannot be assumed that a news system with only a few producers, or even a single dominant one, is necessarily lacking in pluralism. Pluralism may (not necessarily will) emerge from competition among many producers, but it may also be the product of a single, internally pluralist source of news. There are good examples of this in Britain and America—the BBC, PBS, NBC, the main network TV channels in the United States, ITV in Britain, the main newspapers of record in both countries, and the local papers in the United States. Content analysis shows that these produce reliable, accurate, and balanced news, at least as far as election campaigns are concerned, and as far as this is possible in the modern world of tight deadlines and limited resources. The list shows that both commercial and public service organizations can produce internally pluralist news. In the United States and the United Kingdom, one or two internally pluralist sources of news are the mainstay of the news diets of large sections of the populations. In other words, it is not possible to estimate the pluralism of a national news media system simply by counting its producers or by documenting its increasingly concentrated ownership and control.

The third problem concerns biased reporting, especially on the part of the commercial media. Because they are businesses, it is often assumed that they are biased in favor of business interests. If they are part of a multinational multimedia conglomerate, it is often assumed they are biased in favor of big, global business. Yet, as just noted, internally pluralist commercial media exist, and previous chapters recount how Murdoch's papers and television have adopted editorial policies that promote his particular economic interests, not those of the business and corporate world at large. *The Sun* has switched its political party support to keep it in line with the voting intentions of most of its readers; English and Scottish editions of Murdoch's papers strongly advocated contradictory policies during the Scottish independence referendum. Fox News has angered Republican campaign managers by giving a lot of air time to unelectable candidates who were favored by the channel's aging, white, male audience. It seems that commercial news is not necessarily biased and that when it is, it is not necessarily biased in favor of conservative, free-market forces. It can be biased in favor of what its consumers want.

In short, it is wrong to assume that a commercial system is the only way to guarantee pluralist diversity of news and opinion, just as it is wrong to assume that commercial news agencies are inevitably biased in their reporting. Similarly, it is wrong to assume that a news system lacks pluralism because it has few producers or even has a single dominant one. Internally pluralist news is especially important if it is the only or main news for large parts of the population, the more so if that portion gets the rest of its news from a biased source.

Pluralist News Diets

A diversity of news sources is of no consequence if the general population does not also have pluralist news-gathering habits, although a single internally pluralist source is certainly better than none or only a few sources that share the same political bias. Of all the questions to ask about democratic politics and the news, the number and variety of news sources they habitually access and what they make of their news content are among the most important. And yet, these are among the most under-researched topics in media studies. Fortunately, however, there is some good evidence from the United Kingdom and United States that points to similar conclusions.

About one in seven people is a news avoider, taking news in irregularly and infrequently, although probably coming across political information and opinion in other ways. At the other extreme, approximately a quarter to a third of the population uses at least three or four main sources of news most days—mainly television, radio, newspapers, and the web—and another two or three more sporadically. This group includes the news junkies who use three or more main sources daily, sometimes more than once, and up to six, seven, or eight other sources less often, sometimes cross-checking accounts depending on the subject. In between the extremes, the largest group in the population of the United Kingdom and the United States follows the news daily, using two or three sources regularly and a few others more sporadically. In the United Kingdom, a large proportion of the population uses BBC radio and TV and the main commercial TV channels as their main news sources. In the United States, the main terrestrial channels and local papers are the most heavily used sources, and content analysis finds that these are generally internally pluralist, at least in their reporting of election campaigns. Studies in both countries comment on the surprising amount of cross-media usage of news media with different political points of view. Few citizens get their news from a single partisan source, and even those most attached to Fox News in the United States generally get different accounts of the news from other sources.

In general, it seems, most people have a moderately pluralist diet of news just as they demonstrate a moderate amount of political knowledge, interest, and activity—another example of how the media fit the standard model of the behavioral sciences. It might be argued, with good cause, that the mainstream news is not as complete, unbiased, or accurate as it should be, and that most people do not make as much of it as they might, but the evidence suggests that the pluralist glass is around half full, or half empty.

By making it easier, quicker, and cheaper to access news from different and sometimes conflicting sources, the news media system has made it easier, quicker, and cheaper for citizens to diversify their news diet. A majority do so, and some now cross-check items of interest in different news sources—including the most committed partisans of Fox News and young people who happen to come across items of interest on social websites. Distrust of the media, combined with ease of accessing a diversity of sources, has resulted in citizens acting as the nineteenth-century theorists of pluralism would have them behave.

Another consequence of the fragmentation and diversification of the news system is that some sections of the population who used to receive the same news from the limited number of TV channels are gradually being replaced by a more fragmented electorate that bundles different combinations of news from partisan and pluralist sources. This means that there is no such thing as "the media," only a variety of different mediums, and no such thing as "the media audience," only different groups in the population opting for different combinations of news sources. The consequence of this for mass attitudes and behaviors and political integration and stability have yet to be established. Meanwhile, it seems that the old concern over a growing concentration of ownership and control is now less important as myriad partial and impartial news outlets become more widely used. What has undermined "the public sphere," if it ever existed, is not the growing concentration of capitalist ownership and control of the mass media market, but the fragmentation of media systems and the fragmentation of news media audiences resulting from the hyperpluralism of the digital age.

Fake News

Fake news has been a feature of politics at least since Greek and Roman times, but it can now travel faster and farther than before because of the speed and reach of digital communications and the diminishing costs involved in creating and distributing it. There is, however, little hard evidence about its effects on public opinion, partly because little is known about who receives it and from what source and who believes it and acts upon it, and partly because of difficulties with sorting out a morass of possible causes and effects. If fake news is accepted as a short-term belief of convenience that is used to support or hide more deep-seated convictions—a sort of willing suspension of disbelief—it is likely to have little or no impact. This is because core beliefs that predispose people to accept fake news already exist, and because fake news can be easily cast aside—sometimes to be replaced with a new fake story—without any effect on core beliefs. In any case, if the evidence about the impact of real, hard news is taken into account, fake news is likely to have a small impact on public opinion and behavior, if any. The evidence, although there is not much of it, suggests that fake news reaches a small fraction of the population compared with the news of more reliable mainstream media. We have to wait for the beginnings of research, which will be no easy job given problems of data and methods.

Meanwhile, there are hints at some of the reasons for the spread of fake news in recent years. Low and declining trust in the media makes it easier to define real news as fake, and fake news as real. This may leave some undecided about what to believe and others to rely on "my media," which they believe to be trustworthy.

Fake news is not just about individual psychology, nor is it about the willingness of politicians on both sides of the Atlantic to exploit it. Societies that are highly polarized by economic inequality, racial or religious discrimination, geographical cleavages, and deep political differences often generate fake news and conspiracy theories. They also produce political leaders who are willing to use fake news. Those hit hardest by economic hardship, austerity, and discrimination are most likely to believe it. The postmodern idea that everything is subjective and relative, and therefore neither true nor false, does not help—nor does the "have your say" culture that encourages everyone to express an opinion about everything. It is a short step from there to the post-truth society of fake news and alternative facts in which anyone can believe whatever they want and where subjective opinion carries more certainty than objective evidence. As Tony Blair said about his "sexed-up dossier" justifying war with Iraq, "I only know what I believe." Imagine how things would have been different if he'd said "I only believe what I know"?

The Interaction of News Consumers and Producers
Each chapter in this book provides examples of how media effects depend on an interaction between the media and the consumers and how crucial the inputs of the individuals are to the outcome. What people do with any given item of news, if they receive it at all, is heavily dependent on their demographic characteristics, their political values and interests, the trust they

place in a news source, whom they talk to about politics, and their own life experience. These seem to be the strong variables that determine what news people receive, the sources they receive it from, and how they react to it. Consequently, the same message from the same source can be accepted by one group, rejected by another, ignored by a third, and turned around to reinforce its own counter-opinions by a fourth. The message matters, but how different individuals and groups react to it is more important.

There are two sets of interactions to take into account. One concerns how individuals interact with the news they receive, and the other concerns interactions within individuals and groups that determine how they react to the news they receive. For example, those who combine a need to know about politics and high distrust of the media seem to pay more attention to the news than those who combine distrust and low interest. Similarly, politically aware hawks and politically aware doves reacted relatively quickly to the anti–Vietnam War messages of the American news, but in opposite ways, whereas less-aware hawks and doves reacted more slowly and less strongly, also in different ways. Discussion circles can have a powerful effect on how their members react to news items, but the nature of the effect depends on whether the circle is of homogeneous or mixed political opinions. Individuals interact with the media, and how their individual characteristics interact determines how they interact with the media.

The Illusion of Media Power

Sometimes the interaction between media and audiences can produce an illusion of media power when what at first seems to be a strong media effect turns out to be a weaker one that is magnified by audience approval or disapproval. Media messages that resonate with audiences are magnified by that audience, and messages that fail to resonate are either ignored or dismissed. Similarly, trust in the messenger, talk with others, the values and opinions of audiences, and compatibility with life experience can all magnify or diminish media effects. If these sorts of interactions are not taken into account, the media may seem to have powerful effects that are actually as much the product of audiences as of the media.

When the Media Can Be Influential

It would be wrong to draw the conclusion from the evidence in this book that the media never have any effect on mass attitudes and behavior. On the contrary, there is good evidence that they do have an impact, even if a rather small and patchy one. Other things being equal, the more time people spend with the news media, the better informed they are and the more positive their attitudes toward politics, political government, and democracy. The effect is not strong but it does constitute a media effect and it spills over into political behavior, including the inclination to turn out and vote. The positive impacts of newspapers are somewhat stronger than those of television, and the positive effects of TV news apply to those who fall into the news as well as those who seek it out. There is inconclusive evidence that entertainment television undermines democratic attitudes, but, equally, there is evidence that this has more to do with what sorts of individuals watch what kinds of television and with the viewing habits of country populations as a whole. Countries that watch a lot of TV have lower levels of trust than those that watch less.

Public service broadcasting has benefits compared with commercial channels. Its TV news is associated with a better-informed public and a smaller knowledge gap between people who are more and less politically interested. In fact, public service television (and possibly radio, although this has not been examined) has a double virtuous circle effect of mobilizing politically aware citizens who switch on their television to watch the news and those who fall into the news because they watch a lot of television. These effects do not always or only operate directly on the individuals who watch public service television—because individuals in countries with a significant public sector audience have higher levels of social trust, even if they spend most of their time with commercial channels. This rainmaker effect works by helping to create a trustworthy society, which affects all citizens, whatever kind of television they prefer. Once again, public service television effects are small, and the characteristics of audiences and society at large make a bigger difference.

Beyond that, the media, in general, and news media, in particular, may have more influence under the following circumstances: when they are trusted; when they report new political events or issues that the public has not already formed an opinion about; when the issue is not a salient issue or intrusive one; and when the matters reported are not encountered in everyday life—such as news about technical and scientific matters and foreign affairs. Because first opinions can be difficult to change, the first news to arrive may have more of an effect than later reports, even if the intial news misinformed. To this extent, there is a difference between opinion formation and opinion change, and it may be that media influence can be stronger in creating opinions where there are none than in changing those already existing. Fake news may also be accepted if it resonates with an individual's core beliefs and values, although it may create a belief of convenience rather than of conviction.

The News As a Leaky System

The news media form a leaky system akin to a garden hose that is punctured and cracked so that it leaks and squirts water in all directions, sometimes on the flower beds with the desired effect, but also on other places to no or adverse effect. In the same way, the media pour out a rushing flow of news around the clock, but its effects are a hit-or-miss affair. Only a portion of it hits its targets: some people try to avoid politics; some pay close attention to selected subjects; others follow the general news regularly; news junkies get their fix from a daily array of sources. Some accept a given report, some reject it or ignore it, and others turn it around to reinforce their opposite opinion. Some accept information but draw their own conclusions; others reject the facts as lies, propaganda, fake news, or irrelevances. Some misinterpret the message and draw false conclusions, others forget it almost instantly, and the true believers, partisans, and ideologues fit it into their worldview, sometimes with the help of invented facts, false logic, or a handy conspiracy theory. And, not least, some receive, accept, internalize, and act on the information and opinion, often because they were predisposed to do so in the first place. There is also a sleeper effect in which it takes a long time and constant repetition of a message to effect a slow change in public opinion.

Opinions about obtrusive issues are not much influenced by the news media because the public has views of its own, but first reports about unobtrusive matters can take root, making it hard for subsequent corrections to have an effect. News that resonates with an individual's life experience is likely to get more attention than other matters, but given what a person already knows, or thinks they know, they are more likely to react to it in their own way, sometimes without much media input, and sometimes in spite of what the news tells them. The routines of existence, including talking politics with others, can be powerful gatekeeping moderators of the news that amplify or diminish its messages.

People who are politically interested and aware pay most attention to the news, but because they are likely to have well-developed views, they are also likely to react to news in their own way. People who are less aware may be more susceptible to news media influence, but they pay less attention to it. Some accept the political agenda of their favored medium because they trust it; others may distrust a newspaper but read it nevertheless. Another section of the population can trust a news source but pay it little attention. PBS news in the United States is widely trusted but watched by few.

It is well said that most generalizations about the media are wrong, because there is no such thing as *the media,* other than in a purely grammatical sense. *Media* is a collective noun representing a disparate set of agencies with different motives and purposes that produce different content for different audiences to different effect. Besides competing with each other, these agencies must fight for attention with many other sources of information and many other vocal groups—churches, trade unions, professional organizations, interest groups and voluntary organizations, scientists, experts, religious leaders, public figures, and self-appointed opinion leaders. The public also goes to meetings, conferences, and workshops and publishes a vast array of newsletters, leaflets, magazines, bulletins, and press releases as well as producing websites in ever-increasing numbers. The belief that the news media are a powerful influence on what people do and think is inclined to overlook the fact that they are only one among many sources of news, and not necessarily the most influential among them.

The Irony of Pluralist Theory

Pluralist theory argues that the media should provide news from a variety of political perspectives, so that citizens can compare different accounts and make up their own minds. The evidence we have is that news from a wide variety of political standpoints is readily available and that most, not all, citizens do sample a small proportion of it much of the time, though they cannot possibly sample even a small cross section of it all the time. To this extent, the modern news media system is pluralist to a modest degree in respect to the public's use of it. Critics will argue that it is not pluralist enough, and they are probably right, although *enough* may be a shifting utopian ideal, always just beyond the reach of what we have.

In any case, the problem with pluralist theory is that citizens do make up their own minds, but often not in the way that pluralist theory requires and often with results that pluralist theorists dislike. Citizens can use an elaborate array of mental shortcuts, heuristics, and cognitive biases to reach judgments that are mixtures of prejudice, wishful thinking, fantasy, and sheer bloody-mindedness. All citizens are capable of this whatever their education, background, and intelligence and whether or not they are highly paid professionals and distinguished experts or laypeople involved in a bar-room discussion. Politics, the law, science, philosophy, and academia have their share of those who use their mental skills to argue for ideas and theories that have been or will be subsequently killed stone dead by all the evidence and logic. Einstein himself dismissed the idea of continental drift as naive in his introduction to a 1958 book by an eminent geologist friend.[7]

Cognitive bias and belief preservation are part of the human condition, and pluralist theory will have to come to terms with that somehow. Meanwhile, people are reaching their own judgments about politics in their own ways and for their own reasons—which is what the theory requires of them.

Notes

1. Schudson 1995: 22.
2. McGuire 1986: 174.
3. Clarke et al. 2004.
4. Achen and Bartels 2016.
5. Postman 1985.
6. The public service broadcasters discussed here are more or less, if not wholly, independent of government control and follow the model set up for the BBC in 1927. In other words, this discussion does not include the direct state and government control of TV and radio stations found in parts of Russia and Eastern Europe.
7. Marx and Bornmann 2013: 600; S. Krause, "Hapgood's Theory of Earth Crust Displacement," S.Krause, December 6, 1996, http://www.skrause.org/writing/papers /hapgood_and_ecd.shtml. On cognitive bias, expert advice, self-deception, and clever fools, see Crews 2006; Tetlock 2005; Kahneman 2011; Trivers 2011: 36–38.

Postscript:
What Politicians
Should Understand

If men define situations as real, they are real in their consequences.
—*D. I. Thomas and D. S. Thomas,* The Child in America:
Behavior Problems and Programs[1]

When the facts change, I change my mind.
What do you do, sir?
—*Variously attributed to John Maynard Keynes,*
Paul Samuelson, Winston Churchill, and Joan Robinson

Giving evidence to a judicial inquiry into the conduct of the press in 2012, Tony Blair stated that shortly before his first general election as the leader of the Labour Party in 1995, he flew halfway around the world to meet with Rupert Murdoch. His purpose was, as he put it, to persuade Murdoch's papers against "tearing us to pieces." It was important, he said, to get *The Sun* "on board," because "You were in a position where you were dealing with very powerful people. If they were against you, they were all-out against you." What is interesting about Blair's meeting with Murdoch is not that he went to such trouble to set it up, or that Murdoch made his point by obliging Blair to fly to Australia to meet him, or that it was kept secret for many years (though widely rumored) but that it is no surprise that Blair was convinced that Murdoch's approval, or at least Murdoch's neutrality, was essential for his political ambitions.

Blair had good reason to believe this. Murdoch's British papers sold approximately 5 million copies each weekday, with an estimated readership of between 10 million and 15 million readers. Sunday sales were 6 million, with an estimated 12 million to 18 million readers. As owner of *The Sun, Sun on Sunday* (since 2013), *News of the World,* the *Times,* and the *Sunday*

Times, Murdoch controlled about a third of the national newspaper market in the United Kingdom, and he also owned 39 percent of BskyB shares. It is generally thought that he controls the editorial policies of his papers. These had forcefully supported the Conservatives throughout four elections that kept the party in power for 18 years, notably in the previous contest of 1992. John Major won this close contest in the last week of the campaign when *The Sun* threw its full weight behind him. Hence, *The Sun*'s famous headline "It Was *The Sun* Wot Won It."

The Sun then switched from the Conservatives to fulsome support for Blair's New Labour in 1997, which then won a victory of historic proportions. After his meeting with Murdoch in 1995, Blair formed a close personal relationship with Murdoch, but he later stated that the relationship between those in government and the press was "unhealthy." However, the message we take from this close alliance is "keep your friends close and media magnates even closer." For his part, Murdoch has insisted that "I've never asked a prime minister for anything." But Murdoch rang Blair just before the Iraq invasion, urging him to join the Americans in military action.

Blair's personal and political relationship with Murdoch was only the tip of the iceberg of his government's concern with the media. He set up a lavishly staffed and funded communications department with special powers, bought an expensive computer program (Excalibur) to provide instant rebuttals to criticism of the government, and in general displayed an obsessive preoccupation with news management that amounted to what Seymour-Ure calls a "media fixation."[2]

Blair was not the first British prime minister to cultivate a close political understanding with Murdoch, or the last. Documents released by the Thatcher Archive Trust show that she had a secret meeting with him on January 4, 1981, in which they struck a deal: he would support her in the next election in return for her help to buy the *Times* and the *Sunday Times*. Despite his insistence that he never asked a prime minister for anything, this seems to be one more thing Murdoch asked a prime minister to do for him. The purchase was controversial because it would give him control of almost 40 percent of national newspaper sales, but first it had to be agreed by the Monopolies and Mergers Commission, which would require some adroit political maneuvers. Thatcher pushed through her side of the bargain by vehemently denying any such meeting for 30 years, replacing an experienced and knowledgeable government minister charged with referrals to the Monopolies Commission with a compliant and inexperienced one, making sure that he was not properly informed, overloading him with other work, imposing a three-line whip on her party to vote in Parliament for the Murdoch purchase, and then pretending that she had nothing to do with any of it. In their turn, politicians and the Commission had to swallow the idea that the *Times* and the *Sunday Times* had to be saved from financial collapse, whereas, in fact, they were profitable.

After Blair, both Brown and Cameron also took pains to keep Murdoch "on board." Ken Clarke, a senior minister in Cameron's cabinet, said he believed that Cameron had done "some sort of deal" with Murdoch to get his support in the 2010 election campaign. In return, Cameron appointed Andy Coulson, editor of Murdoch's Sunday paper *News of the World,* to be his director of communications, thus putting Murdoch's man at the center of government. Relations between senior government officials and Murdoch's people continued with Christmas parties, personal contacts, and meetings about political matters.

According to Clarke, Cameron arranged a meeting for him with Rebekah Brooks, an ex-editor of the *News of the World,* and of *The Sun* and, at that time, CEO of News International, the holding company of Murdoch's papers. Clarke reports that she described herself as running the government in partnership with Cameron, and the purpose of the meeting was to instruct Clarke about prison policy. Later, Cameron stated that "never again should we let a media group get too powerful . . . we all did too much cosying up to Rupert Murdoch" and "the relationship between ministers and editors/proprietors was too close for the good of the country."[3]

According to the *New York Times,* Murdoch has had a very different set of relations with US presidents. In the 44 years since he bought his first American newspaper, he has failed to cultivate close relations with any presidents—until Donald Trump, that is. The *New York Times* reports that Trump had regular phone conversations with Murdoch in his first months in office to discuss policy matters, including immigration, a new chair of the Federal Communications Commission (FCC), and the sale of major sections of the news and entertainment business. Murdoch is said to have been a close personal friend and confidant of Trump and Jared Kushner.[4] Murdoch's Fox News has been just about the only mass medium in the United States to support Trump, and although the *Wall Street Journal* (also a Murdoch paper) initially endorsed him, the president and the paper had their differences about fake news in 2018. This fits a pattern in which the Murdoch media follow the political interests of their readers and viewers.

Britain and the United States under Trump are not alone. Germany's *Bild* is a close equivalent of *The Sun* and Europe's best-selling daily paper. The two have in common their huge national sales, their sensational content, their punchy style, and strong, populist opinions. *Bild,* it is claimed, is feared by German politicians, including Gerhard Schröder, who said that all he needed for successful government was *Bild* and television.[5]

In Italy, it is believed Silvio Berlusconi rose to power on the back of Mediaset, his own huge media corporation. In Russia, Vladimir Putin and his allies take care to control TV news, the main source of news for most Russians. The Japanese prime minister Shinzo Abe says that he had to tame the *Asahi Shimbun* to stay in power. The *Asahi* has a daily circulation of about 6.6 million and an estimated readership of some 13 million to 18 million, the second largest in the country.

If they do not own the media, top politicians in the United Kingdom, Germany, Russia, Japan, and the United States feel an urgent need to neutralize them or make best friends with them. This distorts the democratic process, placing enormous powers in the hands of people who are not actually powerful, not elected, not accountable, and who speak only for their own political and economic interests. The *belief* that the press is powerful distorts and undermines democracy.

If politicians were to form a more realistic opinion about media power, they might stop cozying up to media magnates and, as Cameron said, this could only be for the good of their country. It would save them time, energy, and money trying to please a handful of people and untie political leaders from the apron strings of media barons, giving them greater freedom to adopt policies in the national interest. It would set them free to reform the media in the national interest, rather than in the interest of a few oligopolies. They could give more time and thought to the content of their public policies, give less time to how they are presented and packaged, and worry less about what the newspapers say about them. When they fall from grace in public opinion, politicians might realize their own part in the process rather than blaming the media for their own faults and failures.

Most of all, they would have a firmer grasp on what really drives public opinion and behavior—not the press, but how people perceive and react to their own circumstances and those around them. This is not to claim that public opinion is always right or that it is based on a correct understanding of problems—far from it. But as long as politicians choose to blame the press, they will not face up to real political problems posed by public opinion and its underlying causes. Politicians often claim to be hard-headed realists, but where the news media are concerned, they are not, and their false beliefs cause them and their countries all sorts of problems.

Mark Twain observed, "What gets us into trouble is not what we don't know. It's what we know for sure that just ain't so." There is a great weight of evidence to show that what politicians and citizens know for sure about the power of the media just ain't so. Many of the conclusions about media power in this book are unexpected, counterintuitive, and contrary to conventional wisdom, and so many who "know for sure" will find them surprising. Is it too much to hope that they will change their minds as the facts change?

Notes

1. Thomas and Thomas 1928: 572.
2. Seymour-Ure 2002: 133.

3. Murdoch's relations with Blair, Brown, Thatcher, and Cameron are outlined in King 2015: 149–158; A. McSmith, "Iraq and the Rupert Murdoch Connection: The Media Mogul's Network of Pro-War Campaigners," *Independent* (London), July 7, 2016, http://www.independent.co.uk/news/media/press/chilcot-inquiry-report-iraq-war-rupert -murdoch-connection-a7125786.html; "Leading Article: Questions for Mr. Blair to Address," *Independent* (London), May 28, 2012, http://www.independent.co.uk/voices /editorials/leading-article-questions-for-mr-blair-to-address-7792581.html; N. Watt, "Rupert Murdoch Pressured Tony Blair over Iraq, Says Alastair Campbell," *The Guardian* (Manchester), June 15, 2012, https://www.theguardian.com/media/2012/jun /15/rupert-murdoch-tony-blair-iraq-alastair-campbell; R. A. Greene, "Rupert Murdoch Put Pressure on Tony Blair, Ex-Prime Minister Says," CNN, May 28, 2012, http://edition .cnn.com/2012/05/28/world/europe/uk-phone-hacking/index.html; P. Owen, "Brown on Murdoch—and Murdoch on Brown," *Guardian* (Manchester), November 13, 2009, https://www.theguardian.com/politics/2009/nov/13/brown-murdoch-on-each-other; J. Martinson, "Murdoch at the Centre of Power Again as Cameron Drops Round for Drinks," *The Guardian* (Manchester), December 21, 2015, https://www.theguardian.com /media/2015/dec/21/rupert-murdoch-david-cameron-christmas-party; "Leveson Inquiry: Tony Blair Defends Murdoch Friendship," BBC News, May 28, 2012, http://www .bbc.co.uk/news/uk-18228898; H. Evans, "How Thatcher and Murdoch Made Their Secret Deal," *The Guardian* (Manchester), April 28, 2015, https://www.theguardian.com /uk-news/2015/apr/28/how-margaret-thatcher-and-rupert-murdoch-made-secret-deal; R. Vaughan, "Ken Clarke: David Cameron Did 'a Deal' with Sun Tycoon Rupert Murdoch," iNews, November 23, 2017, https://inews.co.uk/news/politics/ken-clarke-david-cameron -deal-sun-tycoon-rupert-murdoch/; Cowell and Burns 2012; Wolff 2012.

4. A. Chozick, "Rupert Murdoch and President Trump: A Friendship of Convenience," *New York Times,* December 23, 2017, https://www.nytimes.com/2017/12/23/business /media/murdoch-trump-relationship.html. See also D. Folkenflik, "Murdoch and Trump, an Alliance of Mutual Interest," NPR, March 14, 2017, https://www.npr.org/sections /thetwo-way/2017/03/14/520080606/murdoch-and-trump-an-alliance-of-mutual-interest; E. Louis, "Trump-Murdoch Relationship Raises Conflict-of-Interest Questions," CNN, May 7, 2017, http://edition.cnn.com/2017/05/06/opinions/trump-murdoch-conflicts-opinion -errol-louis/index.html; C. Lima, "The New Murdoch Media—Tucker Carlson Ready for Takeoff—Inside Trump's TV Addiction and Fake War on the Press," *Politico,* April 24, 2017, https://www.politico.com/tipsheets/morning-media/2017/04/the-new-murdoch-media -tucker-carlson-ready-for-takeoff-inside-trumps-tv-addiction-and-fake-war-on-the-press -219916; Barnett 2017.

5. M. Steininger, "German Tabloid Bild Takes Down Politicians with Its Unmatched Megaphone," *Christian Science Monitor,* January 18, 2012, https://www.csmonitor.com /World/Europe/2012/0118/German-tabloid-Bild-takes-down-politicians-with-its-unmatched -megaphone.

Bibliography

Aalberg, T., and Curran, J., eds. 2012. *How Media Inform Democracy: A Comparative Approach.* London: Routledge.

Aalberg, T., Esser, F., Reinemann, C., Strombeck, A., and de Vreese, C., eds. 2016. *Populist Political Communication in Europe.* London: Routledge.

Aalberg, T., Papathanassopoulos, S., Soroka, S., Curran, J., Hayashi, K., Iyengar, S., and Tiffen, R. 2013. "International TV News, Foreign Affairs Interest and Public Knowledge: A Comparative Study of Foreign News Coverage and Public Opinion in 11 Countries." *Journalism Studies* 14:387–406.

Aalberg, T., Van Aelst, P., and Curran, J. 2010. "Media Systems and the Political Information Environment: A Cross-National Comparison." *International Journal of Press/Politics* 15:255–271.

Aaronovitch, D. 2010. *Voodoo Histories: The Role of the Conspiracy Theory in Shaping Modern History.* London: Penguin.

Aarts, K., Fladmoe, A., and Strömbäck, J. 2012. "How the Media Inform Democracy: Media, Political Trust and Political Knowledge: A Comparative Perspective." In *How the Media Inform Democracy: A Comparative Approach,* edited by T. Aalberg and J. Curran, 98–117. London: Routledge.

Aarts, K., and Semetko, H. A. 2003. "The Divided Electorate: Media Use and Political Involvement." *Journal of Politics* 65:759–784.

Abelson, R. P. 1986. "Beliefs Are Like Possessions." *Journal for the Theory of Social Behaviour* 16:223–250.

Achen, C. H., and Bartels, L. M. 2016. *Democracy for Realists: Why Elections Do Not Produce Responsive Government.* Princeton, NJ: Princeton University Press.

Aday, S. 2010. "Chasing the Bad News: An Analysis of 2005 Iraq and Afghanistan War Coverage on NBC and Fox News Channel." *Journal of Communication* 60:144–164.

Alesina, A., and Giuliano, P. 2011. "Family Ties and Political Participation." *Journal of the European Economic Association* 9:817–839.

Allcott, H., and Gentzkow, M. 2017. "Social Media and Fake News in the 2016 Election." *Journal of Economic Perspectives* 31:211–236.

Anderson, C. A., Lepper, M. R., and Ross, L. 1980. "Perseverance of Social Theories: The Role of Explanation in the Persistence of Discredited Information." *Journal of Personality and Social Psychology* 39:1037–1049.

Anderson, C. J., and Paskeviciute, A. 2005. "Macro Politics and Micro-Behavior: Mainstream Politics and the Frequency of Political Discussion in Contemporary Democracies." In *The Social Logic of Politics: Personal Networks as Contexts for Political Behavior,* edited by A. S. Zuckerman, 228–248. Philadelphia: Temple University Press.

Anderson, C. W., Downie, L., and Schudson, M. 2016. *The News Media: What Everyone Needs to Know.* Oxford: Oxford University Press.

Andolina, M. W., and Wilcox, C. 2000. "Public Opinion: The Paradoxes of Clinton's Popularity." In *The Clinton Scandal and the Future of American Politics,* edited by M. J. Rozell and C. Wilcox, 171–194. Washington, DC: Georgetown University Press.

Arceneaux, K. 2006. "Do Campaigns Help Voters Learn? A Cross-National Analysis." *British Journal of Political Science* 36:159–173.

Arceneaux, K., and Johnson, M. 2013. *Changing Minds or Changing Channels? Partisan News in an Age of Choice.* Chicago: University of Chicago Press.

Ariely, D. 2012. *The (Honest) Truth About Dishonesty.* London: HarperCollins.

Arpan, L. M., and Raney, A. A. 2003. "An Experimental Investigation of News Source and the Hostile Media Effect." *Journal and Mass Communication Quarterly* 80:265–281.

Avery, J. M. 2009. "Videomalaise or Virtuous Circle? The Influence of the News Media on Political Trust." *International Journal of Press/Politics* 14:410–433.

Bader, C. D., Mencken, F. C., and Baker, J. O. 2017. *Paranormal America: Ghost Encounters, UFO Sightings, Bigfoot Hunts, and Other Curiosities in Religion and Culture.* New York: New York University Press.

Bagdikian, B. 2004. *The New Media Monopoly.* Rev. ed.), Boston, MA: Beacon.

Barnett, S. 2002. "Will a Crisis in Journalism Provoke a Crisis in Democracy?" *Political Quarterly* 73:400–408.

———. 2017. "Murdoch Has Had Too Many Favours." *British Journalism Review* 28:51–56.

Baron, J. 2007. *Thinking and Deciding.* Cambridge: Cambridge University Press.

Bartels, L. M. 2002. "Beyond the Running Tally: Partisan Bias in Political Perceptions." *Political Behaviour* 24:117–150.

———. 2014. "Remembering to Forget: A Note on the Duration of Campaign Advertising Effects." *Political Communication* 31:532–544.

Bartle, J., Crewe, I., and Gosschalk, B. 1998. "Introduction." In *Political Communications: Why Labour Won the General Election of 1997,* edited by I. Crewe, B. Gosschalk, and J. Bartle. London: Frank Cass.

Baum, M. A., and Groeling, T. 2009. "Shot by the Messenger: Partisan Cues and Public Opinion Regarding National Security and War." *Political Behavior* 31:157–186.

———. 2010. "Reality Asserts Itself: Public Opinion on Iraq and the Elasticity of Reality." *International Organization* 64:443–479.

Bausell, R. B. 2009. *Snake Oil Science: The Truth About Complementary and Alternative Medicine.* Oxford: Oxford University Press.

Beck, P. A., Dalton, R. J., Greene, S., and Huckfeldt, R. 2002. "The Social Calculus of Voting: Interpersonal, Media, and Organizational Influences on Presidential Choice." *American Political Science Review* 96:57–73.

Bell, S. 2000. "Kill the Messenger! The Public Condemns the News Media." *USA Today Magazine,* January, 61–62.

Bennett, S. E. 2002. "Another Lesson About Public Opinion During the Clinton-Lewinsky Scandal." *Presidential Studies Quarterly* 32:276–292.

Bennett, S. E., Flickinger, R. S., Baker, J. R., Rhine, S., and Bennett, L. M. 1996. "The Impact of Personal Characteristics and Mass Media Exposure on Citizens' Knowledge of Foreign Affairs: A Five Nation Study." *Harvard International Review of Press/Politics* 1:10–21.

Bennett, S. E., Flickinger, R. S., and Rhine, S. L. 2000. "Political Talk Over Here, Over There and Over Time." *British Journal of Political Science* 30:99–119.

Bennett, S. E., Rhine, S. L., Flickinger, R. S., and Bennett, L. L. 1999. "Videomalaise Revisited: Reconsidering the Relations Between the Public's View of the Media and Trust in Government." *Harvard International Journal of Press/Politics* 4:8–23.

Bennett, W. L. 2005a. "Beyond Pseudoevents: Election News as Reality TV." *American Behavioral Scientist* 491:364–378.

———. 2005b. "News as Reality TV: Election Coverage and the Democratization of Truth." *Critical Studies in Media Communication* 22:171–177.

————. 2008. "Changing Citizenship in the Digital Age." In *Civic Life Online: Learning How Digital Media Can Engage Youth.* John D. and Catherine T. MacArthur Foundation Series on Digital Media and Learning, edited by L. W. Bennett. Cambridge, MA: MIT Press.

————. 2015. "Changing Societies, Changing Media Systems: Challenges for Communication Theory, Research and Education." In *Can the Media Serve Democracy? Essays in Honour of Jay G. Blumler,* edited by S. Coleman, G. Moss, and K. Parry, 151–163. Basingstoke, England: Palgrave.

————. 2016. *News: The Politics of Illusion.* Chicago: University of Chicago Press.

Bennett, W. L., and Iyengar, S. 2008. "A New Era of Minimal Effects? The Changing Foundations of Political Communication." *Journal of Communication* 58:707–731.

Bennett, W. L., Segerberg, A., and Walker, S. 2014. "Organization in the Crowd: Peer Production in Large-Scale Networked Protests." *Information, Communication & Society* 17:232–260.

Benson, R. 2010. "What Makes for a Critical Press? A Case Study of French and U.S. Immigration News Coverage." *International Journal of Press/Politics* 15:3–24.

Benson, R., and Hallin, D. 2007. "How States, Markets and Globalization Shape the News: The French and U.S. National Press, 1965–1997." *European Journal of Communication* 22:27–48.

Benson, R., and Powers, M. 2011. *Public Media and Political Independence: Lessons for the Future of Journalism from Around the World.* New York: Department of Media, Culture, and Communication, New York University.

Berry, J. M., and Sobieraj, S. 2014. *The Outrage Industry: Political Opinion Media and the New Incivility.* Oxford: Oxford University Press.

Blumler, J. 1970. "The Political Effects of Television." In *The Effects of Television,* edited by J. Halloran, 70–104. London: Panther Books.

Blumler, J., Gurevitch, M., and Nossiter, T. J. 1995. "Struggle for Meaningful Election Communication: Television Journalism at the BBC, 1992." In *Political Communications: The General Election Campaign of 1992,* edited by I. Crewe and B. Gosschalk, 65–84. Cambridge: Cambridge University Press.

Bode, L., and Vagra, E. K. 2018. "Study Politics Across Media." *Political Communication,* 1–7.

Borah, P. 2014. "Does It Matter Where You Read the News Story? Interaction of Incivility and News Frames in the Political Blogosphere." *Communication Research* 41:809–827.

Boulianne, S. 2009. "Does Internet Use Affect Engagement? A Meta-Analysis of Research." *Political Communication* 26:193–211.

Boulton, A. 1998. "A View from Sky News." In *Political Communications: Why Labour Won the General Election of 1997,* edited by I. Crewe, B. Gosschalk, and J. Bartle, 195–204. London: Frank Cass.

Bounegru, L., Gray, J., Venturini, T., and Mauri, M. 2018. "A Field Guide to 'Fake News' and Other Information Disorders: A Collection of Recipes for Those Who Love to Cook with Digital Methods." Public Data Lab, Amsterdam.

Bourdieu, P. 1998. *On Television and Journalism.* London: Pluto Press.

Boxell, L., Gentzkow, M., and Shapiro, J. M. 2017. "Is the Internet Causing Political Polarization? Evidence from Demographics." NBER Working Paper No. 23258, National Bureau of Economic Research, Washington, DC.

Braestrup, P. 1977. *Big Story: How the American Press and Television Reported and Interpreted the Crisis of Tet 1968 in Vietnam and Washington.* Boulder, CO: Westview Press.

Brants, K., and Siune, K. 1998. "Politicization in Decline?" In *Media Policy: Convergence, Concentration and Commerce,* edited by D. McQuail and K. Suine, 128–143. Trowbridge, Wiltshire, United Kingdom: Cromwell Press.

Brabham, D. C. 2015. "Studying Normal, Everyday Social Media." Social Media and Society, 1(1), p.2056305115580484.

Brehm, J., and Rahn, W. 1997. "Individual-Level Evidence for the Causes and Consequences of Social Capital." *American Journal of Political Science* 41:999–1023.

Brundage, M., Avin, S., Clark, J., Toner, H., Eckersley, P., Garfinkel, B., Dafoe, A., et al. 2018. *The Malicious Use of Artificial Intelligence: Forecasting, Prevention, and Mitigation Future of Humanity.* Oxford: Future of Humanity Institute, University of

Oxford, Centre for the Study of Existential Risk, University of Cambridge, Center for a New American Security, Electronic Frontier Foundation, OpenAI.

Burnett, D. 2017. *The Idiot Brain: A Neuroscientist Explains What Your Head Is Really Up To.* New York: W. W. Norton.

Butler, D. 1995. *British General Elections Since 1945.* Oxford: Blackwell.

Butler, D., and Kavanagh, D. 1997. *The British General Election of 1997.* Basingstoke, England: Macmillan.

Calhoun, C. 1988. "Populist Politics, Communications Media and Large Scale Societal Integration." *Sociological Theory* 6:219–241.

Campbell, A. 1966. "Has Television Reshaped Politics?" In *Political Opinion and Electoral Behavior: Essays and Studies,* edited by E. C. Dreyer and W. A. Rosenbaum, 10–13. Belmont, CA: Wadsworth.

Campbell, D. E., and Wolbrecht, C. 2006. "See Jane Run: Women Politicians as Role Models for Adolescents." *Journal of Politics* 68:233–247.

Campbell, J. E. 2005. "The Fundamentals in US Presidential Elections: Public Opinion, the Economy and Incumbency in the 2004 Presidential Election." *Journal of Elections, Public Opinion & Parties* 15:73–83.

Carretta, T. R., and Moreland, R. L. 1982. "Nixon and Watergate: A Field Demonstration of Belief Perseverance." *Personality and Social Psychology Bulletin* 8:446–453.

Carruthers, S. L. 2000. *The Media at War.* Basingstoke, England: Macmillan.

Cathcart, B. 2017. "The *Daily Mail* and the Stephen Lawrence Murder." *Political Quarterly* 88:640–651.

Christen, C. T., Kannaovakun, P., and Gunther, A. C. 2002. "Hostile Media Perceptions: Partisan Assessments of Press and Public During the 1997 United Parcel Service Strike." *Political Communication* 19:423–436.

Clancy, S. A. 2005. *Abducted: How People Come to Believe They Were Kidnapped by Aliens.* Cambridge, MA: Harvard University Press.

Clark, T. N. 1969. *Gabriel Tarde on Communication and Social Influence.* Chicago: University of Chicago Press.

Clarke, H. D., Sanders, D., Stewart, M. C., and Whiteley, P. 2004. *Political Choice in Britain.* Oxford: Oxford University Press.

CNN. 1998. "Poll: Too Much Lewinsky Coverage." January 29. http://www.cnn.com /ALLPOLITICS/1998/01/29/poll/.

Coe, K., Tewksbury, D., Bond, B. J., Drogos, K. L., Porter, R. W., Yahn, A., Zhang, Y. 2008. "Hostile News: Partisan Use and Perceptions of Cable News Programming." *Journal of Communication* 58:201–219.

Cohen, G. L. 2003. "Party over Policy: The Dominating Impact of Group Influence on Political Beliefs." *Journal of Personality and Social Psychology* 85:808.

Cohen, S. 2001. *States of Denial: Knowing About Atrocities and Suffering.* Cambridge: Polity.

Cohn, N. 1970. *The Pursuit of the Millennium: Revolutionary Millenarians and Mystical Anarchists of the Middle Ages.* Oxford: Oxford University Press.

Coll, S. 2014. "The King of the Foxes." *New York Review of Books,* April 3, 6–11.

Compton, J., and Ivanov, B. 2012. "Untangling Threat During Inoculation-Conferred Resistance to Influence." *Communication Reports* 25:1–13.

Compton, J., Jackson, B., and Dimmock, J. A. 2016. "Persuading Others to Avoid Persuasion: Inoculation Theory and Resistant Health Attitudes." *Frontiers in Psychology* 7:122.

Corrigall-Brown, C., and Wilkes, R. 2014. "Media Exposure and the Engaged Citizen: How the Media Shape Political Participation." *Social Science Journal* 51:408–421.

Couldry, N., Livingstone, S., and Markham, T. 2016. *Media Consumption and Public Engagement: Beyond the Presumption of Attention.* Basingstoke, England: Palgrave.

Council of Europe. 2013. *Television News Channels in Europe.* Strasbourg, France: Council of Europe.

Cowell, A., and Burns, J. F. 2012. "At British Inquiry, Cameron Denies 'Deals' with Murdoch." *New York Times,* June 14.

Crews, F. C. 2006. *Follies of the Wise: Dissenting Essays.* Berkeley, CA: Counterpoint Press.

Cronin, T. E., and Genovese, M. A. 1998. "President Clinton and Character Questions." *Presidential Studies Quarterly* 28:892–897.

Cross, K. P. 1977. "Not Can but Will College Teachers Be Improved?" *New Directions for Higher Education* 17:1–15.

Curran, J., Coen, S., Soroka, S., Aalberg, T., Hayashi, K., Hichy, Z., Iyengar, S., et al. 2014. "Reconsidering 'Virtuous Circle' and 'Media Malaise' Theories of the Media: An 11-Nation Study." *Journalism* 15:815–833.

Curran, J., Iyengar, S., Lund, A. B., and Salovaara-Moring, I. 2009. "Media System, Public Knowledge and Democracy: A Comparative Study." *European Journal of Communication* 24:5–26.

Curran, J., and Seaton, J. 2010. *Power Without Responsibility.* 7th ed. Abingdon, Oxford: Routledge.

Curtice, J. 1997. "Is the Sun Shining on Tony Blair? The Electoral Influence of British Newspapers." *Harvard International Journal of Press/Politics* 2:9–26.

———. 1998. "Do Newspapers Change Voters' Minds? Or Do Voters Change Their Papers?" Paper presented at the American Political Science Association Annual Meeting, Boston.

———. 1999. "Was It the Sun That Won It Again? The Influence of Newspapers in the 1997 Campaign." CREST Working Paper No. 75, University of Strathclyde Centre for Research into Elections and Social Trends, Glasgow.

Curtice, J., and Semetko, H. 1994. "Does It Matter What the Papers Say?" In *Labour's Last Chance,* edited by A. Heath, R. Jowell, and J. Curtice, 43–64. Aldershot: Dartmouth.

Cushion, S. 2012. *The Democratic Value of News: Why Public Service Matters.* Basingstoke, England: Palgrave.

D'Alessio, D., and Allen, M. 2000. "Media Bias in Presidential Elections: A Meta-Analysis." *Journal of Communication* 50:133–156.

d'Ancona, M., 2017. *Post-Truth: The New War on Truth and How to Fight Back.* New York: Random House.

Dalton, R. J., Beck, P. A., and Huckfeldt, R. 1998. "Partisan Cues and the Media: Information Flows in the 1992 Presidential Election." *American Political Science Review* 92:111–126.

Daniel, J. H., and Ladd, J. M. 2014. "The Consequences of Broader Media Choice: Evidence from the Expansion of Fox News." *Quarterly Journal of Political Science* 9:115–135.

Darnton, R. 2000. "An Early Information Society: News and the Media in Eighteenth-Century Paris." *American Historical Review* 105:1–35.

Davis, R. 2009. *Typing Politics: The Role of Blogs in American Politics.* New York: Oxford University Press.

Davison, W. P. 1983. "The Third-Person Effect in Communication." *Public Opinion Quarterly* 47:1–15.

Dean, J. 1998. *Aliens in America: Conspiracy Cultures from Outerspace to Cyberspace.* Ithaca, NY: Cornell University Press.

De Camp, L. S. 2012. *Lost Continents.* North Chelmsford, MA: Courier Corporation.

DeFleur, M. H. 1998. "James Bryce's 19th-Century Theory of Public Opinion in the Contemporary Age of New Communications Technologies." *Mass Communication and Society* 1:63–84.

De Hart, J., and Dekker, P. 1999. "Civic Engagement and Volunteering in the Netherlands." In *Social Capital and European Democracy,* edited by J. W. van Deth, M. Maraffi, K. Newton, and P. F. Whitely, 75–107. London: Routledge.

DellaVigna, S., and Kaplan, E. 2006. "The Fox News Effect: Media Bias and Voting." *Quarterly Journal of Economics* 122:1187–1234.

Delli Carpini, M. X., and Keeter, S. 1997. *What Americans Don't Know About Politics and Why It Matters.* New Haven, CT: Yale University Press.

Delli Carpini, M. X., and Williams, B. A. 2001. "Let Us Infotain You: Politics in the New Media Environment." In *Mediated Politics: Communication in the Future of Democracy,* edited by W. L. Bennett and M. L. Entman, 160–181. Cambridge: Cambridge University Press.

De Vreese, C. H. 2007. "A Spiral of Euroscepticism: The Media's Fault?" *Acta Politica* 42:271–286.

De Vreese, C. H., Banducci, S. A., Semetko, H. A., and Boomgaarden, H. G. 2006. "The News Coverage of the 2004 European Parliamentary Election Campaign in 25 Countries." *European Union Politics* 71:477–504.

De Vreese, C. H., and Boomgaarden, H. 2006. "News, Political Knowledge and Participation: The Differential Effects of News Media Exposure on Political Knowledge and Participation." *Acta Politica* 41:317.

Dimitrova, D. V., Shehata, A., Strömbäck, J., and Nord, L. W. 2014. "The Effects of Digital Media on Political Knowledge and Participation in Election Campaigns: Evidence from Panel Data." *Communication Research* 41:95–118.

Dimitrova, D. V., and Strömbäck, J. 2012. "Election News in Sweden and the United States: A Comparative Study of Sources and Media Frames." *Journalism* 13:604–619.

Dimock, M. A., and Popkin, S. L. 1997. "Political Knowledge in a Comparative Perspective." In *Do the Media Govern? Politicians, Voters and Reporters in America,* edited by S. Iyengar and R. Reeves, 217–224. Thousand Oaks, CA: Sage.

Ditto, P. H., and Lopez, D. F. 1992. "Motivated Skepticism: Use of Differential Decision Criteria for Preferred and Nonpreferred Conclusions." *Journal of Personality and Social Psychology* 63:568–584.

Dougan, C., and Weiss, S. 1983. *Nineteen Sixty-Eight.* Boston: Addison-Wesley.

Dowell, B. 2012. "Rupert Murdoch: '*Sun* Wot Won It' Headline Was Tasteless and Wrong." *The Guardian* (Manchester), April 25. http://www.guardian.co.uk/media/2012/apr/25/rupert-murdoch-sun-wot-won-it-tasteless.

Doyle, G. 2002. *Media Ownership.* London: Sage.

———. 2007. "Undermining Media Diversity: Inaction on Media Concentrations and Pluralism in the EU." *European Studies: A Journal of European Culture, History and Politics* 24:135–156.

Doyle, G., and Vick, D. W. 2005. "The Communications Act 2003: A New Regulatory Framework in the UK." *Convergence* 11:75–94.

Drew, D., and Weaver, D. 2006. "Voter Learning in the 2004 Presidential Election: Did the Media Matter?" *Journalism and Mass Communication Quarterly* 83:25–42.

Druckman, J. N., Levendusky, M. S., and McLain, A. 2018. "No Need to Watch: How the Effects of Partisan Media Can Spread via Interpersonal Discussions." *American Journal of Political Science* 62:99–112.

Duffy, B., and Rowden, L. 2005. *You Are What You Read? How Newspaper Readership Is Related to Views.* London: Mori Social Research Institute.

Dunning, D. 2011. "The Dunning-Kruger Effect: On Being Ignorant of One's Own Ignorance." *Advances in Experimental Social Psychology* 44:247–296.

Durante, R., Pinotti, P., and Tesei, A. 2014. "No News, Big News: The Political Consequences of Entertainment TV." Working Papers No. 063, Carlo F. Dondena Centre for Research on Social Dynamics (DONDENA), Milan, Università Commerciale Luigi Bocconi.

Eagly, A. H., and Chaiken, S. 1993. *The Psychology of Attitudes.* Fort Worth, TX: Harcourt Brace Jovanovich.

Ecker, U. K., Lewandowsky, S., Swire, B., and Chang, D. 2011. "Correcting False Information in Memory: Manipulating the Strength of Misinformation Encoding and Its Retraction." *Psychonomic Bulletin and Review* 18:570–578.

Edelman, M. J. 1988. *Constructing the Political Spectacle.* Chicago: University of Chicago Press.

Edwards, K., and Smith, E. E. 1996. "A Disconfirmation Bias in the Evaluation of Arguments." *Journal of Personality and Social Psychology* 71:5–24.

Electoral Commission. 2005. "Election 2005: Engaging the Public in Great Britain." London: Electoral Commission.

Elegant, R. 1981. "How to Lose a War." *Encounter* 57:73–90.

Eliasoph, N. 1998. *Avoiding Politics: How Americans Produce Apathy in Everyday Life.* Cambridge: Cambridge University Press.

Enomoto, C. E., and Baker, N. 2005. "Public Opinion of the Impeachment of President William Jefferson Clinton: A Look Back." *American Review of Political Economy* 3:51–71.

Entman, R. M. 2005. "The Nature and Sources of News." In *Institutions of American Democracy: The Press,* edited by G. Overholser and K. H. Jamieson, 48–65. Oxford: Oxford University Press.

Esser, F., de Vreese, C. H., Strömbäck, J., and van Aelst, P. 2012. "Political Information Opportunities in Europe: A Longitudinal and Comparative Study of Thirteen Television Systems." *International Journal of Press/Politics* 17:247–274.

Eveland, W. P., Hutchens, M. J., and Morey, A. C. 2013. "Political Network Size and Its Antecedents and Consequences." *Political Communication* 30:371–394.

Fenster, M. 1999. *Conspiracy Theories: Secrecy and Power in American Culture.* Minneapolis: University of Minnesota Press.

Fenton, N. 2010. "News in the Digital Age." In *The Routledge Companion to News and Journalism,* edited by A. Stuart, 557–567. London: Routledge.

Fernbach, P. M., Rogers, T., Fox, C. R., and Sloman, S. A. 2013. "Political Extremism Is Supported by an Illusion of Understanding." *Psychological Science* 24:939–946.

Festinger, L., Riecken, H. W., and Schachter, S. 1956. *When Prophecy Fails.* Minneapolis: University of Minnesota Press.

Fine, C. 2006. *A Mind of Its Own: How Your Brain Distorts and Deceives.* London: Icon Books.

Flaxman, S., Goel, S., and Rao, J. M. 2013. "Ideological Segregation and the Effects of Social Media on News Consumption." *Public Opinion Quarterly* 16:298–320.

Fox, R. L., Van Sickel, R. W., and Steiger, T. L. 2001. *Tabloid Justice: Criminal Justice in an Age of Media Frenzy.* Boulder, CO: Lynne Rienner Publishers.

Fraile, M. 2011. "Widening or Reducing the Knowledge Gap? Testing the Media Effects on Political Knowledge in Spain 2004–2006." *International Journal of Press/Politics* 16:163–184.

Fraile, M., and Iyengar, S. 2014. "Not All News Sources Are Equally Informative: A Cross-National Analysis of Political Knowledge in Europe." *International Journal of Press/Politics* 19:275–294.

Freitag, M. 2003. "Beyond Tocqueville: The Origins of Social Capital in Switzerland." *European Sociological Review* 19:217–232.

Fritze, R. H. 2009. *Invented Knowledge: False History, Fake Science and Pseudo Religions.* London: Reaktion Books.

———. 2016. *Egyptomania: A History of Fascination, Obsession and Fantasy.* London: Reaktion Books.

Gabler, N. 1998. *Life the Movie: How Entertainment Conquered Reality.* New York: Knopf.

Gaines, B. J., Kuklinski, J. H., Quirk, P. J., Peyton, B., and Verkuilen, J. 2007. "Same Facts, Different Interpretations: Partisan Motivation and Opinion on Iraq." *Journal of Politics* 69:957–974.

Garrett, R. K., Carnahan, D., and Lynch, E. K. 2013. "A Turn Toward Avoidance? Selective Exposure to Online Political Information, 2004–2008." *Political Behavior* 35:113–134.

Garwood, C. 2008. *Flat Earth: The History of an Infamous Idea.* London: Macmillan.

Gavin, N. T., and Sanders, D. 2003. "The Press and Its Influence on British Political Attitudes Under New Labour." *Political Studies* 51:573–591.

Gelman, A., and King, G. 1993. "Why Are American Presidential Election Campaign Polls So Variable When Votes Are So Predictable?" *British Journal of Political Science* 23:409–451.

Gentzkow, M., Shapiro, J. M., and Sinkinson, M. 2011a. "The Effect of Newspaper Entry and Exit on Electoral Politics." *American Economic Review* 101:2980–3018.

———. 2011b. "Ideological Segregation Online and Offline." *Quarterly Journal of Economics* 26:1799–1839.

Georgiou, M. (n.d.) *Mapping Minorities and Their Media: The National Context—the UK.* London: London School of Economics.

Gerbner, G., Gross, L., Morgan, M., and Signorielli, N. 1986. "Living with Television: The Dynamics of the Cultivation Process." In *Perspectives on Media Effects,* edited by J. Bryant and D. Zillman, 17–40. Hillsdale, NJ: Erlbaum.

Gerbner, G., Mowlana, H., and Schiller, H. I. 2018. *Invisible Crises: What Conglomerate Control of Media Means for America and the World.* London: Routledge.

Gibson, J. L. 2001. "Social Networks, Civil Society and Prospects for Consolidating Russia's Transitions." *American Journal of Political Science* 45:51–68.

Gil de Zúñiga, H., Puig-i-Abril, E., and Rojas, H. 2009. "Weblogs, Traditional Sources Online and Political Participation: An Assessment of How the Internet Is Changing the Political Environment." *New Media and Society* 11:553–574.

Gilens, M. 2001. "Political Ignorance and Collective Policy Preferences." *American Political Science Review* 95:379–396.

Giner-Sorolla, R., and Chaiken, S. 1994. "The Causes of Hostile Media Judgements." *Journal of Experimental Social Psychology* 30:165–180.

Gladwell, M. 2010. "Small Change: Why the Revolution Will Not Be Tweeted." *The New Yorker,* October 4.

Goddard, P., Scammell, M., and Semetko, H. A. 1998. "Too Much of a Good Thing? Television in the 1997 Election Campaign." In *Political Communications: Why Labour Won the General Election of 1997,* edited by I. Crewe, B. Gosschalk, and J. Bartle, 149–179. London: Frank Cass.

Goldacre, B. 2007. "Benefits and Risks of Homoeopathy." *The Lancet*: 1672–1673.

Gooch, A. 2018. "Ripping Yarn: Experiments on Storytelling by Partisan Elites." *Political Communication* 35:220–238.

Goodin, R. E. 2000. "Democratic Deliberation Within." *Philosophy and Public Affairs* 29:81–109.

Gorman, S. E., and Gorman, J. M. 2017. *Denying to the Grave: Why We Ignore the Facts That Will Save Us*. Oxford: Oxford University Press.

Gosnell, H. 1929. *Getting Out the Vote*. Chicago: University of Chicago Press.

Green, A., and Gerbner, D. 1999. "Misperceptions About Perceptual Bias." *Annual Review of Political Science* 2:189–210.

Greenslade, R. 2009. "The *Sun*'s Political Switch Is No Surprise." *The Guardian* (Manchester), September 29.

Guilbeault, D., and Woolley, S. 2016. "How Twitter Bots Are Shaping the Election." *The Atlantic,* November 1, 2016.

Gunther, A. C. 1992. "Biased Press or Biased Public: Attitudes Towards Media Coverage of Social Groups." *Public Opinion Quarterly* 56:147–167.

Gunther, A. C., and Chia, S. C.-Y. 2001. "Predicting Pluralistic Ignorance: The Hostile Media Perception and Its Consequences." *Journalism and Mass Communication Quarterly* 78:688–701.

Gunther, A. C., Christen, C. T., Liebhart, J. L., and Chia, S. C.-Y. 2001. "Congenial Public, Contrary Press, and Biased Estimates of the Climate of Opinion." *Public Opinion Quarterly* 65:295–320.

Gunther, A. C., Miller, N., and Liebhart, J. L. 2009. "Assimilation and Contrast in the Hostile Media Effect." *Communication Research* 36:1–18.

Gunther, A. C., and Schmitt, K. 2004. "Mapping Boundaries of the Hostile Media Effect." *Journal of Communication* 54:55–70.

Gunther, R., and Mughan, A. 2000. "The Political Impact of the Media: A Reassessment." In *Democracy and the Media: A Comparative Perspective,* edited by R. Gunther and A. Mughan, 402–408. Cambridge: Cambridge University Press.

Habermas, J. 1989. *The Structural Transformation of the Public Sphere.* Cambridge, MA: MIT Press.

Haidt, J. 2001. "The Emotional Dog and Its Rational Tail: A Social Intuitionist Approach to Moral Judgment." *Psychological Review* 108:1024–1052.

Hall, L., Johansson, P., and Strandberg, T. 2012. "Lifting the Veil of Morality: Choice Blindness and Attitude Reversals on a Self-Transforming Survey." *PLOS ONE* 7:e45457.

Haller, H. B., and Norpoth, H. 1997. "Reality Bites: News Exposure and Economic Opinion." *Public Opinion Quarterly* 61:555–575.

Hallin, D. C. 1984. "The Media, the War in Vietnam, and Political Support: A Critique of the Thesis of Oppositional Media." *Journal of Politics* 46:2–24.

———. 1989. *The "Uncensored War": The Media and Vietnam.* New York: Oxford University Press.

———. 2006. "The Living-Room War: Media and Public Opinion in a Limited War." In *Rolling Thunder in a Gentle Land: The Vietnam War Revisited,* edited by A. Weist, 76–291. Oxford: Osprey.

Hallin, D. C., and Mancini, P. 2004. *Comparing Media Systems: The Models of Media and Politics*. Cambridge: Cambridge University Press.

Hamilton, J. 2004. *All the News That's Fit to Sell: How the Market Transforms Information into News*. Princeton, NJ: Princeton University Press.

Hamilton, J. T. 2007. "News That Sells: Media Competition and News Content." *Japanese Journal of Political Science* 8:7–42.

Hammond, W. M. 1989. "The Press in Vietnam as Agent of Defeat: A Critical Examination." *Reviews in American History* 17:312–323.

Hanas, J. 1998. "Dog the Wag." *Memphis Flyer: Media Watch,* January 29.

Hansen, K., Gerbasi, M., Todorov, A., Kruse, E., and Pronin, E. 2014. "People Claim Objectivity After Knowingly Using Biased Strategies." *Personality and Social Psychology Bulletin* 40:691–699.

Happer, C., and Philo, G. 2013. "The Role of the Media in the Construction of Public Belief and Social Change." *Journal of Social and Political Psychology* 1:321–336.

Harding, S., Phillips, D., and Fogarty, M. P. 1986. *Contrasting Values in Western Europe: Unity, Diversity and Change*. London: Macmillan.

Harris, P., Fury, D., and Lock, A. 2006. "Do Political Parties and the Press Influence the Public Agenda? A Content Analysis of Press Coverage of the 2001 UK General Election." *Journal of Political Marketing* 5:1–28.

Hastorf, A. H., and Cantril, H. 1954. "They Saw a Game: A Case Study." *Journal of Abnormal and Social Psychology* 49:129–134.

Heald, G., and Wybrow, R. 1986. *The Gallup Survey of Britain*. Beckenham, England: Croom Helm.

Heath, A., Jowell, R. M., and Curtice, J. K. 1985. *How Britain Votes*. Oxford: Pergamon Press.

———. 1994. *Labour's Last Chance? The 1992 Election and Beyond*. Watertown, MA: Dartmouth Publishing Group.

Herbst, S. 2010. *Rude Democracy: Civility and Incivility in American Politics*. Philadelphia: Temple University Press.

Hesmondhalgh, D. 2001. "Ownership Is Only Part of the Media Picture." *Open Democracy,* November 29. https://www.opendemocracy.net/media-globalmediaownership/article_46.jsp.

Hibbs, D. A. 2008. "Implications of the 'Bread and Peace Model' for the 2008 US Presidential Election." CEFOS Working Paper 7, Goteborg, Centre for Public Sector Research.

Highfield, T. 2016. *Social Media and Everyday Politics*. Cambridge: Polity Press.

Hilbert, M. 2012. "Toward a Synthesis of Cognitive Biases: How Noisy Information Processing Can Bias Human Decision Making." *Psychological Bulletin* 138:211–237.

Hill, S. J., Lo, J., Vavreck, L., and Zaller, J. 2013. "How Quickly We Forget: The Duration of Persuasion Effects from Mass Communication." *Political Communication* 30:521–547.

Hillygus, D. S. 2005. "Campaign Effects and the Dynamics of Turnout Intention in Election 2000." *Journal of Politics* 67:50–68.

Hilton, S. 1998. "The Conservative Party's Advertising Strategy." In *Political Communications: Why Labour Won the General Election of 1997,* edited by I. Crewe, B. Gosschalk, and J. Bartle, 45–49. London: Frank Cass.

Hindman, M. 2009. *The Myth of Digital Democracy*. Princeton, NJ: Princeton University Press.

Holbert, R. L. 2005. "A Typology for the Study of Entertainment Television and Politics." *American Behavioral Scientist* 3:436–453.

Holtz-Bacha, C. 1990. "Videomalaise Revisited: Media Exposure and Alienation in West Germany." *European Journal of Communication* 5:78–85.

Holtz-Bacha, C., and Norris, P. 2000. "To 'Entertain, Inform and Educate': Still the Role of Public Television in the 1990s?" Boston: Joan Shorenstein Center on the Press, Politics, and Public Policy.

Hooghe, M. 2002. "Watching Television and Civic Engagement: Disentangling the Effects of Time, Programs, and Stations." *Harvard International Review of Press/Politics* 7:84–104.

Hopkins, D. J., and Ladd, J. M. 2014. "The Consequences of Broader Media Choice: Evidence from the Expansion of Fox News." *Quarterly Journal of Political Science* 9:115–135. http://dx.doi.org/10.1561/100.00012099.

House of Lords Select Committee on Communications. 2008. *The Ownership of the News. Vol. I: Report.* HL Paper 122–I. London: Stationery Office Limited, 32.

Hovland, C. I., Janis, I. L., and Kelley, H. H. 1953. *Communications and Persuasion.* New Haven, CT: Yale University Press.

Howard, P. N., Kollanyi, B., Bradshaw, S., and Neudert, L. M. 2017. "Social Media, News and Political Information During the US Election: Was Polarizing Content Concentrated in Swing States?" Comprop Data Memo 2017.8, Computational Propaganda Research Project, September. https://arxiv.org/ftp/arxiv/papers/1802/1802.03573.pdf.

Howell, W. G., and West, M. R. 2009. "Educating the Public." *Education Next* 9:41–47.

Huckfeldt, R. 2014. "Networks, Contexts, and the Combinatorial Dynamics of Democratic Politics." *Political Psychology* 35:43–68.

Huckfeldt, R., Mendes, J. M., and Osborn, T. 2004. "Disagreement, Ambivalence and Engagement: The Political Consequences of Heterogeneous Networks." *Political Psychology* 25:65–95.

Huckfeldt, R., Pietryka, M. T., and Reilly, J. 2014. "Noise, Bias, and Expertise in Political Communication Networks." *Social Networks* 36:110–121.

Huckfeldt, R., and Sprague, J. 1991. "Discussant Effects on Vote Choice: Intimacy, Structure and Interdependence." *Journal of Politics* 53:122–158.

———. 1995. *Citizen, Politics and Social Communication: Information and Influence in an Election Campaign.* Cambridge: Cambridge University Press.

Humphreys, P. 1996. *Mass Media and Media Policy in Western Europe.* Manchester, England: Manchester University Press.

Hundal, S. 2010. "What Happens to Politics After the Sun Dies?" *New Statesman,* June 3.

Isin, E., and Ruppert, E. 2015. *Being Digital Citizens.* Boulder, CO: Rowman and Littlefield.

Ivanov, B., Miller, C. H., Compton, J., Averbeck, J. M., Harrison, K. J., Sims, J. D., Parker, K. A., and Parker, J. L. 2012. "Effects of Postinoculation Talk on Resistance to Influence." *Journal of Communication* 62:701–718.

Iyengar, S. 1994. *Is Anyone Responsible? How Television Frames Political Issues.* Chicago: University of Chicago Press.

Iyengar, S., Curran, J., Lund, A. B., Salovaara-Moring, I., Hahn, K. S., and Coen, S. 2010. "Cross-National Versus Individual-Level Differences in Political Information: A Media Systems Perspective." *Journal of Elections, Public Opinion and Parties* 20:291–309.

Iyengar, S., and Hahn, K. S. 2009. "Red Media, Blue Media: Evidence of Ideological Selectivity in Media Use." *Journal of Communication* 59:19–39.

Iyengar, S., Peters, M. B., and Kinder, D. R. 1982. "Experimental Demonstrations of the 'Not So Minimal' Consequences of Television News Programs." *American Political Science Review* 76:848–858.

Iyengar, S., and Simon, A. F. 2000. "New Perspectives and Evidence on Political Communication and Campaign Effects." *Annual Review of Psychology* 51:149–169.

Jack, I. 2015. "The Real Deal: The Autobiography of Britain's Most Controversial Media Mogul." *The Guardian* (Manchester), July 4, 7.

Jacobs, L. R., Cook, F. L., and Delli Carpini, M. X. 2009. *Talking Together: Public Deliberation and Political Participation in America.* Chicago: University of Chicago Press.

Jacobs, L., Hooghe, M., and de Vroome, T. 2017. "Television and Anti-immigrant Sentiments: The Mediating Role of Fear of Crime and Perceived Ethnic Diversity." *European Societies* 19:243–267.

Jacobs, L., Meeusen, C., and d'Haenens, L. 2016. "News Coverage and Attitudes on Immigration: Public and Commercial Television News Compared." *European Journal of Communication* 31:642–660.

Jacobsen, G. C. 2008. *A Divider, Not a Uniter: George W. Bush and the American People: The 2006 Election and Beyond.* New York: Pearson Longman.

Jastrow, J. 1935. *Wish and Wisdom: Episodes in the Vagaries of Belief.* New York: Appleton.

Johann, D., Königslöw, K. K. V., Kritzinger, S., and Thomas, K. 2018. "Intra-campaign Changes in Voting Preferences: The Impact of Media and Party Communication." *Political Communication* 35:261–286.

Johansson, P., Hall, L., Sikström, S., and Olsson, A. 2005. "Failure to Detect Mismatches Between Intention and Outcome in a Simple Decision Task." *Science* 310:116–119.

Johansson, P., Hall, L., Tärning, B., Sikström, S., and Chater, N. 2014. "Choice Blindness and Preference Change: You Will Like This Paper Better if You (Believe You) Chose to Read It!" *Journal of Behavioral Decision Making* 27:281–289.

Johnston, R., and Pattie, C. 2006. *Putting Voters in Their Place: Geography and Elections in Great Britain.* Oxford: Oxford University Press.

Jones, A. S. 2009. *Losing the News: The Future of the News That Feeds Democracy.* Oxford: Oxford University Press.

Kaase, M. 2000. "Germany: A Society and a Media System in Transition." In *Democracy and the Media: A Comparative Perspective,* edited by R. Gunther and A. Mughan, 375–401. Cambridge: Cambridge University Press.

Kahan, D. M. 2017. "Misconceptions, Misinformation, and the Logic of Identity-Protective Cognition." Cultural Cognition Project Working Paper Series No. 164, Yale Law School, Public Law Research Paper No. 605, Yale Law and Economics Research Paper No. 575. http://dx.doi.org/10.2139/ssrn.2973067.

Kahne, J., and Bowyer, B. 2018. "The Political Significance of Social Media Activity and Social Networks." *Political Communication* 35:470–493.

Kahneman, D. 2011. *Thinking Fast and Slow.* London: Allen Lane.

Kalmoe, N. P., Gubler, J. R., and Wood, D. A. 2018. "Toward Conflict or Compromise? How Violent Metaphors Polarize Partisan Issue Attitudes." *Political Communication* 35:333–352.

Kamalipour, Y. R., and Snow, N., eds. 2004. *War, Media, and Propaganda: A Global Perspective.* Lanham, MD: Rowman and Littlefield.

Kaminska, I. 2017. "A Lesson in Fake News from the Info-Wars of Ancient Rome." *Financial Times,* January 17.

Katz, E. 1999. "Theorizing Diffusion: Tarde and Sorokin Revisited." *Annals of the American Academy of Political and Social Science* 566:144–155.

———. 2006. "Rediscovering Gabriel Tarde." *Political Communication* 23:263–270.

Katz, E., and Lazarsfeld, P. F. 1955. *Personal Influence: The Part Played by People in the Flow of Mass Communications.* New York: Free Press.

Kellner, P., and Worcester, R. 1982. "Electoral Perceptions of Media Stance." In *Political Communications: The General Election Campaign of 1979,* edited by R. Worcester and M. Harrop, 57–67. London: Allen and Unwin.

Kenny, C. 1998. "The Behavioral Consequences of Political Discussion: Another Look at Discussant Effects on Vote Choice." *Journal of Politics* 60:231–244.

Kevin, D. 2015. *Snapshot: Regional and Local Television in the United Kingdom.* Strasbourg, France: Council of Europe.

Kiewiet, D. R. 1983. *Micropolitics and Macroeconomics.* Chicago: University of Chicago Press.

Killick, A. 2017. "Do People Really Lack Knowledge About the Economy? A Reply to Facchini." *Political Quarterly* 88:265–272.

Kim, J., Wang, C., Nunez, N., Kim, S., Smith, T. W., and Sahgal, N. 2015. "Paranormal Beliefs: Using Survey Trends from the USA to Suggest a New Area of Research in Asia." *Asian Journal for Public Opinion Research* 2:279–306.

King, A. 1997. *New Labour Triumphs: Britain at the Polls.* Chatham, NJ: Chatham House.

———. 2001. "Campaign Is Making No Impact on Voters." Gallup, May 18. https://news.gallup.com/poll/3145/Campaign-Making-Impact-Voters.aspx.

———. 2015. *Who Governs Britain?* London: Penguin Random House.

Klofstad, C. A. 2007. "Talk Leads to Recruitment: How Discussions About Politics and Current Events Increase Civic Participation." *Political Research Quarterly* 60:180–191.

———. 2009. "Civic Talk and Civic Participation: The Moderating Effect of Individual Predispositions." *American Politics Research* 37:856–878.

Klofstad, C. A., McClurg, S. D., and Rolfe, M. 2009. "Measurement of Political Discussion Networks: A Comparison of Two 'Name Generator' Procedures." *Public Opinion Quarterly* 73:462–483.

Klofstad, C. A., Sokhey, A. E., and McClurg, S. D. 2013. "Disagreeing About Disagreement: How Conflict in Social Networks Affects Political Behaviour." *American Journal of Political Science* 57:120–134.

Knobloch-Westerwick, S., Johnson, B. K., and Westerwick, A. 2015. "Confirmation Bias in Online Searches: Impacts of Selective Exposure Before an Election on Political Attitude Strength and Shifts." *Journal of Computer-Mediated Communication* 20:171–187.

Knoke, D., 1990. *Political Networks: The Structural Perspective*. Cambridge: Cambridge University Press.

Kruger, J., and Dunning, D. 1999. "Unskilled and Unaware of It: How Difficulties in Recognizing One's Own Incompetence Lead to Inflated Self-Assessments." *Journal of Personality and Social Psychology* 77:1121–1134.

Kuhn, D. and Lao, J. 1996. "Effects of Evidence on Attitudes: Is Polarization the Norm?" *Psychological Science* 7:115–120.

Kuhn, R. 1997. "The Media and Politics." In *Developments in West European Politics,* edited by M. Rhodes, P. Heywood, and V. Wright, 263–280. Basingstoke, England: Palgrave Macmillan.

Kuklinski, J. H., Quirk, P. J., Jerit, J., Schwieder, D., and Rich, R. F. 2000. "Misinformation and the Currency of Democratic Citizenship." *Journal of Politics* 62:790–816.

Kumlin, S. 2004. *The Personal and the Political: How Personal Welfare State Experiences Affect Political Trust and Ideology.* Basingstoke, England: Palgrave.

Ladd, J. M. 2010. "The Neglected Power of Elite Opinion Leadership to Produce Antipathy Toward the News Media: Evidence from a Survey Experiment." *Political Behavior* 32:29–50.

Ladd, J. M., and Lenz, G. S. 2009. "Exploiting a Rare Communication Shift to Document the Persuasive Power of the News Media." *American Journal of Political Science* 53:394–410.

La Due Lake, R., and Huckfeldt, R. 1998. "Social Capital, Social Networks, and Political Participation." *Political Psychology* 19:567–584.

Larson, M. S., and Wagner-Pacifici, R. 2001. "The Dubious Place of Virtue: Reflections on the Impeachment of William Jefferson Clinton and the Death of the Political Event in America." *Theory and Society* 30:735–774.

Lavine, H. G., Johnston, C. D., and Steenbergen, M. R. 2012. *The Ambivalent Partisan: How Critical Loyalty Promotes Democracy.* Oxford: Oxford University Press.

Lawrence, R. G., and Bennett, W. L. 2001. "Rethinking Media Politics and Public Opinion: Reactions to the Clinton-Lewinsky Scandal." *Political Science Quarterly* 116:425–446.

Lazarsfeld, P. F. 1942. "The Daily Newspaper and Its Competitors." *Annals of the American Academy of Political and Social Science* 219:32–43.

Lazarsfeld, P., Berelson, B., and Gaudet, H. 1968. *The People's Choice.* New York: Columbia University Press.

Lee, G., Cappella, J. N., and Southwell, B. 2003. "The Effects of News and Entertainment on Interpersonal Trust: Political Talk Radio, Newspaper and TV." *Mass Communications and Society* 6:413–434.

Leibowitz, H. 1965. *Visual Perception*. New York: Collier Macmillan.

Lenz, G. S. 2012. *Follow the Leader. How Voters Respond to Politicians' Policies and Performance.* Chicago: University of Chicago Press.

Leshner, G., and McKean, M. L. 1997. "Using TV News for Political Information During an Off-Year Election: Effects on Political Knowledge and Cynicism." *Journalism and Mass Communication Quarterly* 74:69–83.

Levendusky, M. 2017. "Morris Fiorina's Foundational Contributions to the Study of Partisanship and Mass Polarization." *The Forum* 15:189–201.

Lewandowsky, S., Stritzke, W. G., Oberauer, K., and Morales, M. 2005. "Memory for Fact, Fiction, and Misinformation: The Iraq War 2003." *Psychological Science* 16:190–195.

Lodge, M., and Taber, C. S. 2013. *The Rationalizing Voter.* Cambridge: Cambridge University Press.

Lord, C., Ross, L., and Lepper, M. 1979. "Biased Assimilation and Attitude Polarization: The Effects of Prior Theories on Subsequently Considered Evidence." *Journal of Personality and Social Psychology* 37:2098–2109.

Lumsdaine, A. A., and Janis, I. L. 1953. "Resistance to 'Counterpropaganda' Produced by One-Sided and Two-Sided 'Propaganda' Presentations." *Public Opinion Quarterly* 17:311–318.

Lundberg, G. 1926. "The Newspaper and Public Opinion." *Social Forces* 4:709–715.

Lupia, A., and McCubbins, M. D. 1998. *The Democratic Dilemma: Can Citizens Learn What They Need to Know?* Cambridge: Cambridge University Press.

Maarek, P. J. 1995. *Political Marketing and Communication.* London: John Libby.

MacArthur, B., and Worcester, R. M. 1992. "Preaching to the Uninterested." *UK Press Gazette,* April 6.

MacKuen, M. B., Erikson, R. S., and Stimson, J. A. 1992. "Peasants or Bankers? The American Electorate and the US Economy." *American Political Science Review* 86:597–611.

Mancini, P. 2012. "The Berlusconi Case: Mass Media and Politics in Italy." In *Media, Democracy and European Culture,* edited by I. Bondebjerg and P. Madsen, 107–119. Bristol, England: Intellect Press.

Mann, C. C. 2011. *1493: How Europe's Discovery of the Americas Revolutionized Trade, Ecology and Life on Earth.* London: Granta.

Margalit, Y. 2013. "Explaining Social Policy Preferences: Evidence from the Great Recession." *American Political Science Review* 107:80–103.

Margetts, H. 2017. "Why Social Media May Have Won the 2017 General Election." *Political Quarterly* 88:386–390.

Margetts, H., John, P., Hale, S., and Yasseri, T. 2016. *Political Turbulence: How Social Media Shape Collective Action.* Princeton, NJ: Princeton University Press.

Margolin, D. B., Hannak, A., and Weber, I. 2018. "Political Fact-Checking on Twitter: When Do Corrections Have an Effect?" *Political Communication* 352:196–219.

Marwick, A., and Lewis, R. 2017. *Media Manipulation and Disinformation Online.* New York: Data and Society Research Institute.

Marx, W., and Bornmann, L. 2013. "The Emergence of Plate Tectonics and the Kuhnian Model of Paradigm Shift: A Bibliometric Case Study Based on the Anna Karenina Principle." *Scientometrics* 94:595–614.

Massing, M. 2015. "Digital Journalism: The Next Generation." *New York Review of Books,* June 25, 43–45.

———. 2016. "Why Is Digital Journalism So Old and Boring?" Paper presented at Spring 2016 Donoho Colloquium, Dartmouth College, Hanover, NH, May 19.

McChesney, R. W. 1999. *Rich Media, Poor Democracy: Communication Politics in Dubious Times.* Urbana: University of Illinois Press.

McClurg, S. D. 2003. "Social Networks and Political Participation: The Role of Social Interaction in Explaining Political Participation." *Political Research Quarterly* 56:449–464.

McClurg, S. D. 2004. "Indirect Mobilization: The Social Consequences of Party Contacts in an Election Campaign." *American Politics Research* 32:406–443.

———. 2011. "Press Widely Criticized, but Trusted More Than Other Information Sources." *Views of the News Media: 1985–2011.*

McCombs, M. 2014. *Setting the Agenda: Mass Media and Public Opinion.* New York: Wiley.

McCombs, M. E., and Shaw, D. L. 1972. "The Agenda-Setting Function of Mass Media." *Public Opinion Quarterly* 36:176–187.

McGraw, K., and Hubbard, C. 1996. "Some of the People Some of the Time: Individual Differences in Acceptance of Political Accounts." In *Political Persuasion and Attitude Change,* edited by D. Mutz, P. M. Sniderman, and R. A. Brody, 145–170. Ann Arbor: University of Michigan Press.

McGuire, W. 1986. "The Myth of Massive Media Impact: Savagings and Salvagings." In *Public Communication and Behavior,* Vol. 1, edited by G. Comstock, 173–257. Orlando: Florida Academic Press.

McGuire, W. J., and Papageorgis, D. 1961. "The Relative Efficacy of Various Types of Prior Belief-Defense in Producing Immunity Against Persuasion." *Journal of Abnormal and Social Psychology* 62:327–337.

McKie, D. 1998. "The Tabloid Press and the 1997 General Election." In *Political Communications: Why Labour Won the General Election of 1997*, edited by I. Crewe, B. Gosschalk, and J. Bartle, 115–130. London: Frank Cass.

MacKuen, M. 1990. "Speaking of Politics: Individual Conversational Choice, Public Opinion, and the Prospects for Deliberative Democracy." In *Information and Democratic Processes*, edited by J. A. Ferejohn and J. H. Kuklinski, 59–99. Urbana: University of Illinois Press.

McLeod, J. M., Scheufele, D. A., and Moy, P. 1999. "Community, Communication and Participation: The Role of the Mass Media and Interpersonal Discussion in Local Political Participation." *Political Communication* 16:315–336.

McNair, B. 2017. *Fake News: Falsehood, Fabrication and Fantasy in Journalism*. London: Routledge.

McQuail, D. 1977. "The Influence and Effects of Mass Media," in *Mass Communication and Society*, edited by J. Curran, M. Gurevitch, and J. Woolacott, 70–94. London: Sage.

Mercier, H., and Sperber, D. 2017. *The Enigma of Reason*. Cambridge, MA: Harvard University Press.

Meyrowitz, J. 1995. "How Television Changes the Political Drama." In *Mass Media and Politics, Research in Political Sociology*, Vol. 7, edited by P. C. Washburn, 7–12. Greenwich, CT: JAI Press.

Mickiewicz, E. 2008. *Television, Power, and the Public in Russia*. Cambridge: Cambridge University Press.

Miller, A. H. 1999. "Sex, Politics, and Public Opinion: What Political Scientists Really Learned from the Clinton-Lewinsky Scandal." *PS: Political Science and Politics* 32:721–729.

Miller, J. M., and Krosnick, J. A. 2000. "News Media Impact on the Ingredients of Presidential Evaluations: Politically Knowledgeable Citizens Are Guided by a Trusted Source." *American Journal of Political Science* 44:295–309.

Miller, M. C. 2002. "What's Wrong with This Picture?" *The Nation*, January 7, 18–20.

Miller, W. 1991. *Media and Voters*. Oxford: Oxford University Press.

Miller, W., Timpson, A. M., and Lessnoff, M. H. 1996. *Political Culture in Contemporary Britain: People and Politicians, Principles and Practice*. Oxford: Oxford University Press.

Mlodinow, L. 2009. *The Drunkard's Walk: How Randomness Rules Our Lives*. New York: Vintage Books.

Mondak, J. J. 1995. *Nothing to Read: Newspapers and Elections in a Social Experiment*. Ann Arbor: University of Michigan Press.

Moore, R. 2010. *Shrinking World: The Decline of International Reporting in the British Press*. London: Media Standards Trust.

Morris, J. S. 2005. "The Fox News Factor." *Harvard International Journal of Press/Politics* 10:56–79.

Moss, G. D. 1998. *Vietnam: An American Ordeal*. Englewood Cliffs, NJ: Prentice Hall.

Moyers, B. 2009. *Moyers on Democracy*. New York: Anchor Books.

Mueller, J. E. 1973. *War, Presidents and Public Opinion*. New York: Wiley.

Mughan, A. 2000. *Media and the Presidentialization of Parliamentary Elections*. Basingstoke, England: Palgrave.

Mughan, A., and Gunther, R. 2000. "The Media in Democratic and Non-democratic Regimes: A Multilevel Perspective." In *Democracy and the Media: A Comparative Perspective*, edited by R. Gunther and A. Mughan, 1–26. Cambridge: Cambridge University Press.

Müller, P., Schemer, C., Wettstein, M., Schulz, A., Wirz, D. S., Engesser, S., and W. Wirth. 2017. "The Polarizing Impact of News Coverage on Populist Attitudes in the Public: Evidence from a Panel Study in Four European Democracies." *Journal of Communication* 67:968–992.

Munro, G. D. 2010. "The Scientific Impotence Excuse: Discounting Belief-Threatening Scientific Abstracts." *Journal of Applied Social Psychology* 40:579–600.

Mutz, D. C. 1998. *Impersonal Influence: How Perceptions of Mass Collectives Affect Political Attitudes*. Cambridge: Cambridge University Press.

————. 2015. *In-Your-Face Politics: The Consequences of Uncivil Media.* Princeton, NJ: Princeton University Press.

Mutz, D. C., and Martin, P. S. 2001. "Facilitating Communication Across Lines of Political Difference: The Role of Mass Media." *American Political Science Review* 95:97–114.

Mutz, D. C., and Mondak, J. J. 2006. "The Workplace as a Context for Cross-Cutting Political Discourse." *Journal of Politics* 68:140–155.

Mutz, D. C., and Reeves, B. 2005. "The New Videomalaise: Effects of Televised Incivility on Political Trust." *American Political Science Review* 99:1–15.

Negrine, R. 1989. *Politics and the Mass Media in Britain.* London: Routledge.

Neiheisel, J. R., and Niebler, S. 2016. "On the Limits of Persuasion: Campaign Ads and the Structure of Voters' Interpersonal Discussion Networks." *Political Communication* 32:434.

Nelson, J. L., and Taneja, H. 2018. "The Small, Disloyal Fake News Audience: The Role of Audience Availability in Fake News Consumption." *New Media and Society.* doi:10.1177/1461444818758715

Newman, B. 2002. "Bill Clinton's Approval Ratings: The More Things Change, the More They Stay the Same." *Political Research Quarterly* 55:781–804.

————. 2003. "Integrity and Presidential Approval, 1980–2000." *Public Opinion Quarterly* 67:335–367.

Newman, N., Fletcher, R., Kalogeropoulos, A., Levy, D., and Nielsen, R. K. 2018. *The Reuters Digital News Report 2018.* Oxford: Reuters Institute for the Study of Journalism.

Newton, K. 1999. "Politics and the News Media: Mobilization or Media Malaise?" *British Journal of Political Science* 29:577–599.

Newton, K., and Brynin, M. 2001. "The National Press and Party Voting in the UK." *Political Studies* 49:265–285.

Newton, K., and Norris, P. 2000. "Confidence in Institutions: Faith, Culture, or Performance." In *Disaffected Democracies: What's Troubling the Trilateral Democracies?* edited by S. J. Pharr and R. D. Putnam, 52–73. Princeton, NJ: Princeton University Press.

Nichols, T. 2017. *The Death of Expertise: The Campaign Against Established Knowledge and Why It Matters.* Oxford: Oxford University Press.

Nielsen, R. K. 2012. *Ground Wars: Personalized Communication in Political Campaigns.* Princeton, NJ: Princeton University Press.

Nikoltchev, S. 2007. *The Public Service Broadcasting Culture.* Strasbourg, France: European Audiovisual Observatory, Council of Europe.

Norris, P. 1996. "Does Television Erode Social Capital? A Reply to Putnam." *PS: Political Science and Politics* 29:474–480.

————. 2000. *A Virtuous Circle: Political Communications in Postindustrial Societies.* Cambridge: Cambridge University Press.

————. 2001. "Apathetic Landslide: The 2001 British General Election." *Parliamentary Affairs* 54:564–589.

————. 2006. "Did the Media Matter? Agenda-Setting, Persuasion and Mobilization Effects in the British General Election Campaign." *British Politics* 1:195–221.

Norris, P., Curtice, J., Sanders, D., Scammell, M., and Semetko, H. A. 1999. *On Message: Communicating the Campaign.* London: Sage.

Norris, P., and Sanders, D. 2003. "Message or Medium? Campaign Learning During the 2001 British General Election." *Political Communication* 20:233–262.

Nyhan, B. 2010. "Why the 'Death Panel' Myth Wouldn't Die: Misinformation in the Health Care Reform Debate." *The Forum* 8:1–24.

Nyhan, B., and Reifler, J. 2010. "When Corrections Fail: The Persistence of Political Misperceptions." *Political Behavior* 32:303–330.

————. 2012. *Misinformation and Fact Checking: Research Findings from Social Science.* Washington, DC: New America Foundation, Media Policy Initiative.

Ofcom. 2009. *Local and Regional Media in the UK.* London: Ofcom.

————. 2011. *The Communications Market Report 2011.* London: Ofcom.

————. 2012. *Measuring Media Plurality: Ofcom's Advice to the Secretary of State for Culture, Olympics, Media and Sport.* London: Ofcom.

————. 2015a. *The Communications Market Report 2015.* London: Ofcom.

———. 2015b. *News Consumption in the UK: Research Report.* London: Ofcom.

Offit, P. 2013. *Killing Us Softly: The Sense and Nonsense of Alternative Medicine.* New York: HarperCollins.

Packer, D., and Wohl, M. 2017. "Most Republicans Still Say They Support Trump." *Washington Post,* July 20.

Paletz, D. L., and Entman, R. M. 1981. *Media, Power, Politics.* New York: Free Press.

Papageorgis, D., and McGuire, W. J. 1961. "The Generality of Immunity to Persuasion Produced by Pre-exposure to Weakened Counterarguments." *Journal of Abnormal and Social Psychology* 62:475–481.

Papathanassopoulos, S., and Negrine, R. M. 2011. *European Media.* Oxford: Polity Press.

Parenti, M. 1992. *Make-Believe Media: The Politics of Entertainment.* New York: St. Martin's Press.

Park, R. L. 2002. *Voodoo Science: The Road from Foolishness to Fraud.* Oxford: Oxford University Press.

———. 2008. *Superstition: Belief in the Age of Science.* Princeton, NJ: Princeton University Press.

Pattie, C., and Johnston, R. 1999. "Context, Conversation and Conviction: Social Networks and Voting at the 1992 British General Election." *Political Studies* 47:877–889.

Perloff, R. M. 1989. "Ego Involvement and the Third Person Effect of Television News Coverage." *Communication Research* 16:336–362.

Pew Research Center. 1998. "Americans Unmoved by Prospects of Clinton, Lewinsky Testimony." *Philosophy and Public Affairs* 29:81–109.

———. 2008a. *Audience Segments in a Changing News Environment.* Washington, DC: Pew Research Center.

———. 2008b. *Internet Overtakes Newspapers as New Outlet.* Washington, DC: Pew Research Center.

———. 2010. *Americans Spending More Time Following the News.* Washington, DC: Pew Research Center.

———. 2011. *Views of the News Media 1985–2011.* Washington, DC: Pew Research Center.

———. 2012. *Cable Leads the Pack as Campaign Source.* Washington, DC: Pew Research Center.

Pfetsch, B. 1996. "Convergence Through Privatization? Changing Media Environments and Televised Politics in Germany." *European Journal of Communication* 8:425–450.

Philo, G. 2014. *Seeing and Believing: The Influence of Television.* London: Routledge.

Pingree, R. J., and Stoycheff, E. 2013. "Differentiating Cueing from Reasoning in Agenda-Setting Effects." *Journal of Communication* 63:852–872.

Postman, N. 1985. *Amusing Ourselves to Death: Public Discourse in the Age of Show Business.* New York: Viking-Penguin Books.

———. 2000. "The Social Effects of Commercial Television." In *Critical Studies in Media Commercialism,* edited by R. Andersen and L. Strate, 47–53. Oxford: Oxford University Press.

Price, V., and Zaller, J. 1993. "Who Gets the News? Alternative Measures of News Reception and Their Implications for Research." *Public Opinion Quarterly* 57:133–164.

Prior, M. 2005. "News vs. Entertainment: How Increasing Media Choice Widens Gaps in Political Knowledge and Turnout." *American Journal of Political Science* 49:577–592.

———. 2009a. "The Immensely inflated news audience: Assessing bias in self-reported news exposure." *Public Opinion Quarterly* 73:130–143.

———. 2009b. "Improving media effects research through better measurement of news exposure." *Journal of Politics* 71:893–908.

———. 2013. "Media and Political Polarization." *Annual Review of Political Science* 16:101–127.

Putnam, R. D. 1995. "Tuning In, Tuning Out: The Strange Disappearance of Social Capital in America." *PS: Political Science and Politics* 28:664–683.

———. 2000. *Bowling Alone: The Collapse and Revival of Civic America.* New York: Simon and Schuster.

Putnam, R. D., Pharr, S. J., and Dalton, R. J. 2000. "Introduction. What's Troubling the Trilateral Democracies?" In *Disaffected Democracies: What's Troubling the Trilat-*

eral Democracies? edited by S. J. Pharr and R. D. Putnam, 3–27. Princeton, NJ: Princeton University Press.

Quiggin, J. 2012. *Zombie Economics: How Dead Ideas Still Walk Among Us.* Princeton, NJ: Princeton University Press.

Radio Centre. (n.d.). *Action Stations: The Output and Impact of Commercial Radio.* London: Radio Centre.

Rahn, W. M. 1993. "The Role of Partisan Stereotypes in Information Processing About Political Candidates." *American Journal of Political Science* 37:472–496.

Randi, J. 1982. *Flim-Flam! Psychics, ESP, Unicorns, and Other Delusions.* Buffalo, NY: Prometheus.

Ranney, A. 1983. *Channels of Power: The Impact of Television on American Politics.* New York: Basic Books.

Redlawsk, D. P. 2002. "Hot Cognition or Cool Consideration? Testing the Effects of Motivated Reasoning on Political Decision Making." *Journal of Politics* 64:1021–1044.

Richey, S., and Zhu, J. 2015. "Internet Access Does Not Improve Political Interest, Efficacy, and Knowledge for Late Adopters." *Political Communication* 32:396–413.

Robinson, M. J. 1975. "American Political Legitimacy in an Era of Electronic Journalism: Reflections on the Evening News." In *Television as a Social Force: New Approaches to TV Criticism,* edited by D. Cater and R. Adler, 97–139. New York: Praeger.

———. 1976. "Public Affairs Television and the Growth of Political Malaise: The Case of 'The Selling of the Pentagon.'" *American Political Science Review* 70:409–432.

Roessler, P. 1999. "The Individual Agenda-Designing Process: How Inter-personal Communication, Egocentric Networks, and Mass Media Shape the Perception of Political Issues by Individuals." *Communication Research* 26:666–700.

Ronson, J. 2009. *The Men Who Stare at Goats.* New York: Simon and Schuster.

Ross, L., and Anderson, C. A. 1982. "Shortcomings in the Attribution Process: On the Origins and Maintenance of Erroneous Social Assessments." In *Judgment Under Uncertainty: Heuristics and Biases,* edited by D. Kahneman, P. Slovic, and A. Tversky, 129–152. Cambridge: Cambridge University Press.

Ross, L., Lepper, M. R., and Hubbard, M. 1975. "Perseverance in Self-Perception and Social Perception: Biased Attributional Processes in the Debriefing Paradigm." *Journal of Personality and Social Psychology* 32:880–892.

Russell Neuman, W., Guggenheim, L., Mo Jang, S., and Bae, S. Y. 2014. "The Dynamics of Public Attention: Agenda-Setting Theory Meets Big Data." *Journal of Communication* 64:193–214.

Russo, J. E., and Chaxel, A. S. 2010. "How Persuasive Messages Can Influence Behavior Without Awareness." *Journal of Consumer Psychology* 20:338–342.

Sabato, L. J. 2001. *Feeding Frenzy: How Attack Journalism Has Transformed American Politics.* Baltimore: Lanahan Publishers.

Sanders, D., Clarke, H., Stewart, M., and Whiteley, P. 2001. "The Economy and Voting." *Parliamentary Affairs* 54:789–802.

Schama, S. 1988. *The Embarrassment of Riches: An Interpretation of Dutch Culture in the Golden Age.* Oakland: University of California Press.

Schlosberg, J. 2016. *Media Ownership and Agenda Control: The Hidden Limits of the Information Age.* London: Routledge.

Schmitt, K. M., Gunther, A. C., and Liebhart, J. L. 2004. "Why Partisans See Mass Media as Biased." *Communication Research* 31:623–641.

Schmitt-Beck, R. 2003. "Mass Communication, Personal Communication, and Vote Choice: The Filter Hypothesis of Media Influence in Comparative Perspective." *British Journal of Political Science* 33:233–259.

Schmitt-Beck, R., and Farrell, D. 2002. "Do Political Campaigns Matter?" In *Do Political Campaigns Matter? Campaign Effects in Elections and Referendums,* edited by D. Farrell and R. Schmitt-Beck, 183–193. London: Routledge.

Schmitt-Beck, R., and Wolsing, A. 2010. "European TV Environments and Citizens' Social Trust: Evidence from Multilevel Analyses." *Communications* 35:461–483.

Schudson, M. 1995. *The Power of News.* Cambridge, MA: Harvard University Press.

Semetko, H. A. 1996. "Political Balance on Television: Campaigns in the United States, Britain, and Germany." *Harvard International Journal of Press/Politics* 1:51–71.

———. 2000. "Great Britain: The End of *The News at Ten* and the Changing News Environment." In *Democracy and the Media: A Comparative Perspective,* edited by R. Gunther and A. Mughan. Cambridge: Cambridge University Press.

Seymour-Ure, C. 1997. "Editorial Opinion in the National Press." In *Britain Votes 1997,* edited by P. Norris and L. Gavin, 586–609. Oxford: Oxford University Press.

———. 2002. "New Labour and the Media." In *Britain at the Polls, 2001,* edited by A. S. King, 117–142. New York: Chatham House Publishers.

Shah, D. V. 1998. "Civic Engagement, Interpersonal Trust and TV Use: An Individual Level Assessment of Social Capital." *Political Psychology* 19:469–496.

Shah, D. V., McLeod, J. M., and Yoon, S.-H. 2001. "Communication, Context and Community: An Exploration of Print, Broadcasting and Internet Influences." *Communication Research* 28:464–506.

Shao, C., Ciampaglia, G. L., Varol, O., Flammini, A., and Menczer, F. 2017. "The Spread of Fake News by Social Bots." arXiv. https://www.researchgate.net/publication/318671211_The_spread_of_fake_news_by_social_bots.

Shea, D. M., and Fiorina, M. P., eds. 2012. *Can We Talk? The Rise of Rude, Nasty, Stubborn Politics.* New York: Pearson.

Shea, D. M., and Sproveri, A. 2012. "The Rise and Fall of Nasty Politics in America." *PS: Political Science and Politics* 45:416–421.

Shehata, A., Hopmann, D. N., Nord, L., and Höijer, J. 2015. "Television Channel Content Profiles and Differential Knowledge Growth: A Test of the Inadvertent Learning Hypothesis Using Panel Data." *Political Communication* 32:377–395.

Shehata, A., and Strömbäck, J. 2011. "A Matter of Context: A Comparative Study of Media Environments and News Consumption Gaps in Europe." *Political Communication* 28:110–134.

Shepperd, J., Malone, W., and Sweeny, K. 2008. "Exploring Causes of the Self-Serving Bias." *Social and Personality Psychology Compass* 2:895–908.

Shermer, M. 2002. *Why People Believe Weird Things: Pseudoscience, Superstition, and Other Confusions of Our Time.* New York: Macmillan.

Sides, J., and Vavreck, L. 2014. *The Gamble: Choice and Chance in the 2012 Presidential Election.* Princeton, NJ: Princeton University Press.

Singh, S., and Ernst, E. 2008. *Trick or Treatment: The Undeniable Facts About Alternative Medicine.* New York: W. W. Norton.

Skogerbø, E. 1997. "The Press Subsidy System in Norway: Controversial Past—Unpredictable Future?" *European Journal of Communication* 12:99–118.

Sloman, S., and Fernbach, P. 2017. *The Knowledge Illusion: Why We Never Think Alone.* New York: Penguin Random House.

Smelser, N. J. 1965. *Theory of Collective Behavior.* New York: Free Press.

Smith, R. C., and Tambini, D. 2012. "Measuring Media Plurality in the United Kingdom: Policy Choices and Regulatory Challenges." *Journal of Media Law* 4:35–63.

Sonner, M. W., and Wilcox, C. 1999. "Forgiving and Forgetting: Public Support for Bill Clinton During the Lewinsky Scandal." *PS: Political Science and Politics* 32:554–557.

Soroka, S. N. 2012. "The Gatekeeping Function: Distributions of Information in Media and the Real World." *Journal of Politics* 74:514–528.

Soroka, S. N., Andrew, B., Aalberg, T., Iyengar, S., Curran, J., Coen, S., Hayashi, K., et al. 2013. "Auntie Knows Best? Public Broadcasters and Current Affairs Knowledge." *British Journal of Political Science* 43:719–739.

Sprague de Camp, L. 1970. *Lost Continents: The Atlantis Theme in History, Science, and Literature.* New York: Dover.

Srnicek, N. 2016. *Platform Capitalism.* New York: Wiley.

Stephens-Davidowitz, S. 2017. *Everybody Lies: Big Data, New Data, and What the Internet Can Tell Us About Who We Really Are.* London: Bloomsbury.

Sternheimer, K. 2003. *It's Not the Media: The Truth About Pop Culture's Influence on Children.* New York: Basic Books.

Street, J. 2001. *Mass Media, Politics and Democracy.* Basingstoke, England: Palgrave.

Strömbäck, J. 2017. "News Seekers, News Avoiders, and the Mobilizing Effects of Election Campaigns: Comparing Election Campaigns for the National and the European Parliaments." *International Journal of Communication* 11:237–258.

Strömbäck, J., and Dimitrova, D. V. 2006. "Political and Media Systems Matter: A Comparison of Election News Coverage in Sweden and the United States." *Harvard International Journal of Press/Politics* 11:131–147.

Strömbäck, J., Falasca, K., and Kruikemeier, S. 2018. "The Mix of Media Use Matters: Investigating the Effects of Individual News Repertoires on Offline and Online Political Participation." *Political Communication* 35:413–432.

Strömbäck, J., and Shehata, A. 2010. "Media Malaise or a Virtuous Circle? Exploring the Causal Relationships Between News Media Exposure, Political News Attention and Political Interest." *European Journal of Political Research* 49:575–597.

Sunstein, C. R. 2007. *Republic.com 2.0.* Princeton, NJ: Princeton University Press.

Sutherland, S. 2009. *Irrationality.* London: Pinter and Martin.

Taber, C. S., and Lodge, M. 2006. "Motivated Skepticism in the Evaluation of Political Beliefs." *American Journal of Political Science* 50:755–769.

Taplin, J. 2017. *Move Fast and Break Things: How Facebook, Google, and Amazon Cornered Culture and Undermined Democracy.* London: Macmillan.

Taverne, D. 2005. *The March of Unreason: Science, Democracy, and the New Fundamentalism.* Oxford: Oxford University Press.

Tetlock, P. 2005. *Expert Political Judgment: How Good Is It? How Can We Know?* Princeton, NJ: Princeton University Press.

Thomas, D. I., and Thomas, D. S. 1928. *The Child in America: Behavior Problems and Programs.* New York: Alfred A. Knopf.

Thompson, D. 2008. *Counter-Knowledge: How We Surrendered to Conspiracy Theories, Quack Medicine, Bogus Science and Fake History.* London: Atlantic Books.

Thorson, E. 2015. "Identifying and Correcting Policy Misperceptions." Unpublished paper, George Washington University. Available at http://www.americanpressinstitute .org/wp-content/uploads/2015/04/Project-2-Thorson-2015-Identifying-Political -Misperceptions-UPDATED-4-24.pdf.

Tóka, G., and Popescu, M. 2009. "Public Television, Private Television and Citizens' Political Knowledge." EUI Working Papers, RSCAS 2009/66, European University Institute, San Domenico di Fiesole, Italy.

Tomasky, M. 2016. "Can the Monster Be Elected." *New York Review of Books,* July 14–August 17, 43.

Trenaman, J. M., and McQuail, D. 1961. *Television and the Political Image: A Study of the Impact of Television on the 1959 General Election.* London: Taylor and Francis.

Trivers, R. 2011. *Deceit and Self-Deception: Fooling Yourself the Better to Fool Others.* London: Penguin.

Trouche, E., Johansson, P., Hall, L., and Mercier, H. 2016. "The Selective Laziness of Reasoning." *Cognitive Science* 40:2122–2136.

Tsfati, Y. 2003. "Does Audience Skepticism of the Media Matter in Agenda Setting?" *Journal of Broadcasting and Electronic Media* 47:157–176.

Tsfati, Y., and Cappella, J. N. 2005. "Why Do People Watch the News They Do Not Trust? The Need for Cognition as a Moderator in the Association Between News Media Scepticism and Exposure." *Media Psychology* 7:251–271.

Tumminia, D. G. 2005. *When Prophecy Never Fails: Myth and Reality in a Flying-Saucer Group.* Oxford: Oxford University Press.

Underwood, D. 2001. "Reporting and the Push for Market-Oriented Journalism: Media Organizations as Businesses." In *Mediated Politics: Communication in the Future of Democracy,* edited by W. L. Bennett and R. M. Entman, 99–116. Cambridge: Cambridge University Press.

University of Essex, Institute for Social and Economic Research. 2018. British Household Panel Study, 1992, 1997.

Vallone, R., Ross, L., and Lepper, M. 1985. "The Hostile Media Phenomenon: Biased Perception and Perceptions of Media Bias in Coverage of the Beirut Massacre." *Journal of Personality and Social Psychology* 49:577–585.

Vermeule, A. 2011. "'Government by Public Opinion': Bryce's Theory of the Constitution." Harvard Public Law Working Paper No. 11-13, Harvard Law School, Cambridge, MA.

Voltmer, K. 2000. "Structures of Diversity of Press and Broadcasting Systems: The Institutional Context of Public Communication in Western Democracies." WZB Discussion Paper No. FS III 00-201, WZB, Berlin.

Walgrave, S., and Van Aelst, P. 2006. "The Contingency of the Mass Media's Political Agenda Setting Power: Toward a Preliminary Theory." *Journal of Communication* 56:88–109.

Walsh, K. K. 2004. *Talking About Politics: Informal Groups and Social Life in American Politics.* Chicago: University of Chicago Press.

Ward, D. 2005, "Media Concentration and Pluralism: Regulation, Realities and the Council of Europe's Standards in the Television Sector." Venice Commission, T-01-2005, European Commission for Democracy Through Law, T-01-2005, Strasbourg.

Ward, D., Fueg, O. C., and D'Armo, A. 2004. *A Mapping Study of Media Concentration and Ownership in Ten European Countries.* Hilversum, the Netherlands: Commissariaat voor de Media.

Westen, D. 2008. *The Political Brain: The Role of Emotion in Deciding the Fate of the Nation.* New York: PublicAffairs.

Wheen, F. 2005. *How Mumbo-Jumbo Conquered the World: A Short History of Modern Delusions.* New York: PublicAffairs.

Wilken, R. L. 2003. *The Christians as the Romans Saw Them.* New Haven, CT: Yale University Press.

Wlezien, C., and Norris, P. 2005. "Conclusion: Whether the Campaign Mattered and How." *Parliamentary Affairs* 58:871–888.

Wolff, M. 2012. "Tony Blair and the Murdochs: A Family Affair." *The Guardian* (Manchester), May 29, 2012.

Wonneberger, A., Schoenbach, K., and van Meurs, L. (n.d.). "Trends of Exposure to Public-Affairs TV in the Netherlands 1988–2010." Amsterdam: Amsterdam School of Communication Research.

Wood, N. T., and Herbst, K. C. 2007. "Political Star Power and Political Parties: Does Celebrity Endorsement Win First-Time Votes?" *Journal of Political Marketing* 6:141–158.

Woolley, S. C., and Howard, P. N. 2017. *Computational Propaganda Worldwide.* Oxford Computational Propaganda Research Project, Working Paper No. 2017.11, Oxford.

World Radio and Television Council. 2011. *Public Broadcasting Why? How?* Paris: UNESCO.

Wu, T. 2011. *The Master Switch: The Rise and Fall of Information Empires.* New York: Vintage Books.

Wyatt, R. O., Katz, E., and Kim, J. 2000. "Bridging the Spheres: Political and Personal Conversation in Public and Private Spaces." *Journal of Communication* 50:71–92.

Zaller, J. 1992. *The Nature and Origins of Mass Opinion.* Cambridge: Cambridge University Press.

———. 1996. "The Myth of Massive Media Impact Revived: New Support for a Discredited Idea." In *Political Persuasion and Attitude Change,* edited by D. C. Mutz, P. M. Sniderman, and R. A. Brody, 17–78. Ann Arbor: University of Michigan Press.

———. 1998. "Monica Lewinsky's Contribution to Political Science." *PS: Political Science and Politics* 31:182–189.

———. 2001. "Monica Lewinsky and the Mainsprings of American Politics." In *Mediated Politics,* edited by W. L. Bennett and Robert M. Entman, 252–278. Cambridge: Cambridge University Press.

Zhang, W., Johnson, T. J., Seltzer, T., and Bichard, S. L. 2010. "The Revolution Will Be Networked: The Influence of Social Networking Sites on Political Attitudes and Behaviour." *Social Science Computer Review* 28:75–92.

Zucker, H. G. 1978. "The Variable Nature of News Media Influence." In *Communication Year Book 2,* edited by B. Reben, 225–240. New Brunswick, NJ: Transaction Books.

Zuckerman, E. W., and Jost, J. T. 2001. "What Makes You Think You're So Popular? Self-Evaluation Maintenance and the Subjective Side of the 'Friendship Paradox.'" *Social Psychology Quarterly* 64:207–223.

Index

267

About the Book

What role do the media play in influencing political life and shaping public opinion and behavior? Do they support—or undermine—our democratic beliefs and institutions? Claims about the media's powerful influence are frequently made, but where is the evidence?

Kenneth Newton scrutinizes these complex questions. Recognizing that differing forms of political communication have differing effects on differing people around the world, Newton goes further to ask why this occurs, and how. The answers that he presents in *Surprising News* offer a deeply researched, enlightening challenge to conventional wisdom in this age of fake news, post-truth, and claims about how the new digital media have transformed politics.